World Dance Cultures

From healing, fertility and religious rituals, through theatrical entertainment, to death ceremonies and ancestor worship, *World Dance Cultures* introduces an extraordinary variety of dance forms practiced around the world.

This highly illustrated textbook draws on wide-ranging historical documentation and first-hand accounts, taking in India, Bali, Java, Cambodia, China, Japan, Hawai'i, New Zealand, Papua New Guinea, Africa, Turkey, Spain, Native America, South America, and the Caribbean.

Each chapter covers a certain region's distinctive dances, pinpoints key issues and trends from the form's development to its modern iteration, and offers a wealth of study features including:

- Case Studies – zooming in on key details of a dance form's cultural, historical, and religious contexts
- 'Explorations' – first-hand descriptions of dances, from scholars, anthropologists and practitioners
- 'Think About' – provocations to encourage critical analysis of dance forms and the ways in which they're understood
- Discussion Questions – starting points for group work, classroom seminars or individual study
- Further Study Tips – listing essential books, essays and video material.

Offering a comprehensive overview of each dance form covered with over 100 full color photos, *World Dance Cultures* is an essential introductory resource for students and instructors alike.

Patricia Leigh Beaman is on the dance faculty at Wesleyan University and teaches dance history at New York University. As a Baroque and contemporary dancer, she has worked nationally and internationally, and is currently exploring the juxtaposition between historical Baroque and Postmodern dances of the 1960s.

World Dance Cultures
From Ritual to Spectacle

Patricia Leigh Beaman

Routledge
Taylor & Francis Group

LONDON AND NEW YORK

First published 2018
by Routledge
2 Park Square, Milton Park, Abingdon, Oxon, OX14 4RN

and by Routledge
711 Third Avenue, New York, NY 10017

Routledge is an imprint of the Taylor & Francis Group, an informa business

British Library Cataloguing-in-Publication Data
A catalogue record for this book is available from the British Library

Library of Congress Cataloging-in-Publication Data
A catalog record for this book has been requested

ISBN: 978-1-138-90772-0 (hbk)
ISBN: 978-1-138-90773-7 (pbk)
ISBN: 978-1-315-69493-1 (ebk)

Typeset in Helvetica
by Apex CoVantage, LLC

This book is dedicated to Walter Beaman and Jay LaMonica, who both loved the world, and the people in it.

Contents

Figures

Acknowledgements

Writing this book has been a sojourn, and I am fortunate to have been helped by the generosity of so many along the way. I give profound thanks to my editor, Ben Piggott, who gave me this opportunity, as well as to Kate Edwards, Autumn Spalding, and the Routledge editing staff. The brilliant and invaluable Ann Jacoby – who cheerfully read every word – has my eternal thanks and friendship. Going to look for photos in the huge archive that Linda and Jack Vartoogian have amassed over years was always a magical experience. Their superb work graces so much of this text, and they have my deep appreciation and fondness. Much gratitude goes to Deborah Jowitt, who introduced me to global dance on a deeper level, and to Susie Linfield, who taught me to write about what matters. Kay Cummings, James Martin, Catherine Turocy, Julie Malnig, Pedro Alejandro, Gay Smith, Seán Curran, and Hari Krishnan have all been integral to my career, and I am thankful for them, as well as for all my colleagues, past and present, at NYU and Wesleyan.

I also thank, in alphabetical order, these colleagues, photographers, and students for their generosity: Anisha Anantpurkar, Michel Beretti, Janice Boddy, Tanya Calamoneri, Anna Lee Campbell, Barbara Chan, James Cowdery, Djassi DaCosta-Johnson, Jean-Louis Dalbera, Rhea Daniels, Joanna de Souza, Blake Everson, Jean-Louis Fernandez, Carlos Fittante, Martin Garrardo, Céline Gaubert, Richard Glasstone, Jack Gray, Toshinori Hamada, Sean Hamlin, Richard Haughton, Tom Iclan, Karina Ikezoe, Kristin Jackson, Polly Jacobs, Ron Jenkins, William Johnston, Susan Kenyon, Akram Khan, Antonia Lang, Rachmi Diyah Larasati, Kalamandalam Manoj, Dennis H. Miller, Kyle Mullins, Juliet Neidish, Michele Olerud, Eiko Otake, Toni Shapiro-Phim, Emmanuele Phuon, Nellie Rainwater, Natesh Ramasamy, Aparna Ramaswamy, Andy Ribner, Ryan Rockmore, Miriam Rose, Ruthie Rosenberg, Christopher Roy, Moise Sagara, Edward Scheiffelin, Svea Schneider, Hari Setiano, Robert Turnbull, Alarmél Valli, Sividas Vadayath, Kaladharan Viswanath, Dr. Alfred Weideman, Nejla Yatkin, and Yloy Ybarra. Lastly, I thank my dear family – immediate, and extended – and especially my husband, Justin Luchter, whose technical wizardry, humor, and love sustained me through every step of this journey.

Publisher's acknowledgements

The publishers would like to thank all those included in *World Dance Cultures* and acknowledge the following sources for permission to reproduce their work in this volume:

Exploration 1.2 (p. 13): Republished with permission of University of Chicago Press, from "Whatever Happened to the South Indian Nautch? Toward a Cultural History of Salon Dance" by Davesh Soneji in *Unfinished Gestures: Devadasis, Memory, and Modernity in South India* (2011); permission conveyed through Copyright Clearance Center, Inc.

Exploration 1.4 (p. 28): Republished with permission of MIT Press-Journals, from "Who Wears the Skirts in Kathakali?" by Diane Daugherty and Marlene Pitkow in *The Drama Review* vol. 35.2 (1991); permission conveyed through Copyright Clearance Center, Inc.

Exploration 2.5 (p. 51): Republished with kind permission of Ron Jenkins. Excerpt from "Fratello Arlecchino: Clowns, Kings, and Bombs in Bali" by Ron Jenkins.

Exploration 2.6 (p. 60): Rachmi Diyah Larasati, "Introduction: Dancing on the Mass Grave" from *The Dance that Makes You Vanish: Cultural Reconstruction in Post-Genocide Indonesia*. Republished with kind permission of University of Minnesota Press. Copyright 2013 by the Regents of the University of Minnesota. All rights reserved.

Exploration 3.2 (p. 75): Republished with permission of Scarecrow Press, from "Mediating Cambodian History, the Sacred, and the Earth" by Toni Shapiro-Phim in *Dance, Human Rights, and Social Justice: Dignity in Motion*, ed. by Naomi Jackson and Toni Shapiro-Phim (2008); permission conveyed through Copyright Clearance Center, Inc.

Exploration 3.4 (p. 90): Richard Glasstone, excerpt from *The Story of Dai Ailian* (Dance Books, 2007). Reprinted with kind permission of Dance Books Ltd.

Exploration 4.4 (p. 121): Republished with permission of MIT Press – Journals, from "Selections from the Prose of Kazuo Ohno," by Noriko Maehata in *The Drama Review* vol. 30.2 (1986); permission conveyed through Copyright Clearance Center, Inc.

Exploration 5.3 (p. 143): Extract from Jack Gray, "Ko Mitimiti Ahau, I Am (of) the Place, Mitimiti," *Dance Research Journal*, Volume 48(1), pp 33–36, (2016). Republished with permission of Cambridge University Press.

Exploration 5.4 (p. 151): Extract from Edward Schieffelin, *The Sorrow of the Lonely and the Burning of the Dancers* (2005), Palgrave Macmillan US. Reproduced with permission of Palgrave Macmillan.

Exploration 6.2 (p. 164): Extract from Mette Bovin, *Nomads Who Cultivate Beauty* (2001), republished with permission of The Nordic Africa Institute.

Exploration 6.4 (p. 177): Republished with kind permission of Christopher Roy. Excerpt from *Land of the Flying Masks: Art and Culture in Burkina Faso* by Thomas Wheelock and Christopher Roy (Prestel, 2007).

Exploration 7.2 (p. 195): Republished with kind permission of Janice Boddy. Excerpt from *Wombs and Alien Spirits: Women, Men and the* Zar *Cult in Northern Sudan* by Janice Boddy (University of Wisconsin Press, 1989).

Exploration 8.2 (p. 229): From *Killing Custer* by James Welch with Paul Stekler. Copyright © 1994 by James Welch and Paul Stekler. Used by permission of W. W. Norton & Company, Inc. This selection may not be reproduced, stored in a retrieval system, or transmitted in any form or by any means without the prior written permission of the publisher.

Exploration 8.3 (p. 239): Extract from Karen McCarthy Brown, "Afro-Caribbean Spirituality: A Haitian Case Study" in *Vodou in Haitian Life and Culture: Invisible Power* ed. by Claudine Michel and Patrick Bellegarde-Smith (2006), Palgrave Macmillan US. Reproduced with permission of Palgrave Macmillan.

Every effort has been made to contact copyright-holders. Please advise the publisher of any errors or omissions, and these will be corrected in subsequent editions.

An introduction to *World Dance Cultures*

As far back as the fifteenth century, European pursuit of colonies in the New World, Africa, Oceania, Southeast Asia, and Asia was a highly competitive and rapacious endeavor. In their zeal for new territories and treasures, colonialists were largely blind to the ancient wisdom, religions, and cultural practices of the peoples they were invading and/or enslaving, and solipsistic in their view that Christian society was the best. In their "civilizing missions," colonial governments and missionaries regularly targeted cultural traditions, especially dance, as pagan. A conspicuous and disturbing commonality between most of the dances discussed in *World Dance Cultures* is that they were irrevocably altered or damaged through colonial domination; the societies in which they developed often had to fight to survive. In *Custer Died for Your Sins*, the late, great Native American rights activist and scholar Vine Deloria offered a mordant joke that could serve as one for many indigenous peoples. Two Indians are watching Columbus's fleet land. One turns to the other and says, "Maybe if we leave them alone, they will go away."[1] In light of what we know about history, the colonists didn't go away, nor did they leave the inhabitants alone. The fragility of cultural traditions, and in some heartening instances, their resilience, is an important theme throughout this introductory textbook, which delves into the historical, political, economic, and artistic factors that shaped both these cultures and their dances.

During almost two decades of teaching global dance studies at New York University's Tisch Dance, finding a comprehensive textbook has been challenging. By writing one myself, I hope to rectify this problem. *World Dance Cultures* includes a current trends section on each topic, as well as sixteen explorations offering the viewpoints of dancers, anthropologists, and scholars. Photographs enliven each section. For clarity, the chapters are arranged regionally, but are also issue based. Chapter 1 examines *bharatanatyam*, derived from dance that was originally practiced by *devadasis* in Hindu temples and courts of South India; *kathak*, originally entertainment in Hindu and Muslim courts in North India; and *kathakali*, which was performed by male warriors in the courts of Kerala. With the onset of British rule in the mid-nineteenth century, all were altered due to a variety of sociopolitical factors. Chapter 2 focuses upon the dance and the entwined political histories of two Indonesian islands, Bali and Java. In Bali, dancers serve as bodyguards to Hindu-Balinese gods and as spirit-mediums in healing rituals, and perform in dance dramas to keep a community in balance. In Java, the royal *bedhaya* dancers pay tribute to the ruler. In the violent aftermath of a 1965 military *coup d'état* in Indonesia, socialist folk dancers were slaughtered, while Javanese palace dancers were exploited to glorify the militaristic New Order regime.

Chapter 3 investigates how aristocratic dance in Cambodia and China was targeted by the Communist regimes that overtook both countries. During Mao Zedong's Cultural Revolution (1966–1977), educational "model works" such as *The Red Detachment of Women* supplanted *jingju* (Beijing opera), which was banned as elitist; its artists were ostracized or killed. When the Khmer Rouge took power in Cambodia in 1975, all vestiges of the country's aristocratic past such as the ancient court dance, *robam boran*, were eliminated. During this murderous reign, new folk dances became tools of propaganda, while the court dances – and the dancers – disappeared into the Khmer Rouge Killing Fields. Chapter 4 studies the ways that Japanese *noh*, *kabuki*, and *butoh* each reflected the ethos and politics of their respective audiences. Moralistic *noh* plays during a war-torn era became exclusive entertainment for elite *samurai*, while colorful and flamboyant *kabuki* echoed the hedonistic desires of the merchant class. *Butoh* artists in a post-World War II era created brutally frank and subversive works by rejecting Japan's strict social codes and increasingly Western influences.

Chapter 5 examines how Hawaiians, the Māori of Aotearea/New Zealand, and the Bosavi of Papua New Guinea traditionally preserved their cultural folklore through chant and dance. When Christian missionaries arrived in Oceania in the nineteenth century, the sacred *hula* and the Māori *haka* were deemed to be heathen and banned. In the 1930s, arriving missionaries and government officials prohibited the Bosavi's ritual of burning dancers in the cathartic *gisalo*. Chapter 6 demonstrates the vital purpose of dance in African fertility rituals, death ceremonies, and ancestor worship. At an annual Wodaabe festival designed to encourage coupling, men dance in beauty contests, which women judge. In Dogon and Mossi death ceremonies, masks, dancing, and drumming are essential in pointing the soul of the deceased toward the ancestral realm, while Yoruba ancestor spirits physically manifest themselves by descending into the bodies of *Egungun* maskers, who demonstrate their power and presence to their descendants through dance.

How dance functions as a healing ceremony, a form of worship, or a vehicle for personal expression is viewed in Chapter 7. In North Africa, the *zār* is a healing rite in which maladies caused by possession of *zār* spirits are placated through music, dancing, and sacrifices. In Turkey, Mevlevi dervishes of a Sufi Islamic order unite with God through the ritual of *sema*, a whirling dance that creates a state of religious ecstasy. *Flamenco's* long and varied roots tap into the music, song, and dance of Arabs, Jews, and Gypsies who coexisted in Andalusia, and converged into a *Gitano* manifestation of protest against fanatical governmental persecution. Chapter 8 looks at dance in terms of activism, spirituality, and spectacle. Desperate Lakota Sioux believed that by dancing the Ghost Dance, their ancestors and the buffalo would return and the white people would be obliterated. Instead, the US Army massacred hundreds at Wounded Knee in 1890. Decades later, Wounded Knee would become a site of resistance when the activist American Indian Movement took possession of the village. Haitian Vodou, a syncretic religion that evolved from African religions and Catholicism, involves propitiating deities with songs, dances, and offerings. At ritual ceremonies, a deity, if so moved, will take possession of a devotee and appear amongst the community. *Tango* emerged from the dance, music, and singing of European immigrants and Afro-Argentinians in the migrant enclaves of Buenos Aires in the 1880s. Disdained by upper-class Argentinians, *tango* became a sensation in Paris, and then eventually found acceptance at home after 1914.

It is always greatly rewarding to witness the profound awakening that occurs when students who have experienced dance from a largely Western perspective realize how dance functions in innumerable and indispensable ways in other cultures. While dance is often viewed as "art" or entertainment in the West, in other parts of the world, dances of necessity – for healing, purification, or rites of passage – are regarded as communal rituals. As students learn that these unique, codified practices are complex and valid, their respect and appreciation for unfamiliar cultures broaden. In today's politically tense and xenophobic climate, my profound and possibly fanciful wish for this text is three-fold. First, I hope it will allow students and other readers to garner a deep understanding of the dangers that lie in the suppression or banning of a group or an individual's traditions, religion, or lifestyle; second, that they develop an appreciation of the beauty and intricacies inherent in these dances; and third, that through these investigations into the positive and negative actions of others, they will become open-minded, empathetic, and vigilant citizens of the world.

—Patricia Leigh Beaman
New York City, 2017

Note

1 Deloria, Vine, Jr. *Custer Died for Your Sins: An Indian Manifesto*, 148.

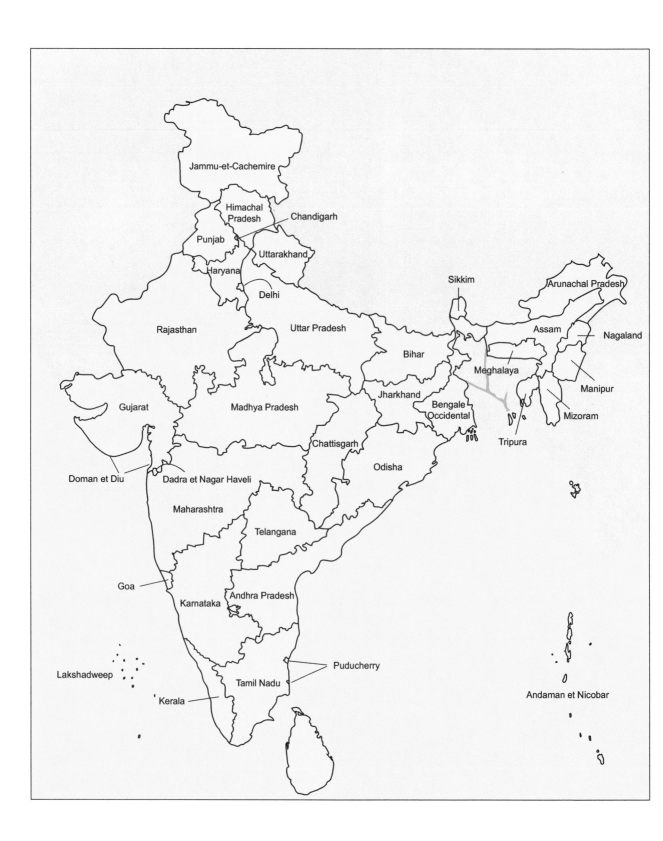

India
Devotion, dance, and mythology

1.1 Overview

After India's long-sought independence from Britain was achieved in 1947, several indigenous genres of dance became institutionalized by its new government and received "classical" designation. In this chapter, *bharatanatyam* of Tamil Nadu, *kathak* of Uttar Pradesh, and *kathakali* of Kerala will be explored. *Bharatanatyam* was historically practiced by *devadasis* – a term that may be translated as "female devotees of god." As a profession, they performed ritual duties in temples and danced as entertainers in royal courts in South India from the sixteenth to the early twentieth century. Similarly, *kathak* derived from the hereditary tradition of *tawaifs*, women who were professional entertainers at the North India courts of Hindu and Muslim rulers during the Mughal Empire. *Kathak* combines Hindu elements with Islamic influences from Persia, Afghanistan, and Turkey. Many parallels to *kathak* can also be seen in the footwork and expressive arms inherent in *flamenco*, a form that many speculate was influenced by Gypsies from North India who migrated to Spain.[1] When *kathakali* originated in the seventeenth century, it was traditionally performed as a dance drama by men and patronized by nobility and wealthy families. Its practitioners were members of a warrior caste, who were highly trained in a martial art that is still currently practiced in *kathakali* institutions.

In all three of these dance forms, royal patronage was crucial in supporting the tradition and profession of the performers. With the onset of British rule in the mid-nineteenth century, the ability of Indian rulers to financially maintain patronage of artists at their courts waned considerably. By the early twentieth century, *tawaifs* and *devadasis* became viewed as "*nautch*" dancers – a pejorative term for a common street dancer and prostitute – and were persecuted in an anti-*nautch* campaign. Although male *kathakali* performers did not suffer disdain, their professions were also affected by the loss of aristocratic support. By the beginning of the twentieth century, all three of these forms were altered or reconstructed due to a variety of sociopolitical factors. Today, *bharatanatyam*, *kathak*, and *kathakali* have become systematized and designated as "classical" Indian dance, and what was once a hereditary profession, passed between generations, is apt to be learned in an academic institution. These genres are global and continue to evolve through the innovations of vital artists who are honoring the cultural specificity of their respective discipline, yet transcending its boundaries in myriad ways.

Case study: British interests and rule in India

When Christopher Columbus inadvertently encountered the New World in 1492, his intended destination was India, and he called the indigenous people "Indians," a misnomer that persists today. Portuguese explorer Vasco da Gama had more success: by circumnavigating Africa in 1498, he reached India's

Malabar Coast. Soon, other European powers such as the Dutch, Danish, French, and British followed, all coveting spices. In 1600 the British East India Company was formed and came to rule most of India, demonstrating an unprecedented and unrestrained desire for supremacy and profit. After an Indian rebellion occurred in 1858, the British government officially took control of the country, which was known as the British Raj ("rule"). In 1947, after years of fervent nationalist activity by political luminaries such as Mohandas Gandhi and Jawaharlal Nehru, India finally gained its hard-won independence.

1.2 *Bharatanatyam*: concertizing a sacred form from South India

Key points: bharatanatyam

1 *Bharatanatyam* is derived from *sadir*, a devotional dance form from South India practiced by *devadasis*, who performed ritual duties in temples and danced as professional entertainers in royal courts from the sixteenth to the early twentieth century.
2 Traditionally, *devadasis* lived in extended family households run by female elders and had a lifestyle with more economic stability and rights than those of married women. Normally, Hindu households followed patterns of patrilineal inheritance, but *devadasis* could pass on both their land and wealth to their daughters.
3 At puberty, a *devadasi* was symbolically "married" to a Hindu temple deity. This prohibited her from marrying a mortal man, but she could maintain a lucrative courtesan relationship with an upper-caste male patron, chosen by her female elders.
4 In 1892, an "anti-*nautch*" campaign was launched against *devadasis* by the Indian Women's Movement and British colonial rulers, which condemned their courtesan lifestyle and profession and led to the demise of the *devadasi* profession. Anti-dedication legislation was passed in 1947.
5 The anti-colonial Indian nationalist movement took pride in indigenous arts, and reformists restructured *sadir* into *bharatanatyam*, a new symbol of Indian cultural identity. This label justified the dance by associating its origins with principles of Sanskrit drama and Carnatic music found within the ancient *Bharata Natyasastra*, an ancient dramaturgical text.

Our class is mentioned in all the works of literature and religion of our country through its various epochs . . . Everyone will readily admit that we have been the guardian angels of two of the most useful of arts to modern civilization: Music and Dancing.[2]
—From a 1927 petition by the Madras Devadasis' Association

Devadasis were women whose lives were dedicated to serving Hindu temples in the South Indian province of Tamil Nadu from the sixteenth to the early twentieth century. Literate at a time in which many in India were not, these highly accomplished women were versed in song, dance, and music. Performing ritual functions as a *devadasi* in the temple was a hereditary profession, but families could also offer a young daughter to serve. Starting around age seven, a *devadasi* would be rigorously trained in music and the solo form of *sadir*, also called *dasiattam* (dance of *devadasis*) by male teachers called *nattuvanars*. At the conclusion of her formal training, a *devadasi* would perform an *arangetram* – a solo dance before the main deity in the temple. At puberty, a *devadasi* would be symbolically "married" to the deity in a dedication ritual known as *pottukkattutal* that served as her initiation into full temple duties. After a priest tied a necklace (*pottu*) around a girl's neck, she symbolically entered into a divine marriage that ensured her the status of *nityasumangali* – an eternally auspicious woman.[3] In Hindu society, a wife's social welfare depended upon her husband being alive; unlike most married women, a *devadasi* was freed from the hardship of widowhood by being wedded to an immortal spouse.

Case study: Hindu gods: Brahma, Shiva, Vishnu, and Krishna

In Hindu mythology, deities are like normal people: they can feel jealousy, anger, and passion, and have spouses, lovers, and enemies. In order to facilitate their missions among mortals, they may be incarnated as avatars into other gods, goddesses, children, or animals. Some gods who appear frequently in mythology are Brahma, Shiva, Vishnu, and Krishna. Brahma is known as the Creator, while Shiva, the Destroyer, is also known as Lord of the Dance in his incarnation as Nataraja. In this guise, he destroyed the old world through his forceful dancing called *tandava*, allowing Brahma to create a new one. Vishnu is the Preserver and has ten avatars – incarnated beings that help him in his role as protector. Krishna, Vishnu's eighth incarnation, is one of the most widely worshiped gods in the Hindu pantheon. Stories abound of his antics as a butter-stealing child and as heartthrob of the *gopis* – the milkmaids he enchants by his flute playing.

Devadasis received salaries from the temple, supplemented with money earned from special performances. They lived with their children in extended family households run by female elders, following a lifestyle that deviated considerably from traditional Indian values. Normally, Hindu households followed patterns of patrilineal inheritance, but *devadasis* could pass on both their land and wealth to their daughters. Since females continued the hereditary profession, *devadasi* families preferred their children not to be boys and could adopt girls whom they would train in temple service. As a symbolic bride of a deity, a *devadasi* was not expected to remain sexually abstinent, but could have liaisons with a wealthy upper-caste Hindu male patron selected for her by the elder women of the household.[4] Her dedicated status made it a privilege for him to maintain her. In this lucrative arrangement as a courtesan, a *devadasi* lived independently and did not do domestic tasks for her patron. Many achieved considerable wealth through this lifestyle.

The Thanjavur court, salon performances, and the attack on *devadasi* tradition

By the seventeenth century, *devadasis* had begun to perform at the royal courts of Indian rulers, who displayed their political and moral responsibility as protectors of the society through their patronage of temples.[5] At the Thanjavur court in the nineteenth century, King Serfoji II and his heir Sivaji II employed numerous temple dancers and innovative composers, notably the Thanjavur Quartet (1802–1865), founded by four brothers working as *nattuvanars*. Their experimental collaborations radically altered music and dance by creating new repertory and compositions, codifying the dance lessons, and integrating *sadir* into a coordinated performance order still followed today. In the mid-nineteenth century, Thanjavur court dancers and musicians began to appear in salon performances in homes of wealthy landowners and elite Brahmins of Madras. In these intimate settings, far from the temple or a king's court, a new secular system of patronage developed between the dancers and their hosts that ignited the ire of some members in Indian society.

Figure 1.1 (p. 4)
Aparna Ramaswamy depicting Shiva on Nandi, the bull that is the bearer of truth.
Image: Amanulla.

Figure 1.2
Meenakshi Sundareswarar Temple in Tamil Nadu is dedicated to the goddess Parvati and her consort, Shiva.
Image: Natesh Ramasamy.

Case study: The caste system

For thousands of years, the caste system in Hindu India determined a person's social class at birth. Castes existed in four levels, or *varnas*. At the top, the venerated Brahmin caste comprised highly educated priests who presided over religious ceremonies and served as spiritual guides to rulers. Just below on the echelon was the Kshatriya class, which included princes, warriors, and landowners. Further down, skilled workers such as artisans, merchants, and farmers were of the Vaishya caste, while unskilled laborers and servants belonged to the Shudra class. Excluded from the caste system were the "untouchables," or Dalits, an ostracized group whose unsavory labors involved stripping skin from animal carcasses and cleaning up human waste. Dalits were barred from temples, forbidden to gather water from public wells, and could not be cremated after death. During the colonialist era, the British maintained the Indian caste system as a means of social control. During the campaign for India's independence, Mohandas Gandhi advocated for Dalits, calling them *harijan*, or "children of god." Although the caste system was outlawed in the 1950s, today many Dalits continue to live in poverty. Great strides in shattering social barriers were made when K. R. Narayanan, born into a Dalit family, was democratically elected and served as president of India from 1997 to 2002.

The profession of the *devadasis* came under fire from several factions. Instigated by members of the Indian Women's Movement, Hindu Brahmins, and British colonial officials, this movement called into question the *devadasis'* vocation as entertainers, and the ritualistic and financial connections between the rulers and temples sustaining the *devadasi* system. Under British colonialism, Indian kings were reduced to acting as figureheads in palaces and forced to answer to foreign bureaucracy that effectively reduced their financial means to continue their patronage of dancers at royal courts and temples. "*Nautch*," derived from *nāch* – the Hindi word for dance – was a derogatory term denoting common prostitutes who danced in the streets. It became routinely used by British colonialists in referring to the dance of any professional female entertainers in India, regardless of their artistry or social status.[6] In 1892, an "anti-*nautch*" campaign against *devadasis* was launched. This crusade, which condemned their courtesan lifestyle and their ritual profession, contributed catastrophically to their demise. The Indian Women's Movement – another

opposing faction – emerged alongside the anti-colonial Indian nationalist movement for independence.[7] Its determination to end temple dedication was part of a larger complex of reforms relating to women's rights, such as bans on patriarchal traditions of female infanticide and compulsory *sati*, which forced a widow to be burnt alive on her husband's funeral pyre. The movement also called for the legalization of remarriage for widows and advocated raising the age of consent for marriage – long encouraged by English missionaries and colonial officials in their "civilizing mission" in India.[8]

A powerful proponent of *devadasi* reform was Dr. Muthulakshmi Reddy (1886–1968), a female physician born to a *devadasi* mother and a Brahmin father, who provided her with an elite education. During her tireless campaign, Reddy wrote the Madras *Devadasis* Prevention of Dedication bill, which aimed at freeing *devadasis* from ritual service and sexual patronage so that they could legally enter conventional, monogamous marriages. In a letter to Gandhi during the campaign for Indian independence, she wrote, "I place the honour of an innocent girl, saving her from an inevitable life of shame and immorality, even above that of Swaraj [self-rule] . . . I will value Swaraj in as much as it gives protection to these girls and women."[9] Reddy considered her fight to end temple dedication as a movement to challenge women's oppression.

Case study: Mohandas Gandhi (1869–1948)

After training as a lawyer in London, Mohandas Gandhi worked in South Africa, where he first employed his concept of nonviolent civil disobedience while fighting to obtain civil rights for expatriate Indians. He was imprisoned for his efforts. After returning home, Gandhi became head of the Indian National Congress in 1921, and as a fervent leader in the Indian Independence Movement he fought for *swaraj* (self-rule) and for the rights of Dalits and women. Although he had married and had children, Gandhi later adopted a pure life of celibacy and vegetarianism, and followed *satyagraha*: adherence to truth. Consequently, he earned the reverential title *Mahatma*, or "great soul." In 1948 – a year after India's independence was won – a Hindu nationalist assassinated Gandhi. Prior to his demise, he had been the target of five other unsuccessful attempts upon his life.

As the war against their profession continued, some *devadasis* showed their mettle by forming the Madras Presidency *Devadasis'* Association. In 1927, they petitioned the government, claiming that their profession was both crucial to Hindu tradition and Indian nationalism. They argued that temple devotion didn't necessarily result in a courtesan arrangement and that legislation could actually promote prostitution because it would leave them without a source of income.[10] Retired *devasdasi* B. Varalakshmamma

Think about:
What were the pros and cons for *devadasis* being freed from ritual service so that they could enter into monogamous marriages?

wrote to Reddy, stating that since only *devadasis* possessed training in the artistic practices outlined in the Hindu *sastras* (scriptures), abolishing temple dedication would effectively eliminate this knowledge. Varalakshmamma advocated for an emancipatory shift: education for *devadasis* that would provide them with new autonomy, fostered through scholarships.[11] Despite the efforts of *devadasis*, ultimately the victors were the anti-*nautch* campaign, the Indian Women's Movement, and British colonial rulers, and by the early twentieth century, *sadir* was in danger of dying. When the Madras *Devadasis* Act of 1947 was passed four months after India's independence, temple dedication was officially declared illegal.

The emergence of *bharatanatyam*

Despite opposing forces, *devadasi* dance had its defenders. In the 1920s and 1930s, the nationalist fervor championing indigenous Indian traditions inspired some non-*devadasi* dancers to resurrect *sadir*. This theoretic reformation was championed by members of the Madras Music Academy, which was founded in 1927 by a group of anti-colonial activists such as E. Krishna Iyer (1897–1968). A Brahmin lawyer who had studied *sadir* while training in drama, Iyer lectured and performed *sadir* dressed like a *devadasi* throughout South India, and successfully convinced audiences that he was a temple dancer.[12] Iyer challenged Reddy's efforts to abolish *sadir* head-on, which resulted in a heated two-sided debate through spirited letters, published in newspapers.

At Iyer's urging, in 1931 the Madras Music Academy began to present *sadir* concerts. As respect for the form grew, in 1933 the decision was made to change the name *sadir* to *bharatanatyam*. This new moniker gave validity to the dance by associating its origins with principles of Sanskrit drama and Carnatic music found within the ancient *Bharata Natyasastra*, a dramaturgical text written by the sage Bharata in the second century.[13] The "tarnished" *sadir* of the *devadasis* was restructured into *bharatanatyam*, a new symbol of Indian cultural identity. In 1933, when the Academy presented the dancer Tanjore Balasaraswati, her artistry electrified the public and inspired middle-class Brahmin women such as Rukmini Devi to study the dance.

Figure 1.4
Two *devadasi*, circa 1920.
Image: Photographer unknown.

Rukmini Devi (1904–1986)

Born to a Brahmin family, Rukmini Devi was versed in drama, Sanskrit scholarship, and music. Her father was a member of the Theosophical Society, which fostered the study of philosophy, science, and the arts. At sixteen, when Devi married Society member George Arundale, she became an active member, directing theatrical productions. The couple befriended renowned Russian ballerina Anna Pavlova in 1928, when she toured India and captivated many with *Hindu Wedding* and *Radha-Krishna*. These "Oriental" dances had been choreographed in London in collaboration with Uday Shankar, an early innovator in Indian dance. Her artistry inspired Devi to study ballet, but Pavlova, who had been disheartened at her inability to see any *devadasi* dance in India, urged Devi to pursue Indian dance. In 1933, Devi began to train in earnest in a *guru-shishya* (teacher-student) relationship with *nattuvanar* Meenakshi Sundaram Pillai, a descendant of the Thanjavur Quartet. Foreshadowing her inclination to break with tradition, Devi committed an unthinkable transgression when she arranged her own *arangetram* debut in 1935 without the customary approval from her *nattuvanar*, who did not yet think she was ready.

In 1936, Devi and Arundale established Kalakshestra. In this Western-style conservatory, *bharatanatyam* became institutionalized, with newly invented pedagogy that resourced Sanskrit sources. In her crusade to reinvent tradition, Devi's methods at Kalakshestra proved influential. Originally, the aesthetic of *sadir* in the temple and salon embraced musicality, individual expressionism, and a nuanced embodied understanding of the dance, its poetry, and its eroticism. At Kalakshestra a dancer's technical ability became the focus, facial expression and the lines of the body were exaggerated, and tempo of the music increased, supplanting former aesthetic principles. To make *bharatanatyam* socially acceptable, *sringara* – the expression of love in song, danced out by a *devadasi* in *sadir* – was absent in Kalakshestra training and in Devi's group dance dramas. Instead, she emphasized spiritual devotion, or *bhakti*, by placing a statue of Shiva as Nataraja, Lord of the Dance upon the stage, saying, "My intention was that dance, now abolished in the temple, should create the temple atmosphere on stage."[14] As a result, *bharatanatyam*, as we know it now, reifies religiosity, unlike *devadasi* dance, in which the ethos was about sensual love. Devi also defied the long-held method of *guru-shishya* training when she fired the seasoned *nattuvanars* teaching at Kalakshestra, and students themselves began to conduct the music at concerts.

Tanjore Balasaraswati (1918–1984)

Tanjore Balasaraswati descended from a family of Thanjavur court *devadasis* and musicians, and trained in traditional Carnatic music with her celebrated grandmother and mother. She studied *bharatanatyam* with *nattuvanar* Kandappa Pillai, and made her formal *arangetram* debut under his tutelage. When the 15-year-old Balasaraswati appeared at the Madras Music Academy in 1933, her dancing enthralled many, including Uday Shankar. Both Devi and Balasaraswati were fundamental in the exposure of *bharatanatyam*, but each differed greatly in her aesthetic approach. Unlike Devi, a Brahmin who began training at age 29, Balasaraswati was born into a family whose traditions of music and dance had been the focus of life for generations. She was opposed to breaking her lineage by enhancing, sanitizing, or modernizing the dance. In her performances, Balasaraswati embraced *sringara*, the *devadasi* expression of love so rejected by Devi. She claimed, "The sringara we experience in bharata natyam is never carnal – never, never, never. For those who have yielded themselves to this discipline with total dedication, dance, like music, is the practice of presence, it cannot merely be the body's rapture."[15] While Devi had eradicated *sringara* and reduced the art of *abhinaya* to mere storytelling, Balasaraswati was unparalleled in her performance of poetic metaphorical vignettes about love and eroticisim, conveyed through her deep understanding and sophisticated relationship between music and dance. Balasaraswati enjoyed an international career until the 1970s and then settled and taught in the United States. Her performances made deep impressions upon many, ranging from ballerina Margot Fonteyn and historical modern dancers Ted Shawn and Ruth St. Denis, to avant-garde choreographer Merce Cunningham.

Bharatanayam technique

In *bharatanatyam* a dancer imparts narratives that often come from poems, or *puranas* – Hindu mythological stories. In a solo performance, the dancer can portray a scenario between a woman and the deity she loves, and artfully go between enacting the god as well as the woman. In order to do this, the dancer employs an energetic, masculine style called *tandava*, legendarily danced by Shiva in his manifestation as Nataraja, Lord of the Dance. *Lasya*, the feminine style, is much gentler, sensual, and sometimes erotic. Since its reconfiguration into *bharatanatyam*, both of these stylistic terms were adopted for use, but originally had no connection to *devadasi* dance at all.[16] Another of the many changes has been that the dance is no longer the sole domain of women, but is widely practiced by men as well. Both women and men perform *tandava* and *lasya* as they dance out various characters of the narrative.

Figure 1.5
Uday Shankar.
Image: photographer unknown. Courtesy of the John Martin Collection.

Nritta and *abhinaya*

In performance, *bharatanatyam* has two aspects: abstract dance, called *nritta*, and narrative dance, known as *abhinaya*. *Nritta* interludes showcase the clarity of a dancer's technique – the performer does precise, rhythmic footwork in time to the music, and executes ornamental arm and hand gestures that have no specific meaning. Using basic steps called *adavu*, these pure dance sequences are meticulously choreographed and do not allow for improvisation. *Abhinaya*, which translates as communication, is the method in which a dancer uses gestures, poses, and facial expressions to convey the emotions and portrayal of the metaphoric text-based poetry. In this narrative component of *bharatanatyam*, the dancer is free to interpret the words set to music and can improvise if desired. *Abhinaya* is divided into four categories, which are utilized in all classical Indian dance forms: *angika*, *aharya*, *satvika*, and *vachika*.

Angika abhinaya concerns the movements of the whole body. *Mudras* (sometimes called *hastas*) are codified hand gestures that can communicate words, feelings, or concepts in conjunction with the lyrics of a song. To do so, a dancer masters twenty-four basic single-hand *mudras* and twenty-eight double-hand *mudras*. The articulate movements of the head, neck, and eyes are called *bedhas*. A dancer uses quivering lips to convey sadness, tightens the cheeks to show disgust, opens the eyes widely to display anger, or raises the eyebrows in surprise. *Aharya abhinaya* encompasses decorative aspects such as costumes, jewelry, and make-up. In traditional *bharatanatyam*, a female dancer wears a silk *sari* that features a tight scooped-neck bodice with short sleeves, often crossed with a sash. The dancer is often in loose leggings, draped with a pleated apron. The ankle bells, or *salangai*, are stitched onto padded leather in rows. The dancer's hair bun is adorned with a corona of white jasmine buds, from which emerges a *chauri* – a long braid attachment studded with gold ornaments that extends down to the waist, typically worn by brides. The *chutti pattam* jewelry covers the middle part of the hair and frames the top of the forehead. Bell-shaped earrings are worn along with nose rings, bangles, and a gold necklace, and the eyes are accentuated with thick black eyeliner. A *bindi* – an auspicious red dot traditionally worn by a bride – is placed on the forehead. The palms, tips of the fingers, and the outline of the feet are accentuated with *alta*, a red dye.

Satvika abhinaya is the representation of the deep psychic condition of a character through facial and bodily expression. A dancer's innermost feelings in conveying a story are portrayed through a concept called *rasa*, which translates as emotion, or taste. In Indian classical dance, there are nine human expressions of emotion called *navarasas*: love, laughter, sorrow, anger, heroism, fear, wonder, disgust, and serenity. In expressing these, the *rasa* of a skilled dancer will create mood, or *bhava*, in the audience, and is a sought-after quality in their *abhinaya*. *Navarasas* are shown through facial expression and body language; for instance, in displaying laughter, a dancer crosses the arms, the torso shakes, the eyes narrow, and the lips twitch.

Vachika abhinaya is verbal expression through spoken syllables, poetry, song, or music. Carnatic music, which accompanied *sadir* and continues the tradition with *bharatanaytam*, is played by a small orchestra that includes a singer, melodic instruments such as flute and violin, a double-headed *mridangam* drum, and a drone instrument called a *tambura*. In performance, a *nattuvanar* will guide the rhythm of the orchestra by beating together small cymbals called *nattuvangam*. Aside from singing rhythmic syllables during the abstract *nritta* sections, a *nattuvanar* also sings lyrical Sanskrit verses called *slokas* that convey a metaphoric vignette during an *abhinaya* interlude.

Figure 1.6
Aparna Ramaswamy in a *mudra* portraying a deer.
Image: Amanulla.

Figure 1.7 (p. 10)
Alarmél Valli expresses beauty and joy using a *tambracuda mudra* hand gesture.
Image: S. Anwar

Bharatanatyam training

Traditionally, a *nattuvanar* is male, and in his role as *guru* he serves as choreographer, rehearsal director, and orchestra leader. A *nattuvanar* controls the rhythm of the dancing by beating a *kattai kuchi* – a rectangular piece of wood – and reciting syllables called *sollukattus*, such as "*dhit-dhit-teis, dhit-dhit-teis.*" The dancer pairs their *adavu* step patterns to these sounds and dances them in three speeds, accelerating from slow, to medium, and then to fast before returning to medium, then to slow. While performing this footwork, the student is in *araimandi*, or half-seated position: the feet are turned out with the heels touching, and remain flat on the floor, while a diamond shape is created in the legs as the knees bend out to the side. The pelvis tips back, resulting in a slight arch in the lower back, and the backs of the hands rest on each side of the waist. In *araimandi* the level of the torso stays constant as the dancer transfers weight to one leg, lifts the other high with the foot reaching up toward the buttock, and then slaps the foot flat on the ground. Other basic positions include *mandi*, a full-seated posture in which the dancer sinks down low and perches on the balls of the feet, and *samapadam*, a standing position in which parallel feet and legs touch. *Anga suddha* translates as "clean body line." This aesthetic aspect of *bharatanatyam* calls for a dancer's precision and sense of proportion in extending the limbs of the body, beating the feet on the ground in time with the music and articulating *mudras* between the rhythms, text, and song. The ideal aesthetic is for the dancer to perform the complex technique with crisp clarity that is pleasing to the eye.

In *bharatanatyam* concerts today, the musicians sit in a line on stage right, facing stage left. In *puja*, a salutation to Mother Earth before and after dancing, the dancer descends to the ground, touches the floor, and raises the palms to the eyes in a gesture of deference. The order of a traditional two-hour concert includes seven sections: *alarippu*, *jatisvaram*, *sabdam*, *varnam*, *padam*, *javali*, and *tillana*. In the *alarippu*, a dancer makes an invocation to a god, followed by the *jatisvaram* in which the dancer explores variations on a choreographic pattern. The *sabdam* introduces *abhinaya* through a mythological story, mimed to a song. The *varnam* is a lengthy, intricate combination of *nritta* and *abhinaya*. It focuses on the feelings of the *Nayika*, or heroine, who might express her love, or dismay at having to wait for her lover. In the love song of a *padam*, a dancer portrays a woman pining for her unfaithful lover. This mood is quickly replaced by the *javali*, an erotic song in which *sringara* is expressed through *abhinaya*. Lastly, the exuberant *tillana* is a rhythmic abstract display that closes the concert.

Current trends

The complex journey from *devadasi* performance to *bharatanatyam* has led to a global proliferation of dance artists and choreographers who have taken the form in innovative directions. One early maverick was Chandralekha (1928–2006), who studied with *nattuvanar* Ellappa Pillai but was not content to stay within the strict parameters of the Indian classical form. In the 1970s, she began choreographing dances reflecting her deep personal concerns. She radically combined martial arts with *bharatanatyam* in controversial works such as *Angika*, *Sri*, and *Sharira*, which championed equality, women's rights, and the environment. Mallika Sarabhai uses her art to instigate social change through her dance company and school, Darpana, which she co-directs with her mother, renowned dancer Mrinalini Sarabhai. In the 1980s, after playing Drapaudi in Peter Brook's legendary production of *The Mahabharata*, Mallika began creating socially relevant dances. Recent works include *Unsuni*, a work about social injustice, and her film, *Women with Broken Wings*, which spotlights gender inequality and violence.

Born in Chennai, Shobana Jeyasingh founded her company in London in 1988. Her highly physical work is often site specific: *Counterpoint* features fifteen dancers amidst fifty-five fountains at Somerset House, and *TooMortal* is staged in historical churches. In *Bayadère – The Ninth Life*, she illuminates the Western fascination with

India during the nineteenth century, drawing on Marius Petipa's original ballet and the visit of the "temple dancers" to Europe in 1838. Jeyasingh is currently exploring the interaction between humans and robotic systems in collaboration with King's College.

Born in Singapore, choreographer and dancer Hari Krishnan studied in India with the late *nattuvanar* Kittappa Pillai and courtesan dancer R. Muttukannamal from the *devadasi* community. In his choreographic work for his Toronto-based company, inDance, Krishnan creatively straddles the divide between the classical and contemporary worlds through hybrid works informed by critical history. The eroticism and sexuality that were inherent in courtesan dance are central to his inquiry, which has informed his own complex understanding of gender and identity. *Skin; Quicksand; I, Cyclops;* and *Bollywood Hopscotch* are examples of his vibrant and highly technical dances that delve into issues such as post-colonialism, sexuality, gender, and pop-culture in a subversive and provocative way.

Malavika Sarrukai and Alarmél Valli continue their respective careers as highly respected international artists of *bharatanatyam*. Recently, two documentaries have been produced on each: Sarrukai's *The Unseen Sequence* charts her journey as a dancer and choreographer, and Valli's *Lasya Kavya* explores her aesthetic world in which traditional dance is fused with modernity. Valli – celebrated for her musicality, precision, and the purity of her *abhinaya* – is an influential teacher in Chennai. Aparna Ramaswamy, a protégée of Valli, is choreographer and co-director of the Minneapolis-based Ragamala Dance Company. Her recent solo work, *They Rose at Dawn*, explores women as guardians of ritual. Carnatic music merges with jazz in *Song of the Jasmine* and with Japanese *taiko* drums in *1,001 Buddhas: Journey of the Gods*.

Figure 1.8
Hari Krishnan's inDance performs *Quicksand*.
Image: Andy Ribner

1.2 Exploration: excerpt from *Unfinished Gestures: Devadasis, Memory, and Modernity in South India* by Davesh Soneji[17]

In this account of a private "nautch" performance in 1838, given in honor of an Englishman, Davesh Soneji notes that the inclusion of acrobatic feats performed enabled devadasis *and* nattuvanars *to thrive amongst the competition in Madras, and posits that the social reform movement directed toward* devadasis *was a result of these private performances, rather than their temple service.*

Colonial engagements with cultural forms such as music and dance are documented as early as 1727 . . . From at least this time onward, the South Indian salon dance or "nautch" was canonized as *the* most viable expression of elite sociopolitical authority. In some contexts, the space of the salon served to cement relations between Indian elites and Europeans in the sociological theater of colonial Madras. To be sure, women who performed in these contexts were not only objectified sexually by both groups, but were also racialized by Europeans across axes of imperial power . . . I will turn now, therefore, to some representative examples in which salon performances are described by colonial administrators.

The European gentlemen were about sixty in number . . . and several ladies were present also. The following programme exhibits the entertainment above stairs:

- A set of three Mahomedan dancing women, dancing in a circular form round the hall.
- A young Hindoo girl, dancing on the sharp edges of swords, which are fixed in a ladder, at the same time cutting pieces of sugar-cane, applied below her feet.
- A set of eight Hindoo dancing women, each of them holding a string fixed in the ceiling, dancing in different ways and forming the strings into nets, ropes . . . at the same time singing and beating time with their feet and hands.
- A set of three Hindoo dancing girls, dancing in the Carnatic form.
- A Hindoo dancing girl, dancing in the Hindoo form, to an English tune.

. . . It was said that the value of the jewels on three of the girls . . . could not have been less than ten thousand pagodas! They were literally covered with brilliants, not excepting their noses, which were positively tortured with precious stones. The rather alarming exhibition of a young girl dancing on the edges of sharp swords, which formed the second act, was repeated late in the evening; but on this occasion, she cut limes with her heels . . . It appears hardly credible that a delicate little girl should be able to stand on the edge of a sharp sword, and at the same time . . . cut a lime in two on the same instrument.

This description captures the complexities of European representations of native dancers and their arts. There is certainly a fascination, usually erotic . . . with any of the visual markers of difference – in this case, with the dancers' jewels that subtly evoke an exotic sexuality. But this is immediately juxtaposed with a moral judgment. The observer is simultaneously disturbed by the risks posed to the "delicate little girl" who dances on the edge of swords. These kinds of representations are best understood as metonymic; the elements of any single version parallel those of imperial adventure in the male imagination: the confrontation, rescue, reform, and conquest of natives all live through these tellings.

Discussion questions: *bharatanatyam*

1 The Indian Women's Movement sought many reforms for what they saw as women's rights, such as bans against female infanticide, compulsory widow-burning, and an end to temple dedication. Could a solution have been found for keeping their hereditary profession of *devadasis* intact?

2 The experimental collaborations of Thanjavur Quartet instigated many influential changes in *sadir*. While the dance, and the dancers, proved to be threatening to the public, why is it that music did not?

3 While Rukmini Devi, a Brahmin, eradicated *sringara* (expression of love) and reduced the art of *abhinaya* to mere storytelling, Balasaraswati, a hereditary performer, was unparalleled in her metaphorical vignettes about devotional love and eroticisim. Discuss these binary approaches of two performers in terms of purification, or tradition.

1.3 *Kathak*: entertainment for Hindu *Maharajas* and Muslim *Moghuls*

Key points: *kathak*

1 Kathak derived from the tradition of the *tawaifs*, female performers who were professional entertainers at the North India royal courts during the Mughal Empire. These women danced and sang, accompanied by male musicians known as *Kathaks*, or "storytellers," at gatherings of nobility and upper-class men.

2 *Kathak* features virtuosic rhythmic interplay between musicians and, traditionally, a solo dancer, who employs mesmerizing footwork in pure dance sections called *nritta* and elegant lyrical dancing during narrative interludes known as *abhinaya*.

3 *Kathak* combines both Muslim and Hindu influences, and is performed to Hindustani music. The Islamic influence can be seen in spins called *chakkara*, which may have derived from the dance of the Sufi dervishes in Turkey. It shares many similarities with *flamenco*, originally a Gypsy form of dance and music from Spain.

4 British administrators pejoratively referred to *tawaifs* as "nautch dancers," a distortion of the Sanskrit word *nāch*, or dance. The status of these formerly elite artists was debased by the government: they were classified as "public women and whores" in census reports, and subjected to health inspections.

5 The ancestry of current dance masters in *kathak gharanas* (stylistic schools) can be directly traced to the Hindu *Kathaks* employed at royal courts. Although the origins of *kathak* dance are often attributed to these men, the contributions of female Muslim *tawaifs* have been largely overlooked.

> **There are always and everywhere women of loose character. In India all professional singing and dancing, when performed by women, with very few exceptions, is performed by prostitutes . . . They are frequently hired together, the Kathaks to play on instruments, the women to dance and sing.[18]**
> **—1872 British census report of "tribes and castes"**

Kathak, from North India, is a synthesis of diverse origins and artistic elements that emerged from Muslim courts and Hindu palaces during the Mughal Empire. From the sixteenth to the nineteenth century, rulers who were lavish patrons of the arts engaged elite dancers and musicians from India and central Asia as court entertainers. The ancestry of current dance masters in *kathak's* three existing *gharanas*, or stylistic schools – Jaipur, Benares, and Lucknow – can be directly traced to male court performers known as *Kathaks*, or "storytellers."[19] Although the origins of *kathak* dance are often attributed to these Hindu hereditary entertainers, the contributions of female Muslim performers called *tawaifs* – who were often courtesans of nobility – have been largely overlooked. Other forms of Indian classical dance have been linked to the dramaturgical rules within the ancient Sanskrit *Bharata Natyasastra*, yet *kathak*, as a codified dance form, actually emerged during the twentieth century and is now danced professionally on concert stages.[20] Today, men and women perform the same material in *kathak*, although its teachers are predominantly male and its practitioners female.

Kathak features virtuosic rhythmic interplay between musicians and, traditionally, a solo dancer, who employs mesmerizing footwork and electrifying spins in pure dance sections called *nritta*, as well as elegant lyrical dancing during narrative interludes known as *abhinaya*. The narrative is conveyed through the use of facial expressions and gestures that enable the dancer to incarnate characters and animals from mythological tales in Indian epics. *Kathak* has links to both Hindu and Muslim culture, and is the only classical dance form accompanied by Hindustani music. Although traces to its past as the courtesan art form of *tawaifs* are not emphasized, a legacy of conveying beauty exists nonetheless in its subtle swaying, the use of the eyes, and themes of love explored.

Figure 1.9
Kathak dancer Mahua Shankar, a disciple of Pandit Birju Maharaj, performs with the Maharaj Kathak Dance Ensemble.
Image: Jack Vartoogian, Front Row Photos.

The Mughal Empire

The emperors of the Islamic Mughal Empire were descendants of Genghis Khan, the mighty *Moghul* of the Mongol Empire. Its golden age is considered to be during the reign of Akbar the Great, who became Emperor in 1556. Although the Empire tripled in size due to his conquests, this influential leader was respectful of local artistic and religious customs, and within his court all traditional and sacred festivals were celebrated. To further secure his authority, the *Moghul* forged many marital and cultural alliances with the Hindu Rajput princes of Rajasthan. Akbar became a generous patron of musicians and dancers who migrated from Hindu temples to his sumptuous court, enticed by financial gain. Love was another way in which dancers, albeit inadvertently, came under his domain: when Akbar became enamored of Roopmati, a Hindu singer and wife of an Afghan sultan living in the fortified city of Mandu, he seized it in order to abduct her. Although Roopmati poisoned herself rather than be captured, Akbar managed to carry off 350 dancers from the sultan's harem – new additions to the fertile artistic environment already flourishing at his palace.[21]

At Akbar's court, the secular environment and the diversity of the dancers brought new influences. In Mughal miniature paintings, court entertainers are depicted in an upright stance characteristic of Persian dance, rather than in the typical position of traditional Indian forms in which the legs are turned out and the knees flexed. This verticality lent itself to new possibilities in rhythmic footwork and in spins called *chakkars*, possibly derived from the dance of Turkish Sufi dervishes. A scholar visiting at Akbar's court described the movements of the Persian dancers as imitating a peacock, fish, or deer; he also recounted watching a veiled dancer perform a gentle dance with a gliding gait.[22] The fusion of Muslim and Hindu traditions in Akbar's court led to the nascent emergence of what is now recognized as *kathak* dance. Further efflorescence occurred in the court of *Nawab* Wajid Ali Shah, who ascended to the throne at his court in Lucknow in 1847.

The *nawab*, a compassionate ruler, enjoyed writing plays and musical compositions. In the cultural haven of his court, he employed *Kathaks* – men who sang, played instruments, told stories, and sometimes dressed as women when enacting Hindu devotional tales about Radha and Krishna. *Tawaifs* were also engaged as court entertainers. Unlike the majority of women of their day, *tawaifs* were highly literate and owned property they could pass on to female relatives. In addition to singing and dancing, *tawaifs* were gifted conversationalists, versed in poetry and politics. They were so respected that young princes were sent to their salons to learn social etiquette and manners, and women imitated their outfits, hairstyles, and jewelry.[23] At *mehfils* – intimate performances of poetry, music, and dance in the music rooms at court or at homes of noble patrons – a *tawaif* would begin her performance seated, accompanied by *Kathaks* playing *tabla* drums and a *sarangi*, an upright violin. As she sang *thumri*, poetic songs about love with lyrics ranging from sacred to sexual, she interpreted the words through her *abhinaya* gestures, boldly making direct eye contact with the male audience before rising to dance. Like a *devadasi*, a *tawaif* could work as a courtesan and gain large fortunes from a male patron, whose own social standing was enhanced through his liaison with her. It is important to note that the *tawaifs* were not considered to be common prostitutes; they enjoyed an elite status, and were generally kept by only one patron at a time.[24]

The British Raj and the demise of the *tawaifs*

In 1858, a year after the suppression of the Sepoy Rebellion – an Indian uprising now referred to as the First War of Independence – Britain declared rule over India by establishing the British Raj. As royal palaces began to be annexed by the colonial government, aristocratic power eroded and artistic patronage subsequently waned. The exiled *Nawab* Wajid Ali Shah and court performers migrated to cities such as Kolkata (Calcutta), capital of the British Raj, where dancers and musicians found employment as entertainers at lavish gatherings in the homes of wealthy Bengali *zamindars* (landowners).[25] Victorian administrators, frowning at the profession of *tawaifs*, pejoratively referred to them as "*nautch* dancers," a distortion of the Sanskrit word na̅ch, or dance. The government debased the status of these formerly elite artists: they were classified as "public women and whores" in British census reports and subjected to enforced health inspections. When the Cantonment Act of 1864 established regulated prostitution for the British army, *tawaifs* became housed in military brothels and were reduced to sexually serving a regiment.[26] Although the anti-*nautch* campaign begun in 1892 opposed prostitution and was aimed at the social reformation of *devadasis* temple dancers in South India, the *tawaifs* also became marginalized when their profession was targeted. As the reputation of *tawaifs* became tainted in the public eye and their presence diminished, some had the fortune of becoming successful singers and musicians in the nascent radio industry, while those who weren't often fell into common prostitution.

Resuscitation of *kathak*

An integral aim of the anti-colonial Indian nationalist movement of the early twentieth century was the revitalization of indigenous arts. Although music was much less negatively affected by colonialism, as their financial and societal support crumbled, female dancers suffered changes that drastically altered their profession and social status. In South India, elite Brahmins transformed *sadir* into the "respectable" form of *bharatanatyam*. *Devadasis* were disassociated from the dance, yet male *nattuvanars* retained their presence as teachers and music masters. This same phenomenon occurred when "*nautch*" became refashioned as *kathak*. The Muslim *tawaifs* were replaced by their former accompanists – men from Hindu *Kathak* families formerly employed at royal courts, who now became the performers, as well as teachers of young middle-class women. The Lucknow *gharana*, which emerged from the court of *Nawab* Wajid Ali Shah, had three renowned male hereditary *gurus* and performers: the Maharaj brothers Acchan, Lachhu, and Shambhu. Today, Acchan's son, acclaimed *kathak* dancer Birju Maharaj, presides over the Lucknow g*harana*, which is famous for its lyrical style and sensuous, expressive movement. Today, male *gurus* are largely transmitting the inherited legacy of *kathak* to the next generation. Yet scholars such as Margaret Walker and Pallabi Chakaravorty have shed light on the important role that female performers have played in the

Figure 1.10
Legendary Birju Maharaj, *guru* of the Lucknow *gharana*.
Image: Jack Vartoogian, Front Row Photos.

development of the form, and argue that attributing the dance's origins solely to the Hindu hereditary male *Kathaks* disregards the history and artistic contributions of the *tawaifs* in the development of classical *kathak*. Walker writes:

> These men are still considered authorities on kathak's authentic style . . . Although one cannot deny the involvement of these male musicians and dancers in north Indian dance, their largely unchallenged hegemony through the twentieth century belies the influence of women, hereditary and non-hereditary, on the development of kathak dance.[27]

Just as in the separation of the *devadasi* from their dance, the reformed *kathak* abandoned any aspects associated with *tawaif* courtesan performance. Like *bharatanatyam*, validated by its new alliance with ancient Sanskrit sources such as the *Natyasastra*, certain *hasta* hand gestures used in *kathak* began to be referred to in Sanskrit terms, and Hindu devotional expressions – such as the *anjali* double-handed prayer gesture – replaced the Muslim one-handed *salaam*, or salutation.[28]

Think about:
Does the dominance of male *gurus* in the three *gharanas* of *kathak* perpetuate colonial tropes towards women?

Case study: Orientalism

Indian dancers have long been a source of fascination for Western writers and choreographers. With their mystic portrayals of the East, nineteenth-century French writers Victor Hugo and Gustave Flaubert helped ignite an Oriental craze. At the center of this obsession was the stereotypical, exotic temple dancer, known by the French term *bayadère*. In *Le Dieu et la Bayadère* (1830), Paris Opera ballerina Marie Taglioni and the female *corps de ballet* inspired effusive critic Théophile Gautier to describe temple dancers as "those voluptuous enchantresses gilded by the sun's rays, who sound the silver bells of their bracelets before the door of the hot rooms and on the steps of the pagodas."[29] In 1838, a European tour presented four *devadasis* as "real *bayadères*" in *The Hindoo Widow*. In the plot – a perfect exemplification of the "civilizing mission" of colonialism – a widow is saved from the funeral pyre by British troops.[30] In 1877 in Imperial Russia, Marius Petipa choreographed *La Bayadère*, still widely performed today. American dancers Ted Shawn and Ruth St. Denis, a duo who specialized in transforming themselves into dancers of other cultures, piqued the curiosity of the Indian public during a 1926 tour. In *The Cosmic Dance of Shiva*, Shawn appeared as the "Lord of the Dance" in the center of a circle of "fire" and wearing only a small bejeweled loincloth and a conical headpiece. For her *Nauch Dance* and *Radha*, St. Denis conducted research by watching the "Hindoo Dancers" at the sideshow at Coney Island amusement park in Brooklyn, New York.

Although by the twentieth century hereditary male performers had become the keepers of the dance of the *tawaifs*, an Indian dancer named Leila Sokhey championed *kathak* by developing the glamorous persona of Madame Menaka. She followed a similar path to that of Rukmini Devi, who devoted herself to establishing *bharatanatyam* as a reputable art form. Just as Devi eradicated *sadir's* erotic element of *sringara* from the new *bharatanatyam*, Menaka replaced the suggestive *thumri* love songs of *tawaif* courtesans with spiritual Sanskrit dance dramas, and used modern stagecraft in her productions. Menaka became a cultural ambassador of sorts for India when her troupe – composed exclusively of girls from upper-class families – toured Europe and America to great acclaim.

In 1941, Menaka founded her school, Nrityalayam, and developed a curriculum taught by *Kathak* male dancers and musicians; *tawaifs*, however, were excluded. Although Nrityalayam lasted only a few years, her initiatives influenced other institutions such as the Sangeet Natak Akademi. These schools hired *gurus* such as the legendary Maharaj brothers of the famous Lucknow *gharana* and began to receive support from the newly formed Indian government, the new "patron" of the art. Eventually, as the standardizations of the technique and order of the solo performance were codified in these academies, this revised form of *kathak* became categorized as a classical dance of India.

Costuming

In the Hindu style of costuming, a female *kathak* dancer dresses in a tight bodice with short sleeves called *choli*, and a *dupatta*, or scarf, over the shoulder and across the torso. She wears *chudidaar* pants and topped with a *lehenga* – a long, full skirt. In the Muslim style, an *angarakha*, a long-sleeved dress cinched at the waist that flares out widely during spins, is worn, along with an *odhni*, or veil, and a peaked cap. In both styles, jewelry is worn around her neck and wrists, as well as in her hair, which is pulled back in a bun or a braid. Men wear a *dhoti*, a single cloth that is wrapped around the legs and pleated at the waist, and a long *kurta* shirt that comes to the knees. *Ghunghru* ankle bells are woven along a string and tied on. Children start with twenty-five, while adults might wear as many as 150 or more on each leg.

Music and technique

Traditionally in a *kathak* solo, the dancer directs the evolution of the different musical compositions through communication with the musicians. The Hindustani musical accompaniment to *kathak* includes the bowed *sarangi*, *tabla* hand drums, the deeper-toned *pakhavaj* drum, and the harmonium. The dance and music share a similar progression: pure dance patterns are mathematically set to *talas*, rhythmic metric cycles played by the drums. Abstract vocal syllables called *bols*, such as *ta thei thei tat-ta thei thei tai*, are recited by the dancer to a *tala* cycle before beginning the solo – a link to the former singing of the *tawaifs*. There are many varieties of complex footwork, which are executed to the cycle of a *tala*. Ankle bells add to the percussion; a dancer skillfully controls their amplification, ranging from delicately soft to resoundingly loud. In contrast to the rhythmic footwork, a dancer improvises with his or her upper body, moving in a stream of graceful, flowing movements.

As a solo unfolds, *abhinaya* acting and the abstract dance of *nritta* are interwoven. In *abhinaya* the dancer interprets the lyrics of the poetic songs through the movements of the eyes and symbolic *hasta* hand gestures, while *nritta* features virtuosic footwork, turns, and jumps. In these abstract sections, a dancer creates numerous rhythmic patterns to repetitive metric *tala* cycles within musical compositions that can transition between three speeds, or *layas*, and directs the musicians in changing the tempo. An example of this progression is a *tukra*, which is first danced to the slow tempo of the *vilambit laya*, doubles in speed in the *madhya laya*, and then quadruples in the *drut laya*. At the culmination of a dance sequence in the fast *drut laya* tempo, dynamic multiple *chakkara* spins occur. To execute these, a dancer maintains an upright torso and puts weight on one foot while the other rhythmically paddles, propelling the turns. Although *kathak's* energetic spins are anticipated by informed audiences today, this account, written during *kathak's* nascence as a classical form, shows an audience's surprise: "In the Allahabad Music Conference in 1937 . . . a female *Kathak* dancer in the course of her demonstration whirled at such a terrific speed that the spectators thought she had two heads."[31] Another dynamic feature in *kathak* is *utplavanas* – jumps that shoot up vertically, with the legs bent.

During the *abhinaya* narrative sections, facial movements are more subtly executed compared to other forms of classical Indian dance, but the eyes often widen as the eyebrows move up and down repeatedly, and the neck and the head also move rhythmically, shifting from right to left. The narratives and emotions within the lyrics of poetic songs such as *thurmi* or *ghazal* are interpreted through the improvisatory *abhinaya* of the dancer. A *thumri* is Hindu based, with lyrics expressing the amorousness between two mortal lovers – often with double-entendres – or the devotional love of a woman for a god, such as that of Radha for Krishna. Poets such as Rumi, a Sufi Mevlevi dervish, wrote many beautiful *ghazals* in Persian during the twelfth century that are odes to both love and the bittersweet pain of separation. *Gat bhaav*, performed to melodic songs without words or *bols*, are short narrative pieces in which a dancer pantomimes episodes from a mythological legend, such as Krishna as a mischievous, butter-stealing child. In *abhinaya* sequences, the dancer has enormous improvisational freedom.

Current trends

In India today, Rajendra Gangani of the Jaipur *gharana* trains students traditionally, but takes an experimental, contemporary approach in his choreographic work. Shambhu and Birju Maharaj of the Lucknow *gharana* have been *guru* to many. In the 1960s, Kumudini Lakhia, who studied with Shambhu, departed from traditional *kathak* by developing works such as *Duvidha*, a portrayal of a woman's struggle between independence and duty. In 1967, she established Kadamb, her school in Ahmedabad, and trained Aditi Mangaldas, as did Birju Maharaj. In her choreography, Mangaldas creates a contemporary vocabulary incorporating the aesthetic elements of *kathak*, such as in *Footprints on the Water* and *Silence of Rhythm and Sound*. Another student of Kumudini Lakhia and, later, Birju Maharaj is Daksha Sheth.

Figure 1.12

Akram Khan combines *kathak* and contemporary dance in *Gnosis*, his 2010 work inspired by a *Mahabharata* tale.
Image: Richard Haughton. Courtesy of Akram Khan Company.

Rooted in Indian traditions, Sheth's choreography is a blend of martial arts, yoga, and, more recently, aerial dance in works such as *Bhukham* and *Shiva Shakti*. Her daughter, Isha Sharvani, is a lead dancer in Daksha Sheth Dance Company. Maya Rao, a renowned *kathak* dancer who trained with Shambhu Maharaj, was also an esteemed teacher and founder of the *Natya* Institute of *Kathak* and Choreography in New Delhi. Her student and daughter, Madhu Nataraj, established STEM Dance Kampni in 1995 as a contemporary wing of the institute. Nataraj runs workshops addressing deep social issues in rural areas for children, the disabled, and women's organizations.

UK dance artist Akram Khan, of Bangladeshi parentage, was born in London and trained in *kathak* as a child. At thirteen, he toured in Peter Brook's production of *The Mahabharata*. After being exposed to contemporary dance, Khan began choreographing in the 1990s. He maintains his troupe, the Akram Khan Company, but is also a solo performer engaged in intriguing collaborations that include artists such as ballerina Sylvie Guillem (*Sacred Monsters*) and *flamenco* dancer Israel Galván (*Torobaka*). Khan recently made *In the Shadow of Man* for UK dance artist Aakash Odedra's *Rising*, a production featuring solos that blend Odedra's background in *kathak* and *bharatanatyam* with contemporary dance.

Pandit Chitresh Das (1944–2015) founded his school, Chhandam, and the Chitresh Das Dance Company in San Francisco in 1979. *Indian Jazz Suites* – his collaboration with tap artist Jason Samuels Smith – was recorded in the 2011 film *Upaj*. Joanna de Souza trained extensively in India and later trained and performed with Pandit Das. She runs her school, M-DO/Kathak, and the Chhandam Dance Company in Toronto.

Discussion questions: *kathak*

1 When the Cantonment Act of 1864 established regulated prostitution for the British army, the formerly elite *tawaifs* were housed in military brothels. What does this say about colonialism, and what might have been done to help these women?
2 Due to the anti-*nautch* movement, the *tawaifs* were replaced by their former male accompanists, who then became the performers and the teachers of the dance. What might have been gained by continuing to have the contributions of *tawaifs*?
3 *Kathak* is a synthesis of Muslim and Hindu influences. What elements do you see as being of Turkish or Persian culture? And if you are familiar with *flamenco*, what similarities exist?

1.4 *Kathakali*: narrative dance theater from Kerala

Key points: *kathakali*

1 Originating in seventeenth-century Kerala, *kathakali* is traditionally a male form that emerged from an ancient theatrical form and from religious folk rituals, and features plays inspired by the Hindu epic, the *Mahabharata*. Originally held at a *raja's* court or at temple festivals before an audience of mixed social classes, the outdoor performances typically lasted all night.
2 *Kathakali* was originally performed by men rigorously trained in *kalaripayattu*, a martial art practiced by the warrior caste. Traditionally, students pursued a one-on-one *guru-shishya*, or teacher-student tutorship, but today, training occurs predominantly in institutions such as the Kerala Kalamandalam.
3 Ranging from gods to kings and demons, *kathakali's* stock characters are identified by the audience through their elaborate make-up, vibrant costumes, and giant headpieces. During the long make-up process, the actors are said to "become" the character and leave the "green room" transformed.

4 On stage, percussionists accompany vocalists who sing the story line, which is simultaneously interpreted by the performers through *abhinaya* acting, succinct *mudra* hand gestures, and dance.

5 Due to colonialism, patrons of *kathakali* lost their ability to fund their troupes and, by the twentieth century, the form was endangered. The establishment of the Kerala Kalamandalam was key in revitalizing the form.

What is unraveled is a world of might and power where light and darkness, good and evil, wage a titanic conflict, in which great aspirations, noble endeavors, massive achievements, loves and hatreds, struggles, failures and victories tell their imperishable tales . . . What is seen on the stage is a world of dreams, and they are dreams of our deepest longings.[32]

—K. Iyar

Kathakali, which translates as "story-play," is a classical dance drama of Kerala, located in southwest India. Formerly known as the Malabar Coast, this beautiful region of beaches, mountains, and forests has had a long history of trading spices with the Greeks, Egyptians, Chinese, Phoenicians, Romans, Portuguese, and the Dutch. Although Hindu is the local religion, Jews, Muslims, and Christians have long been a vital part of the populace. Just as Kerala demonstrates a mix of many influences, *kathakali* dance drama originated from an amalgam of several artistic and militaristic practices, and began flourishing under the patronage of nobility and wealthy landowners in the seventeenth century. It is traditionally performed by men rigorously trained in *kalaripayattu*, a martial art practiced by the *Nayar* warrior caste that dates back to the thirteenth century.

Ranging from celestial gods to heroic kings and immoral demons, *kathakali* stock characters are easily identified by Kerala audiences through their elaborate make-up and vibrant costumes. Its plays, written in a mix of Sanskrit and the local language of Malayalam, are based on mythological tales from the *Mahabharata*, the *Ramayana*, and other epic Hindu *puranas* (scriptures). On stage, percussionists accompany vocalists who sing the story line, which is simultaneously interpreted by the performers through *abhinaya* acting, *mudra* hand gestures, and dance. These dance dramas, originally held at a *raja*'s court or outside at a temple festival before a mixed audience of social classes, would typically last throughout the night. Today, they may occur in a theater and trimmed to be less than four hours.

Origins of *kathakali*

The rich, operatic spectacle of *kathakali* evolved from folk forms, theatrical traditions, and *kalaripayattu*. Its roots can be seen in *theyyam* ritual folk dance, in which deities are honored by performers who wear enormous headpieces, voluminous costuming, and have painted orange faces. In Hindu temples of Kerala, spiritual Sanskrit dramas were recited by *cakkyars*, hereditary Brahmin actors famous for their *abhinaya* acting and dance. Their art evolved into *kuttiyattam*, a theatrical form that became a progenitor of *kathakali*, and thrived under royal patronage. Not surprisingly, subjects were tailored to display the courage and power of rulers, who regularly showed their might by pushing the boundaries of a neighboring prince's lands. Scholar Phillip Zarrelli notes, "Given the vagaries and bellicosity of the exercise of power in medieval Kerala, it is not surprising that one of the central anxieties and concerns for *kathakali's* ruling, landholding patron-connoisseurs was that of exploring the nature of the 'heroic.'"[33] In this aristocratic entertainment, even the most refined noble character was capable of committing the most barbarous acts in the name of honor. An example is seen in *The Dice Game* from the *Mahabharata*, in which the Pandava brothers are cheated by the Kauravas, their evil cousins. Consequently, the Pandavas lose their kingdom, as well as Draupadi, their common wife. After she is publicly humiliated by their cousin Dussasana, who attempts to disrobe and rape her, the revengeful Bhima savagely disembowels him through the use of fake blood and entrails.

Case study: Theyyam

Theyyam, or "dance of the gods," is a form of ritual folk dance to propitiate deities, performed by dancers with intricately painted orange faces who wear voluminous straw costumes and impressive headpieces. *Theyyam* has a dangerous element: while dancing, flares that are imbedded in the large headpiece are lit, as are wicks that protrude from the huge skirt. This lighting of the spiritually cleansing fire entices the deity of the shrine to "come alive" in the body of the flaming dancer. While ablaze, a dancer ritually repeats eight steps forward and eight steps back, a pattern reminiscent of *kalaasams*, the repetitive footwork in *kathakali*.

Two rulers contributed to the development of *kathakali* during the seventeenth century. Manaveda, the *Zamorin* of Kozhikode, wrote in Sanskrit on the life of Krishna in *Krishnattam*, while *Raja* Kottarakara Tampuran wrote *Ramanattam* in the local language of Malayalam, based upon the epic *Ramayana*. The success of *Ramanattam* inspired other plays in Malayalam, which made them more accessible to the less educated. Later innovations came from Prince Vettathu Tampuran, who deviated from *kuttiyattam* by directing the performers to act silently through gestures,

Think about:
Can showing violence in art actually keep a society from being violent?

Figure 1.13
Theyyam (a ritual folk dance) performed at Vilangad Bhagavathi Temple in Kadavathur village near Thalassery, Kerala, India.
Image: Jack Vartoogian, Front Row Photos.

Figure 1.14 (p. 23)
Kalamandalam Gopi as Bhima, disemboweling Dussasana, played by Padnamabhan Nair, in "Dussasana Vadham" (The Annihilation of Dussasana) from *The Dice Game*.
Image: Jack Vartoogian, Front Row Photos.

facial expressions, and dance, and employed background singers to vocalize the plot.[34] Gradually, influenced by *kuttiyattam*, *theyyam*, and *kalaripayattu*, *kathakali* emerged as a form, patronized by nobility and wealthy landlords for performances at court, private homes, and temple festivals.

Training and technique

Kathakali students start training in childhood, for a minimum of six years. Traditionally, a pupil seeks out a *guru* at a *kalari* gymnasium and requests a *guru-shishya* (teacher-student) tutorship. If accepted, the student gives a small gift to the teacher, who will then bless his student with a prayer, and present him with a *kacha* – a loincloth worn for training. Today, this same reverent relationship exists, but now more often occurs within one of the many academies found in Kerala (and elsewhere in India) such as the Kerala Kalamandalam. Founded by Vallathol Narayana Menon in 1930 at a time when *kathakali* was in decline due to lack of patronage by princes and the wealthy, this academy offers institutional training in *kathakali* and *kuttiyattam*.

At the Kerala Kalamandalam, training begins at 4:30 in the morning and continues throughout the day. Physical discipline is mastered through complete training of facial expressions, *mudra* hand gestures, and the movements of the limbs and torso through dance training and *kalaripayattu*.[35] As students gain proficiency in technique, they begin to study character expression, percussion, vocalization, and interpretation of the texts. To encourage suppleness in the hips, a student oils his body, and lies flat on the floor while his *guru* administers massage with his feet, controlling the pressure by supporting himself by a hanging rope. Afterward, the student rubs the *guru's* calves in thanks, and then performs post-massage exercises – splits, leg swings, flips, and circular movements of the spine.

Since *kathakali* is concerned with imparting narratives through *abhinaya*, the training of the face and head – eyes, eyebrows, cheeks, lips, chin, and neck – along with the hands, is detailed and rigorous. In order to make the eyes expressive, exercises called *nritta drishti* (dance of the eyes) are performed daily. Holding each eye open with the thumb and index finger, a student follows a *guru's* hand gestures and makes the eyes vibrate, move in a circle from side to side, up to down, diagonally, in a square, or zigzag. Various glances of the eye and articulations of the eyebrows are also mastered. Advanced students are able to open their eyelids so widely that the white surrounding the whole iris is exposed, and can roll them upward so only that only the whites of the eyes are seen. These isolation exercises enable a pupil to express the nine *navarasas* (love, humor, sadness, anger, courage, fear, disgust, wonder, and serenity) and the overall *bhava*, or emotional state of a character. The hands are trained to perform *mudras* – symbolic hand gestures that can be representative of the words of a text, or suggest an idea or feeling. From the single- or double-hand formations of twenty-four basic *mudras*, hundreds of words expressing actions, situations, animals, plants, or flowers can be conveyed in tandem with facial expressions, body positions, and dance to impart a narrative. As training advances, a *guru* improvises a story as his student interprets the words using only his eyes and *mudra* gestures. Later, movements of the body are added.

Discipline of *angika abhinaya*, or action of the limbs, is largely obtained through arduously training in *kalaripayattu*. A student performs a series of deep lunges, high kicks, circular movements of the spine into backwards arches, head balances, flips, jumps, and leg splits, which develop both flexibility and determination in this training, originally for *Nayar* soldiers. The basic stance in *kathakali* is that of a warrior: the chin is held tightly against the throat, the arms extend forward, the legs are spread wide apart with the knees bent, and one moves with the weight placed predominantly on the outside edges of each foot as the toes curl inward. The torso is upright and the buttocks are pushed slightly backward, forming a curve in the spine. This posture, in addition to the contracted feet, is said to create a stance that allows any movement to happen with militaristic alacrity and promotes agility.[36] As rhythmic training, a student performs dance movements in this stance to three speeds of *tala*, or rhythm, with the hands and the feet following the slow, medium, or fast beat.

Figure 1.15
Kerala Kalamandalam actors as the Pandavas and Kauravas, playing a fateful game of dice.
Image: Jack Vartoogian, Front Row Photos

This rigorous training of physical exercises and massage, which render great strength and extraordinary flexibility, has instigated comparisons between a *kathakali* actor and a *yogi* – one who follows the path of yoga, or union – because of the mental concentration and focus that develop. Physically mastering the body leads to mental and spiritual control: although the extreme splits and gyrations of the torso done in *kalaripayattu* are never seen on stage, the training allows the performers to endure the long hours of preparation, promotes the ability to profoundly embody a character, and instills a deep, life-long discipline. As a result, many *kathakali* artists enjoy long careers.

Think about:
How does the arduous
training of *kathakali*
performers reflect the
culture of Kerala?

Character types, make-up, and costuming

A *kathakali* student initially explores all the stock character roles and then specializes in the most suitable one. Some of these types include *pacca* (green), *katti* (knife), *tati* (bearded), *kari* (black), *minukku* (radiant), and *teppu* (special). All are distinguished by specific costuming and make-up, which enables immediate audience recognition. Preparations for a show take at minimum three hours and occur in the "green room," a hallowed space that might be a room backstage or a makeshift tent. No matter the venue, the green room is considered to be the sanctum of Durga, the patron deity of *kathakali*, and her presence instills an austere atmosphere. Here, a performer arrives as an ordinary human and, over the next several hours, exits for the stage as an extraordinary god, a resplendent woman, or a terrifying demon.

In creating the elaborately painted faces of *kathakali* performers, the outline of the intricate patterns is first traced on by the actor and then filled in by experts who paint the faces of the performers as they lay on fiber mats, meditating upon transformation into their character. The red, green, yellow, white, and black pigments – formerly ground from stones such as lapis lazuli and turquoise – are mixed with coconut oil and then meticulously painted on with bamboo slivers. In order to enhance the expressions of their eyes and allow them to be more easily seen, *kathakali* performers redden them by placing a crushed *cuntappuvu* seed under each eyelid, which supposedly causes no discomfort to the actor.[37]

The green face of a *pacca* type symbolizes the heroism and moral excellence inherent in gods, kings, and heroes known as *satvik*, or virtuous characters. His face is embellished with a red bow-shaped mouth and a mark of Vishnu painted in white and red in the middle of a yellow patch on his forehead, while his eyes and eyebrows are elongated with thick black lines. On his jaw a *chutti* beard – crafted from thick white paper and affixed with rice paste – gives the actor a superhuman appearance. Ravana, the arrogant ten-headed king and abductor of Sita in the *Ramayana*, is an example of the *katti* (knife) type. His green face and white *chutti* beard indicate a noble character; however, the red lines resembling bent daggers that thrust up from his nose onto his forehead and splay across his moustache indicate his flawed nature, as do two *chutti* knobs that sit awkwardly on his forehead and the tip of his nose.

The *tati* characterization comprises three bearded types: red, white, and black. A red-beard is an evil character, such as Dussasana, enemy of the Pandava brothers. He has a formidable demeanor: his face is red, his eyes and lips are blackened, and he wears an oversized *chutti* moustache. Like the *katti* type, *chutti* balls sit like warts on his face, but are bigger. The black-beard type, with his dark face and a white *chutti* flower on his nose, represents hunters and dwellers of the forest, as well as schemers. The beloved monkey general Hanuman, a beneficent character and hero in the *Ramayana*, is an example of the white-beard type. He wears *chutti* side-burns and his chin is painted white, black, and red, with a small marking of green on his snout. *Kari* types represent demonesses; their faces are painted black and ornamented with red and white markings. *Kari* witches and terrifying red- and black-beard types may have fangs and make undisciplined groans and grunts. In contrast, the golden facial make-up of *minukku* characters indicates their gentle nature. Female characters and Brahmin priests all fall into this category, as do *lalitas* – *kari* demonesses masquerading as beautiful women. Their make-up merely accentuates the eyes. The last type is *teppu*, which includes masked animal characters such as lions or birds.[38]

All male performers (excluding ascetic Brahmin priests) wear an enormous skirt that bells out on all sides. To create this silhouette, an actor ties a multitude of stiffly starched cloth strips around the waist to create a sort of petticoat and then dons an overskirt that goes to mid-calf, with a pair of white leggings underneath. On top, a jacket is worn – red for heroes, blue for Krishna, and fur for Hanuman and the red-bearded types. The chest is covered with a breastplate and many necklaces hang round the neck, along with scarves ending in large cupped tassels that have mirrors concealed inside. If necessary, in the midst of a performance, an actor can turn a tassel right side up to do a surreptitious make-up check.

The *Bharata Natyasastra* makes note of the types of headgear for gods and kings, which have been modified over time. The glittering *kiritam* headpiece is a tiered tower that fits over the head, backed by a large circular disk painted in a mix of gold, green, and red, and adorned with small mirrors that sparkle. *Pacca* characters wear these, as do *tati* red-bearded types, but their disk is substantially larger. Divine characters such as Shiva or Rama wear a *muti* – a conical headpiece decorated with silver spangles that vibrate as the character moves. The wide brim of Hanuman's hat is trimmed with silver, while those worn by the *kari* types, or ogresses, are bucket-shaped and widen at the top. Below all these, a waist-length black fiber wig is worn. Further ornamentation includes round disc-shaped earrings called *kundala*, arm bangles, armlets, and *nupura* – ankle bells. The fingers of the left hand on most male characters are capped with long silver fingernails that enhance the *mudras*, but can also be used destructively, like claws.

Kathakali music

A *kathakali* percussion orchestra performs on stage right, while two to three singers stand center stage behind the actors. The Carnatic musical ensemble is made up of a *maddalam* drum, a *cenda* drum, a metal gong, a pair of cymbals, and a conch shell. The double-headed *maddalam* blends especially well with *minnukku* female voices, while the more forceful *cenda* highlights turbulent scenes and is not generally played for female characters unless they are evil *kali* types. The gong and cymbals provide accompaniment for dance interludes called *kalasams* that punctuate the verses. Since *kathakali* has recurring themes of battle and bloodletting, the drums will foreshadow these violent scenes with a crescendo of clashing drums and cymbals. The *kathakali* singers lead the actions of the performer, who acts out every lyric with *mudras*, word by word. *Kathakali* texts alternate between *slokas* – narrative sections that describe situations or surroundings, and *padams*, a dialogue or soliloquy in first-person narration that accompanies dance passages, set to specific rhythmic patterns called *tala*.

The preliminary performance and the *kathakali* stage

A *kathakali* stage is a sacred spot where the gods are entertained. An outdoor stage is on the same level as the audience, who sit on mats covering the ground. A canopy, supported by four poles and decorated with palm leaves and flowers, is suspended above and a waist-high brass lamp and a stool are placed downstage center. The use of props is minimal, although fake blood, cudgels, and entrails do make frequent appearances. In this relatively bare performance space, it is the actors who will conjure up the characters and their surroundings through their skillful *abhinaya*. The rank of a character is indicated by his placement on stage: characters of higher social status will always be placed on the audience's left.[39]

Kathakali scholar Phillip Zarrilli lived in India and studied the form during the 1980s. In *The Kathakali Complex* he describes the long attention span local audiences displayed in watching a *kathakali* play, when performances normally lasted sixteen hours and beds were brought for small children. He vividly describes in detail the proceedings for a performance during a temple festival in a village in Kerala.[40] Before a show, the actors arrive at approximately five o'clock at the green room

Figure 1.18
Kalamandalam Manoj as the mythological half-man, half-lion Narasimha, an avatar of Vishnu and killer of Hiranyakashipu.
Image: Sividas Vadayath

Figure 1.19
Kalamandalam Manoj as a disturbed king of the *katti* type in a revealing "curtain look."
Image: Sividas Vadayath

to begin their transformation. Meanwhile, an image of the temple deity is paraded throughout the town on an elephant. At sunset, the musicians begin to "announce" the show by playing their drums, gongs, and cymbals in the performance space. This *keli*, or calling of the audience, can be heard for miles, and engenders excitement. At eight o'clock, the lamp on stage is lit and the audience gathers.

A unique aspect to a *kathakali* is a pre-performance of sorts that is not always visually accessible to spectators. A *therissila* – a portable rectangle silk curtain hand held by two men – is used in various ways. At the beginning of a *kathakali* show, student dancers obscured by the curtain are given the opportunity to perform on stage, albeit unseen, in a preliminary devotional dance called the *todayam*. The curtain is then lowered part way so the audience may see the *purapattu* – a duet danced by a *pacca* hero and his companion. After the *purapattu*, the curtain is used for the *tira-nokku*, or curtain look, which creates an atmosphere of tension and dread by giving the audience a glimpse of the evil characters. As the drums wildly pound, shrieks, growls, and other disturbing sounds are heard. Standing on the stool, an actor will grip the top of the *therissila*, revealing ferociously long fingernails, and ominously lower the curtain. Gradually, the terrifying face of the character, eerily lit from underneath by the lamplight, reveals its menacing nature to the audience. At nine o'clock, the musicians play the first rhythmic prelude announcing the start of the play. The curtain is dropped and the show begins.

Current trends

For over three centuries, men performed female roles in *kathakali* because women were not considered to possess the stamina and strength to train in *kalaripayattu*, wear heavy costumes, and endure long performance hours. In the last few decades, however, female training in *kathakali* has increased, refuting these suppositions, and considerable contributions by women have been made to the form. Founded in 1975 by legendary male *kathakali* artist Padmasri Kalamandalam Krishnan Nair, the forty-member Tripunithura Kathakali Kendram Ladies Troupe (TKK) is currently led by Parvati Menon, an original member.

French actress Annette Leday began studying *kathakali* in Kerala in the 1970s. Today, she directs Annette Leday/Keli Company, which features both Indian and Western dancers in productions that have received international acclaim, such as *Kathakali King Lear* (1989) co-directed with David McRuvie. Her newest work, *Mithuna* (2014), performed by a French and Indian cast, draws inspiration from erotic couplings carved on ancient Indian temples and explores questions of gender and sex. Another artist pushing the boundaries is Maya Krishna Rao, who as a child trained at the International Centre for *Kathakali* in New Delhi. Her landmark solo performance, *Khol Do* (1993), featured *kathakali* movement to the music of Phillip Glass, and addressed the devastating riots that followed the partitioning of India and Pakistan. In a more recent work, *Ravana Nama*, Rao controversially chose to take on the male role of Ravana, abductor of Sita, and paired *kathakali* with the pop songs of Michael Jackson, backed by computer-generated images. *Walk*, her gripping monologue about the 2012 gang-rape on a bus that killed a young woman, is dance per se, but the physicality of her gestures shows a power garnered from concentrated training and demonstrate her deeply fervent concerns and razor-sharp skewering of ineffectual and corrupt politicians.

1.4 Exploration: excerpt from "Who Wears the Skirts in Kathakali?" by Diane Daugherty and Marlene Pitkow[41]

The Tripunithura Kathakali Kendram Ladies Troupe, based in Kerala, is active today.

For three centuries *kathakali* performance was the domain of upper-class male-members of Kerala's warrior and priestly castes. After the caste system was legally abolished in 1947, boys of all backgrounds were permitted to train at the arts academies. Indian girls, however, were still restricted to private instruction. In 1975 a group of highly skilled young women formed an all-female troupe, the Tripunithura Kathakali Kendram Ladies Troupe [TKK]. All TKK members are from the castes who were traditionally *kathakali* patrons and performers . . . Forming the TKK was a pragmatic, not political, decision; its perpetuation shows a commitment to the art, not to any ideological position. The TKK women chose to practice *kathakali* instead of the regional female performance forms . . . not because they wanted to infiltrate a male-dominated performance tradition, but because they consider *kathakali* a more highly developed and challenging art. But performing with men on a regular basis would expose her to lewd gossip or the improper advances of drunken actors, as endured by Chavara Parukutty, the only woman to attempt to earn her living as a *kathakali* performer in Kerala.

Before the institutionalization of *kathakali* in the 1930s, knowledge was passed directly from teacher to pupil, a process known as the *gurukula* system. . . The shift to academy training was the first step toward *kathakali's* secularization. Mahakavi Vallathol – Kerala's poet laureate, who founded the Kerala Kalamandalam – once remarked to a friend . . . K. Krishnan, that he did not think a Kerala girl could possibly do *kathakali*. Krishnan, hearing this as a challenge, hired a teacher to train his eight-year-old daughter, Radha. When Radha performed for Vallathol, the poet took back his disparaging remarks. Later Radha performed for Jawaharlal Nehru, and the Prime Minister gave Krishnan a grant to found an academy for training girls in *kathakali*.

Today, foreign women enjoy a special status. They are the only women allowed to study *kathakali* alongside the boys at the Kalamandalam. One TKK member who applied for admission was turned down because, the chairman of the governing board told us, the presence of an Indian woman in class would disrupt the learning process . . . Some men question the importance of the *uzhicchal* [massage] . . . The massage, which begins when a boy is eight years old, molds and reshapes the body, so that he can assume the difficult positions . . . one male aficionado observed that a woman's body is "like a banana plant – so soft and supple that there is no need for females to have the massage." Radhika [a TKK member] believes that the massage is unnecessary for women because they are naturally more flexible than men. "Men's body construction is different . . . At puberty men become very stiff and this is why they need *uzhicchal*. Without massage we can do what men do after massage."

Padmanabhan Nair, a former principal of the Kerala Kalamandalam, also articulated reservations about women performing *kathakali*. Biologically, he claims, women lack the power and energy necessary. He maintains that since the female roles were designed for the male body, only men can effectively play them. And, because it is socially unacceptable for women to exhibit the darker emotions in daily life, it would be difficult for them to play roles which demand that they show anger or disgust. "It is true, we are expected to control anger," Geetha [a TKK member] laughed. "Your mother and the culture say do not get angry, do not get angry. So when we get a chance to get angry onstage, full anger comes out."

Discussion questions: *kathakali*

1 Despite the arduous training of a *kathakali* student in *kalaripayattu*, a performer on stage in his large costume and headpiece never performs choreography that even faintly matches the splits, high kicks, and jumps practiced in the martial art. Why is this extreme mastering of the body pursued?

2 For over three centuries, men performed female roles in *kathakali* because women were not considered to possess the stamina and strength to train in *kalaripayattu*, wear heavy costumes, and endure long performance hours. Discuss how and why this has changed.

3 Today, *bharatanatyam*, *kathak*, and *kathakali* have become systematized and designated as classical Indian dance, and what was once a hereditary profession – passed between generations – is apt to be learned in an academic institution. What perhaps has been lost here and what gained?

Notes

1 Phillips, Miriam. "A Shared Technique/Shared Roots? A Comparison of Kathak and Flamenco Dance History," 47.
2 Sreevinas, Mytheli. "Creating Conjugal Subjects: Devadasis and the Politics of Marriage in Colonial Madras Presidency," 79.
3 Kersenboom, Saskia C. "The Traditional Repertoire of the Tiruttani Temple Dancers," 57.
4 Srinivasan, Amrit. "Reform or Conformity?," 142.
5 Sreevinas, 66.
6 Chakravorty, Pallabi. "Dancing into Modernity: Multiple Narratives in India's Kathak Dance," 116–117.
7 Hubel, Teresa. "The High Cost of Dancing: When the Indian Women's Movement Went after the *Devadasis*," 161.
8 Srinivasan, 140.
9 Sreevinas, 69–70.
10 O'Shea, Janet, *At Home in the World: Bharata Natyam on the Global Stage*, 31.
11 Sreevinas, 77–78.
12 O'Shea, 35.
13 Meduri, Avanthi. "Bharatanatyam as World Historical Form," 255–256; O'Shea, 36–37.
14 Allen, Matthew. "Rewriting the Script for South Indian Dance," 226.
15 Katrak, Ketu H., *Contemporary Indian Dance: New Creative Choreography in India and the Diaspora*, 31.
16 Hari Krishnan, personal communication, November 21, 2015.
17 Soneji, *Unfinished Gestures*, 75–79.
18 Walker, Margaret E., *India's Kathak Dance in Historical Perspective*, 77.
19 Although each *gharana* originally had very different traits, today these seem to be converging as people train with different schools. Personal communication with Anisha Anantpukar, December 28, 2016.
20 Ibid., 134.
21 Vatsyayan, Kapila, *Indian Classical Dance*, 85.
22 Walker, 43.
23 Katrak, 31.
24 Walker, 92.
25 Chakravorty, 117.
26 Walker, 94.
27 Walker, Margaret. "Courtesans and Choreographers: The (Re)Placement of Women in the History of *Kathak* Dance," 280.
28 Chakravorty, 119.
29 Gautier, Théophile, *The Romantic Ballet*, 23.
30 Bor, Joep. "Mamia, Ammani, and Other *Bayadères*," 29.
31 Devi, Ragini, *Dances of India*, 61.
32 Iyer, K., *Kathakali: The Sacred Dance-Drama of Malabar*, 24.
33 Zarrilli, Phillip, *Kathakali Dance Drama: Where Gods and Demons Come to Play*, 23.
34 Pandeya, *The Art of Kathakali*, 37.
35 See *The Kathakali Complex: Actor, Performance, and Structure* by Phillip Zarrilli for an extensive description on Kathakali training, costuming, music, and performance.
36 Zarrilli, Phillip, *The Kathakali Complex,* 155.
37 Zarrilli, Phillip, *Kathakali Dance Drama: Where Gods and Demons Come to Play*, 57.
38 Ibid., 53–55.
39 Ibid., 51.
40 Zarrilli, 161.
41 Daugherty, Diane and Marlene Pitkow. "Who Wears the Skirts in Kathakali?" 138–156.

Bibliography

Visual sources

YouTube

"Alarmel Valli: Tillana Bharatanatyam," YouTube video, 6:50, posted by "Moni Mishrakeshi," January 14, 2015, www.youtube.com/watch?v=XVNKUbxiGas&index=5&list=PLmsfZEGhTh-vs-3e9JAEONsz7kWsrngqD

"Bala (1976) – Satyajit Ray Documentary on T. Balasaraswati," YouTube video, 31:17, posted by "Muntiri Kkottai," March 22, 2012, www.youtube.com/watch?v=ak_a1RJ2DZc

"Kalaripayattu: The Secret of Kundalini 2," YouTube Video, 3:23, posted by "Sangam Institute of Indian Martial Arts," November 21, 2012, www.youtube.com/watch?v=ZioVSjjC0Jg

"Kalyanasougandhikam in Kathakali, Pt. 1, Invis Multimedia, DVD," YouTube video, 9:57, posted by "indavideodotorg," October 18, 2010, www.youtube.com/watch?v=YEwn3fCwhRw

"Pt. Birju Maharaj at Carnegie Hall, 1," YouTube video, 14:03, posted by "tripmonk0," October 12, 2011, www.youtube.com/watch?v=IUkpUkkrBc8

"Pt. Birju Maharaj at Carnegie Hall, 2," YouTube video, 14:58, posted by "tripmonk0," October 12, 2011, www.youtube.com/watch?v=mXxQuGhZlqA

"T. Balasaraswati Documentary," YouTube video, 10:26, posted by "Parisumuthu Kannan," November 11, 2011, www.youtube.com/watch?v=ibSmDqm-k3o

"Ted Shawn's Cosmic Dance of Shiva," YouTube Video, .41, posted by "Kauai's Hidden Monastery," October 1, 2009, www.youtube.com/watch?v=M1jyD0QiTsQ

Written sources

Allen, Matthew Harp. "Rewriting the Script for South Indian Dance." In *Bharatanayam: A Reader*, edited by Davesh Soneji, 205–252. New Delhi: Oxford University Press, 2010.

Bor, Joep. "Mamia, Ammani, and Other *Bayadères*." In *Bharatanayam: A Reader*, edited by Davesh Soneji, 13–52. New Delhi: Oxford University Press, 2010.

Chakravorty, Pallabi. "Dancing into Modernity: Multiple Narratives in India's Kathak Dance." *Dance Research Journal*, Vol. 38, No. 1–2 (Summer–Winter 2006): 115–136. Accessed November 11, 2015. Stable URL: www.jstor.org/stable/20444667.

Daugherty, Diane and Marlene Pitkow. "Who Wears the Skirts in Kathakali?" *The Drama Review*, Vol. 35, No. 2 (Summer, 1991): 138–156. Accessed December 28, 2015. DOI: 10.2307/1146093.

Devi, Ragini. *Dances of India*. New York: Books for Libraries, 1980.

Gautier, Théophile. *The Romantic Ballet*. Translation: Cyril Beaumont. London: Cyril Beaumont, Publisher, 1947. Republished by Dance Horizons, New York, 1972.

Hubel, Teresa. "The High Cost of Dancing: When the Indian Women's Movement Went After the *Devadasis*." In *Bharatanayam: A Reader*, edited by Davesh Soneji, 205–252. New Delhi: Oxford University Press, 2010.

Iyer, Bharatha K. *Kathakali: The Sacred Dance-Drama of Malabar*. London: Luzack and Company Ltd., 1955.

Jonas, Gerald. *Dancing: The Pleasure, Power, and Art of Movement*. New York: Harry N. Abrams Inc., 1992.

Jowitt, Deborah. *Time and the Dancing Image*. Berkeley: University of California Press, 1988.

Katrak, Ketu H. *Contemporary Indian Dance: New Creative Choreography in India and the Diaspora*. New York: Palgrave Macmillan, 2011.

Kersenboom, Saskia C. "The Traditional Repertoire of the Tiruttani Temple Dancers." In *Bharatanayam: A Reader*, edited by Davesh Soneji, 53–68. New Delhi: Oxford University Press, 2010.

Meduri, Avanthi. "Bharatanatyam as World Historical Form." In *Bharatanatyam: A Reader*, edited by Davesh Soneji, 53–68. New Delhi: Oxford University Press, 2010.

Narayanan, Mundoli. "The Politics of Memory: The Rise of the Anti-Hero in Kathakali." In *Dance Matters: Performing India*, edited by Pallabi Chakravorty and Nilanjana Gupta, 237–263. New Delhi: Routledge Press, 2010.

O'Shea, Janet. "Dancing Through History and Ethnography: Indian Classical Dance and the Performance of the Past." In *Dancing from Past to Present: Nation, Culture, Identities*, edited by Theresa Jill Buckland, 123–152. Madison, WI: University of Wisconsin Press, 2006.

O'Shea, Janet. *At Home in the World: Bharata Natyam on the Global Stage*. Middletown, CT: Wesleyan University Press, 2007.

Pandaya, Avinash C. *The Art of Kathakali*. New Delhi: Munshiram Manoharlal Publishers, 2nd ed., 1999.

Phillips, Miriam. "A Shared Technique/Shared Roots? A Comparison of Kathak and Flamenco Dance History." *Proceedings from Society of Dance History Scholars* (Winter, 1991): 47–53. http://worldartswest.org/plm/guide/locator/KFHistory1991.pdf.

Reddy, S. Muthulakshmi. "Why Should the Devadasi Institution in the Hindu Temples Be Abolished?" In *Bharatanatyam: A Reader*, edited by Davesh Soneji, 115–127. New Delhi: Oxford University Press, 2010.

Soneji, Davesh. "Critical Steps: Thinking Through Bharatanatyam in the Twenty-First Century." In *Bharatanatyam: A Reader*, edited by Davesh Soneji, xi–li. New Delhi: Oxford University Press, 2010.

Soneji, Davesh. *Unfinished Gestures: Devadasis, Memory, and Modernity in South India*. Chicago: University of Chicago Press, 2012.

Sreevinas, Mytheli. "Creating Conjugal Subjects: Devadasis and the Politics of Marriage in Colonial Madras Presidency." *Feminist Studies*, Vol. 37, No. 1 (Spring 2011): 63–92. Stable URL: www.jstor.org/stable/23069884.

Srinvivasan, Amrit. "Reform, or Conformity? Temple Prostitution and the Community in the Madras Presidency." In *Bharatanatyam: A Reader*, edited by Davesh Soneji, 53–68. New Delhi: Oxford University Press, 2010.

Vatsyayan, Kapila. *Indian Classical Dance*. New Delhi: Publications Division, Government of India, 1974.

Walker, Margaret E. "Courtesans and Choreographers: The (Re)Placement of Women in the History of *Kathak* Dance." In *Dance Matters: Performing India*, edited by Pallabi Chakravorty and Nilanjana Gupta, 279–293. New Delhi: Routledge Press, 2010.

Walker, Margaret E. *India's Kathak Dance in Historical Perspective*. Burlington, VT: Ashgate Publishing Company, 2014.

Zarrilli, Phillip B. *The Kathakali Complex: Actor, Performance, and Structure*. New Delhi: Abbinav Publications, 1984.

Zarrilli, Phillip B. *Kathakali Dance Drama: Where Gods and Demons Come to Play*. London and New York: Routledge Press, 2000.

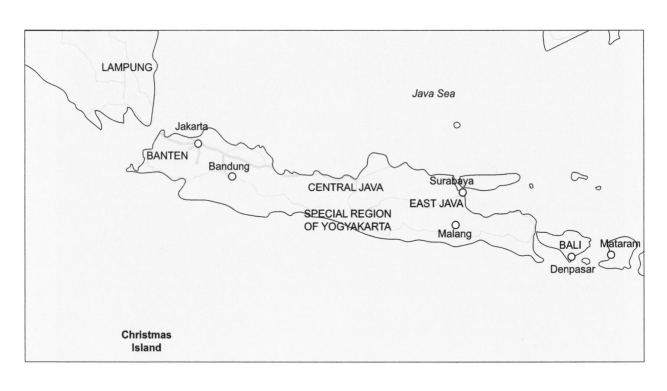

Bali and Java
From temple, to village, to court

In Balinese thought, evil can never be entirely defeated, only propitiated and, to a limited extent, controlled. It is necessary, therefore, to attend very frequently to bringing the divine and the demonic into balance.
—I Madé Bandem and Fredrik Eugene deBoer[1]

2.1 Overview

Bali and Java are two islands of many thousands that make up the 3,000-mile-wide archipelago of Indonesia in Southeast Asia. A Hindu-Buddhist kingdom formerly ruled each, and this syncretism (merging of religious beliefs) reflecting the significance of Hindu mythology and Buddhist philosophy from China influenced dance in both places. Based in Java, the powerful Majapahit Empire expanded into Bali in the fourteenth century, and the erudite ethos of Majapahit-Hindu culture profoundly influenced Balinese temple architecture, literature, and dance dramas. When this prosperous Empire fell to Muslim invaders in the early sixteenth century, the top echelon of Javanese society – priests, aristocrats, artisans, dancers, musicians, and scholars – escaped to Bali and set up a Hindu stronghold that has resisted conversion to Islam or Christianity to this day.[2]

Although Holland dominated other parts of Indonesia in the nineteenth century, the Balinese fought fiercely against colonization and maintained their independence until 1908. With the intent of making Bali a tourist destination, the Dutch banned slavery and widow sacrifice, as well as phased out opium use.[3] By the 1920s, Bali had become a haven for expatriate artists, musicians, and anthropologists. The Japanese invasion during World War II put an end to this society, as well as to Dutch colonial rule. Indonesia received independence in 1945.

When an abortive *coup d'état* took place in 1965, General Suharto and his military forces blamed the Indonesian Communist Party (PKI) and began a societal purge. From 1965 to 1966, an estimated two million suspected communists were murdered or incarcerated across Indonesia. Suharto became dictator of what he named the New Order and ruled Indonesia with an iron hand from 1967 until 1998. At the time, the US government was embroiled in a war against communists in Vietnam and supported Suharto's anti-communist regime. Although many were victimized, dancers were particular targets and women from communist-affiliated social groups were slaughtered on the basis of their "unclean" folk dancing.[4] Yet Suharto used the court dances of the Yogyakarta and Surakarta palaces as political propaganda, demonstrating the power of his militaristic regime in which torture, forced silence, and accusations without trial abounded.[5]

Although these devastating events have left deep scars on the Indonesian people who survived these times, there has been tremendous effort to resurrect their cultural traditions. The revival of folk dances and the expression of contemporary artists have contributed to the resurrection of old forms and the creation of new ones. There is a Norwegian folk proverb: "Where song is, pause to listen. Evil people have no song." If we substitute the word "dance" for "song," we can now pause to watch, as these are better times.

Balinese ideology

When India's prime minister Pandit Nehru visited Bali in the 1950s, he immortalized it as a tropical paradise by describing it as "the morning of the world." The inhabitants of Bali actually do call their home "Island of the Gods," or *Pulau Dewata*, and believe the deities live atop the sacred Mount Agung, an active volcano. The Balinese use it to orient themselves in a unique way, known as the *kaja* and *kelod* axis. *Kaja* means "toward the mountain" and is a sacred, positive direction, while *kelod*, meaning "toward the ocean," is a dangerous and negative trajectory since demons inhabit the sea. For example, in any village, the most holy sanctum of a temple will be aligned toward Mount Agung in a *kaja* orientation, while the graveyard will be situated on the outskirts of a village in a *kelod* direction, toward the ocean.

Figure 2.1
Gunung Agung, Bali's sacred volcano.
Image: Martin Garrido (Flickr. Published under a CC BY 2.0 license).

Bali is the only island in the predominantly Islamic Indonesian archipelago where Hinduism remains the dominant religion. Honoring deities is a part of the daily lives of many, and dance and music are considered to be divine offerings. Trance occurs in certain dances and is a religious experience, as it allows for communication with ancestors, gods, and spirits. In times of need, the spirits are propitiated with dances and offerings. If pleased, a spirit will manifest itself in the body of a dancer, who will then "speak" for the deity, answering questions on how to eradicate any misfortune. Trance states may also be induced by wearing holy masks – infused with magical power through the blessings of a priest – which are reverently stored in temples.

Balinese temples are called *pura* and have three courtyards in which three categories of dance are performed. The most inner courtyard, closest to Mount Agung, is where sacred, or *wali* dances occur. In the second, semi-sacred or *bebali* dances are performed, such as *topeng*, masked dance dramas (a rich Balinese tradition, worthy of study). In the outer courtyard, secular ceremonies of the *bali-balihan* category are held. During temple celebrations known as *Odalan* it is believed that the gods descend from Mount Agung and enter the sanctuary. One of the largest *Odalan* occurs at the sacred Pura Besakih, perched high on the mountainside of Mount Agung. When the volcano last erupted in 1963, Pura Besakih was in grave peril and local dancers performed a *baris gede*

Figure 2.2
Pura Besakih on the slopes of Mount Agung is Bali's holiest temple.
Image: Sean Hamlin (Flickr. Published under a CC BY 2.0 license).

to appease the deities. The molten rivers of lava fortunately parted, sparing the mountainside temple – an act the Balinese regarded as a wondrous miracle from their gods.

While much of Indonesia converted to Islam, Bali maintained Hindu beliefs originating from India, but its creed had become its own syncretic mix. In the ideology of the Hindu-Balinese religion, Brahma, Vishnu, and Shiva are mentioned in prayers, but ancestral worship is the strongest aspect of their belief system. The dead are cremated in elaborate rituals and later honored as deities in family shrines. If they are remembered properly through offerings, they will help their descendants, but if forgotten, they might bring great misfortunes to the family.

Case study: The importance of death rites in Bali

In Bali, death rituals are properly followed so that the spirits of the dead are freed from their earthly ties. If not, there is a Balinese belief that they can potentially cause great harm. Between 1965 and 1966, the Indonesian Army and civilian death-squads killed over a million suspected communists. Because the victims' bodies disappeared, no death rites could be carried out. In researching how the Balinese responded to the massacres by using ritual as a healing process, anthropologist Angela Hobart states that many Balinese believed that the spirits became *buta*, unruly demons that threatened families. This was the plight of the family of leftist Balinese governor Anak Agung Bagus Suteja, whose disappearance in 1966 left them bereft and unsettled. Forty years later, after his son had consulted many mediums, Suteja's spirit entered a village priest who, while in trance, gave directions on how to conduct a cremation so that Suteja's soul could be released. A masked *topeng* dancer performing as the monkey god Hanuman led the funeral procession for the cremation, during which an effigy of Suteja was burned in a spectacular ceremony, thereby freeing his soul.[6]

The Balinese believe in reincarnation; when a child is born it is thought that the character of an ancestor reappears in them.[7] Another Balinese ideological belief is that opposing forces – good and evil, female and male, day and night – cannot exist without one another, and that equalizing these entities maintains harmony in the community. All sickness or affliction is attributed to the actions of evil spirits, but if offerings are made and their demands are satisfied, chances are the appeased interlopers will retreat and bad fortune will abate.[8]

Think about:
How do various rules inherent in Balinese culture influence and enforce correct societal behavior in communities?

Balinese dance

In Bali, children are exposed to dance at an early age. Adults take infants on their laps and teach them to "dance" by moving their small hands and arms while bouncing them in time to music. Later, they are taught to dance in a hands-on manner, in which the teacher stands behind the students and rhythmically manipulates their arms and heads, as well as shifts their torsos, putting them into postures with chest and shoulders lifted high.

The *agem* is the fundamental stance of Balinese dance. Although balance and harmony are important tenets, this is an asymmetrical posture. In a right *agem*, both legs are bent with the majority of the weight on the right foot, while the left foot is turned out and placed in front of the right. The torso and head are shifted to the right, while the arms are bent and held horizontally at shoulder height with the right hand held at ear level and the left at chest height. As in classical Indian dance, the hands are extremely expressive, but unlike the *mudras* of *kathakali* and *bharatanatym*, few gestures have symbolic meaning. Instead, they often reflect nature or animals – water, flowers swaying in the wind, or flying birds or bees. Ideally, the palms flex and face down so that the fingers arch upward, trembling and fluttering in a technique known as *geirahan*. The refined, elegant dance forms are called *alus*, while the

Figure 2.3
Ida Bagus Putrus Kenaka performs *kebyar duduk* (seated *kebyar*) with the Children of Bali Ensemble.

Figure 2.4
Balinese children of the village of Sanur learning the *agem* position.

strong and forceful ones are categorized as *keras*. Women and men perform both styles, depending on the nature of the dance. All movements stem from the *agem*, and mastering this asymmetrical pose demonstrates the power to rectify imbalance – a principle of Balinese philosophy.

Facial expressions communicate emotions in Balinese dance. A dancer should never show any teeth, but keep the lips together in a semi-smile. When a dancer expresses anger or fear, the shape of the mouth becomes neutral and the eyes take on an intense, wide-eyed stare, known as *nelik*. *Seledet* are rapid eye movements that dart up and down or right to left in time to the music, while *angsel* are sudden bursts of movements that highlight the percussive accelerations of the *gamelan* orchestra.

Case study: The *gamelan* orchestra – an Indonesian tradition

In a legend about the origin of the *gamelan*, a god named Sang Hyang Guru ruled Java from the top of Mount Lawu. He created a gong that he could strike from his lofty realm to summon the other gods, thereby crafting the first *gamelan*. Composed of percussive instruments such as xylophone-like metallophones, gongs, stringed instruments, drums, and a few flutes, they are considered to be *pusaka* – an heirloom endowed with supernatural power. In Bali, cymbals are used often, and the music is filled with different tempos, rhythmic changes, and sudden dynamics. In Java, *gamelan* players produce a more tranquil sound by using padded mallets. Colin McPhee, an expatriate composer in Bali in the 1930s, described the difference as such: "While the classic calm of Javanese music and dance is never disturbed, music and dance in Bali is turbulent and dramatic, filled with contrast and bold effects. Javanese musicians find the music of Bali barbaric. Balinese complain that the music of Java 'sends them to sleep.'"[9]

Head movements can turn suddenly to the right or left, or be beautifully fluid, with side-to-side motions that give the illusion of the head floating on the neck. In Balinese dance, *taksu* is a charismatic performance quality that every dancer aspires to gain. Mastering all these technical elements helps the dancer to attain this compelling quality.

2.2 The *baris* dancers: bodyguards of Balinese gods

Key points: *baris*

1 The *baris*, an ancient devotional warrior dance that derived from martial arts, originated in Indonesia in the sixteenth century during the powerful Majapahit Empire. In Bali, soldiers performed the *baris* as a martial exercise in defense of their kings as well as of their gods.
2 Since the *baris* is an act of dedication to the temple, performed by a dancer carrying his weapon, it is categorized as *wali*, or sacred. All *wali* dances take place in the *jeroan*, the inner most courtyard of the temple.
3 *Baris* translates as "line" and *baris gede*, a dance for men in a group ranging anywhere from four to sixty, means "great line." All *baris* gede dances are accompanied by the *gamelan*, a large percussion orchestra.
4 Today, over thirty types of *baris* exist and are an essential part of *Odalan* temple ceremonies. They are also performed at cremations.
5 *Baris tunggal* is a solo dance that is often taught to a young boy as his first formal dance. All its forceful warrior-like movements are derived from the sacred *baris gede*, but the solo allows for greater liberty in the choreography and no weapon is carried.

An indispensable part of the ritual feast of the old villages is the baris gede, a stately war dance in which ten or twelve middle-aged warriors with their heads covered with flowers, wearing magic scarves, and carrying long spears . . . dance in double line, grimacing and striking heroic poses until the music becomes violent, when they enact a sham battle with their spears.[10]
—Miguel Covarrubias, 1932

As a martial exercise in defense of their kings and their gods, Majapahit soldiers danced *baris*, a devotional warrior dance originating in the sixteenth century. *Baris* translates as "line" and *baris gede*, a dance for men in a group ranging anywhere from four to sixty, means "great line." Today, over thirty types of *baris* exist and are an essential part of *Odalan* temple ceremonies and cremations. (The "Kidung Sunda," a Javanese poem from 1550 recounting the cremation of a great king, a gruesome slaughter, and the subsequent mass ritual suicide of widows, mentions seven types of *baris* being performed.) The *baris* is an act of dedication to the temple and therefore it is categorized as *wali*, or sacred, and takes place in the *jeroan*, the innermost courtyard of the temple. Dancers carry weapons such as spears, shields, daggers, or offerings of flowers. The name of the weapon, offering, or function informs what kind of *baris* it is: in a *baris tumbak*, long lances called *tumbak* are carried, while in *baris pendet* offerings are held. All these fall under the category of *baris gede*, or ritual group *baris*.

The *baris* and *Odalan* temple ceremonies

An *Odalan* is a tribute to the gods in which theatrical performances and dances such as the *baris* are religious offerings. An *Odalan* occurs every 210 days (half a year in the Balinese calendar) and lasts from a few days to more than a week, depending on a temple's importance. Everyone in the village takes part in the elaborate preparations. Dancers and musicians rehearse, children gather flowers and palm leaves for the sumptuous temple decorations, and others prepare feasts and construct towering platters of fruits and flowers as divine offerings. Outside the temple, evil spirits are placated with offerings of food strewn on the ground and the spilt blood from a cockfight that occurs during the ritual of inviting the deities to descend from Mount Agung.[11]

Hindu-Balinese followers believe that when the gods descend, they enter wooden doll-like effigies called *pratima*. *Baris* dancers serve as bodyguards for these deities, and during the conclusion of an *Odalan* they lead a procession to a sacred spring where the *pratima* are ritually cleansed. Escorted out of the temple in portable shrines, these holy sculptures are accompanied by the entire temple congregation. The *baris gede* dancers guard the *pratima* with their weapons, protecting them as the direction of the procession goes from a positive to negative *kaja-kelod* trajectory. The *pratima* are bathed by the priests and then re-enshrined in the temple. A priest then offers dedicatory prayers in Sanskrit while gesturing *mudras* with his hands, and the ringing of his temple bell marks the end of the *Odalan*.

Costuming and make-up

The magnificent *baris gede* costume is a variation on what Majapahit soldiers wore centuries ago. A dancer dresses in white pants and a white cotton shirt – a color denoting heroism and honor. A cloth strip called a *setagen* wraps around his chest, allowing him to carry his *keris*, a large dagger, on his back. Layers of shimmering cloth panels called *awiran* dangle from the dancer's body, silk-screened with gold and edged with a colorful pom-pom fringe. His chest, shoulders, and upper back are covered by a bib-like "armor" called a *bapang* that may be embedded with colored stones or elaborately embroidered. Tight black velvet cuffs decorated with gold and red trimming cover his wrists and ankles. A triangular headpiece called a *gelungan* is adorned by hundreds of mother-of-pearl shell fragments attached to springs that allow each piece to shimmy as he dances. All these costume elements make the dancer larger than life, presenting him as a daunting foe to the enemy.

Make-up in Balinese dance also helps create a superhuman effect. The quick *seledet* movements of the eyes, so essential to the dance, are enhanced by thick black charcoal eyeliner and vivid eye shadow. Pink blush is applied to the cheeks and lipstick to the mouth. A white dot drawn in between the eyebrows represents the Hindi concept of the "third eye." Traditionally, this white make-up, made from a white clay powder, protected dancers from any black magic directed at them. Today, dancers use toothpaste, which arguably has its own merits but may not stand up against human evil.

Case study: *Baris tunggal* – solo baris

Baris tunggal is often the first dance a young boy is taught. Its forceful, warrior-like movements are derived from the *baris gede*, but the solo allows for greater liberty in the choreography and no weapon is carried. Although there is no direct narrative, *baris tunggal* depicts a proud warrior: as he meets his invisible enemy, his facial expressions communicate his myriad emotions and actions. *Seledet* eye movements are extremely pronounced – the sudden, darting movements of the dancer's eyes are intermingled with stares so wide that the eyes literally bulge in their sockets. The *gamelan gong kebyar* accompanies the *baris tunggal*. *Kebyar*, which translates as "bursting into flames," is a style that developed in Bali in the 1920s and remains popular today.

Baris gede

All *baris gede* dances are accompanied by the *gamelan gong gede*, a large orchestra including thirty to fifty percussionists. The entrance of *baris* dancers into the *jeroan* of the temple is a formidable show of might. Sometimes holding weapons, they take a crouching, stylized walk in unison called *pedjalan*. Stepping down onto a slightly bent knee, they sink their weight into their hip, lift the other leg up to the side at an angle, and then quickly swing the heel in to touch the knee of the bent standing leg before taking the next step. They may also take *pedjalan* at a faster tempo,

Figure 2.6
I Made Basuki Mahardika performs *baris tunggal* with the Children of Bali Ensemble.
Image: Linda Vartoogian, Front Row Photos.

adding a repetitive bounce to the walk. Their arms, held out to the side, are tensely bent at the elbow with the palms down and fingers curved upward. This walking is punctuated by moments when they rise up high onto the balls of their feet, elevate their shoulders, and then drop down with their legs in a deep straddle while letting out a deep, intimidating grunt.

In a *baris gede* normally one dancer emerges as leader and conducts a group prayer in a circle. Then, a call-and-response drill begins as the leader grunts "uuhhh" and the group replies "yyeee" several times. In some forms of *baris*, the men divide in two groups and attack each other in a unison mock battle, grunting and colliding. In every move, their footsteps are steady and firm, and they maneuver their weapons in a drill-like way. At the conclusion of a *baris*, the warriors face the main shrine, bow, and make their exit, having done their duty to the gods.

Discussion questions: *baris*

1 Can parallels be drawn between the *baris* and military displays of might in countries today?
2 The *baris tunggal* solo form is often danced by a child. What are the social implications – is this done merely as an early lesson in dance, or can it impart cultural messages to a child? If so, what messages?
3 How do the disciplines of martial arts and dance in the *baris* merge?

2.3 The *sanghyang dedari*: child mediums to the spirit realm

Key points: *sanghyang dedari*

1 *Sanghyang* are ancient, sacred dances involving ritual possession by either demonic or celestial deities for the purpose of exorcising illness.
2 In the *sanghyang dedari*, meaning "Honored Goddess Nymphs," pre-pubescent girls (also called *sanghyang*) become possessed by divinities. When the little girls are in trance, they are oracles for celestial beings that descend into their bodies.
3 A *sanghyang* must abide by a strict code of behavior: she cannot use bad language or be argumentative, crawl under a bed or eat the remains of a meal, and must avoid clotheslines and dead flesh. Unlike accomplished *legong* dancers, who also retire at puberty, they receive no dance training.
4 A traditional *sanghyang dedari* begins at night in the inner temple courtyard. As the priest prays, the girls kneel and begin to inhale incense. When they fall into trance, he has them walk through burning embers; if they are impervious to the heat, he judges that the trance has fully set in, enabling the girls to become mediums to the gods.
5 Once it is established that possession has occurred, the male *cak* chorus replaces the women's ensemble. The small goddesses are then transported throughout the village to the crossroads by the graveyard. The *sanghyang* make repelling gestures and sprinkle holy water toward evil spirits in the graveyard, while the priest prays to exorcise them.

Gods are like children, and children are like gods.[12]

—Balinese proverb

Sanghyang are ancient dances involving ritual possession by spirits or celestial deities for the purpose of exorcising illness. In Bali, over twenty types of *sanghyang* exist, danced by boys or girls who become channels for animal spirits who drive away demons such as monkeys, pigs, or horses. In the *sanghyang dedari*, meaning "honored goddess nymphs," pre-pubescent girls become possessed by divinities.

This altered somatic state, known as *kerawuhan*, translates as "to be entered." When the little girls, who are also called *sanghyang*, are in *kerawuhan*, they are oracles for celestial beings that descend into their small bodies. Strange voices emerge from the *sanghyang* as the spirits communicate through them, answering questions on how to eradicate disease or rectify imbalance in the community. While they perform this duty, the *sanghyang* are regarded as goddesses and are able to dance in trance nightly for a month or more in times of calamity. Once a *sanghyang* reaches puberty, she retires from her position, but many go on to study classical dance, such as the courtly *gambuh* or the popular *legong*, which was inspired by the *sanghyang dedari*. Performed in times of need to ward off illnesses such as smallpox or cholera, it is considered to be *wali*, and photography is normally not allowed during the sacred ritual. However, just as other *wali* dances have been adapted for tourism, secularized versions of *sanghyang* dances abound every night in Ubud, Batubulan, and other tourist areas in which the trance is omitted, or possibly feigned, and photography is permitted.

Figure 2.7
Two girls possessed by celestial spirits in the purifying ritual of the *sanghyang dedari*.
Image: photographer unknown. Courtesy of Tropenmuseum, part of the National Museum of World Cultures. Published under a CC BY-SA 3.0 license.

Although the girls generally dance in pairs, villages usually keep four or five of them in service in a *sanghyang* "club." The girls are specially selected by a priest not for their dancing skills, but for their natural ability to become possessed. Their service to the village starts when they are about eight years old and ends abruptly at puberty. The family of a *sanghyang* is released from all duties in the temple and village, but the girl herself must abide by a strict code of behavior: she cannot use bad language or be argumentative, and must avoid lurking spirits by not crawling under a bed or a clothesline, eating the remains of a meal, or touching dead flesh. *Sanghyang* tend shrines at the temple, where they are educated in singing sacred *kidung* poems. Unlike accomplished *legong* dancers, they receive no dance training, yet the grace and skill that they exhibit while in trance is believed by the Balinese to be proof that a deity has entered them. The little girls improvise while possessed, imitating the head, hand, and arm movements and the asymmetrical stances all Balinese children are exposed to from an early age. One *sanghyang*, who only danced when in trance, said she had the sensation of being led by an invisible teacher, whose steps she followed.[13]

The *sanghyang dedari* ritual

A traditional *sanghyang dedari* is performed at night in the presence of the entire village in the *jeroan*, the inner temple courtyard. The priest, a female chorus, and the *sanghyang* pair gather by a shrine, where offerings to the gods have been placed. As the priest prays, the girls kneel together in front of a brazier filled with incense and inhale the purifying smoke. The chorus invites the goddesses to descend, slowly singing sacred *kidung* that steadily increase in tempo as possession approaches. When the girls enter *kerawuhan*, they sway backward and forward, murmuring in voices unlike their own. The priest has them walk through burning coconut shells; if they are impervious to the heat, he judges that the trance has fully set in, enabling the girls to become mediums for the gods.

Think about:
Why is a trance state more easily attained in certain cultures?

Once it is certain that possession has occurred, the male *cak* chorus replaces the women's ensemble. They energetically chant the monosyllable "cak" (pronounced "chak") repeatedly in interlocking rhythms. This mesmerizing polyphony helps keep the *sanghyang* in *kerawuhan*, and is thought to please the spirit that has descended into each girl. The *sanghyang* are then dressed in ceremonial outfits and headpieces and taken out of the temple, either hoisted up onto the shoulders of a man, carried on a horizontal bamboo pole, or paraded in a portable chair throughout the village. Perched high, they sway from side to side or arch dangerously backward, improvising in a bending movement called *ngelayak*, which translates as "tree laden with blossoms swaying in the wind." Often they keep their eyes closed as their small hands make articulate gestures and their heads bob side to side. The purifying journey from the temple through the village culminates at the crossroads, where the *sanghyang* make repelling gestures toward the evil *buta* spirits that hang about in the graveyard. They are then taken back to the temple, where the priest brings them out of trance by sprinkling holy water on them. Unlike other forms of trance, *sanghyang* dancers never seem exhausted after being in this dissociative state, but are more like children awakening from sleep.

Behavior of *sanghyang* in *kerawuhan*

While *sanghyang* are deep in *kerawuhan*, the celestial mood of the normally dutiful little girls can become unpredictable, and they have been known to behave with unusual aggression if their will is not obeyed. They may become annoyed by the *gamelan*, refusing to dance to a particular melody, or reject a man who attempts to carry one of them. One dancer who fell off the shoulders of a man slapped him in the face and scolded everyone around her.[14] As the advice of the gods is greatly needed, the villagers try to cater to the divine whims of the *sanghyang*, who will only deliver messages if content. Anthropologist Jane Belo, in her observations on their possession trance, said they were "very much like children – capricious, gay, difficult by turns."[15]

Belo, a part of Margaret Mead and Gregory Bateson's anthropological team in the 1930s, researched *sanghyang dedari* in Bali. In her book, *Trance in Bali*, she witnessed the power of a *sanghyang* to *njawat*, or "touch," another *sanghyang* who was off duty, which caused the girl to go into trance. She describes two *sanghyang* partners, Tjibloek and Renoe. When Tjibloek suddenly began menstruating, she could not perform that night, or indeed ever again. Because of this abrupt onset of puberty, Renoe was told to perform solo, which made her temper rise. Belo recounts:

> Misi was a member of another *sanghyang* club . . . Renoe fell upon her and shook her furiously, nearly pulling her head off. Misi went into trance almost immediately, went limp, and was carried over and dressed hastily, with eyes closed, in a position of petulance, occasionally stamping and waving her fan. From then on, the girls were partners.[16]

Belo also revealed that the club would fine Renoe if she didn't dance. Although many accounts exist of placating the little goddesses, it is worth noting that even before financial gain from tourism was fully entrenched in Bali, the capriciousness of the *sanghyang* could be kept in check by the threat of a fine.

Sanghyang also have demonstrated a clairvoyant sense. Beryl de Zoete and Walter Spies each spent several years researching dances in Bali, and co-authored *Dance and Drama in Bali* in 1938. They describe a remarkable meeting of two *sanghyang*:

> Once a *sanghyang* was dancing in Soekawati. She stopped and sat down . . . and made signs that she wanted to be carried in a certain direction . . . they met another procession carrying a *sanghyang* from another village. The two *sanghyang* descended . . . Though they did not know each other and had never danced together before, they danced in perfect unison as if they had been two *legongs*. After about a quarter of an hour the guest stopped dancing of her own accord, and was led out . . . and carried away.[17]

This account of two unacquainted *sanghyang* dancing in an almost identical fashion leads us to question what is learned behavior and what is innate – or perhaps the Balinese would ask, what is of this world and what is divine? As the petite, mortal bodies of the *sanghyang* act as hosts for the deities, the realms of the earthly and the celestial unite in their divine dance of purification.

Discussion questions: *sanghyang dedari*

1 Even though the *sanghyang* do not receive formal dance training, while in trance they perform elaborate swaying dances, perched on top of precariously high places. How much of this is innate behavior and how much of this is absorbed from the dances Balinese children see from an early age?
2 How does the music accompanying the *sanghyang* support the girls in their passage from their normal state into *kerawuhan*? And how does it reflect the Balinese principle of the duality of opposing forces?
3 During the *sanghyang*, the girls travel to several places. How is the positive-to-negative *kaja* and *kelod* axis exemplified in the various venues during the *sanghyang*, and do you recognize any symbolic or metaphoric use of space in your own culture?

2.4 The *legong*: when sacred dances become secular

Key points: *legong*

1 The *legong* originated in the nineteenth century and was traditionally danced at court by pre-pubescent girls. This dance of the secular *bali-balihan* category derives from the sacred *wali* dance of the *sanghyang dedari*.
2 Once just courtly entertainment, today the *legong* is one of the most well-known forms of dance entertainment in *Bali*, and is performed at temple festivals and in tourist venues.
3 Like the *sanghyang dedari*, a traditional *legong* features pre-pubescent girls, called *legong*, who retire at puberty. But unlike *sanghyang*, *legong* are highly trained and not considered proficient unless they have had at least two or three years of training. While performing they neither speak nor enter into trance.

The Balinese are eager for new effects and are not afraid of mixing incompatible elements.[18]

—Beryl de Zoete and Walter Spies

The *legong*

The elegant and refined *legong* originated in the nineteenth century, and was traditionally danced at court by young girls chosen for their beauty and grace. This dance of the secular *bali-balihan* category is a mixture of the swaying movements of the sacred *wali* dance of the *sanghyang dedari*, and the classical court dance drama, *gambuh*. In the royal courts of pre-colonial Bali, it was known as *legong keraton*, which translates as "palace *legong*." A *Radja* (king) would search his kingdom for the most beautiful girls, regardless of their social caste. These sumptuously dressed dancers were given bodyguards, who protected them with spears whenever they ventured out in public.[19] Once courtly entertainment, today the *legong* is one of the most well-known forms of dance entertainment in Bali and is performed at temple festivals and in tourist venues. Versions with narratives are cut down to fifteen minutes or so, and much older dancers have replaced little girls.

Figure 2.8
Legong dancer Anak Agung Sri Utari in an *agem* stance, backed by the *gamelan* orchestra.
Image: Jack Vartoogian, Front Row Photos.

Like the *sanghyang dedari*, a traditional *legong* features pre-pubescent girls, also called *legong*, who retire on the onset of their menstruation. But unlike *sanghyang*, *legong* are highly trained and not considered proficient unless they have had at least two or three years of training. While performing they neither speak nor enter into trance. An older form of percussion orchestra called *gamelan pelegongan* accompanies the *legong*, and often a narrator will guide the audience through the tale since it is sung in the archaic language of Kawi. Although many types of stock *legong* narratives exist, some versions are abstract, in which the girls represent butterflies, herons, or monkeys.

Legong costuming

A *legong* dancer's feet are bare, but the rest of her body is regally bedecked in gold, colorful silk, and two "horns" of frangipani blossoms emerge from her golden leather headdress, or *gelungan*. These protrusions are topped with two red blooms on springs that quiver during the dance. Suspended from the crown and dangling down the sides of the dancer's temples are two red tassels that bounce and sway. The *kain* is a long piece of silk fabric, stamped with gold batik patterns, that winds tightly around her body. Running down the center of her long-sleeved blouse is a silk *lamak*, a long, fringed golden panel. The dancer manipulates a colorful bamboo fan, which adds another layer of movement.

The legong Lasem

The story behind the extremely popular *legong Lasem* is from *Malat*, an ancient Javanese poem, in which the king of Lasem meets Langkesari, a beautiful princess,

Figure 2.9
The *congdong*, or maidservant in the *legong*, also portrays a fierce crow.
Image: Dennis H. Miller.

and her maidservant (the *congdong*) in the forest. Although he already has a queen, he intends for the princess to be his second wife and abducts her against her will – but she is in love with another and repelled by her kidnapper. Her brother, the king of Daha, declares war against Lasem. To his queen's sorrow, Lasem goes to fight, but a bad omen occurs: a black crow attacks him and, consequently, he dies during the fighting. In the *legong Lasem*, three little girls enact this narrative – a pair in green and soloist in red. At times, the pair will portray one character – and, switching roles without a costume change – will then take on the roles of the king and the princess. The solo dancer in red plays the role of the *congdong* maidservant and the crow. Their style of dancing – strong, or refined – along with their facial expressions – indicate whether the indignant princess, the sad queen, the imperious king, or his brave attendant is being played.

Although older dancers perform the *legong* for tourists today, traditionally, the dancing life of a *legong* ended with the onset of puberty and her subsequent marriage. Often a *legong* married a man of a higher caste because of her beauty and status as a member of the Radja's court. After colonization, when the rulers became figureheads but lacked the funds to keep a full stable of court performers, many former *legong* returned to their birthplaces, where they taught the court dance to their fellow villagers. Others became professional dancers in forms such as *gambuh* and *wayan wong*, in which ageism does not exist.

Discussion questions: *legong*

1 The *legong* derived from the sacred *sanghyang dedari*. Can transforming a sacred form into a secular one lead to a denigration of the form, an artistic innovation, or something in between?
2 Compare the lifestyles, careers, and prospects of *sanghyang* and *legong* performers.

2.5 The *calonarang*: keeping a community in balance

Key points: *calonarang*

1 The *calonarang* is a ritualistic dance drama that serves as a way of driving off negative powers in a community. The main protagonists are the widow Rangda, a black-magic witch who represents destruction, and the Barong Ket, a lion-like creature representing protection.
2 China's influence can be seen in the Barong Ket mask. In addition to his role in the *calonarang*, every New Year's Day the Barong parades in the *kaja*-to-*kelod* direction through the village in order to steer evil spirits back into the graveyard and the ocean, and to counteract the power of *leyaks* (witches).
3 Rangda's power induces the *kris* dancers to fall into trance and turn their *krisses* (daggers) upon themselves. In this self-stabbing called *ngoerek*, they hold the sharp daggers with both hands and push them into their chests while rocking back and forth violently.
4 The power of the Barong enables the *kris* dancers to emerge unharmed from their self-mutilation. The attendants carry the stiff, contorted bodies of the *kris* dancers into the temple courtyard, where they will be revived with holy water and incense.
5 The *calonarang* was a subject of great fascination to Western anthropologists such as Margaret Mead and Jane Belo. It continues to be a sought-after ritual on the Balinese tourist circuit.

All of Bali was a stage, and the nights were full of young foaming males in cataleptic contortions, each turning a razor-sharp kris against his glistening belly . . . while Rangda, the witch, cavorted to claim her victims in vain.[20]
—Josef von Sternberg

The Balinese believe that celestial good and demonic evil are two inevitable forces that coexist in all of us. They greatly fear people who practice black magic to transform themselves into *leyaks* – harmful witches who convene in the graveyard and appear in the guise of animals. *Buta* are malevolent demons, bringing evil and misfortune. Although the Balinese believe that evil can never be eradicated, these entities may be kept at bay if ritually propitiated with offerings. One such offering is the *calonarang*, a ritualistic dance drama that serves to drive away negative powers in a community. The main protagonists are Rangda, a witch who represents destruction and controls *leyaks*, and the Barong Ket, a lion-like creature who keeps demonic forces in check.[21] A battle ensues between them and, although neither can vanquish the other, a temporary balance is restored. By performing the *calonarang* in dangerous places, such as at the crossroads and in the graveyard of the village, supernatural evil entities are met on their own turf. When performed as an exorcism in the context of village life, the *calonarang* is considered to be *wali*, or sacred. However, today, this dance drama has been condensed to an hour and packaged in wildly popular tourist excursions. The masks used in these shows are not sacred and the trance state of the performers is questionable.

Think about:
Should sacred and healing traditions of a community be held sacrosanct, or is change through tourism a necessary evil?

The Barong Ket and Rangda

Although the influence of India is strongly present in Balinese dance, China's influence can be seen in the Barong Ket mask, which has its origins in the Chinese Lion Dance. On New Year's Day, the Barong parades in the *kaja*-to-*kelod* direction through a village in order to steer malevolent spirits back into the graveyard and the ocean. As he brings blessings to the people for the New Year, they treat him as a deity and bow as he passes. If there is sickness in a village, the long beard of the Barong, made from human hair, is dipped in water by the priest, which transforms it into holy water used for healing.

Think about:
Is fear of widows really fear, or a way of controlling women in a patriarchal society?

Underneath the magnificent Barong Ket is a bamboo frame shaping its body and curved tail, which is covered with "fur" made from palm fibers. Its broad shoulders are protected by golden leather armor studded with mirrors, and its headdress has protruding eyes and a gaping mouth with movable jaws. It takes two strong *baris* dancers to perform as the four-legged creature. The man in the rear must remain bent over the entire time, while the lead dancer clacks the jaws and moves the bulbous eyes of the mask. As the shaggy Barong prances and sways to the *gamelan*, he might preen at times, shaking off flies, or turn backward to admire his long tail. He also teases the musicians, stretching out on an instrument while one attempts to keep playing, or will rest a foot on a drum, all to the audience's delight.[22]

Figure 2.10
The beloved Barong Ket brings blessings to the Balinese.
Image: Dennis H. Miller.

Contrary to the beneficent Barong, Rangda is old crone who has the power to transform herself into the *calonarang*, a fearsome witch. The word "*rangda*" translates as widow. Although ritual suicide for Balinese widows is no longer practiced, formerly, a wife would have followed her dead husband into the underworld. As a living widow, Rangda is the wife of a spirit; therefore, her continued existence makes her highly dangerous.[23] Her terrifying mask features a sinister, gaping mouth with sharp fangs, a long, protruding tongue, and bloodshot bulging eyes. Hairy gloves with extremely long fingernails cover her hands, and she carries a magic white cloth believed to cause harm to people by its touch. Only a man of great spiritual strength wears the *calonarang* mask, since he must be able to withstand the forces that might be unleashed by its presence. The battle between Rangda and the Barong with his followers, the *kris* dancers, evokes so much emotion that these players fall into trance during the drama.[24] Therefore, those performing these roles must practice a cleansing ritual called *mewinten*, which entails following a special diet, abstention from sexual activity, and avoidance of corpses for at least twenty-four hours before performing.

Performing the *calonarang*

The *calonarang* is inspired by an ancient Hindu-Javanese story. In the basic plot, the widow Rangda is the *calonarang*, a monstrous witch. Enraged that no man will marry her daughter, she has taught her *sisya* (students of black magic) to change into *leyaks*. Together, they have brought plague and pestilence to the village. The Barong and his loyal devotees arrive to combat the *calonarang*. In most endings, the Barong is successful in his attack, ridding the village of plaguing entities, but the understanding remains that this struggle between good and evil will never be over. The Barong, in his role as protector of the community, counteracts the malevolence of Rangda, however temporary it may be.

Although more modern footage of a *calonarang* performance can be found, *Trance and Dance in Bali* was filmed in 1939 by anthropologists Margaret Mead and Gregory Bateson. In the film, as her *sisya* disciples dance, Rangda, with her sagging breasts, long fingernails, and hairy leggings, barges into their circle, unmasked. As revenge for the king refusing to marry her daughter, the irate Rangda directs the women and a few children to transform into evil *leyaks*. A pregnant woman (played by a man) enters and mimes giving birth. A witch child steals the baby, kills it, and gleefully tosses it to the grieving mother. Rangda returns in her frightening mask, now in her supernatural state as the *calonarang*. She dances wildly, taking high-spirited, awkward prances while brandishing her magic white cloth and menacingly vibrates her long fingernails. The Barong appears and charges through the space toward the *calonarang*. They quarrel heatedly in Kawi, the ancient Balinese language, and then Rangda stuffs her magic white cloth into the Barong's mouth, signifying his defeat.[25] Not ready to concede, the Barong waddles off to rally his devotees. Twelve appear, barefooted and wearing white loincloths. As this vigilant army dances a stylized march with the legs turned out and the knees bent, they grip metal *kris* daggers in their right hands, while their left arms are held out rigidly to the side. They charge forward to attack, but the *calonarang* repels them and they retreat, collapsing to the ground. They rally again and begin to stab her two by two, but her formidable power induces them to fall into trance upon contact. Soon, all have succumbed, and in this altered state, they turn their *krisses* upon themselves. In this self-stabbing called *ngoerek*, they point the sharp blades into their chests while violently rocking back and forth, then stagger and fall to the ground, quivering and convulsing in an unconscious state. One man twitches uncontrollably, holding a *kris* now bowed from the intense pressure of his stabbing. Attendants to the *kris* dancers rush in; we see five to six of them attempting to wrestle a *kris* from the abnormally strong grasp of one entranced man's fist. Although the power of Rangda has sent them into a frenzied trance, the power of the Barong enables them to emerge unharmed from their self-mutilation. No blood has been shed and they are impervious to pain. The attendants carry the stiff, contorted bodies of the *kris* dancers into the temple courtyard, where they will be revived with holy water and incense.

Traditionally, at the end of a *calonarang*, the witch is tackled and doused with holy water and guided back to the temple, where the mask will be carefully stored, while the priest dips the Barong's beard in water to render it holy. Those who have fallen into trance are brought out through the sprinkling of this holy water and all go home at dawn. Jane Belo, an anthropologist who wrote extensively on trance in Bali, observed that the ritual purification a *calonarang* provided to the community seemed to give the Balinese a feeling of comfort: "After such a performance everyone goes home feeling perfectly great and at peace with the world."[26]

Current trends

In Bali, tourism continues to support the dance forms discussed in this chapter, as well as others such as the *kecak*, which enacts the abduction of Sita from the *Ramayana*. *Kecak kontemporer,* a contemporary iteration, draws more of a Balinese audience. One innovator in the *kecak* is choreographer Sardono Kusumo, who departed from its traditional movements by using those inspired by nature. Other experimental choreographers furthering contemporary innovations in Balinese dance include I Wayan Dibia, and I Madé Sidia, both important teachers at *Institut Seni Indonesia* in Denpasar. I Wayan Dibia has been committed to instigating a renaissance in Bali's performing arts. To this end, he founded the Bali Arts Festival to provide a venue and an audience for both new and old forms of Balinese dance, which has been attracting artists and tourists since it was established in 1979. In a country where dances abound in tourist venues, the festival has become of great interest to the Balinese themselves. After losing favor to the faster *kebyar* dances, a revival of the *legong* was spearheaded in the 1990s by *Tirta Sari*, a professional *legong* dance company from Peliatan, run by Anak Agung Gede Oka Dalem, and today is ubiquitously performed in Bali.

2.5 Exploration: excerpt from "Clowns, Kings, and Bombs in Bali" by Ron Jenkins

Ron Jenkins, a former Guggenheim Fellow, has written several books on Balinese performing arts with the support of the Asian Cultural Council, the Watson Foundation, and a Fulbright Research Grant. Published courtesy of Ron Jenkins.

Whenever historical chronicles are re-enacted in the Balinese plays known as "Topeng," it is the clowns who make the metaphoric connections between the past and the present. In the period after the Bali terrorist bombings of 2002 that shattered the island's tourist-driven economy, clowns took on the responsibility of performing plays that told stories of people surviving disaster and recovering their fortunes . . . In August, 2003, shortly after the trial that condemned the Muslim extremist Amrozi bin Nurthasyim to death for his role in the bombing, a troupe of clowns put on a historical drama . . . a few miles away from the site of the tragedy. The plot was based on a fifteenth century story about a disastrous situation under the rule of King Medang Kemulan. No one in the market could sell any of their products and the King's subjects became desperately poor. The solution proposed by the priest in the story, after he was possessed by a visit from a goddess, was to tell the people that they had become too greedy, focusing more on making money than honouring their gods. When the people gave up their selfish ways and made offerings to their forgotten gods, prosperity returned to the kingdom.

The audience of villagers watching the play had suffered a similar economic tragedy, so the story's metaphor hit them close to home. Many of them were descendants of King Medang Kemulan, and some of them responded to the performance by going into trances that were manifested by weeping and convulsions that continued until a priest blessed them with holy water and mantras. These blessings took place at the same time that a masked figure in the play called Sidha Karya . . . was performing similar rituals of blessing for the characters in the story. Before long Sidha Karya was chanting mantra and sprinkling holy water over the audience as well as the actors. The boundaries between the emotional world of the play and the emotional world of the village had dissolved in tears. The conflated realms of historical fiction and contemporary reality shared the sadness caused by economic disaster and both realms resolved the problem through ritual.

This play and countless others performed during that period advocated an extraordinary response to the terrorist bombings. Instead of demonising and attacking the bombers and other Muslims as the Americans had done after the September 11 bombings, the Balinese clowns were suggesting that their fellow islanders follow an example from past history in which the Balinese responded to disaster by looking inward to their own flaws and examining the possibility that they themselves might be partially responsible for the era of destruction because they had created an environment of spiritual imbalance in which religious devotion was eclipsed by conspicuous consumption.

As usual the clowns had made the connections between the past and present clear with their extra-narrative improvisations. One clown in the fifteenth century story wearing a buck-toothed mask came out stuttering and lunged into the audience. He immediately apologized for his aggression by reassuring the public: "Don't worry. I'm not Amrozi." Another clown jumped at the sound of a slamming door. "Whenever somebody farts," he said, "I think it's a bomb."

After the performance, Ketut Jagra, who played the central role of clown narrator in the drama reflected on the intensity of the audience's response. "The trance is proof and witness that the ceremony was successful," noted Jagra. "Maybe the bomb was a warning to the Balinese to wake up and pay more attention to worship and 'yadnya' " (ritual obligations to the gods).

Discussion questions: *calonarang*

1 The often-convulsive trance state and self-stabbing that occurs in the *calonarang* might be a disquieting experience for the uninitiated, yet the Balinese feel a sense of comfort after a *calonarang* performance. Since being out of control is not normative in the Balinese demeanor, could witnessing this have a cathartic effect? Is there a ritual or dance drama in your culture that provokes this range of feelings?
2 Western anthropologists and artists commissioned "ordered performances" from the Balinese. Can these be considered as being less authentic, and how much do you think taking a ritual out of its context alters its validity?
3 The Balinese believe that evil spirits can never be eradicated, and therefore propitiating these spirits maintains peace in the community and creates a balance between destructive and positive forces. How do the opposing characters of Rangda and the Barong maintain their relevance in Balinese society today, and why?

2.6 Javanese *bedhaya*: celestial palace dance

Key points: *bedhaya*

1 In both the Surakarta and the Yogyakarta palaces, the *bedhaya*, traditionally danced by nine highly trained women, pays tribute to the glory of the ruler and exemplifies the serene self-containment of the Javanese way of life, in which emotion is held in check.
2 The origin of the *bedhaya* is an abstraction of the love story between the Sultan Agung and Ratu Kidul, the Goddess of the South Sea, a powerful and fearsome deity of destruction who dwells in the Indian Ocean.
3 In the *kraton* (palace), a *bedhaya* is traditionally performed in a spectacular outdoor dance pavilion called a *pendopo*. Its acoustics are ideal for the *gamelan* orchestra and the chorus accompanying the dance.
4 An important manifestation of Hindu thought in the *bedhaya* is in the concept of *semadhi*, through which intense religious focus leads to a mystical union with

the divine. Many court dancers and musicians in Java claim that they do not perform for money or professional recognition, but that it is an act of *semadhi* – divine service or worship.

5 The *bedhaya* typifies the smooth, refined *alus* style, and is the root from which all other Javanese court dances, or *tari kraton*, have evolved. Due to its slowness, specificity, and duration, the *bedhaya* is the most difficult of the female dance techniques.

The bedhaya strives to affect all the senses in a pleasurable manner, dissolving any discord or disharmony through a sensation of supreme and sparkling, yet distant beauty.[27]

—Clara Brakel-Papenhuijzen

Located between Sumatra and Bali, Java is the fifth largest island in the Indonesian archipelago, and home to half the Republic's population. It has long maintained economic domination over the rest of Indonesia. Since the eighth century, Java was ruled by Hindu-Buddhist kingdoms and later became the center of the powerful Majapahit Empire. After Islam became the dominant religion in Java during the sixteenth century, the Mataram Sultanate emerged, which resulted in the fall of Majapahit and the migration of its Hindu nobility to Bali. When the Dutch later began to control Java in the seventeenth century, they permitted compliant rulers to serve as district officials under colonial supervision and allowed them to reside in their *kraton*, or royal palaces.[28] Although their supreme power had been seized, the fact that these sovereigns could serve as figureheads within the *kraton* helped preserve their aristocratic traditions such as the ceremonial female *bedhaya* and *srimpi* dances, the *wayang wong* dance dramas based on the Hindu *Mahabharata* and the *Ramayana*, and the *wireng*, a male combat dance. A mere forty miles separate the courts of Yogyakarta and Surakarta in Java, but their royal dances differ in style, music, and dance technique. However, in both palaces, the *bedhaya*, traditionally danced by nine highly trained women, pays tribute to the glory of the ruler and exemplifies the serene self-containment of the Javanese way of life, in which emotion is held in check.

The legend of the *bedhaya*

The *bedhaya* was created in the seventeenth century during the reign of Sultan Agung (1613–1645), and involves the love story between the sultan and Ratu Kidul, the Goddess of the South Sea. This powerful and fearsome deity of destruction dwells in the Indian Ocean and reigns over aquatic demons that have powers to invoke pestilence and disaster. After becoming infatuated with Ratu Kidul during his meditations by the shore, the sultan willingly followed her beneath the waves to her palace and lived with her there until his royal duty compelled him to return. Because of their romantic alliance, the sultan had access to her great powers of destruction, which he used to vanquish his enemies and expand his realm. Here the myth diverges: in one version, the goddess created the *bedhaya* song and movement for him, and he ultimately took this with him as parting gift; another claims that the second sultan of Yogyakarta created the *bedhaya* in the eighteenth century to commemorate the meeting between his ancestor and the goddess. No matter which version is followed, the Javanese are fearful of Ratu Kidul and treat her with devout respect. *Bedhaya* musicians

Figure 2.12
Dancers perform for Sri Sultan Hamengku Buwono X at the court of Yogyakarta in the "Harjuna Wijaya" *bedhaya*.
Image: Hari Setiano.

and dancers purify themselves before every performance by fasting and reciting special prayers. They also present flowers, food, cigarettes, or incense, as well as beauty items such as combs, hand mirrors, or hairnets as ritual offerings to insure the deity will be pleased. If this protocol is neglected, the palace and its inhabitants risk terrible misfortune. Since the *bedhaya semang* of Yogyakarta and the *bedhaya ketawang* of Surakarta are both representations of the legend of the sultan and Ratu Kidul, they are considered to be *pusaka* – sacred and treasured royal heirlooms. A legend claims that sometimes the goddess appears in the *kraton* and joins in with the dancers. The *bedhaya* has a divine association with the gods, and is a dance of love.

The *bedhaya* at the courts of Yogyakarta and Surakarta

In 1755, a dispute caused a division of the Mataram Sultanate, based in the court of Surakarta, and gave rise to the equally powerful court of Yogyakarta. Later, a further split led to the founding of two additional minor courts. As a result, all four *kraton* actively cultivated their respective lineages and distinctive court dances, called *tari kraton*.[29] New *bedhaya* were created for resident court dancers, who were often the ruler's relatives. However, these newer forms were never considered to be as hallowed as the seventeenth-century *bedhaya semang* of Yogyakarta, which almost fell into oblivion until its recent reconstruction, or the ongoing *bedhaya ketawang* of Surakarta, which can only be rehearsed every thirty-five days and performed once a year to commemorate the coronation of the ruler.

Stylistically, the disciplined and vigorous court dances of Yogyakarta express the martial ethos of the court's rebellious history. The early Sultans of Yogyakarta allegedly took male and female *bedhaya* dancers with them when they waged war, and although now it is a solely a female form, the dancers often carry weapons. In Surakarta, the dancing has remained much more gentle and sensual. In both cases, the *bedhaya* is a court tradition that qualifies being called *kelangenan dalem*, or "royal delight." Clara Brakel-Papenhuijzen, a scholar and practitioner of Javanese dance, writes:

> In fact, the Javanese word *kelangenan* implies something more, and partly something different from what is referred to by the English word, "entertainment." The word may be also used for a mistress or non-official wife, or in general for anything that creates intense pleasure.[30]

With its nine dancers dressed as royal brides, the *bedhaya* is divine entertainment for the ruler, who the Javanese believe to be the closest link to the gods. Through his meditation and devotion to ceremonial rituals, he possesses a kind of benevolent magic that maintains a healthy equilibrium in the kingdom. In the *kraton*, a *bedhaya* is traditionally performed in a spectacular dance hall called a *pendopo*, an outdoor open-walled temple-like structure in which decorative pillars support a high, peaked roof that covers a marble floor. The ruler and his guests sit on three sides. Out of deference, seating is arranged so that the guests' heads remain at a lower level than his.[31]

Think about:
How does noble patronage affect the purity of an art form and the attitudes of the professionals?

Hindu influence in the Muslim court: concept of *semadhi* and the number nine

Vestiges of Hindu tradition manifest themselves in several ways within the *bedhaya* of the Muslim *kratons*. There are versions of the dance that depict scenes from the Sanskrit *Mahabharata* and *Ramayana*, and mystical numbers in Hindu-Buddhist philosophy have retained importance within its highly symbolic choreographic formations. For example, the *ragit tika-tika* is a pattern in which nine *bedhaya* dancers line up in three rows of three, reflecting the auspicious nature of that number in Hindu culture as well as the sacred trinity of Shiva, Vishnu, and Brahma.

Figure 2.13 (p. 55)
Bedhaya dancers in a trio formation.
Image: Hari Setiano.

Another important manifestation of Hindu thought in the *bedhaya* is the concept of *semadhi*, the Javanese form of the Sanskrit word *samadhi*, through which intense religious focus leads to a mystical union with the divine. Many court dancers and musicians in Java claim that they do not perform for money or professional recognition, but as an act of *semadhi* – divine service or worship.[32] Mangkunagoro VII, an early twentieth-century prince compelled by its mystical aspects, wrote:

> Semadhi is . . . achieved after long and persistent exercises while assuming a certain body posture and after one has tested one's mastery over one's own lower "ego." The guru . . . teaches us that in this state one can have experiences of which one is not capable of in the usual state of full consciousness.[33]

In the *bedhaya*, this philosophical concept of *semadhi* is witnessed in the choreographic patterns. As the nine dancers move in unison, they represent one human body and its nine orifices. When they all merge into a straight-line formation, it symbolizes that the *semadhi* of the practitioner is complete; all the openings of the body are closed and one has achieved inner balance because of inner discipline.[34] Since this happens in unison, it is a powerful moment that adds to the sacredness of the dance.

Figure 2.14
Court dancers of the Sultan's Palace in Yogyakarta perform a straight-line formation signifying unity in the *bedhaya*.
Image: Jack Vartoogian, Front Row Photos.

The *bedhaya* style

India's influence on the *bedhaya* is recognizable in the eloquent hand gestures and the articulate head and neck movements of the dancer. However, the rapid eye motions and pronounced facial expressions so prevalent in the Hindu traditions of Indian or Balinese dance are noticeably absent in this dance form. Despite variations in court performance styles, the *bedhaya* typifies the smooth, refined *alus* style and is the root of all other Javanese court dances. Due to its slowness, specificity, and duration, the *bedhaya* is the most difficult of the female techniques, in which dancers are trained to move effortlessly in a liquid fashion.

Case study: The *bedhaya* during Suharto's New Order

During the 1965–1966 purges, terrifyingly waged against approximately a million suspected communists by General Suharto, thousands of female folk dancers – perceived as leftist for supporting the rights of working-class women – were incarcerated or murdered. To project the power of his autocratic New Order regime, Suharto repackaged certain dances for export that idealized Indonesia's *luhur*, or noble culture, and chose to utilize female dancers in his campaign of propaganda. Javanese court dances such as the *bedhaya* were taken out of their palace contexts and were taught to female civil servants who performed them on international cultural missions to demonstrate Indonesia's cultural sophistication. In order to be hired, the dancers had to pass a background screening in order to insure their "clean status." Today, half a century later, many still-fearful Indonesians are reticent to face their losses and memories of the past, as seen in Joshua Oppenheimer's 2014 film, *The Look of Silence*, and in Rachmi Diyah Larasati's *The Dance that Makes You Vanish*, excerpted at the end of this chapter.

The *bedhaya* is considered to be *luhur* – high and noble – and emblematic of court etiquette. Since expressions of emotion in daily life are not considered aristocratic, this dance does not display emotion or passion, but rather a refined, understated

Figure 2.15
A low, introverted gaze is characteristic in Javanese dance.
Image: Dennis H. Miller.

elegance. Throughout the *bedhaya*, a dancer reflects this social tenet by maintaining a serene facial expression, an almost imperceptible smile, and a lowered gaze, deep and penetrating. Despite the fact that the legend behind the *bedhaya* is based on the carnal union between the sultan and the Goddess of the South Sea, the movement should not be seductive. To create an aesthetic effect of sexual detachment and self-containment, a dancer fixes her gaze to a low point on the floor in front of her. In performing the refined *alus* style, the dancer must strike a balance between tension and fluidity in a concept called *kenceng*. In order to pass gracefully through these fluctuating states, the dancer's knees are constantly bent, allowing the torso to incline forward. This stance enables the hips to initiate constant weight shifts that result in a smooth, controlled swaying from side to side, which is occasionally interspersed with vertical motions as the legs straighten.

Think about:
How do the values of the Javanese court manifest themselves in both the *bedhaya* and in a dancer's demeanor?

Bedhaya costuming

The bridal-like costuming and pronounced facial make-up is identical for all nine *bedhaya* dancers, enforcing the concept that when they move in unison, they represent aspects of a single person, characteristic, or an idea.[35] Each dancer is tightly wrapped in a *dodot* – a skirt of batik cloth that trails to the floor. A fabric panel running down the front extends in a long train that drifts backward in between the ankles as she moves. *Bedhaya* dancers are highly skilled in deftly flicking it out of their way with their bare feet as they take articulate, deliberate steps. A *sampur* scarf tied around the waist falls to the floor and a gold belt, bracelets, and decorative armbands are worn. A few sartorial differences have evolved between the courts: in the *bedhaya semang* of Yogyakarta, a headdress of gold with a feather in front is worn, a *keris* dagger is carried in the belt, and the velvet blouse, embroidered with gold, has capped sleeves. In the *bedhaya ketawang* of Surakarta, a scalloping effect enhancing the hairline is painted high on the forehead, a beaded net covers the large hair bun, and the velvet blouse is strapless.

The decline and return of the *bedhaya*

When the Dutch colonized Java in the seventeenth century, its royalty – reduced in power, but rich in cultural artifacts – focused on refining the language and etiquette of court. An atmosphere of exclusivity enveloped the *bedhaya* and, since it was not performed or taught outside of the *kraton*, very few outsiders ever saw it. Brakel-Papenhuijzen, citing the decline of political power and the economy as causing a regression of cultural court activities, writes:

> Knowledge of the art form was restricted to the performers and their dance or music masters, all of whom were attached to the court either as relatives of the ruler, or as court servants . . . The dances are considered sacred, not only because they are assumed to embody esoteric spiritual values. The compositions are based on Javanese concepts of mysticism, beauty, and power, which are not usually expressed in words, and certainly not to the uninitiated outsider, but are treasured as an esoteric science. Their very sacredness made the dances so inaccessible to the general public, that they were in serious danger of falling into oblivion since the *kratons* lost their political function.[36]

After 1917, the elegant, refined *bedhaya semang* of Yogyakarta was no longer being performed.

In the 1970s, after a rare notation was discovered, the Yogyakarta *kraton* began reconstructing the sacred *bedhaya semang*.[37] The militaristic dance style of the Yogyakarta court is apparent as nine splendidly costumed women approach the *pendopo*, each with a *keris* dagger tucked diagonally in her belt. With an air of intense concentration, they slowly enter in a formation emulating a dagger: a straight line of seven dancers creates the blade; the two dancers flanking the second one in line form the hilt above the grip; and the first dancer is the handle of the sword. Walking in perfect unison, they lift their flexed feet with the toes curling sharply upward and then rotate them outward before stepping heel first. The undulating effect of these turned-in, turned-out steps is so fluid that it brings to mind the aquatic legend behind the *bedhaya*. Upon reaching the center of the *pendopo* they stop, and with their arms held out at forty-five degrees, they sway in place to the hypnotic rhythm of the *gamelan*, then sink to a seated position with knees raised and bring their palms in front of their face in *sembah*, a salutation of prayer. The chorus sings lyrics that refer to the dancers as heavenly nymphs and metaphorically describe their movements as "fluttering insects" or "reeds in the wind."[38] The dancers glide through formations with a downcast gaze, moving their necks and heads in a floating serpentine fashion in a technique called *toya mili*, or "flowing water." As they skim across the floor, they make their costumes "dance" as well. Each dancer delicately picks up one half of the *sampur* scarf hanging from her waist and lets it cascade to the side as a percussive note strikes, adding a visual effect that accentuates the music.

Midway through, six dancers pull *keris* daggers from their belts and "fight" each other in a mock battle, all while maintaining their elegant, luxuriously unhurried demeanor – there is no attempt to make this skirmish realistic. Two then emerge for a duet: one is the *batak*, who represents the human soul and is overseer of the five senses, and the other is the *endel*, the symbol of human will and material desires. These metaphysical ideas are not overtly displayed in this enactment of a love duet between the sultan and the Goddess of the South Sea. As the two dancers come together, fingers curled, they touch the insides of their wrists together in a gesture that denotes "beauty," but also could be interpreted as a sensual union. The dancers display no emotion, but remain serene, inwardly focused, and demure:

Figure 2.17 (p. 59)
Indonesian choreographer and dancer Sardono Kusumu performs *Passage Through the Gong* with the Sardono Dance Theater.
Image: Jack Vartoogian, Front Row Photos.

exemplars of the regal Javanese demeanor. These nine women dancing in unison, with their flowing, delicate arm movements, hypnotic tilts of the head and body, and indistinguishable facial expressions, create a feeling of tranquility. For both performers and audience alike, the mesmerizing *bedhaya* is a meditative process that leads to an elevated spirit.

Current trends

Due to initiatives by the Yogyakarta *kraton*, there has been much resurgence in *bedhaya* since the 1970s. Today, the *Konservatori* and the *Akademi Seni Tari Indonesia* train dancers of non-noble backgrounds. Since ascending the throne in 1989, Sultan Hamengku Buwono X has invigorated the tradition by commissioning three new *bedhaya* for the Yogyakarta *kraton*. In Surakarta, two dance institutions were founded within the *kraton* grounds in the 1970s: the *Pusat Kebudayaan Jawa Tehgah* (Cultural Center for Central Java) and the *Akademi Seni Karawitan Indonesia*. Susuhunan Paku Buwana XII granted permission to the director of the *Akademi* to perform new versions of the *bedhaya* so that the original choreography would remain exclusive to the *kraton*.

Several contemporary Indonesian choreographers are using traditional *tari kraton* as a point of departure. The forerunner of this trend was Bagong Kussudiardja (1928–2004), a renowned classical dancer and teacher who studied Japanese and Indian dance and trained under Martha Graham. Kussudiardja was a prolific and sometimes controversial choreographer. In 1980, he created *Bedhaya Genden*, in which he subtly criticized the ritualistic nature of the court dance by presenting the dancers as mechanical pawns of the aristocracy. His student, the classically trained Retno Maruti, was also a protégé of Surakarta palace instructors and founded the *Padnecwara* school. Maruti, known for her depictions of the struggles of female characters from Hindu epics, collaborated with Balinese choreographer Bulantrisna Djelantik in *Bedhaya Legong Calonarang* (2006) and combined the female forms of *bedhaya* and *legong*. Classically trained Javanese court dancer Sardono Kusumo is internationally known as a contemporary choreographer. In 2010, Kusumo mounted *Opera Diponegoro*, which he based on the courageous story of Prince Diponegoro, who led his people in a fight against Dutch colonization. In theatricalizing the power struggle between the Javanese and their colonizers, Kusumo presented the prince as a symbol of the new Java – a cultural hero, rather than a warrior.

The next generation includes Eko Supriyanto and Martinus Miroto, both classically trained dancers who each have companies in Java. After receiving their respective Master's degrees from UCLA in the United States, Miroto performed with Pina Bausch's *Tanztheater Wuppertal* and Supriyanto toured with pop-star Madonna. Miroto has drawn on the Javanese mask traditions, as seen in his *Dancing Shadows*. In Supriyanto's *Flame On You* (2012) he addresses feminist issues through an episode from the *Ramayana*, in which Rama requests his wife to set herself on fire to prove her loyalty. Rachmi Diyah Larasati, a dance artist and scholar now residing in the United States, has created highly politicized works such as *Tembok Mari Bicara* (Talk to the Wall) that challenged censorship imposed by the Indonesian government. Those entering the theater lobby were met by an installation she created that featured a sculpture of a dead dancer in an open coffin in a museum-like display, reminding the audience of the many who were lost.

2.6 Exploration: excerpt from *The Dance that Makes You Vanish: Cultural Reconstruction in Post-Genocide Indonesia* by Rachmi Diyah Larasati[39]

Reprinted with kind permission from University of Minnesota Press

Javanese dancer and scholar Rachmi Diyah Larasati's grandmother was a member of Gerwani, a socialist pro-woman's group who performed folk dances in large leftist

rallies. During the 1965–1966 massacres of suspected communists by Suharto's "New Order" government, many disappeared, including Gerwani dancers. Although Suharto resigned in 1998, the perpetrators have never been brought to trial and many still-haunted Indonesians remain reluctant to speak out about the brutal mass murders.

From within the relative safety and obscurity of my grandmother's yard, where I learned to dance, my life began to change quickly and permanently. I rarely looked back, as new alliances were formed and old ones erased and forgotten. After performing nationally for a few years as a teenager, one day I was told to undergo a *skrening* (screening), after which I received a kind of agreement letter to become a government employee of Indonesia. During the *skrening* I was asked to make a diagram of my family tree, to see if there were any connections to the Communist party in my family; even a distant relative known to have been in an "affiliated" organization would have disqualified, and probably blacklisted me, or far worse. This was my final test, and with . . . Mr. Soek's signature, my "dirty" genealogy was officially made invisible, obscuring my connection to a disappeared grandfather and many other "subversive" relatives. Soon afterward, I was inducted as a member of the civil service and began teaching at the Indonesian State Institute of the Arts (ISI) in Yogyakarta, where President Suharto, the person mainly responsible for the killings in 1965 and the "antisubversive" policies that followed, visited in 1984 for the opening ceremony. By that time I had become a member of the Indonesian Cultural Mission, an official, state-sanctioned dance troupe whose function was to promote Indonesia's national identity abroad. Thus, drawing on my experience as a dancer, civil servant, and national cultural representative, and my transformation from a so-called unruly, unwanted body, I looked at the study of travel and mobility, of "feminist" resistance and co-optation from a dislocated perspective . . . During one such cultural mission in 1994, in a corner of a library in Europe, I found a picture from 1973 of dancers who were identified as Indonesian "political prisoners." Recognizing the style and location as close to home, I moved closer, thinking I might pick out some familiar faces; instead, I found something that made me begin to question aspects of my education, particularly much of the history I had learned in school along with my fellow Indonesian citizens over the past few decades . . . I was suddenly struck by an awful realization, as I was flooded again with memories of my neighbors, many of them dancers like myself and my family, who had disappeared and never returned . . . my sense of historical identification was radically reoriented, as I read that in 1965, more than a million Indonesians were killed and thousands more imprisoned without trial on isolated islands. When I returned to Indonesia in 1998, with much of the "common sense" I had developed as a child and young woman altered or lost, I began to ask questions. Many people were shocked that I would even speak of such matters, others told their stories and versions of events excitedly, and others simply refused to respond or react in any way at all.

Discussion questions: *bedhaya*

1 Discuss the Hindu traditions that are manifested in the *bedhaya* through the choreographic patterns and philosophy of the dance.
2 The *bedhaya* is a rare example of a dance that has survived both colonialism and the massacres of Suharto's regime. Why do you suppose this is the case, and what does it say about royal patronage and politics?
3 Discuss the similarities, differences, and roles of Ratu Kidul, the Javanese Goddess of the South Sea, and Rangda, the Balinese witch, or *calonarang*.

Notes

1 Bandem and deBoer. *Balinese Dance in Transition*, 102.
2 Vickers, Bali, a Paradise Created, 2.
3 Ibid., 102.
4 Larasati, Rachmi Diyah. *The Dance that Makes You Vanish*, 5.
5 Hobart, Angela. "Retrieving the Tragic Dead in Bali," 309.
6 Ibid., 124, 307–336.
7 Ibid., 78.
8 De Zoete and Spies. *Dance and Drama in Bali*, 86.

 9 McPhee, Colin. "The Five-Toned Gamelan: Music of Bali," 250–281; 251.
10 Covarrubias. *Island of Bali,* 187.
11 Belo, Jane. *Bali: Temple Festival,* 258.
12 Belo, Jane. *Trance in Bali,* 181.
13 Ibid., 71.
14 De Zoete and Spies, 69.
15 Belo, 180.
16 Ibid., 187.
17 De Zoete and Spies, 72.
18 Ibid., 221.
19 Bandem and deBoer, 73.
20 Von Sternberg, Josef. *Fun in a Chinese Laundry,* 77.
21 Belo, Jane. *Bali: Rangda and Barong,* 11.
22 Ibid., 93.
23 Ibid., 95.
24 De Zoete and Spies, 97.
25 Belo, 105.
26 Ibid., 12.
27 Brakel-Papenhuijzen, Clara. *The Bedhaya Court Dances of Central Java*, 7–8.
28 Murgiyanto, Sal. *Moving Between Diversity: Four Indonesian Choreographers*, 22.
29 Hughes-Freeman, Felicia. "Constructing a Classical Tradition: Javanese Court
      Dance in Indonesia," 60.
30 Brakel-Papenhuijzen, 4.
31 Jonas, Gerald. *Dancing: The Pleasure, Power, and Art of Movement*, 95.
32 Ibid., 7.
33 Morrison, Miriam J. "The Bedaya-Serimpi Dances of Java," 202.
34 Ibid., 203.
35 Jonas, 89.
36 Ibid., 2.
37 www.youtube.com/watch?v=55JWE0if4ZM
38 Brakel-Papenhuijzen, 8.
39 Larasati, Rachmi Diyah, *The Dance that Makes You Vanish: Cultural
      Reconstruction in Post-Genocide Indonesia*, xviii–xx.

Bibliography

Visual sources

YouTube

"Bali Dance 'Tari baris Tunggal,' " YouTube video, 8:15, posted by "ojisannd 2,"
      November 30, 2011, www.youtube.com/watch?v=1gEoielJDdl
"Bali Danza baris gede Covarrubias Bali 1932," YouTube video, 1.22, from a 1932
      film by Miguel Covarrubias, posted by "gustavothomastheatr," November 26,
      2009, www.youtube.com/watch?v=EF6sle_44Bo
"Bali, Indonesia – The Sacred Sanghyang Trance, 1925, Bali, Kuno," YouTube video,
      5:16, posted by "Timescape Indonesia," December 1, 2012, www.youtube.com/
      watch?v=BERKBHbVcy0
"Bali legong Lasem, Balenag Mandera Stage, Ubud," YouTube video, 22.48, posted
      by "Yendorphine BALI@GAMELAN," December 30, 2010, www.youtube.com/
      watch?v=IUCRRamjHVQ
"baris gede di Klungklung," YouTube video, 10:32, posted by "tropikamanis,"
      August 31, 2009, www.youtube.com/watch?v=U6H0FsQe75Q
"bedhaya Ketawang," YouTube video, 8.34, posted by "indotravel," August 27, 2012,
      www.youtube.com/watch?v=OOu2b7_G_2k
"Barong and Kris Dancers," YouTube video, 20:56, posted by "Chaine de pavdb092,"
      August 27, 2013, www.youtube.com/watch?v=t7CMss4oO2l
"sanghyang dedari," YouTube video, 9:51, posted by "TonyGWilliam," April 22, 2013,
      www.youtube.com/watch?v=t7CMss4oO2l
"Sultan Palace," YouTube video, 40:17, of performance of *bedhaya Semang* at
      Yogyakarta Palace, posted by "TherBeginning," April 18, 2012, www.youtube.
      com/watch?v=55JWE0if4ZM

"Tari bedhaya Ketawang," YouTube video, 5:35, posted by "kratonpedia,"
    September 15, 2011, www.youtube.com/watch?v=zlpoG5urKa4
"Tarian sanghyang dedari," YouTube video, 12:18, posted by "Rais Abduh,"
    October 9, 2013, www.youtube.com/watch?v=-l70fdzNjtw

Film

Bateson, Gregory, and Margaret Mead. *Trance and Dance in Bali*, 1952. Film, 21
    minutes. State College, Pennsylvania: Pennsylvania State University Media
    Sales.
Snyder, Richard, Producer. *Gods of Bali*, 1952. DVD, 56 minutes. Chatsworth, CA:
    Milestone Film and Video, 2004.

Written Sources

Adi, Nugroho Ganug. "Retno Maruti: A Maestro of Classical Dance." *Jakarta Post*,
    May 29, 2012, www.thejakartapost.com/news/2012/05/29/retno-maruti-a-maestr
    o-classical-dance.html.
Bandem, I. Madé. "The Baris Dance." In *Dance in Africa, Asia, and the Pacific*,
    edited by Judy Van Zile, 36–42. New York: MSS Information Corporation, 1976.
Bandem, I. Madé, and Fredrik Eugene deBoer. *Balinese Dance in Transition*. Kuala
    Lumpur: Oxford University Press, 1981; 2nd ed., 1995.
Belo, Jane. *Bali: Rangda and Barong*. New York: J. J. Augustin Publishing, 1949.
Belo, Jane. *Bali: Temple Festival*. New York: J. J. Augustin Publishing, 1953.
Belo, Jane. *Trance in Bali*. New York: Columbia University Press, 1960.
Brakel-Papenhuijzen, Clara. *The Bedhaya Court Dances of Central Java*. Leiden/New
    York/Koln: Brill, 1992.
Covarrubius, Miguel. *Island of Bali*. New York: Knopf, 1937.
Davies, Stephen. "Balinese *legong*: Revival, or Decline?" *Asian Theater Journal*, Vol.
    23, No. 2 (Fall 2006): 314–341. Accessed September 8, 2015. Stable URL: www.
    jstor.org/stable/4137057.
Davies, Stephen. "The Origins of Balinese *legong*." *Bijdragen tot de Taal-, Land- en
    Volkenkunde*, Vol. 164, No. 2/3 (2008): 194–211. Accessed September 8, 2015.
    Stable URL: www.jstor.org/stable/2786848.
De Zoete, Beryl, and Walter Spies. *Dance and Drama in Bali*. London: Faber and
    Faber, 1938.
Dibia, I. Wayan. "Odalan of Hindu Bali: A Religious Festival, a Social Occasion, and
    a Theatrical Event." *Asian Theater Journal*, Vol. 2, No. 1 (Spring 1985): 61–65.
    Accessed September 8, 2015. URL: www.jstor.org/stable/1124507.
Dibia, I. Wayan, and Rucina Ballinger. *Balinese Dance, Drama, and Music: A Guide
    to the Performing Arts of Bali*. Singapore: Periplus Publishing Group. 2004.
Hobart, Angela. "Retrieving the Tragic Dead in Bali." *Indonesia and the Malay
    World* (August 2014) 42: 124, 307–336. Accessed September 8, 2015. DOI:
    10.1080/13539811.2014.933503.
Hobart, Mark. "Rethinking Balinese Dance." *Indonesia and the Malay World*
    35 (April 10, 2007): 101, 107–128. Accessed September 8, 2015. DOI:
    10.1080/13638910701233979.
Hughes-Freeman, Felicia. "Art and Politics: From Javanese Court Dance to
    Indonesian Art." *The Journal of the Royal Anthropological Institute*, Vol. 3, No. 3
    (September 1997): 473–495. Accessed September 8, 2015. Stable URL: www.
    jstor.org/stable/3034763.
Hughes-Freeman, Felicia. "Constructing a Classical Tradition: Javanese Court Dance
    in Indonesia." In *Dancing from Past to Present*, edited by Theresa Jill Buckland,
    52–74. Madison, WI: University of Wisconsin Press, 2006.
Jonas, Gerald. *Dancing: The Pleasure, Power, and Art of Movement*. New York: Harry
    N. Abrams, Inc. 1992.
Kuncoro, Sir. "Harjuna Wijaya, bedhaya Dance: Level of Human Perfection."
    Indonesian Culture: Social Culture Tour, 4th edition (August 23, 2010): 5–27.
    Indonesia Culture.ne.
Larasati, Rachmi Diyah. *The Dance That Makes You Vanish: Cultural Reconstruction
    in Post-Genocide Indonesia*. Minneapolis: University of Minnesota Press, 2013.
McPhee, Colin. "The Five-Toned Gamelan: Music of Bali." *Musical Quarterly*, Vol. 35
    (1949): 250–281.

Morrison, Miriam J. "The Bedaya-Serimpi Dances of Java." *Dance Chronicle*, Vol. 2, No. 3 (1978): 188–212. Accessed September 8, 2015. URL: www.jstor.org/stable/1567381

Putra, I. Nyoman Darma. "Modern Performing Arts as a Reflection of Changing Balinese Identity." *Indonesia and the Malay World*, Vol. 36 (April 10, 2008): 104, 87–114. Accessed September 8, 2015. DOI: 10.1080/13639810802017842

Sorrel, Neill. *A Guide to the Gamelan*. London: Faber and Faber, 1990.

Sumarsam. *Introduction to Javanese Gamelan*. Middletown, CT. Wesleyan University Course Pamphlet, 1998. http://sumarsam.web.wesleyan.edu/Intro.gamelan.pdf.

Vickers, Adrian. *Bali: A Paradise Created*. Ringwood, VIC: Penguin, 1989.

Von Sternberg, Josef. *Fun in a Chinese Laundry*. San Francisco: Mercury House Publishing, 1965.

Cambodia and China
Dance as a political tool

3.1 Overview

Although China and Cambodia may differ in numerous ways, during the twentieth century they both experienced political horrors – incomprehensible in scope – that greatly affected the people and their culture. During Mao Zedong's long rule as Chairman of the People's Republic of China (1949–1975), one of his most devastating political moves was launching the Cultural Revolution in 1966. In this decade-long purge, citizens who were suspected of being religious, educated, prosperous, or artistic were tortured, imprisoned, or murdered. Entertainment was also forced to adapt to new ideological reforms. *Jingju*, also known as Peking or Beijing opera, was populist entertainment that also found royal favor in mid-nineteenth-century China. During the Cultural Revolution, *jingju* – targeted as elite – was banned for over a decade and its artists suffered persecution. *Jingju* was supplanted by works such as *The Red Detachment of Women*, a revolutionary dance drama that served as a political and educational tool for the masses. Remarkably, *jingju* survived and is thriving today in China, while *The Red Detachment of Women* is standard repertory in the Chinese Central Ballet Company.

In Cambodia, after a 1975 military *coup d'état* expelled its king, the Khmer Rouge gained power. As in Chairman Mao's China, this Communist regime aimed to strip Cambodia of any vestige of its aristocratic past and to eliminate class differences. During its diabolical four-year reign, the Khmer Rouge ruthlessly murdered ninety percent of Cambodia's professional artists, musicians, and dancers. New folk dances were performed as tools of propaganda, while the court dance – and their dancers – disappeared to the Killing Fields, where they were executed. Since the 1980s, due to the diligence of the surviving dancers, a new generation is learning traditions that were nearly destroyed and the Royal Ballet of Cambodia has been resurrected.

3.2 Cambodia's royal dancers: survivors of the Khmer Rouge

Key points: *robam boran*

1 Cambodia's *robam boran* is one of the oldest court dance traditions of Southeast Asia. The sacred female dancers of the king ritualistically performed dances as offerings to please ancestral spirits, asking them for rainfall to bring fertility and food to the Khmer (Cambodian) people.
2 Khmer kings expressed their spiritual devotion by building magnificent Hindu temples, such as Angkor Wat, which has many carvings of dancing celestial apsaras. Since their dance was a link between the human and the divine, the king's dancers emulated these sacred icons in their temple ceremonies.

3 In the king's all-female troupe, women play men. Subject matter includes ancient ritual dances and dance dramas based on the *Reamker*, the Cambodian version of the *Ramayana*. Many more modern dances were added in the 1950s and 1960s, such as *Apsara Dance*.
4 As in Indonesia, girls and boys begin their training as young children, with their teachers manipulating their hands, feet, and backs into highly flexed positions that make their joints hyper-mobile.
5 During its diabolical reign, the Khmer Rouge brutally murdered ninety percent of Cambodia's professional artists, musicians, and dancers in just four years. Ten percent of the king's royal troupe survived. Those who returned to Cambodia have made it a mission to revive the classical form.

Three hundred to five hundred palace maidens, gaily dressed, with flowers in their hair and tapers in their hands, are massed together in a separate column. Close behind come the royal wives and concubines, in palanquins and chariots . . . From all this it is plain to see that these people, though barbarians, know what is due to a Prince.[1]
—Chinese emissary Chou Ta Kuan, in 1296

Robam boran, the refined classical dance of Cambodia, is one of the oldest court traditions of Southeast Asia. The *lakhon lueng*, sacred female dancers of the king, resided at the palace and performed dances as offerings to ancestral spirits. As intermediaries between the ruler and the gods, the dancers asked the deities for rainfall to bring fertility to the land, and as a result, food to the Khmer (Cambodian) people. At royal funerals, wearing ghostly white make-up associated with the spirit world, they escorted the king's body to his cremation, and danced to please the spirits so that his soul would be allowed to enter the ancestral realm.[2] In the nineteenth century, the French also admired their grace. When Cambodia was made a French Protectorate in 1863, the administrators preserved the luxurious Khmer tradition of a royal court ballet troupe, which performed ancient ritual dances and dance dramas based on the *Reamker*, the Cambodian version of the *Ramayana*.[3] The *lakhon lueng* electrified France in 1906 and 1931 when they were featured in its *Exposition Coloniale*, which showcased not only the dancers' "exoticism," but also the glory of France, as Cambodia's "protector."

Legend of the *apsaras*

The royal *lakhon lueng* performers were considered to be living symbols of the mythological, divine *apsara* dancers. The Khmer creation myth concerning the birth of the *apsaras* is told in the *Churning of the Sea of Milk*, and depicted in a stone bas-relief in the colossal Hindu temple of Angkor Wat. In the center, a *naga* – a huge sea serpent – is being fought over by two opposing forces. On the left, ninety-two *yakkha* (ogres) pull on his multiple heads, while on the right, eighty-eight *deva* (gods) pull on his tail. The *naga* is wound around a stone and, due to this winding effect and the lashing of his body, the ocean churns with foam. From the frothy liquid, thousands of *apsara* emerge. According to legend, the queen *apsara* descended into *Apsara* Mera, daughter of the powerful *naga*. When the beautiful Mera united with Prince Kambu, the Khmer people were spawned and the Kingdom of Cambodia was founded. Just as *apsara* carvings adorn numerous pillars, niches, and walls of Angkor Wat, the early kings surrounded themselves with thousands of female dancers, who were concubines in their royal harem – a tradition maintained until 1970, albeit on a much lower scale.

Cambodian history and ideology

The Angkor Empire began in the ninth century, and developed into a powerful and glorious Khmer civilization that dominated mainland Southeast Asia for the next

Figure 3.1
Apsara Mera (Chap Chamroeunmina) and Prince Kambu (Chen Chansoda) of the Royal Ballet of Cambodia in *The Legend of Apsara Mera*.
Image: Jack Vartoogian, Front Row Photos.

six centuries. Its kings expressed their spiritual devotion by building magnificent Hindu temples, with the crowning achievement being the twelfth-century Angkor Wat, created in honor of the deity Vishnu, and considered to be one of the seven architectural wonders of the world. Since their dance was a link between the human and the divine, the king's *lakhon lueng*, surrounded by carvings of the celestial *apsaras*, emulated these sacred icons in their lavish temple ceremonies. In the twelfth century, King Jayavarman VII installed almost three thousand dancers in royal temples to please the gods, who would then provide rain to bring fertility to the land and to his people. One specific ceremony to bring rainfall was the *Buong Suong Tevoda*, which translates as "paying respect to heavenly feminine spirits." This dance was performed as an offering in the court or the temple. Although the public never saw this ceremony until after 1970, peasants used to beseech the king to have it performed during times of drought.[4]

The Angkor Empire met its end in 1432, when Siamese armies sacked the country and abducted thousands of accomplished Khmer artists, musicians, and dancers. The Cambodian royal dance tradition remained there for several centuries, which influenced Siamese court dance.[5] In 1847, King Ang Duong, the founder of the present Cambodian dynasty, brought the classical ballet of the Khmer royalty home. He founded a palace school in Phnom Penh and began reconstructing the choreography, music, costumes, and ritual elements of the traditional ballets.

Robam boran training

In Cambodia, children begin training at an early age with their teachers, who manipulate their hands, feet, and backs into highly flexed positions to make their joints hyper-mobile. A dancer must master balancing for long stretches, as in a "flying position," with one turned-in leg raised behind and bent at the knee in an angle, while the supporting leg is bent, and the foot turned out. The arms are held away from the body, often with the elbows at shoulder height, while the hands are in one of four characteristic gestures that represent either a leaf, a flower, a tendril, or a fruit held in the palm, with the fingers articulately bent backward. These gestures can be combined with arm movements to make numerous images, such the head or tail of the mythical serpent *naga*.[6] These representations of nature are also seen in the standing positions, which are inspired by wave-like movements, or those of trees. A dancer learns to move the head and neck slowly in a horizontal figure-eight that creates a magical floating effect. In the dance dramas of the all-female *robam boran*, in which women play men – and the all-male form, *lakhon khol*, in which men play women – characters of both genders move identically, although the men's gestures are more pronounced. Dancers will specialize in one of the four main *robam boran* roles, which are *neay rong* (male), *neang* (female), *yeak* (ogres or giants), and *sva* (monkeys).

Spiritual practice is an integral part of a dancer's training and performing. The respectful *sampeah* gesture to the forehead, in which the palms meet and the fingers arch to create a V shape, is incorporated into every dance. The formal aspects inherent in *robam boran* choreography – the ritual offerings made by the dancers to the four cardinal directions, the symbolic serpentine floor patterns representing *naga*, and the interaction of harmonic female and male energies (despite being

Think about:
In other cultures, the channeling of divine spirits while dancing involves trance. Does the fact that *robam boran* is a court form preclude this phenomenon from happening?

Figure 3.2
The Hindu temple Angkor Wat.
Image: Sam Garza.

Figure 3.3 (p. 71)
Meng Chan Chara of the Royal Ballet of Cambodia in a "flying position".
Image: Jack Vartoogian, Front Row Photos.

danced by women) – all create an atmosphere of otherworldliness. There is a belief that the dancers channel divine spirits: when they go on stage, the Khmer term used is *chaen*, "to go out," while when one exits the stage the term is *chol*, or "to enter." The implication is that when the dancer performs, she enters another realm, and when exiting the stage, she returns to her normal somatic state.[7] A weekly salutation to the spirits called *Tway Kru* was traditionally performed by the king's dancers, which assured good health for the people. Today, dancers perform a weekly ceremony called *Sampeah Kru* to honor their teachers and the spirits of deceased dancing masters.

Music and costuming

The *Pin Peat* orchestra accompanies *robam boran*. This ensemble of eight musicians plays drums, gongs, xylophones, and the *sralay* – a four-reed instrument. Choral singing and chanting, usually done by women, imparts the narrative and the dialogue. The merging of the high tones of the leader's chant with the *sralay* is a distinctive feature in the style. *Pin Peat* compositions are offerings to the ancestral spirits, as is the dance, and also accompany shadow puppet-theater, male *lakhon khol* dance drama, and Buddhist temple ceremonies.

Costuming a classical dancer is an elaborate and painstaking affair since a dancer must be sewn into a costume. Female characters first don a tight silk bodice, and then a *sampot* – a long piece of brocade – is wrapped around the waist and pleated in front. Another length of fabric called a *sarabap* is worn over the left shoulder; the right shoulder is bare. A collar, belt, multiple arm bracelets, anklets, and earrings further adorn the dancer. The golden *mkot* female headdress rises to a tall, single spire at the top, with a tassel extending down one side by her cheek. Because of the mirrors imbedded in the leather, the headdresses are extremely heavy, but less so today, since they are no longer crafted from gold. Since the head of a dancer is considered to be the most sacred part of the body, an offering is made just before the fully dressed dancer has it placed on her head. A single flower is slipped behind one ear and blossoms cascade down her long hair. Women playing male roles wear a *sampot* wound around the legs and tied at the waist to form pantaloons. A tight, long-sleeved brocade jacket features two pointed epaulettes that jut upward from the shoulders. The gold crown for male roles is taller and a mask is worn in the ogre and the monkey roles. The monkey, of course, also wears a tail.

Until the mid-twentieth century, the make-up that *robam boran* dancers applied was a toxic mixture of rice powder and lead that had an ill effect on some dancers. Since white is the color associated with funerals in Asia, this pallor gave the dancers an otherworldly, spirit-like appearance.[8] Teeth would be blackened and lips stained red. Today, the make-up is still pale, but less so, and the eyes are enhanced with colored shadow and dark liner.

The independence years

The independence period (1953–1970) was an innovative time for Cambodian classical dance. Queen Kossamak, the wife of King Sihanouk, aimed to take *robam boran* outside the exclusive palace and into the world. She expanded the possibilities for receiving a formal education in dance by establishing the Conservatoire National in 1964 and the Royal University of Fine Arts in 1965. During this period, a whopping twenty-five percent of Cambodia's budget supported their Ministry of Fine Arts, and the queen made 250 palace dancers into civil servants, whose monthly salaries were the equivalent of 800 US dollars today.[9] The queen choreographed fifteen new dances emblematic of ancient Angkor glory for the modern stage and brought in males to play the monkey roles. Her *Apsara Dance*, or *Robam Tep Apsara*, became an iconic cultural

Figure 3.4
Royal Ballet of Cambodia dancers in the battle between the gods and the giants in *The Legend of Apsara Mera*.
Image: Jack Vartoogian, Front Row Photos.

Figure 3.5
Classical dancers as Sita and Ravana in the *Reamker*, the Cambodian version of the *Ramayana*.
Image: Francis Alexandre Decoly. (PD-US) Wikimedia Commons (public domain).

symbol of Cambodia. Its star was the king's daughter, Princess Norodom Buppha Devi, who became the renowned face of Cambodian dance when the Royal Ballet began its tours abroad. Until 1970, this female troupe lived in the palace until a *coup d'état* occurred and the royal family was exiled to Beijing. This political shift gave rise to a terribly bloody and gruesome time in Cambodian history, which lasted for over two decades.

The Khmer Rouge years

The establishment of the ruthless Khmer Rouge regime in 1975 was due to both overt and covert political operations. In 1970 King Sihanouk was ousted by a *coup d'état*, which precipitated a brutal civil war between the new pro-US government and the Khmer Rouge, an insurgent Communist faction. During this time, a US covert operation dropped 2,756,941 tons of bombs on Cambodia – more than during all of World War II – that killed an estimated 100,000 civilians.[10] From his government in exile, King Sihanouk vehemently urged his people to fight against the United States by siding with his former enemy, the Khmer Rouge. In a meteoric rise, new members joined the organization, which was especially successful in radicalizing rural youths; many were less than fifteen years old.[11] Led by Pol Pot, who had been educated in France and was an admirer of Mao Zedong and his Communist model, they launched a civil war and won in 1975. When the Khmer Rouge marched into Phnom Penh, many people thought this revolutionary regime would usher in an era of peace and rebuilding. Instead, the city was emptied at gunpoint and its people sent to labor in collective farms in the countryside.

A cold-blooded Khmer Rouge slogan was *tuk min chamnenh, dak chenh ka min khat: to keep you is no profit, to kill you is no loss.* The age-old ethos in Cambodia was to respect elders, but in a cruel twist, the party became the parent and it was young people who gave brutal orders and doled out punishment to older people. Emulating Communist China, the Khmer Rouge extolled ignorance and inexperience, favoring youths who were, in Mao's phrase, "poor and blank" to those tainted by free enterprise or extensive education.[12] A massive propaganda campaign indoctrinated people through revolutionary songs relentlessly played on loudspeakers, along with public displays of new "folk dances" exemplifying the communal work ethic, in which dancers would mimic toting hoes or shovels, blacksmiths working bellows, or farmers cutting crops.[13] The palace dancers were the antithesis of all this. Their refined training and royal patronage led to them to their doom as they were hunted down and horribly executed.

In 1979, the Vietnamese army invaded Cambodia and ousted the Khmer Rouge. The world began to learn the extent of the horrors committed by the regime when two Vietnamese journalists discovered Tuol Sleng, Pol Pot's interrogation center. Taken away under the cover of night, accused families would be brought to this veritable torture chamber, once a former high school. Prison officials photographed them, leaving a record of haunted faces without names.[14] After interrogating the father, who was brutally forced to make false confessions and to implicate as many people as possible, the family would be carted off to the Killing Fields, where they were made to dig their own graves before being executed. Reading these confessions from "Cambodian bodies with Vietnamese minds" was a favorite pastime of Pol Pot.[15] Of the 14,000 estimated prisoners there between 1975 and 1979, only seven survived. Today, the prison is now the Tuol Sleng Museum of Genocide.

Think about:
Why is the dancing body so often subjected to being used as a powerful tool of propaganda?

Dance in the camps

In 1975, thousands of Cambodians fleeing the Khmer Rouge began to arrive in refugee camps set up in Thailand by the United Nations. One camp known as Site Two became a haven for dance when former royal dancers Voan Savay and Meas Van Rouen started to teach children.[16] The advent of dance created a strong sense of community and hope, even after so many years of censorship. The power of sacred dance had not been forgotten and was recognized as a necessary ritualistic act that helped a long-suffering people to look ahead. When they could finally return to Phnom Penh, many of the dancers walked home – some of them barefoot – aiming to find one another. Out of three hundred palace dancers, only thirty returned. Those who survived were compelled to resuscitate their life's work, which had been so brutally interrupted. Although one could never do justice in giving credit to all the artists who so devotedly participated in reviving classical Khmer dance from the brink of extinction, Em Theay, Chea Samy, Chheng Phon, Pitch Tum Kravel, Proeung Chhieng, Sam Satthya, and Sophiline Cheam Shapiro are some who have been so vital to this resurrection. Several of them appear in *Continuum: Beyond the Killing Fields*, a film by Ong Keng San.

Current trends

Princess Norodom Buppha Devi taught dance during her many years living in exile in France and also at the border camps in 1982. When she returned to Cambodia in 1991, dance masters joined the princess to help re-establish the Royal Ballet to revive a number of key dances. Today, approximately eighty percent of the former repertory has been recreated and notated.[17] *The Legend of Apsara Mera*, choreographed by Princess Buppha, was a spectacular 2010 touring production by the Royal Ballet of Cambodia that received much acclaim.

Sophiline Cheam Shapiro was one of the first dancers to train at the University of Fine Arts when it re-opened in 1980. Today, she runs the Los Angeles-based Khmer Arts Academy and choreographs cutting-edge works that uphold the cultural specificity of classical Cambodian dance, but carry deep messages. *Samritechak*, her adaptation of Shakespeare's *Othello*, is in reaction to those Khmer Rouge members still at large; *Pamina Devi* merges Mozart's *The Magic Flute* with the *Reamker*; and *The Glass Box* deals with female abuse. *Fire Fire Fire* is her recent collaboration with

Figure 3.6
The Royal Ballet of Cambodia in *The Legend of Apsara Mera*.
Image: Jack Vartoogian, Front Row Photos.

Pichet Klunchun and Eko Supriyanto, two renowned dance artists from Thailand and Indonesia. Despite Shapiro's popularity, her work has come under the scrutiny of Cambodia ministerial officials.[18]

Amrita Performing Arts was founded by Fred Frumberg in Phnom Penh in 2003, who resolved to foster a contemporary form of Cambodian dance that was evolving from the country's classical dance tradition. Through classes, workshops, and performances, it has nurtured the careers of choreographers such as Chey Chankethya (*My Mother and I*); Peter Chin (*Olden New Golden Blue*); Chumvan Sodhachivy (*Bach Cello Suites*); and recently helped sponsor *Khmeropédies* by the French-Cambodian choreographer Emmanuele Phuon.

Although dance is thriving in Cambodia, it is rare to find a professional dancer today who makes their living by performing. Of the seven hundred artists of RUFA and the Department of Performing Arts, the two professional companies, dancers make salaries that range between fifteen and twenty-five US dollars a month.[19] The link between culture and economics is largely dependent upon tourism, especially in Siem Reap, where busloads travel from Angkor Wat to restaurants offering "*Apsara* Dances," accompanied by canned music and laser lights. But the fact that there is dance at all in a country whose cultural traditions faced near annihilation is something to be celebrated, not maligned, and is a testament to the miraculous rebirth of Cambodian culture.

3.2 Exploration: excerpt from "Mediating Cambodian History, the Sacred, and the Earth" by Toni Shapiro-Phim[20]

In 1989, when the Vietnam army withdrew from Cambodian soil, the political faction controlling the refugee camp Site Two sent approximately thirty dancers and musicians through mine fields into Cambodia under military escort. The artists performed a sacred ritual as an offering to the deities and to sanctify the land as Khmer. Cultural anthropologist Toni Shapiro-Phim, who worked in the camps, describes this brave venture.

We went there to ask the *tevoda* (celestial beings) to bring peace and prosperity to the people. "They need the dancers for that," several artists explained upon their return to Site 2. The dancers had journeyed from the other side of the border to make a request and an offering to the deities on behalf of western Cambodia. Divine help was sought to break the cycle of war and deprivation afflicting this land and its people, to stop the loss of life that results from incessant war. The ritual was also a means to ask that the people of Site 2 be able to go back to Cambodia soon.

Surrounded by villagers, with musicians seated on mats to one side having begun the rippling melodic phrases on their xylophones and gong circles, the lead dancer, visiting the "Liberated Zone" from Site 2, stepped into the performance space, dressed as a heavenly being. With a golden crown rising to a narrow point, a velvet sash over one shoulder embroidered in sequined patterns, a brocade skirt reaching to her feet, and wrists and ankles wrapped in elaborate bracelets, she resembled the carved and painted images of celestial beings to whom Cambodians address some of their prayers . . . As she balanced on one foot, lifting the bent left leg behind and up, sole of the foot facing the sky, toes flexed, she manipulated an open fan in each hand. Still on her right leg, with that knee slightly bent and her back deeply arched, she gently pulsed up and down as if she were floating through the clouds. When she stepped forward on her left leg, weight centered and low . . . she all the while exuded an extraordinary lightness. Eleven other dancers followed her onto the stage, moving in a figure-eight pattern across the space, recreating the shape of the *naga* (sacred serpent). Performing male and female roles, ultimately in pairs, they danced a piece from the classical repertoire, *Robam Phlet* (Fan Dance) which reflects upon the history of the Khmer, as part of their ritual prayer for peace.

Discussion questions: *robam boran*

1 The theatrical concept of *chaen*, or "to go out," is used to imply that when a dancer goes on stage, she enters another realm, and when exiting, the term *chol*, or "to enter," infers that she returns to her normal somatic state. Have you ever experienced this idea in performing – whether it be dance, theater, music, sports, or delivering a speech?

2 Discuss the political messages and metaphors that were conveyed in the new dances that Queen Kossamak choreographed for the Royal Ballet. How did she use mythology and personality in her *Apsara Dance*?

3 What do you consider rituals, as well as contemporary dances, to have contributed to the healing process of the Khmer people after such devastation, or is healing ever possible?

3.3 *Jingju*: Chinese Beijing opera – stylized beauty, staged

Key points: *jingju*

1 *Jingju*, also known as Peking or Beijing opera, is a highly stylized genre of popular entertainment that emerged in mid-nineteenth century China. The conventional costuming and facial make-up of its stock characters indicate their rank, temperament, and motivations. Plots impart moral messages of loyalty, filial piety, benevolence, and justice, and range from military battles to domestic dramas.

2 Rigorous *jingju* training in singing, dancing, and martial arts begins in childhood and is either learned from a family member, by apprenticing, or by joining an official school. Children are eventually given the role that is most suitable for their appearance, demeanor, and voice. Elderly artists are regarded as having the most skill and command great respect.

3 After women were banned from the stage on the grounds that they were an immoral influence on the audiences, men began playing female, or *dan,* roles. By employing a stylized form of speech, singing, and movement in their portrayal, *dan* actors created symbolic versions of women that exceeded simple imitation.

4 *Jingju* performers bring symbolism to the stage through conventional acting "tricks" that include fan manipulation and artful pantomime. An actor opens a make-believe door, walks through it, and then closes it; mounts an imaginary horse and gallops; or mimes catching butterflies. A fan is an important prop for demonstrating actions, such as the thrusting of a sword.

5 The orchestra is divided into two categories: the elegant *wen chang* music supports the emotion behind the melodic singing, while robust *wu chang* music accompanies recitation, dancing, and scene changes. Its percussive orchestra also controls the timing and rhythm of the actors' gestures and acrobatics in militaristic fight scenes and dances.

> **Once my teacher, always my father.**
>
> **—Chinese proverb**

Jingju, also known as Peking or Beijing opera, is a highly stylized genre of popular entertainment that emerged in mid-nineteenth-century China during the Qing Dynasty (1644–1911). Its plays dispense with realism in order to convey a symbolic form of beauty through singing, dancing, acting, spectacular acrobatics, stunning costumes, and elaborate make-up. The conventional costuming and make-up of its stock characters are indications of their rank, temperament, and motivations – brave warriors, comic peasants, cruel landowners, or arrogant nobles are all easily identified by an informed audience. Themes range from historic military battles to domestic dramas that instill moral messages of loyalty, filial piety, benevolence, and justice. Rigorous training for *jingju* begins in childhood and can be learned from a family member, by apprenticing in a master-student relationship, or by joining one of the official schools established during the twentieth century. It is considered that a good performer gets better with age – elderly artists are regarded to have the most skill and command great respect.

Jingju evolved from *huabu* opera, based on historical folktales and loved by working classes, and *kunqu* opera – highly sophisticated literary and aristocratic entertainment originating in the fourteenth century. When popular troupes from Anhui province came to Peking (now Beijing) in 1790 to perform for the eightieth birthday celebration of Emperor Qianlong, they settled in the bustling city and *jingju* evolved, taking on characteristics of these operatic genres.[21] Early *jingju* performances were held outdoors at temple fairs and New Year celebrations, and later, during the nineteenth century, in teahouses called *xiyuanzi*.

Politics and *jingju*

Jingju emerged during a difficult political period, when diplomatic conflicts erupted between China and European colonial powers in pursuit of silk, porcelain, and tea.[22] Clashes escalated with the British, who were financially profiting by inundating China with opium grown in India, which generated massive addiction in the population. As a result, the Opium Wars of the mid-nineteenth century ensued, leaving the country badly defeated. This marked the beginning of the Chinese rebellion against imperialism, which was first aimed at European colonial aggression, and later against the Qing Dynasty. In this atmosphere, *jingju* plots began to reflect the bellicose trends of wartime society. Dreamy stories – such as a lovesick nun escaping from her convent in *Longing for Worldly Pleasures* – were supplanted by militaristic plays such as *Water Margin*, which featured acrobatic movements derived from martial arts.[23] These popular stories also appealed to the aristocracy, especially to the Empress Dowager Cixi (1835–1908), who became a great patroness of *jingju* and brought several acclaimed actors to live at her court. The fall of the Qing Dynasty in 1911 also raised the popularity of *jingju*. When the Republic of China (1912–1949) was founded and political power was squarely placed into the hands of the people, many traditional values were rejected and sophisticated art forms such as *kunqu* opera were seen as antiquated. *Jingju* became extremely sought after, and by the 1930s, it was thriving in Chinese opera houses in Beijing, Shanghai, and Tianjin.

Stock characters in *jingju*

There are four main character roles in *jingju*: *dan* is a female; *sheng*, a male; *jing*, a painted face type; and *chou*, a clown. Each role type has sub-genres. In the *dan* characters, *quigyi* is a virtuous woman of high status; *huadan*, a beautiful, flirtatious female; *lao dan*, an elderly lady; and *wu dan* is an acrobatic female warrior. For *sheng* characters, *lao sheng* is a middle-aged to elderly man; a *wu sheng* possesses martial skills; and a *xiao sheng* is young and handsome. The bombastic nature of *jing* characters is manifested in the outlandish patterns and colors of their painted faces – they are always male, loud, and rough, and can represent characters such as judges, landowners, outlaws, or supernatural beings. The *chou* serves as a humorous foil to a leading character and can be of any social rank, age, or gender.

Women – many of them courtesans – performed in Chinese opera until 1772, when Emperor Qianlong banned them on the grounds that they were an immoral influence on the audiences. This resulted in men playing *dan* roles. By employing a stylized form of speech, singing, and movement in their portrayal, *dan* actors created symbolic versions of women that exceeded simple imitation. At the end of the nineteenth century in Shanghai, women began to reappear in *jingju*, and the reforms of 1912 allowed female actors to make their official reappearance in Beijing. Today, both men and women assume *dan* or *sheng* roles.

Figure 3.7
King and *chou* characters.
Image: Jean-Pierre Dalbera

Make-up and costuming

The sumptuous costuming of *jingju*, with its voluminous layers, fabrics, and patterns in a glorious riot of colors, evokes the eras of the Ming and Qing Dynasties, when the styles and colors people wore indicated their status and occupation.[24] An emperor wears a *mang* – a long yellow silk robe embellished with embroidered pythons. High-ranking characters are dressed in purple, virtuous characters wear red, and military officials wear blue or black. A warrior wears a suit of armor called a *kao*, complete with four martial flags projecting vertically from its back. Headdresses and wigs are always worn, regardless of a character's rank. For *dan* characters, the face is framed by hair painted on the cheeks and flower patterns adorn the forehead.

Sleeves, pheasant plumes, and beards are all costume elements incorporated into choreography. A *dan* character's hands are hidden under long, flowing "water sleeves" which are flicked in time to the music while singing, or to emphasize an action, such as hiding the face during emotional turmoil. Two long pheasant plumes decorate a warrior's headdress, which are removed and manipulated by the actor in a show of skill and virtuosity while dancing. A mature male *sheng* wears a beard that is attached to a wire frame that hangs off the ears and covers the mouth. The beards vary from character to character: a king will wear a long, dignified black beard, while a *jing* character will

show his volatile nature by wearing a red one. While singing, an actor will flick the beard aside, toss the hair in a circle, or stroke it to demonstrate a pensive state.[25]

The colorful facial make-up in *jingju* is purposefully exaggerated, especially for the *jing* and *chou* types. The numerous facial patterns representing characters are called *lianpu* and range from a solid color to several within a design: a red face indicates a loyal, brave person; black indicates a tough but honest character; white indicates treachery; and grotesque patterns connote wickedness. *Chou* characters often have a single round patch of white that encircles the bottom of the nose and finishes just below the eyebrows. The faces of *dan* characters are pale, the lips are red, and the eyes are highlighted with a deep pink.

Think about:
Where lies the irony in actors being relegated to such a low level of society?

Jingju training and acting techniques

Before the Communist takeover in 1949, all *jingju* performers were members of troupes that were run on the principle of a master-apprentice relationship. The master, or *ban zhu*, would act as director, playwright, composer, and teacher of apprentices. He decided when actors had finished their indentures and if they would attain status as a "professional," also known as "diving into the sea."[26] Troupes would tour from city to city, living in tents. Despite the demand for them in aristocratic courts and wealthy circles, actors were low on the societal scale, regardless of their fame. Due to severe poverty, many sold their children to acting companies to become apprentices; accounts abound of the harsh exploitation of these children, who seldom reunited with their families. Cheng Yanqiu, a famous *dan* performer, was an example of this brutal system of acquiring children, which was abolished in the 1950s.[27]

Case study: *Farewell My Concubine*

In his 1993 film, *Farewell My Concubine*, Chen Kaige delivers a harrowing view of the life of *jingju* performers. Through a gorgeous cinematic lens, we are shown the grueling training and the tyrannical, punishing relationship between a master and his male students, two of whom find great acting success as a duo of the King and Beauty Yu in the opera *Farewell My Concubine*. During their careers, which span fifty years of Chinese history, they weather the brutal vagaries of the political climate – the Japanese invasion, World War II, the Communist takeover, and the Cultural Revolution – all of which profoundly affect their artistic and personal lives. The *jingju* actor Mei Lanfang co-wrote *Farewell my Concubine*, and Beauty Yu was one of his most famous roles. Chen Kaige further examined Mei's world in his 2008 film, *Mei Lanfang, Forever Enthralled*, a biographical portrait of the actor's life and career.

Professional *jingju* institutes emerged in the twentieth century, such as the Beijing Theater School, founded in 1930 and run by actor Cheng Yanqiu. In this six-year program, boys and girls were given free room and board. Vocal training started at five in the morning. After breakfast came dance practice, with emphasis on flexibility exercises. Renowned performer Mei Lanfang remembered one difficult maneuver:

> The two legs were placed firmly apart at a distance of twelve inches. Both hands were lifted over the head, palms outward with eyes focused on the thumbs. The body was then bent over backwards; if you could grasp your ankles with both your hands your technique was considered good.[28]

Students also practiced stillness in preparation for the characteristic ending poses in *jingju* stage movement, acrobatics were performed with weights on the body for endurance, and rhythmic combat was practiced with bamboo sticks. The methods of this rigorous conservatory became the basis of *jingju* training. Today, students must master singing, dancing, gymnastics, martial arts, facial expression, and gestures of the fingers and hands, and skillfully manipulate stage weapons during stylized acrobatic combat. Children explore all character types and are eventually given the role most suitable for their appearance, demeanor, and voice.

Jingju performers bring symbolism to the stage through *juehuo* – conventional acting "tricks" that include fan manipulation and artful pantomime. An actor opens a make-believe door, walks through, and then closes it; mounts an imaginary horse and gallops; mimes catching butterflies; "steps" over a threshold by lifting a leg; or walks around in a circle to indicate going a far distance. In a bygone *juehuo* called *jiaogong*, a male actor would portray a woman with bound feet by walking on thin wooden supports – a feat that took two to three years to master. Pantomime is used in tandem with tangible stage props: the actor will hold a real shoe to sew, but mimes having a real needle, or will use a riding crop on a reluctant "horse."

Figure 3.10
The characters of King Xiang and Concubine Yu in *Farewell My Concubine*.
Image: Jean-Pierre Dalbera

Jingju music and orchestra

The musical style of *jingju* is called *pihuang*. The orchestra is divided into two categories: *wen chang* and *wu chang*. The graceful and elegant *wen chang* music supports the emotion behind the melodic singing, and features string and wind instruments such as bamboo flutes; a *yuequin*, similar to a mandolin; the *pipa*, a four-stringed lute; and the *jinghu*, a fiddle-like instrument. Every well-known performer has his own personal *jinghu* player, who "announces" the actor he serves with entrance and exit music and accompanies the character's songs. *Wu chang* is robust music that accompanies acting, recitation, dancing, acrobatic fighting, and scene changes. Its percussive orchestra includes various gongs, wooden clappers, drums, and cymbals. The lead drummer controls the timing and rhythm of the actors' gestures and acrobatics in militaristic fight scenes and dances, and adds to the excitement of the drama.

While an actor's recitation (*nian*) imparts the narrative, singing conveys emotions. There are two main styles of song: *xi pi* is animated and can express happiness or anger, and the more subdued *er huang* communicates melancholy or deep sadness. Chinese vocal style, with its complicated rhythms and irregular phrasing, complements each character role, as do the costumes and the facial designs. An aggressive rough character sings in a strong tone, a young man sings in a high register, a young woman sings in a falsetto, while an old woman uses a natural voice. Recitation and singing, synchronized with a performer's formalized movements and gestures, are at the heart of *jingju*.

The traditional jingju stage

As *jingju* grew in popularity, players moved out of the teahouses into old-style opera theaters, such as the Huguang Guildhall and the Zheng Yi Ci. Both venues feature a pointed roof supported by four columns covering a square stage, surrounded on three sides by the audience. An embroidered curtain hangs across the back that has two curtained "doors," one for entrances and one for exits. An actor strides through the lifted curtain, walks along a curved path and stops at center stage, striking a pose. This is called *liangxiang* and is met with enthusiastic cheers of "*hao.*" Sometimes an anticipated actor sings a line from behind the curtain and won't appear before evoking applause. The characters verbally introduce themselves, declaring their role and intentions. The exit of an actor through the curtain signifies a transition in the play. While these old-style theaters were typical in Beijing, many stage innovations were spawned in the cosmopolitan city of Shanghai. The modern Shanghai New Stage, built for *jingju* in 1908, introduced a proscenium arch with a revolving stage, novel lighting, and scenery equipment.

The *jingju* set is a "room" created by the placement of a table and two chairs used symbolically in a multitude of ways: in an emperor's palace, the tablecloth will be embroidered with imperial dragons, and the chairs will be placed behind the table,

Huguang Guildhall, an old *jingju* theater.

as if court were being held. To indicate an ordinary household, the tablecloth will be less ornate and the chairs will be placed in the front. Two upturned chairs can represent prison gates, while the table can act as a bed, a bridge, or a mountain. Traditionally, a stage hand would be present on stage to rearrange the table and chairs in between acts in full view of the audience, indicating a change in place and time. Since the 1950s, a large silk curtain is used to open and close the show and, between acts, a second inner curtain conceals the relocation of the chairs and table.

Jingju actors

Many famous twentieth-century actors were trained in Anhui opera or *kunqu* before taking up *jingju*. Cheng Changgeng (1811–1880), considered to be the founding father of the Peking Opera, was first a performer of Anhui and Han opera. He played venerable "old male" *lao sheng* roles and famously performed for the emperor, who couldn't repress his shouts of appreciation.[29] Cheng's apprentice was Tan Xinpei (1847–1917), a *lao sheng* actor who had a softer style of singing and ultimately established the Tan school of training. Tan's apprentice was the renowned Yang Xiaolou (1878–1936), a militaristic *wu sheng* male character. The legendary Mei Lanfang led the fourth generation, made *dan* roles as important as their male counterparts, and introduced *jingju* to the world outside China.

Mei Lanfang (1894–1961)

Internationally recognized as one of the greatest actors of the twentieth century, Mei Lanfang came from a family of famous opera performers. His training included the refined form of *kunqu* and, by age eleven, he debuted as a *dan* player in Beijing. In 1913, Mei's performances in Shanghai caused a sensation. His portrayal of the essence of femininity sparked this popular saying: "A good wife should be like Mei Lanfang." The progressive nature of *jingju* in Shanghai inspired Mei to settle there. In collaboration with theater scholar Qi Rushan (1875–1962), they developed the psychological landscapes and social ranks of characters in experimental plays.[30] Mei's methods produced significant innovations in singing, dancing, facial expression, music, and costuming. Fluid, graceful movements were also incorporated into his signature dances, which became more important than acrobatic fighting in his plays. He introduced the lower toned *erhu* (two-stringed Chinese fiddle) into the orchestra as an enhancement to the *jinghu* fiddle that accompanied his famous singing.

By the 1920s, Mei was recognized as "The Foremost of the Pear Orchard," a title meaning "the finest actor in the land." He toured to Japan in 1919 and then to the United States in 1930, where he enthralled audiences in sold-out theaters. Some of his greatest roles were in *The Drunken Beauty* (*Gui Fei Zui Jiu*) and *Farewell My Concubine* (*Ba Wang Bie Ji*), which he co-wrote. In 1935, his performances in the Soviet Union profoundly influenced Russian actor/director Vsevolod Meyerhold and the playwright Bertolt Brecht, in exile from Germany.

During World War II when Japan occupied China, Mei was commanded to perform. Afterward, he retreated from society, grew a beard, and chose to live in poverty until 1945. After the Communist takeover in 1949, the new regime found *jingju* incompatible with its revolutionary ideology. Mei weathered the political change by making alterations in *jingju* plays to feature workers, peasants, and soldiers as heroes and heroines. Mei died in 1961 – five years before the Cultural Revolution would denounce him as a reactionary artistic authoritarian. He has since been re-enshrined as one of China's greatest actors.

Current trends

The Chinese government today is introducing new and younger audiences to *jingju* by including *jingju* songs in the music curriculum at elementary schools, and plays are performed on university campuses. CCTV-11 is a television channel that broadcasts Chinese opera exclusively and airs amateur *jingju* talent competitions. During the last decade, the Ministry of Culture announced its support of eleven national prominent *jingju* theaters, including the Shanghai *Jingju* Theater, founded in 1955. This experimental company is known for modern adaptations such as *Hamlet*, which toured in Europe in 2005, and the 2011 multimedia production of *The White Goddess*, in which Western and *jingju* orchestras played together. Another is Tianjin New Generation Peking Opera Troupe, founded in 1994 and run by Zhang Junqiu. This award-winning troupe was featured at the Oregon Shakespeare Festival in 2012. Two lasting aspects of Mei Lanfang's legacy are the establishment of the Mei School of *jingju* performance and the Mei Lanfang *Jingju* Troupe, which is headed by his youngest son, Mei Baojiu, also a noted performer of female roles. In 2003, the Guangzhou Ballet Troupe portrayed his life and career in *Mei Lanfang* and brought the ballet to the University of California at Berkeley in 2007. Many Westerners fascinated by *jingju* have studied the form in China and subsequently produced plays elsewhere. The UK Peking Opera Society, founded by Ione Meyer, is based in London. Professor Elizabeth Wichmann-Walczak, a scholar and practitioner of *jingju*, has staged several productions that have been performed at the University of Hawai'i as well as in China.

Discussion questions: *jingju*

1 A *jingju* performer is considered to improve with age, which is also a concept widely held in Japan and other Asian countries. Does this reverence for age exist in the theatrical genres you are familiar with, and if not, what might this indicate about that particular culture?

2 *Jingju* evolved from both highbrow and lowbrow entertainment, and was embraced by middle classes as well as nobility. Can you equate this phenomenon to other popular theatrical forms, and discuss why they are so appealing to both classes?

3 After the Communist takeover in 1949, Mao Zedong's government swiftly implemented invasive ideological reforms targeting artistic, educational, and religious institutions. Revered actor Mei Lanfang had to weather the theatrical reforms by revising the content of *jingju* plays. Discuss the concept of artistic "conforming" and its effects on the art form, the actors, and the audience.

3.4 Mao's Cultural Revolution and
The Red Detachment of Women

Key points: the Cultural Revolution

1 Although theater reforms began when the Communist People's Republic of China was founded in 1949, this reformation of artistic and educational traditions escalated in 1966 when the Cultural Revolution was launched. Mao Zedong placed his wife, Jiang Qing, along with three others, in charge. They became known as the "Gang of Four." Madame Mao took control of theater, music, and dance.

2 The Gang of Four spearheaded a crusade against "The Four Olds": old ideas, old customs, old habits, and old culture. Ancient, venerable Chinese temples were raided and destroyed, as were educational institutions and the homes of business people, intellectuals, artists, and wealthy landowners.

3 Thousands of artists, scholars, and wealthy people were persecuted, tortured, or murdered for their bourgeois affiliations by the Red Guards, a vigilante group of high-school-aged youths. Many of these victims, along with their children, were sent from their urban homes to be "re-educated" by peasants in the "Down to the Countryside" movement starting in 1968.

4 Maoists believed that theater should be an educational tool and serve the interests of the masses of workers, peasants, and soldiers. Madame Mao banned all forms of theatrical entertainment except the eight "model works" that espoused Mao's political ideology. The eight *yangbanxi* were the only approved stage performances available to the Chinese population during the decade-long Cultural Revolution.

5 Two of the *yangbanxi* were ballets: *The Red Detachment of Women* (1964) and *The White-Haired Girl* (1964). These "model revolutionary dance dramas" for China's Central Ballet Company, which are still popular today, supplanted classical ballets such as *Giselle* and *Swan Lake*, which Madame Mao found full of romance and deemed anti-revolutionary.

Young people of the whole country, bestir yourselves![31]
—Mao Zedong, 1939

After the 1911 overthrow of the Qing Dynasty toppled centuries of imperial rule, the Republic of China (1912–1949) was initially led by Sun Yat-sen (1866–1925) and the Nationalist Kuomintang party (KMT). Sun attempted to modernize China by looking to the West as a model. Some intellectuals and reformists were also inspired by Marxism and the Russian Revolution, and in the early 1920s, the nascent Communist Party of China (CPC) became a left-wing faction within the KMT. When the right-wing KMT leader Chiang Kai-shek (1887–1975) moved to sideline the CPC, the two parties officially split in 1927. Mao Zedong (1893–1976), an avid member of the CPC, was made commander of its Red Army. His Communist ideology differed somewhat from that of Karl Marx and Vladimir Lenin, who believed that social and economic equality was achieved by a worker's revolution against the rich upper classes and aristocracy. In Mao's vision, the workers were not factory laborers, but rural peasants working in agriculture. When Mao led the Red Army during the Long March (1934–1936), he recruited scores of peasants to the CPC's cause. When the Japanese occupied China from 1937 to 1945, Chiang and Mao banded their respective forces together to fight their mutual enemy, but once the Japanese were ousted, a bloody civil war ensued between the parties. Ultimately, the Red Army led the CPC to victory, and in 1949 the People's Republic of China was established. Mao realized that the road to a classless society required strong state control in order to educate the masses and to discourage any dissent. Putting his charismatic, cult-like personality at the epicenter, Chairman Mao became known as "The Great Helmsman" and was slavishly followed by millions who were eventually required to read and recite daily from *Quotations from Chairman Mao Tse-tung*, also known as the *Little Red Book* (1964).

Jingju and the CPC

Mao's new government swiftly implemented
ideological reforms targeting artistic, educational, and
religious institutions. Maoists believed that theater
should be an educational tool and serve the interests
of the masses of workers, peasants, and soldiers.[32]
Jingju was recognized as a popular art, but in need of
reform: between 1949 and 1950, twenty-six *jingju*
plays containing stories of murder, revenge, adultery,
and ghosts were banned as unsuitable for "the spirit of
the people's arts."[33] Concerned, Mei Lanfang – the
country's greatest actor and the head of the China
Beijing Opera Theater – put forth his conviction that
"Moving forward does not require a change of form."
When met with criticism, he altered it by stating,
"Moving forward necessitates change of form."[34] Mei
learned how to walk the ideological line. When one of
his signature works, *The Drunken Concubine*, was
denounced for its pleasure-seeking and sexual
suggestiveness, Mei transformed the concubine into
an "oppressed woman in the palace," representing the
ideology that long-suffering women in the old society
had been liberated by the Communists.[35] Other *jingju*

artists also survived by adapting plays to reflect patriotic, realistic, and revolutionary
themes, full of heroic workers, peasants, and soldiers. One positive note amidst
theater reform was that an actor, once at the bottom of the social ladder, was
elevated to being a "people's artist." With this new level of respect, performers were
also expected to hold up the ideals of the CPC – an actor's "incorrect" political
affiliations and actions could negatively impact their lives and those of their families.
This reforming of artistic and educational traditions by the CPC escalated in 1966,
when the Cultural Revolution ignited into a decade-long bonfire of political purges,
persecution, and violence. Millions of innocent Chinese died from hardships, torture,
or suicide.

The Cultural Revolution (1966–1976)

The Cultural Revolution was Mao's attempt to re-establish his iron grip on China after
The Great Leap Forward (1958–1961), his massive and unsuccessful endeavor to
expand agricultural production in which exhaustive toiling and famine caused the
death of an estimated ten million Chinese.[36] Facing political criticism, he launched
a campaign for cultural and artistic reform known as the Cultural Revolution and
recruited his fourth wife, Jiang Qing (1914–1991), to lead it. Madame Mao, along
with three fellow henchmen – Zhang Chunqiao, Yao Wenyuan, and Wang Hongwen –
became known as the "Gang of Four." In their crusade against "The Four Olds" –
old ideas, old customs, old habits, and old culture – ancient, venerable Chinese
temples were raided and destroyed, as were educational institutions and the homes
of business people, intellectuals, artists, and wealthy landowners. At Mao's urging,
thousands of young people joined the Red Guards, who publicly humiliated and
tortured offenders, making them wear dunce caps and sign boards proclaiming their
"crimes" as they endured savage beatings. Many of these victims were sent from
cities to be "re-educated" by peasants in the "Down to the Countryside" movement
starting in 1968. Brutal purges were carried out with chilling efficacy by the Red
Guards – young vigilantes, intoxicated by the cult of Mao.

Case study: Li Yuru

Li Yuru (1923–2008) was a female *jingju dan* performer who joined the
co-educational Beijing Theater School under Cheng Yanqiu at age 10. After
graduation, Li became a disciple of Mei Lanfang. When the People's Republic was

founded in 1949, Li was found to have a "clean" personal background and was therefore eligible to be a "people's artist." Although she was grateful to the regime for placing actors on an equal par with other citizens, she was coerced into making confessions about her bourgeois lifestyle, love affairs, and penchant for make-up and stylish clothing. Denounced during the Cultural Revolution, Li was imprisoned and her two young daughters were sent to the countryside to be re-educated by peasants. Her mother died after severe beatings by the Red Guards, who occupied and ransacked her house for a week. When Li's *jingju* acting skills were needed in the revolutionary model operas, she was released in 1970 to perform. Mao's death in 1976 allowed Li to return to her famous roles, but much of the repertory, its "bourgeois" characters, and the acting skills from this living tradition had been lost. Teaching these became her mission. In 2007, Li Yuru was awarded a Great Achievement in Performing Arts award for her career in *jingju*.

Despite attempts by *jingju* artists to adapt to the CPC's ideology, Madame Mao, a former actress herself, expressed her vitriolic views in this famous passage:

> It is inconceivable that, in our socialist country led by the Communist Party, the dominant position on the stage is not occupied by the workers, peasants, and soldiers, who are the real creators of history and the true masters of our country . . . So we can say that the modern drama stage is also occupied by ancient Chinese and foreign figures. Theaters are places in which to educate the people, but at present the stage is dominated by emperors, princes, generals, ministers, scholars, and beauties – by feudal and bourgeois stuff.[37]

Jingju, along with all Western music, ballets, and films, was banned in 1966. Madame Mao subsequently launched into promoting her husband's Communist ideology by developing eight state-sponsored *yangbanxi*, or "model works," which were the only approved stage performances available to the Chinese population during the decade-long Cultural Revolution. The themes of these works – five operas, one symphony, and two ballets – broadcasted a revolutionary and educational message that violent rebellion against authority would result in freedom and

Figure 3.13
The National Ballet of China performing *The Red Detachment of Women*, a condoned dance drama during the Cultural Revolution.
Image: Linda Vartoogian, Front Row Photos.

illustrated the class struggle and heroic triumphs of workers, peasants, and soldiers combatting landowners or other enemies of the revolution. *The Red Detachment of Women* (1964) and *The White-Haired Girl* (1964) were "model revolutionary dance dramas" for China's Central Ballet Company that supplanted Soviet-staged classical ballets such as *Giselle* and *Swan Lake*, which Madame Mao deemed as anti-revolutionary. Dai Ailian, the Artistic Director of the Central Ballet Company, initially conducted rehearsals for *The Red Detachment of Women*, but Madame Mao soon took command. Ballet dancers found themselves giving up fluffy tutus for revolutionary uniforms in *The Red Detachment of Women*.

The Red Detachment of Women

The plot of *The Red Detachment of Women* was inspired by true events that took place on Hainan Island during the Chinese Civil War. Wu Qionghua is a peasant who escapes from Nan Batian, her cruel, enslaving landlord. He hunts her down, beats her, and leaves her for dead. Two passersby (on a secret military mission) direct her toward the all-female Red Detachment of the Chinese Communist army. Wu Qionghua becomes a courageous fighter and, eventually, an army leader. The choreography, a collective endeavor by Li Chengxiang, Jiang Zuhui, and Wang Xixian, presented ballet – a dance with aristocratic origin – in a radically new way. The Red Detachment, costumed in unfeminine gray army uniforms, gray knee socks, and toe shoes, projected military might. Traditionally, dancing *en pointe* makes ballerinas look ethereal, yet these women, who needed no male partners, executed gestures and pointe steps that demonstrated strength and portrayed might, power, and ideological fervor. With military precision, the gun-toting female soldiers leaped in precise formations while aiming their bayonets at the imaginary enemy. While

Think about:
When does propaganda become art, and vice versa?

Figure 3.14
Wu Qionghua, played by Zhang Jian, joins the Red Detachment.
Image: Linda Vartoogian, Front Row Photos.

sword dances (a tradition borrowed from Beijing opera) and folk dances were performed by the townsfolk, balletic movement was reserved for the female troops of the Detachment.

In the ballet, when Wu Qionghua meets the Detachment in a delirious state after her traumatic beating and flight from the wicked Nan Batian, she is offered to drink from a coconut. This transformative gulp inspires her – ideologically and physically – and she dances defensively with her arms bent at the elbows and her hands in fists, as if ready to fight. Soon, her long braid is replaced by a bobbed hairstyle, and she wears the Red Detachment uniform. Wu Qionghua becomes a brave fighter, but makes the mistake of impulsively shooting Nan Batian without having received orders to do so. She is punished, but after learning this ideological lesson, her gun is returned and she returns, ultimately vanquishing her enemy. In preparation for wielding weapons, the dancers of the Central Ballet Company were sent to Hainan Island to "learn from the people" and were taught by the Chinese army how to handle rifles realistically.[38]

Figure 3.15
Zhang Jian as Wu Qionghua in a liberating "pointing to the mountain" pose.
Image: Linda Vartoogian, Front Row Photos.

"Make the old serve the new, and things foreign serve things Chinese" was a famous Mao slogan that might explain the seemingly ironic incorporation of Western orchestral music and classical ballet into the hybrid mix of Chinese music, regional folk dances, and *jingju* acrobatics found in *The Red Detachment of Women*. Scholar Paul Clark posits that the merging of various dance elements actually led to a modernization of Chinese culture. He notes, "A ballet step combined with a shifting of the neck in Mongolian style, for example, nicely combined something deemed Chinese with international, modern dance language."[39] However, Madame Mao, who was known to entertain herself in her private quarters with Western music and Hollywood films such as *The Sound of Music*, made sure that Western elements incorporated into *yangbanxi* suited her rebellion. Thinking trombones had an anti-revolutionary sound, she ordered the conductor to get rid of them, but was persuaded that the offending sound emanated from tubas, which were dispensable.[40] She also banned certain ballet steps such as *pas de basque* and *entrechat*, and changed the French terminology of ballet: "stance of the heron bird" replaced *en attitude*, *arabesque* became "spreading your wings in the open breeze," and a high *écarté* side extension of the leg was "pointing to the mountain."

Although *The Red Detachment of Women* and other *yangbanxi* were popular and remain so until this day, the persecution of more traditional artists during the Cultural Revolution was cruel and relentless. Although Mei Lanfang's death in 1961 allowed him to escape this fate, too many in China, including *jingju* artist Li Yuru and ballet director Dai Ailian, did not. Both women were denounced and "sent down" to the countryside for re-education during the Cultural Revolution.

The end of the Cultural Revolution

Less than a month after Chairman Mao's death in 1976, the members of the Gang of Four were put on trial, and jailed. Swift changes occurred in Chinese theater, and the *yangbanxi* model works that had been the standard fare for a decade quickly fell from favor. Efforts to salvage *jingju* began, but it was not performed again until the late 1970s. After the Cultural Revolution, *dan* actress Li Yuru persevered to revive *jingju* acting skills associated with roles that had been banned, such as the "water-sleeve" manipulations of the flirtatious *huadan* character. She recalled what was gained, but also what was lost, saying:

> We tended to think that in the new society everything was bound to be new and we had to learn to adapt ourselves . . . It is very sad . . . I don't know what I can say to my predecessors when I see them in the other world.[41]

In 1977, China held its first nationwide university entrance examination since 1965. Of the five million who took the test, five percent won admission and became known as the class of 1977 – China's "best and brightest." Some of the artists that emerged from the class included filmmakers Chen Kaige (*Farewell My Concubine*) and Zhang Yimou (*Raise the Red Lantern*). Although the years of the Cultural Revolution were undeniably devastating in myriad ways, for so many who had been denounced and "sent down," the opportunity to have a fresh start ultimately led to a great deal of revitalizing creativity. Ironically, many of those who emerged from the Cultural Revolution as innovators shared a commonality with its intended ideology: that art has the power to educate, and transform.

Current trends

After the end of the Cultural Revolution, many condemned artists endeavored to resuscitate their art forms. The Beijing Dance Academy began offering Chinese traditional folk dance along with classical ballet. Although once forbidden works such as *Swan Lake* are performed today by the Central Ballet Company, *The Red Detachment of Women* has a prominent place in the repertory and was recently performed in New York City in 2015. In the 1990s, when this ballet was being restaged, lyrics that might be offensive to wealthy viewers were initially changed, but nostalgic audiences demanded the original words. The proliferation of Cultural

Revolution theme restaurants, which offer evenings of musical theater sing-alongs for diners, demonstrate the degree to which *yangbanxi* political songs had been the soundtrack of many people's youth and remain a strong touchstone for them today.

3.4 Exploration: excerpt from *The Story of Dai Ailain* by Richard Glasstone[42]

Reprinted with kind permission from Dance Books, Ltd.

Dai Ailain (1916–2006) was Artistic Director of the Central Ballet Company until condemned by Madame Mao in 1966 and "sent down" for re-education by peasants, which she recalls in this excerpt. She was eventually released to her former students on the grounds that she was a national treasure.

They [CPC officials] made me write out my history from my birth to the present day . . . again and again during the next four or five years. And they cross-questioned me about everything I wrote. I was also made to do manual work, cleaning out the ballet studios and the school dormitories. I was ordered to cut my long hair, and they threatened to shave my head if I did not cut my hair short myself.

The workers and the army were now in charge. During one of my interrogations sessions a certain Chinese word was used which I did not understand. It turned out to be something to do with my army rank . . . I was surprised, as I had never joined the army; but because I had lived for some time in Chongqing, the city in which the opposition military leader, Chiang Kai-shek, had had his military base during the Japanese invasion, they suspected me of having been in the Kuomintang army. I told them I had never joined any army, so I could not answer questions about my military life.

First I was sent to an experimental agricultural unit. I was over fifty years of age, so they thought I was too old to learn. I was told to tidy the orchard, to pick up leaves and twigs. They said I was too stupid to learn how to do it. Madame Mao had also taken control of the Beijing Opera Company, and among the artists she had sent to work on the land was a very famous opera singer whom I knew well . . . Now I saw this distinguished artist carrying heavy loads and working in the fields during midday heat. Whenever I greeted him, he would look around nervously to make sure we were not being watched. I heard later that he had been savagely beaten by the Red Guards.

Later, together with a Ballet Company unit of about thirty people, I was sent to another farm . . . I caught cold and was bed-ridden three times in one year . . . I was described as a monster and was sent off to look after the pigs. I liked my pigs . . . Some of the other workers took pity on me. One of these was the old Ballet Company chauffeur. He would sometimes secretly slip a cake into my pocket. Another worker, a plumber, laid a pipe to transport the water I had previously had to carry in two buckets attached to a long pole held across my shoulder. We all tried to help one another, but those were hard times, especially in winter. I was given a large pile of pointe shoes to darn and was forced to stay awake several days, until the job was done. All I was given to eat was a bowl of beans at midnight. I was then allowed to rest for two days before being given another batch of pointe shoes to darn. I ended up with a frozen shoulder.

Discussion questions: the Cultural Revolution

1 Madame Mao famously said, "Theaters are places in which to educate the people." In *The Red Detachment of Women*, what lessons were learned by the performers, and by the audience? Should theater, music, and dance serve an educational purpose in society, and if so, why?

2 Today, *The Red Detachment of Women* has a proud place in the repertory of the Central Ballet Company, and musical sing-alongs of *yangbanxi* political songs are popular in certain theme restaurants in China. Discuss your thoughts on the continued popularity of art made in an era of repression.
3 In the "Down to the Countryside" movement, people were taken away from their families, their schooling, and their careers for years in order to be re-educated by peasants. If this had been your fate, when you were allowed to resume your former life, what lessons do you think you would have learned, and how would these have affected your reintegration into society?

Notes

1 Heywood, Denise. *Cambodian Dance: Celebration of the Gods*, 34.
2 Cravath, Paul. "The Ritual Origins of the Classical Dance Drama of Cambodia," 127.
3 Heywood, 39.
4 Cravath, 195.
5 Turnbull, Robert. "A Burned-Out Theater: The State of Cambodia's Performing Arts" 141.
6 Phim, Toni Shapiro. "Mediating Cambodian History, the Sacred, and the Earth," 316.
7 Cravath, 190.
8 Heywood, 126.
9 Turnbull, 142.
10 Widyono, Benny. *Dancing in Shadows: Sihanouk, the Khmer Rouge, and the United Nations in Cambodia*, 24.
11 Heywood, 208.
12 Chandler, David. *Voices from S-21: Terror and History from Pol Pot's Secret Prison*, 33.
13 Phim, Toni Shapiro. "Dance, Music, and the Nature of Terror in Democratic Kampuchea," 183.
14 Widyono, 11; Linfield, Susie. *The Cruel Radiance: Photography and Political Violence*, 54.
15 Widyono, 28.
16 Phim, Toni Shapiro. "Mediating Cambodian History, the Sacred, and the Earth," 309.
17 Turnbull, Personal Communication, May 16, 2015.
18 Shapiro, Sophiline Cheam. "Cambodian Dance and the Individual Artist," 166.
19 Turnbull, 137.
20 Phim, Toni Shapiro. "Mediating Cambodian History, the Sacred, and the Earth." In *Dance, Human Rights, and Social Justice: Dignity in Motion*, edited by Naomi Jackson, and Toni Shapiro-Phim, 304–322. Lanham, MD: Scarecrow Press Inc, 2008, 316–318.
21 Makerras, Colin. "The Drama of the Qing Dynasty," 103.
22 Tian, Min. *Mei Lanfang and the Twentieth-Century International Stage*, 2.
23 Xu, Chengbei, Peking Opera, 92; Makerras, 105.
24 Scott, A. C. "The Performance of Classical Theater," 133–134.
25 Ibid., 132.
26 Ibid., 120.
27 Xu, 29.
28 Scott, 122.
29 Xu, 81.
30 Tian, 4.
31 www.marxists.org/reference/archive/mao/selected-works/volume-2/mswv2_13.htm
32 Makerras, Colin. "Theater and the Masses," 166.
33 Li, Ruru. *The Soul of the Beijing Opera*, 126.
34 Tian, 8; Ruru, 120.
35 Ruru, 141.
36 Hay, Jeff, Ed. *Perspectives on Modern History: The Chinese Cultural Revolution*, 23.

37 Ch'ing, Chiang. "Revolution of Peking Opera," 20.
38 Glasstone, Richard. *The Life of Dai Ailian*, 51.
39 Clark, Paul. *The Chinese Cultural Revolution*, 256.
40 Glasstone, 62.
41 Ruru, 132.
42 Glasstone, Richard. *The Story of Dai Ailian*. Hampshire: Dance Books, Ltd., 2007, 65–66.

Bibliography

Visual sources

YouTube

Cambodia

"Cambodia: 1920s Khmer in Color," YouTube video, 6:06, posted by "The Informer," January 18, 2008, www.youtube.com/watch?v=fxLQ1_SDksE
"Princess Buppha Devi Performs Apsara," YouTube video, 14.23, posted by "prasatevoda's channel," April 16, 2012, www.youtube.com/watch?v=Oi7s9J8GCsc#t=687
"Robam Chouy Chai, danced by Sophiline Cheam Shapiro," YouTube video, 9:20, posted by "Ichan90a," January 21, 2010, www.youtube.com/watch?v=-czq_LDBdVY

China

Jingju

"An Excerpt From *The Drunken Beauty* by Mei Lanfang," YouTube video, 1.38, posted by "Bu Er Magazine," September 15, 2014, www.youtube.com/watch?v=3Q4kAcYUlmQ
Mei Lanfang, *Farewell My Concubine, "Dance of the Swords"* (1956), YouTube video, 1.11, posted by "gustavothomasteatro," February 10, 2010, www.youtube.com/watch?v=M2Su0ryXaZc
"Mei Lanfang Classics" Beijing Opera, YouTube video, 5:34, posted by "The POLOARTS," March 22, 2011, www.youtube.com/watch?v=aGCrdxOpkiU

The Red Detachment of Women

"Punainen Naiskomppania" (*The Red Detachment of Women*), performed by the China Central Ballet Troupe in Helsinki, YouTube video, 9:58, posted by, "Harri Liedes," August 24, 2015, www.youtube.com/watch?v=XqZzi6oYdLI

Written Sources

Chandler, David. *Voices from S-21: Terror and History from Pol Pot's Secret Prison*. Berkeley: University of California Press, 1999.
Chengbei, Xu. *Peking Opera*. Cambridge: Cambridge University Press, 2012.
Chevrier, Yves. *Mao and the Chinese Revolution*. Gloucestershire, UK: Arris Books, 2004.
Ch'ing, Chiang. "Revolution of Peking Opera." *Social Education*, Vol. 1 (1973): 20–25.
Clark, Paul. *The Chinese Cultural Revolution*. Cambridge: Cambridge University Press, 2008.
Cravath, Paul. "The Ritual Origins of the Classical Dance Drama of Cambodia." *Asian Theater Journal*, Vol. 3, No. 2 (Fall, 1986): 179–203. Accessed September 8, 2–15. www.jstor.org/stable/1124400.
Diamond, Catherine. "Emptying the Sea by the Bucketful: The Dilemma in Cambodian Theatre." *Asian Theatre Journal*, Vol. 20, No. 2 (2003): 147–178. Accessed September 8, 2–15. Stable URL:www.jstor.org/stable/1124595.
Ebihara, May, and Judy Ledgerwood. "Aftermaths of Genocide: Cambodian Villagers." In *Annihilating Difference: The Anthropology of Genocide*, edited by Alexander Laban Hinton, 272–283. Berkeley: University of California Press, 2002.

Glasstone, Richard. *The Story of Dai Ailian*. Hampshire: Dance Books, Ltd., 2007.

Heywood, Denise. *Cambodian Dance: Celebration of the Gods*. Bangkok: River Books, 2008.

Jonas, Gerald. *Dancing: The Pleasure, Power, and Art of Movement*. New York: Harry N. Abrams, Inc. 1992.

Li, Ruru. *The Soul of the Beijing Opera*. Hong Kong: Hong Kong University Press, 2010.

Linfield, Susie. *The Cruel Radiance: Photography and Political Violence*. Chicago: University of Chicago Press, 2010.

Mackerras, Colin. *The Chinese Theater in Modern Times*. London: Thames and Hudson, 1975.

Makerras, Colin: "The Drama of the Qing Dynasty." In *Chinese Theater*, edited by Colin Makerras, 92–117. Honolulu: University of Hawaii Press, 1983.

Makerras, Colin: "Theater and the Masses." In *Chinese Theater*, edited by Colin Makerras, 145–183. Honolulu: University of Hawaii Press, 1983.

Nut, Suppya Helene. "The Legend of Apsara Mera: Princess Norodom Buppha Devi's Choreography for the Royal Ballet of Cambodia." *Asian Theater Journal*, Vol. 31, No. 1 (Spring 2014): 279–289. DOI: 10.1353/atj.2014.0025.

Phim, Toni Samantha, and Ashley Thompson. *Dance in Cambodia*. New York: Oxford University Press, 1999.

Phim, Toni Shapiro. "Dance, Music, and the Nature of Terror in Democratic Kampuchea." In *Annihilating Difference: The Anthropology of Genocide*, edited by Alexander Laban Hinton, 179–193. Berkeley: University of California Press, 2002.

Phim, Toni Shapiro. "Mediating Cambodian History, the Sacred, and the Earth." In *Dance, Human Rights, and Social Justice: Dignity in Motion*, edited by Naomi Jackson and Toni Shapiro-Phim, 304–322. Lanham, MD: Scarecrow Press Inc, 2008.

Scott, A. C. "The Performance of Classical Theater." In *Chinese Theater*, edited by Colin Makerras, 118–144. Honolulu: University of Hawaii Press, 1983.

Shapiro, Sophiline Cheam. "Cambodian Dance and the Individual Artist." In *Dance, Human Rights, and Social Justice: Dignity in Motion*, edited by Naomi Jackson, and Toni Shapiro-Phim, 166–168. Lanham, MD: Scarecrow Press Inc; Rowman and Littlefield Publishing Group, 2008.

Terzuolo, Chiara Park. "Opera and Politics: The Twain Shall Meet." *Greater China* (Winter 2009): 39–45. Accessed September 8, 2–15. Stable URL: https://web. stanford.edu/group/sjeaa/journal91/china2.pdf.

Tian, Min. *Mei Lanfang and the Twentieth-Century International Stage*. New York: Palgrave Macmillan, 2012.

Tuchman-Rosta, Celia. "From Ritual Form to Tourist Attraction: Negotiating the Transformation of Classical Cambodian Dance in a Changing World." *Asian Theater Journal* Vol. 31, No. 2 (Fall 2014): 524–544. DOI: 10.1353/atj.2014.0033.

Turnbull, Robert. "A Burned-Out Theater: The State of Cambodia's Performing Arts." In *Expressions of Cambodia: The Politics of Tradition, Identity and Change*, edited by Leakthina Chau-Pech Ollier and Tim Winter, 133–149. New York: Routledge, 2006.

Widyono, Benny. *Dancing in Shadows: Sihanouk, the Khmer Rouge, and the United Nations in Cambodia*. Lanham, MD: Rowman and Littlefield Publishers, 2008.

Xu, Chengbei. *Peking Opera*. Cambridge: Cambridge University Press, 2010.

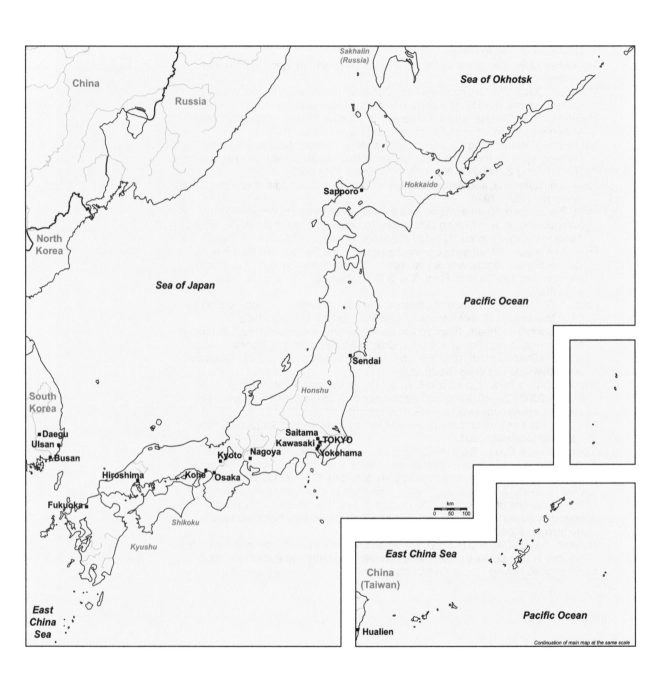

Japanese *noh*, *kabuki*, and *butoh*
Entertaining *samurai*, merchants, and rebels

4.1 Overview

This chapter examines how Japanese *noh*, *kabuki*, and *butoh* reflect the ethos and political landscape from which they arose. During a fractious period of civil wars, Japan's Emperor was reduced to a mere figurehead when a military *Shogunate* government emerged in Kyoto in 1603. The *Shogun*, or "great general," presided over the *samurai*, a society of warriors who lived by *bushido* – a strict moral code upholding attributes of obedience, frugality, loyalty, honor, and Buddhism. In facing dishonor or failure, the only path toward valor was to commit *seppuku* – ritual suicide – in which a warrior would slice his own abdomen with a sword, thereby freeing his spirit. Moral laws governed all aspects of people's lives, even decreeing what fashions, colors, and patterns they wore. *Noh* reflected the ethos of the *Shogun* and his elite *samurai* class, and its moralistic plays became their exclusive entertainment.

While *noh* plays served as spiritual release for *samurai* during a war-torn era, colorful and flamboyant *kabuki* plays of the peaceful seventeenth century echoed the hedonistic desires of a rising merchant class. Its plots featured tormented conflict between one's passions and temptations, and the duty to family or society. *Butoh* evolved in a post-World War II Japan reeling from atomic horrors and defeat. Artists of all sorts rebelled by rejecting traditional forms, Western influences, and Japan's strict social codes, creating brutally frank and subversive works.

4.2 *Noh* theater: entertaining *samurai*

Key points: *noh*

1 *Noh* is an ancient theatrical form, originally enjoyed by the lower classes, that evolved from harvest songs and dances, Shinto fertility rituals, and acrobatic, comic entertainment. At first women and men performed *noh*, but after women were banned from the stage, men played female characters by wearing masks.
2 When *noh* became entertainment exclusively for the elite *samurai* warrior class, playwrights such as Zeami created refined narratives about brave warriors and the salvation of souls that reflected the ethos of this culture.
3 *Noh* is sometimes called "the art of walking." An actor moves along the polished stage in a slow, gliding walk called *suri-ashi*. *Noh kata* – movement patterns, poses, or actions – can be realistic, symbolic, or abstract, but are all highly stylized: anger is shown by slightly moving the head side to side; a fan can be used to indicate the pouring of *sake* or the thrust of a sword.
4 In each of the five plays within a *noh* cycle, the onstage chorus chants the narrative. After the story is introduced, the *shite* (lead actor) enacts a dramatic

transformation offstage and returns in a different guise, often masked as a ghost or a creature.

5 Official *noh* schools, or *ryu*, were established in the fourteenth century, and are still run by the *iemoto* system, in which master teachers pass the tradition down through their biological or adopted heirs.

Even if only unconsciously, the public go to noh theatre as an act of spiritual salvation.[1]

—Mutsuo Takahashi

Noh – with its deliberate slowness, symbolic gestures, and intensely calibrated movements – developed into a highly refined aristocratic entertainment in fourteenth-century Japan. Ironically, *noh* derived from two popular forms of folk entertainment, *dengaku* and *sarugaku*. *Dengaku* was a musical offering to the gods by rice farmers wanting to insure a good harvest. Rooted in Shinto fertility rites, it evolved into a raucous ritual that unleashed brazen female sexuality and impelled people to dance half-naked in public places.[2] *Sarugaku* was acrobatic entertainment imported from China and grew into a form of humorous mime presented at Shinto shrines or Buddhist temples to expel evil spirits and bring good fortune. Interspersed with austere temple dances, *sarugaku* offered the respite of comically vulgar interludes ridiculing outcasts, misfits, and others derided by society. Although these unfortunate beings had been socially rejected, dramas concerning their salvation began to be created. A father and son associated with a famous *sarugaku* troupe from Yamoto were Kan'ami Kiyotsuga (1333–1384) and Zeami Motokiyo (1363–1443). They began to blend mimetic drama with refined dancing and poetic chanting, and became forerunners of *noh*.

Kan'ami and Zeami, and the rise of *noh*

In 1374, when *Shogun* Ashikaga Yoshimitsu saw the talented 12-year-old Zeami perform *sarugaku* with his father, the ruler immediately became the troupe's patron. Under this sponsorship, Zeami received an artistic education and matured into a consummate professional actor and author. As *sarugaku* became refined, Zeami was elemental in the crystallization of a new dramatic male genre called *noh*, a term meaning "skill" or "faculty." He eventually wrote forty plays and several treatises on *noh* acting, such as *Kadensho* (*Book of the Transmission of the Flowers*), helping to codify the form.

Kan'ami and Zeami lived during the turbulent Muromachi Period (1392–1573), when civil wars raged in Japan. The salvation of souls and the Buddhist tenets of *karma*, in which sins govern one's reincarnation status, became of great concern to battling warriors. Zeami and his father penned dramas tailored to the *samurai* audience, who faced numerous moral questions. Tragic and spiritual characters such as phantom warriors, itinerant priests, bereft women, desolate elders, kidnapped children, and demons were woven into stories of hatred, sorrow, vengeance, jealousy, and repentance, and presented in a highly stylized, restrained form. Throughout *noh*, both noble and common characters are concerned with purification, the afterlife, and the power of Buddha, and there is an overall hatred of killing. Ultimately, its dramas are about salvation of souls.

Almost two centuries after Zeami's time, the Ashikaga *Shogunate* of Kyoto was defeated in 1603 by the Tokugawa *Shogunate*, based in Edo (today's Tokyo). To insure security, the new *Shogun* drastically curtailed the social mobility of the people and established four distinct classes, forbidden to intermarry: *samurai*, farmers, craftsmen, and merchants. Christianity was banned and registration at a Buddhist temple or Shinto shrine required. In a drastically isolating move known as *sakoku* that lasted over two centuries, *Shogun Iemitsu* expelled all missionaries and most foreigners before sealing off Japan's borders in 1635. The popularity of *noh* prevailed and five *noh* schools were established, with the *Kanze* school officially appointed as the leading troupe. Many actors finally had a livelihood and received the honorary rank of samurai. During the Tokugawa Era (1603–1863), also known as the Edo period, *noh* theater became reserved exclusively for the *samurai* warrior class. In one incident, commoners erected a stage disguised by day and held clandestine *noh* performances at night. Once discovered, they were severely punished and their theater destroyed.[3]

Case study: Noh schools

The first *noh* school, or *ryu*, was the *Kanze* school, founded by Kannami, Zeami's father, in the fourteenth century under the protection of the Ashikaga *Shogunate*. During the Edo period, the *Kanze* school oversaw three other *ryu*: the *Hosho*, *Konparu*, and *Kongo*, while the *Kita* school developed later. Each continues to be run by the *iemoto* system, in which a family "head" is the supreme authority, approving all licenses issued to professional performers and passing down the tradition to the next appropriate relative or an adopted member. Each family has developed its own style of singing, acting, dancing, and costuming, guards its heritage, and takes pride in owning ancient masks and costumes.

Think about: Despite Japan's act of avoiding any threat of colonialism by sealing its borders, is it ironic that it enforced many similar punishing forces on its people?

The *noh* stage

Made of unfinished Japanese cypress with little ornamentation, no sets, and no frontal curtain, the simplicity of the *noh* stage (*butai*) imparts a feeling of peaceful refuge. The square stage has a peaked roof, supported by four corner pillars, and references the architecture of a Shinto shrine. The stage extends frontally into a pebble "moat" where the audience sits, facing the center and the left of the performance area. The stage, so highly polished that it reflects a performer's figure, is a percussive instrument in itself: huge earthenware pots below the surface produce resonant reverberations from stamping feet during a dance. Performers enter and exit via the *hashigakari* passageway that connects the stage and the dressing room, which is symbolic of a bridge spanning the realm of spirits (backstage) to this world (the stage). Three pine trees lining the edge of the *hashigakari* help orient a masked actor taking dramatic pauses along the way. On the wall upstage center, a painting of a sprawling pine tree represents nature and longevity. The musicians sit upstage center, while the chorus sits on the right-hand side of the stage, facing the performers. Behind the musicians sits the *koken*, who is an attendant to the *shite* (pronounced *shee-tay*), the lead actor on stage. He emerges to handle the few properties used, changes costume accessories for the *shite*, and prompts the actors in a normal voice if a line is forgotten. Although the *koken* remains largely in the background, he is a *noh* master, senior to the *shite*, who can take over a role if necessary.

Noh characters/common dramatic structure

Although all professional *noh* players end up in their respective roles as musician, chanter, or actor, each has been fully trained in each discipline from early childhood, generally by male teachers from a *noh* family. Traditionally, men play *noh* and, for the most part, that has remained the case. Many plays feature female protagonists, but unlike *kabuki*, *noh* actors never embody a female persona – the walk is no different and the voice is not disguised. Only the mask, wig, and robe indicate that the character is female, and the same applies when a monster or god is played. Out of respect, child actors (*kokata*) normally portray emperors or nobles, since it would be disrespectful to have a grown man play someone of such high rank.

Case study: Women in *noh*

Although men continue to dominate the field of *noh*, accounts of accomplished Japanese female *noh* actors exist in fifteenth-century royal diaries. Their presence on stage ended in 1629, when the Tokugawa *Shogunate* outlawed women from performing publicly in order to discourage prostitution. This ban affected *kabuki* as well, and men began to portray female characters in both forms. The *Shogunate* supported the formation of male *noh iemoto* schools and transformed what was formerly a populist pursuit performed by both genders into an elite male practice for an aristocratic audience. After World War II, the *iemoto* of the *Hosho-ryu* feared that the democratization of Japan would lead to the decline of *noh*, which impelled him to train both male and female amateurs. The first female professional actor, Tsmura Kimiko, made her stage debut in 1939. Currently, Kinue Oshima is an active female *shite* actor and teacher from the Oshima Family *Noh* Theater, a branch of the *Kita* school. Still, professional recognition is difficult for women to attain; as of 2013, only fifteen percent of the *Nohgaku* Performers' Association was female. Today in Japan however, the majority of amateur *noh* actors are women over the age of fifty.

In *noh*, the *waki* is a secondary actor serving as foil to the *shite*. Each play is divided into two parts, and the *shite* generally appears in different guises in each – youthful, and then elderly, or sometimes living, and then as a ghost. He may also have companions, known as *tsure*. The *waki* appears as an unmasked mortal and never plays a female. He enters first, often playing an itinerant monk on a pilgrimage to a historical place, and walks as the chorus chants a traveling song. Once the *waki* arrives at his destination, the *shite* then enters in a disguise and, through a dance supported by the chorus's narration, relates a tragic story about a person who died there. The *shite* confesses to being that very person's ghost and then mysteriously

Figure 4.1
Katayama Kuroemon, Living National Treasure of Japan, (left) performs with Urata Yasuchika in *Koi no Omoni (The Heavy Burden of Love)*.
Image: Jack Vartoogian, Front Row Photos.

exits down the *hashigakari*. Backstage, the *shite* dramatically transforms via mask, wig, and costume into a drastically different guise, from an old man into a gallant young god, or from a beautiful young woman into the ghost of a warrior. In the meantime, the *waki* meets a local person, a comedic *kyogen* actor called the *ai*. In cruder jargon, the *ai* confirms the legend of the death and suggests that the *waki* pray for the ghost he has just encountered. The *shite* will then reappear, transformed.

Typically, a cycle of *noh* theater comprises a sacred invocation, or *okina*, five plays, and two comic interludes called *kyogen* (mad words). In the *okina*, a dancer symbolizes the descent of a god by donning an *okina* mask – the face of a wizened old man – and performs a *kamigaku* (divine dance). Another then breaks into a *sanbaso* – a lively dance with leaps, stamps, and the shaking of bells to send the god off royally. A *kyogen* is a short comic duet or trio that has antecedents in the humorous form of *sarugaku*. These interludes involve zany situations, such as a master-servant relationship in which a servant tricks his lord out of *sake* or sugar, or avoids hard work. Other objects of ridicule are bumbling priests, blind men, or unfaithful husbands. Bridegrooms are also targeted. In *Futari-Bakama* (*Two in One Pair of Trousers*), a groom and his father pay a visit to his fiancée's family. Although they only have one pair of formal trousers, they are anxious to make a good impression, so each man occupies a pant leg.

The first of the five plays is called *kami-mono* (god play) and involves a deity who descends to bestow blessings on mortals. The second is *shura-mono* (warrior play) involving a fallen hero, while in the third type, *kazura-mono* (woman play), a lovelorn female is wronged or abandoned by her lover. The fourth is *monoguri-mono* (madness play) in which the protagonist, often a woman, is driven to a deranged state by extreme duress or jealousy. Lastly, in the faster-paced *kiri-mono* (demon play), evil beings preside, or sometimes magical animals. Spectators follow scripts, since the archaic language chanted by the chorus is often incomprehensible to modern Japanese audiences.

Noh plays can exist in two temporal planes. *Genzai* (realistic) *noh* involves a living protagonist, who suffers tremendously from the loss of a spouse or a child. Their tortured life makes them a deranged outcast who exists in a mortal "limbo" that is close to a death-like state. In *mugen* (fantasy) *noh* plots, a sleeping *waki* sees a ghost in a dream. In a flashback, the *shite* relives the suffering he or she endured while living, as well as the present agony of their tortured soul, and begs the monk to pray for their salvation. The *waki* prays until the ghost, set free by prayers, performs a joyful dance and then slowly and silently departs. When the *waki* awakens, foggy from his dream, it is daytime and the ghost is nowhere to be seen.

Figure 4.2
Kankuro and Tomijuro perform *Bo-Shibari*, a *kyogen* in which two servants attempt to drink their master's sake, despite being tied up.
Image: Jack Vartoogian, Front Row Photos.

Figure 4.3
In the *kiri-mono* play of *Tsuchigumo*, a man transforms into a spider. Umewaka Rokuro (left) as the spider and Kakuto Naotaka as Lord Minamoto Raikou.
Image: Jack Vartoogian, Front Row Photos.

Think about:
How does a typical *noh* cycle of five plays, along with its *okina* and *kyogen* interludes, reflect the religious syncretism of Shinto and Buddhism?

Noh aesthetic concepts and technique

Jo-ha-kyu is a crucial aesthetic concept in *noh*. *Jo* means preparation or beginning; *ha* means breaking; and *kyu*, rapid, or urgent. The contained energy within the

introduction, development, and conclusion of *jo-ha-kyu* governs the gradual
acceleration of a walk or movement within in eight counts, the sections of each *noh*
play, and the order of the five within a full cycle. It also defines three areas of the
stage and the *hashigakari* (with the farthest area from the audience being *jo*, the
middle, *ha*, and the one closest to the audience, *kyu*), and determines the pace, with
the fastest action happening on *kyu*.[4] This far-ranging principle exists in other forms
of Japanese music, theater, and dance. Sometime translated as "invisible beauty,"
yugen is another aesthetic concept. *Yugen* and *hana* both mean beauty, but the
connotation of *yugen* is more esoteric – it is a quality that is enhanced by an actor's
experience and age. Author Mutsuo Takahashi explains this phenomenon, using the
term *hana*:

> The natural aura of a youthful body was known as *jibun no hana* (momentary
> blossom), whereas the spiritual aura acquired through years of training, that
> is, long after the body had lost its youthfulness, was called *makoto no hana*
> (the true blossom). Because of the value placed on *makoto no hana*, Noh has
> become uniquely suited to performances by actors whose bodies are past
> their prime, and it even makes a positive virtue of old age.[5]

Roles featuring elderly *shite*, such as *Sekidera Komachi*, are considered more
difficult and are only played by seasoned actors, since *yugen* is crucial to the
interpretation.

Noh is sometimes called "the art of walking." Its characteristic gliding gait, *suri-ashi*,
requires steady concentration and is executed while in the basic *noh* stance (*kamae*)
in which the torso is tilted forward, the knees are slightly bent, and center of gravity is
low. The arms stretch forward, describing an oval, with the palms facing each other.
In *suri-ashi* the feet glide in alternating sequences: in taking one step, as the foot
slides along the floor, the ball of the foot rises with the toes slightly curled upward
and then flattens out on the ground. The performer must move on the same horizontal
plane, with no deviations up and down. When changing direction, one stops, lifts
the ball of a foot and turns on the heel, rotating the body toward the new direction in
a fashion that modern audiences might call a "robotic action." This is most clearly
seen in the locomotion of the *shite* who moves in zigzag lines, while the traveling
patterns of the *waki* curve. Actors use moments of stillness and variations of speed in
their walk to express modulations in emotion: a few backward faltering steps reveal
disappointment, while two or three rapid steps forward imply excitement.[6]

The daily practice of a *noh* actor includes vocal exercises designed to facilitate
kabuittai, a combination of singing and dancing. Words are learned in tandem with
movements that are performed in precise, codified ways, leaving little opportunity for
a *noh* performer to improvise or introduce personal gestures. *Noh kata* – movement
patterns, poses, or actions – can be realistic, symbolic, or abstract, but are all highly
stylized. Actions such as scooping water, pouring sake, thrusting a sword, reading a
book, or writing are executed with a fan. Abstract *kata* are included in dancing, and
include zigzag traveling patterns and stamping.[7] In *noh*, it is what the actor leaves
out that is most important, because our minds will fill in the blanks. For example, a
few steps can represent a character's long pilgrimage, while the brushing of kimono
sleeves together shows affection between lovers. In more symbolic actions such as
weeping, the *kata* has three degrees: slightly bowing the head indicates sadness; in
more pronounced sorrow, one upraised palm moves to the eye, while both palms are
raised in extreme suffering.

There are various terms for "dance" in Japanese. *Mai* is the term for the dance of
noh, indicating that it is contained – the knees are bent and the motion is low and
grounded rather than being airborne. A *jo-no-mai* is a quiet, graceful dance for a
female character performed to instrumental music, while a *kakeri* is an agitated
dance, done by warriors and madwomen (as seen in *Sumidagawa*) to depict their
mental suffering. In the dance sequences, a sense of dramatic power and gravity
is also conveyed through the rhythm of *jo-ha-kyu*, in which the *kata* begin slowly,
gradually increase in speed and tension, reach a climax, and then come to an abrupt
halt. Action in *noh* is balanced by moments of stillness.

Figure 4.4
In *noh*, the simple lifting of the hand to the eye signifies weeping. Katayama Shingo performs as Lady Rokujo in *Aoi no Ue (Lady Aoi)* by the Kashu-Juku *Noh* Theater of Kyoto, Japan.
Image: Jack Vartoogian, Front Row Photos.

Case study: *Sumidagawa* (Sumida River)

Sumidagawa, written in the fifteenth century by Zeami's son, Motomasa, is the deeply sad story of a woman in search of her kidnapped son. Deranged by grief, she arrives at the Sumida River, where a ferryman is taking customers across to a Buddhist ceremony for a boy who died on the riverbank a year ago. He agrees to ferry this madwoman across, but on the condition that she amuse the crowd with her frenetic dancing. Soon realizing that her unbalanced state is the result of deep emotional scarring, he takes pity upon her. During the crossing, he tells his passengers the unfortunate story of the dead boy. After being kidnapped by a slave trader, the child fell sick and was abandoned on the riverbank. Despite being cared for by the locals, he died and was buried there. At the rite, it becomes evident to the madwoman that this boy was her son and, as she prays over his grave, her phantom child emerges. As she reaches out to hold his hand, he disappears and she weeps bitterly. The piece concludes with her dance, in which she asks the birds if her son has found peace. *Sumidagawa* is performed by both *noh* and *kabuki* troupes, and modern iterations exist in *butoh* and in Western opera.

Noh musicians

Noh music is known as *hayashi* and its musicians are called *hayashi-kata*. The *jiutai* is the chorus, which is made up of six to ten men who intone vocal music called *utai*. Similar to a Greek chorus, their unison chants introduce the characters, narrate the encounter between the *shite* and the *waki*, and describe the mental landscape of the *shite*. The accompanying instruments include a shoulder drum (*ko-tsuzumi*), a small drum (*taiko*) played on the knee, a hip drum (*o-tsuzumi*), and a shrill bamboo flute (*nohkan*, or *fue*). A characteristic of *hayashi* is *kake-goe* – meaningless syllables that are called out by drummers before certain beats in the music. These have nothing to do with the action on stage, but add an element of urgency to the atmosphere of the performance. The deep, resonant cries of *kake-goe* act as signposts in leading the rhythm, and one drummer may make them repeatedly as a signal to speed up the tempo. Throughout the performance all musicians kneel, except for the shoulder and hip drummers, who are seated on stools.

Noh costumes and masks

The dazzling, colorful silk *shozoku* robes of *noh* theater are richly embroidered with silver and gold, and reference the elite dress of fourteenth-century nobility. In preparation for putting on a majestic *shozoku*, a performer wears a white cotton undershirt and tights, a padded silk robe, and, if playing a male character, a small pillow to round out the abdomen. The outer robe can be wrapped in various ways and then tied around the hips with an *obi* cloth band, which allows for tucking a fan in front of the abdomen. *Noh* performers wear white ankle-height *tabi* socks that are split in between the first and second toe. Wigs, and sometimes hats, are worn with masks, while unmasked characters wear no make-up.

Noh masks, or *omote*, are vital in the dramatic transformation of a character. These treasured objects, carved by master sculptors from cypress wood and painted in great detail, are priceless heirlooms. Female and male masks are classified in age groups ranging from young to old, and specific categories exist for gods, demons, and ghosts. When an actor dons an *omote* in the mirror room just off stage, he makes a dramatic transcendence by meditating upon a face of heaven or of hell. The *omote* serves as a means for *noh* actors to deeply embody their role, rather than to guide the audience in character recognition. In fact, the narrow masks are not designed to conceal the whole face, and an actor's jaw-line is often visible. An actor magically enables the *omote* to convey a variety of expressions by merely changing the angle of the gaze. One "brightens" the mask by tilting the face upward to show happiness or "clouds" it by lowering the chin to convey sadness. Moving it quickly right and left indicates anger, while rotating side to side slowly and repeatedly signifies searching.

The pace of *noh*

In all *noh* plays except for the demon type, actions move at a glacial pace. Once *noh* became official entertainment for the *samurai* class during the Edo period, many demanded to be trained by the actors. Consequently, *noh* became more solemn and ritual-like, and plays began to be performed approximately three times slower than during Zeami's era.[8] Kunio Komparu, a descendant of a famous *noh* family, claims that since many plays are situated in a *mugen* fantasy realm that transcends the normal boundaries of time, a semi-dozing state is encouraged in the *noh* audience:

> By extinguishing momentarily the bright flame of realistic consciousness and darkening the mind, one will enable the deeper consciousness to surface. This is very close to the state of sleep, but the state of being half awake and half asleep, this feeling of being halfway between dreaming and reality on the territory of time and space where the nonrealistic consciousness of Noh dwells.[9]

Komparu suggests that modern audiences should embrace this opportunity to leave the tensions of the world behind and to bask in this feeling of repose.

Figure 4.5 (p. 103)
Katayama Shingo as Lady Rokujo transforms into a demon in *Aoi no Ue (Lady Aoi)* by the Kashu-Juku *Noh* Theater of Kyoto, Japan.
Image: Jack Vartoogian, Front Row Photos.

Current trends

In 2001, UNESCO designated *noh* as an Intangible Cultural Heritage of Humanity. In Japan, in addition to the hereditary *iemoto* schools, Tokyo's National *Noh* Theater is a vital center for studying *noh* and *kyogen*. Many amateurs practice in cultural centers throughout Japan, which is extremely popular among women over fifty. One *noh* school well-attended by women that has several branches throughout Japan is Sumire Kai, founded in 1986 by Tsurumi Reiko, a female master teacher in the *shite* category.

Recent departures in *noh* include *Sanbaso, Divine Dance* (2013), a site-specific performance held recently in the Guggenheim Museum's rotunda in New York City, in which Nomura Mansai performed the *sanbaso* from the ancient *okina* ritual as a tribute to *Ultramodern Sanbaso*, a 1957 play by avant-garde artist Shiraga Kazuo. Other manifestations of *noh* include the ongoing theatrical works of the *Yugen* Theater of Beauty, based in San Francisco for over thirty years. Their recent production of *Mystical Abyss* (2015) combined *noh* and Native American performers in a cross-cultural work that examined the cyclical nature of death and rebirth. *Hagoromo* (2015), adapted from the ancient *noh* play, featured former New York City ballet dancers Wendy Whelan and Jock Soto. Soto played the *waki*/fisherman, who finds a beautiful robe made of feathers on the beach belonging to the *shite*/angel, played by Whelan. Unmasked, they performed slow, contemporary movement on a stark stage, accompanied by a Japanese *bunraku* puppet, whose masked face was a reproduction of Whelan's. *Pagoda* (2009) is an original *noh* play and a collaboration between British playwright Janette Cheong and Richard Emmert, director of Theater *Nohgaku*. Kinue Oshima, a female *noh* actor and master teacher, played the *shite* role. *Pagoda* toured widely in Japan and China. In addition to his work in Japan, Emmert directs the Noh Training Project, a six-week summer intensive offered in the United States.

4.2 Exploration: excerpt from "Import/Export: Artistic Osmosis Between Japan, Europe, and the United States" by Patricia Leigh Beaman

In 1854, after two centuries of the closed-door, isolationist policy of *sakoku*, Commodore Matthew Perry brazenly sailed US Navy ships into Edo Bay and leveled their cannons, thereby forcing Japan to resume trading with the outside world. After the Emperor Meiji was restored to power, foreigners were invited to Japan in a move to "modernize" the country, and exchanges of all sorts between the East and the West began. Japan's cultural treasures tremendously impacted European artists, such as Impressionist painters Claude Monet, Édouard Manet, and Vincent Van Gogh. By the twentieth century, *noh* had substantially influenced Western dance, theater, and music.

In the 1920s, Arthur Waley's English translation of *The No Plays of Japan* was published, and dramatist Paul Claudel became the French ambassador to Japan. Many became curious about *noh* through Claudel's writings, including renowned French actor Jean-Louis Barrault, who eventually toured Japan in 1960, visited the *Kanze* school, and learned its gliding walk. The inclusion of *noh* elements in Barrault's productions introduced many to the ancient form, and he and British director Peter Brook established a company of international performers that included *noh* actor Yoshi Oïda. British composer Benjamin Britten based his opera *Curlew River* (1964) on *Sumidagawa* (*Sumida River*). He employed an all-male cast, and incorporated *noh* treatment of theatrical time and Japanese instruments into his composition. Japanese author Yukio Mishima wrote *Modern Noh Plays* in the 1950s, which continue to be performed internationally. Mishima suggested that his *noh* adaptations be performed on a bench in Central Park in New York City.

Modern dance pioneer Martha Graham was a great admirer of Japanese and Greek theater, and skillfully melded the two in *Night Journey* (1947), based on the Greek classic *Oedipus Rex*. The dance opens dramatically at the very moment of Jocasta's suicide by hanging. Suddenly, the rope falls to the floor with a loud thud. In a sort of *noh* flashback, Graham transports us backward to Jocasta's entanglements with her son/husband, and then to her ultimate demise. Graham often collaborated with Japanese-American sculptor Isamu Noguchi, whose sparse set for *Appalachian Spring* (1944) referenced a *hashikagari* ramp.

During the 1950s, Japanese modern dancers such as Eguchi Takaya and Ando Mitsuko brought German *neue tanz* (new dance) to Tokyo. Its pioneers were Rudolph Laban and Mary Wigman, who in the early twentieth century explored angular, percussive movement that displayed tension, effort, and defied conventional ideals of balletic beauty. By the 1930s, Hitler's Nazi regime condemned the form, deeming it to be "degenerate art." Not surprisingly, the *neue tanz* expression of the dark side of human nature attracted postwar dancers in Japan such as Kazuo Ohno and Tatsumi Hijikata, the future founders of *butoh*. Hijikata explored French Dadaism and Surrealism through writers such as Jean Genet, Antoine Artaud, Henri Michaux, and Georges Bataille. The aberrational worlds these writers conjured up, full of rebels, indigents, erotic deviance, death, and obfuscations of reality, resonated immensely with Hijikata as he began to conjure his raw, subversive *butoh* dances.

Discussion questions: *noh*

1 The *samurai* code of fighting for honor, loyalty, and maintaining Buddhist belief is reflected in *noh* plots. Can you juxtapose *noh* with another theatrical form that embodies the respective tenets of its culture?
2 Two humorous *kyogen* are interspersed amidst a typical cycle of five *noh* plays. Discuss why and how humor is integral to this art form.
3 *Yugen*, or "invisible beauty," is an attribute every *noh* actor should possess, and is considered to grow stronger with age, rather than fade. Can you equate this reverence for age with a theatrical tradition that is a part of your own culture?

4.3 From pleasure women's *kabuki* to Grand *Kabuki* Theater

Key points: *kabuki*

1 *Kabuki*, now a cultural treasure of Japan, actually started as a rebellious and irreverent theatrical form in Kyoto during the seventeenth century. *Kabuki* today is an all-male form; however, it was originally a theatrical entertainment started by a woman named Okuni.
2 While *noh* was the upper-class entertainment for the *samurai*, male *kabuki* emerged as entertainment for the merchant class, approved by the *Shogunate*. Like *noh*, *kabuki* training and artistic traditions are preserved by the *iemoto* system, in which the head of an acting family passes on his name to his son, or to an adopted male.
3 Some *kabuki* plots are adapted from *noh*, but most are domestic dramas or historical plays drawn from real-life situations reflecting the environment from which they arose. Kyoto's *wagoto*, or "soft style" performance, features gentle, romantic heroes, while in Edo, a bombastic style called *aragoto* (rough style) displays a macho warrior spirit.
4 Wigs, make-up, and costuming are essential components in portraying a *kabuki* character. As in *noh*, character transformation is a thematic element, but no masks are worn in *kabuki*. Instead, shedding a costume to reveal one's true nature happens directly on stage with the assistance of a *koken* attendant, who maintains an "invisible" presence.
5 The enormous *kabuki* stage is full of devices such as rotating stages, trap doors, and rigging that allows a character's spectacular flight. The *hanamichi*, or "flower walk," is an elevated ramp for actors' entrances and exits extending from the back of the theater onto the stage, and gives the audience the opportunity to see the actor up close.

Art lies somewhere in the shadowy frontiers between reality and illusion.
– Chikamatsu Monzaemon

Kabuki history

Kabuki, which translates as "song, dance, skill," is a cultural treasure of Japan, but it actually arose as a rebellious and irreverent theatrical entertainment in Kyoto during the seventeenth century. *Kabuki* today is a male form; however, its founder was a woman named Okuni, whose first performances were held on the banks of Kyoto's Kamo River in 1586. Okuni was an iconoclast who dressed in men's pants and wore foreign hats. She claimed to be a temple dancer, but perhaps this was to facilitate financial compensation, since one could only be paid to dance in the interest of raising money for a temple or shrine. What we do know is that her dance drew from serious temple dances, but was interlaced with seductive humor and pantomime. Okuni began presenting novel outdoor skits with her troupe, in which women performed as men, and became especially famous for portraying a handsome man who makes passionate love to a courtesan. Raucous audiences of commoners flocked to see her bawdy lustiness and explicit pantomime. As her popularity grew, her audience attracted high-class *samurai* who disguised themselves to conceal their identity. Okuni's fame purportedly prompted both the Emperor in Kyoto and the *Shogun* in Edo to summon her for command performances.[10] When she died in 1610, *kabuki* had become her legacy.

When the Tokugawa *Shogunate* took power in 1603, the capital shifted from Kyoto to Edo (now Tokyo) and performers migrated to the new center of power. During this era, *kabuki* became associated with offbeat, unconventional behavior. *Kabuki mono* were rebels roaming in gangs, the majority of whom were *samurai*, idle after the death of their *daimyōs*, or lords. They defied social order by flaunting outlandish outfits and hairdos and smoking four-foot-long tobacco pipes. Their legendary exploits were often woven into early *kabuki* shows and their outrageous fashion was imitated throughout Japan.[11] *Kabuki mono* were seen by the regime as being a subversive, immoral, and dangerous presence that resulted in the emergence of strict policies to control all levels of society.

In an effort to contain rapidly growing moral vice in Edo, the *Shogunate* confined theaters and teahouses – the working venues of prostitutes – to an area known as the "pleasure quarter." All actors and prostitutes were required to be licensed and to live and work within its limits. *Kabuki's* popularity brought many pleasure seekers to this quarter, and their rivalries over the performers sometimes caused violent brawls in the audience. Because some players were also *yuna* – public bathhouse girls who would massage clientele and entertain them in various ways – *kabuki* became regarded as a rampant vehicle for prostitution and was called *yu-jo kabuki*: "pleasure women's *kabuki*." Attempting to rein in *samurai* who were mixing with the lowest class of society, the *Shogunate* levied a ban on all female stage performers in 1629. Despite government censorship, *kabuki* remained popular and young boys replaced women in *wakashu kabuki*, or "young men's *kabuki*." This, however, did not stop the flow of men – many of them *samurai* – from finding the attractive boys even more enthralling than the women. Finally, in 1652, the *Shogunate* decreed that only mature males could be *kabuki* players and *yaro kabuki*, or "men's *kabuki*," was established, which has continued to this day.

Once *kabuki* became the domain of men, the convention of the *onnagata* emerged, in which highly trained actors specializing in female roles offered a hyper-real version of a woman in looks, gesture, voice, and movement. Unlike the aristocratic *noh* theater audience, in which a male actor played a female character simply by putting on a mask without elevating the pitch of his voice, rowdy *kabuki* audiences demanded more. Through stylized feminine costuming, elaborate wigs, whitened faces, falsetto voices, and the slightly pigeon-toed gait that led the shoulders to sway seductively, *onnagata* were idealized creatures who carried this idealization into their daily lives. Offstage, early *onnagata* dressed as women and, in speaking, used female pitch and intonation, as well as the vocabulary and verb endings inherent in Japanese women's language.

Think about:
Can *kabuki* be thought of as an ancient forerunner of other transgressive movements, such as punk?

Figure 4.6
A seventeenth-century print of a *kabuki* stage in Edo by Toyokuni III.

By the latter half of the seventeenth century, male *kabuki* had emerged as entertainment for the lower merchant class and became officially condoned by the *Shogunate*. Of the four licensed *kabuki* theaters, the biggest seated 1,000 and ran plays from dawn to dusk.[12] Merchants flocked to shows dressed in the drab-colored *kimonos* of their rank, but once inside, would remove them to reveal brilliantly colored under-robes. Although *noh* was the upper-class entertainment for the *samurai*, curious *Shogunate* officials could be discerned in *kabuki* theater boxes, hidden behind screens.

Dramatic subjects

Although some *kabuki* plots were adapted from *noh*, most of its 350 plays, which include *sewamono* (domestic dramas) or *jidaimono* (historical plays), were drawn from real-life situations reflecting the environment from which they arose. The two main centers of *kabuki* were the imperial city of Kyoto, and Edo, a frontier town swarming with sword-wielding *samurai*. Not surprisingly, two styles of *kabuki* began to emerge. In refined Kyoto, Chikamatsu Monzaemon (1653–1724) created a realistic *kabuki* genre known as *wagoto*, or "soft style" performance, whose gentle, meek hero was desired by the most popular courtesans in the pleasure district. Monzaemon wove scandalous and poignant human-interest stories of the day into his innovative plays in a disguised manner, since depiction of the contemporary exploits of the upper classes was illegal. Setting the story in the distant past and altering names of people and places, Monazemon wrote deeply humanistic and complex stories ranging from ill-fated lovers to tormented *samurai*. Nothing was worse both financially and morally than losing one's master and surviving him, and these lord-less *samurai*, called *ronin*, became subjects of *kabuki* plays. One example is *Goban Taiheiki*, or *The Go Board Chronicle*, the true story of forty-seven *samurai* who tragically committed *seppuku* (suicide) in 1702 to avenge the loss of their *daimyō* lord.[13]

Monzaemon also specialized in love-suicide plays. The ethos of loyalty to family and duty to society often conflicted with personal desires. A scenario in several of his *kabuki* plots involved family debt, such as a destitute husband selling his wife into prostitution. She falls in love with a poor customer, who is unable to buy her out of

Think about:
What did kabuki themes provide Japanese middle classes with that noh lacked?

her servitude. If she escapes, she will disgrace her family, as will he if he abandons his life for one in the pleasure quarter. Death is their only way out. The highpoint of the play is the final *michiyuki*, or traveling scene, in which the couple dresses in their finest clothes in a sort of heroic send-off before committing double *seppuku*.

In contrast to heart-rending stories reflecting life in Kyoto, Edo's militaristic atmosphere elicited warrior stories filled with villains, bravado fighting, and beheadings. An actor named Ichikawa Danjuro I (1660–1704), known as "The Flower of Edo," introduced a bombastic, macho style of acting called *aragoto* (rough style). Wearing exaggerated make-up, actors strutted and swaggered on stage, contorting their faces while projecting their lines in booming voices. In a society in which *samurai* were permitted to carry two swords, an *aragoto* actor carried three. In plays such as *Shibaraku* (*Wait a Moment!*), heroism, foolishness, bellicosity, and evil are all inflated in this acting style, which brought Danjuro I great fame.[14] This was the origin of the renowned Ichikawa family acting tradition, whose lineage has continued through twelve generations.

Kabuki training

Like *noh*, *kabuki* artistic traditions are preserved by the *iemoto* system, in which the *iemoto* – the head of an acting family – controls who can become a *kabuki* actor, and how far they can advance. Traditionally, *kabuki* is passed on from father to son or to an adopted male who will inherit the father's name after death. Actors train in music, dance, and martial arts, and must master sitting in *seiza*, a formal kneeling pose, for as long as an hour. *Suri-ashi*, the basic gliding walk of *noh*, is learned and then embellished to create a *samurai*'s arrogant strut, the shuffling plodding of a farmer, or the turned-in sauntering of an *onnagata*. *Onnagata* training is especially difficult, and begun early. The hyper-feminine, stylized gait is taught by holding a sheet of paper between the knees while walking. An *onnagata* often wears platform shoes and walks with the feet slightly turned in, which causes the shoulders to sway gently, while the heavy wig worn causes the head to bobble subtly. An actor keeps his bent elbows against the body, and to give the illusion of small hands, the fingers are held closely together with the thumbs bent, and barely emerge from the *kimono* sleeves. *Onnagata* must dance with their legs in a slightly bent and lowered position, which is very difficult. An especially beautiful moment is when an *onnagata* faces upstage and reveals the back of the neck – considered to be a highly attractive part of a woman's body – and then bends slowly backward from the waist until the audience can see down the actor's *kimono*. This pose has strong erotic connotations for the Japanese.[15]

Kabuki technique

Kabuki's stylized movement and dance is learned through *kata*, codified movement patterns. *Kata* sequences move from one pose to another, are interspersed with momentary pauses called *ma*, and culminate in a frozen dynamic pose called a *mie* (mi-yeh). *Ma* is used in terms of dramatic timing and can be translated as "the space

Figure 4.7
Japanese Living National Treasure Danjuro XII displays his *mie* as Kagemasa, an *aragoto* character, in *Shibaraku (Wait a Moment!)* with the Grand *Kabuki* of Japan.
Image: Jack Vartoogian, Front Row Photos.

Figure 4.8 (p. 109)
World-famous *onnagata* Bando Tamasaburo V performs a dance in *Kanegamisaki (The Cape of the Temple Bell)*.
Image: Jack Vartoogian, Front Row Photos.

between." The *mie* is a dramatic pause at a highpoint in *kabuki* that heightens the emotion and dramatic tension. As the music builds in intensity, an actor will move his arms, legs, and head in rhythmic circular motions, and then freeze in an expressive pose for several seconds while staring at the audience. Although the *mie* originated in *aragoto* acting, it is executed with grace and refinement in the *wagoto* style. In the *aragoto* style, a warrior will pose with his legs apart, his fists clenched, and his eyes crossed (*nirami*) to make his face more formidable.[16] *Mie* reveal the inner torment of a brave character to the audience, such as in *The Village School*, when a *samurai* must confirm that an execution has occurred by looking into a box carrying the severed head, which he knows is actually that of his own child. He inspects it, then turns to the audience and strikes a *mie*, conveying his deep feelings over his loss.[17] Another *kabuki* technique revealing the inner landscape of a character is *roppo*, which translates as "six directions." Accompanied by the rapid sounding of wooden clappers, an actor will make a spectacular entrance or exit via the *hanamichi*. These vary from a "flying *roppo*" of a boisterous *aragoto* actor who runs with legs akimbo and arms flailing, to *roppo* that imitate characteristics of a fox or a ghost.

Figure 4.9
Ebizo Ichikawa Danjuro XII in the title role of *Narukami*, performed by the Grand *Kabuki* of Japan.
Image: Jack Vartoogian, Front Row Photos.

Figure 4.10
Ebizo Ichikawa Danjuro XII as Mitsukuni and Utaemon VI (right) of the Grand *Kabuki* of Japan as Kisaragi/Princess Takiyasha in a fight scene in *Masakado*.
Image: Jack Vartoogian, Front Row Photos.

Tachimawari is the term for stage acrobatics and combat, which are largely based on martial arts that were of supreme importance in the days when *samurai* were poised for battle. *Kabuki* reflects this culture by featuring spectacular, tightly choreographed fight scenes. One *kata* is the *miso suri*, a term meaning "bean paste being ground." A performer gets on his hands and knees, shifts the weight of his body to one knee, and extends the other leg behind him at hip level. He then uses his hands to spin around on his knee as his leg whirls behind him, creating a daunting blur of activity. In some *tachimawari* fights, made up of *kata* called *tate*, opponents attack each other in slow motion and end in a group *mie* tableau. Once a *kabuki* hero has reached star status, he does not endanger himself by performing acrobatics, but simply poses heroically amidst his warriors during combat scenes. If attacked, he majestically defeats his enemies without contact – a brief wave of his hand sends his opponents tumbling or into acrobatic somersaults that symbolize their end.

Classical *kabuki* dance, known as *kabuki buyo*, has evolved from the contributions of three styles: *mai*, *odori*, and *furi*. *Mai* is a type of stately and grounded dance, derived from the slow glides and pivots of *noh* and solemn shrine dances, while *odori* originated from lively folk dances that were rhythmic and airborne. *Furi* is a pantomimic form in which the dancer uses properties such as a fan to represent a falling leaf, a sake cup, a letter, the moon rising, a flute, or a sword. Musical instruments are also employed in *furi*. All *kabuki* actors learn to play the *shamisen*, while *onnagata* also master the *koto* (zither) and the *kokyu*, a bowed version of the *shamisen*.[18]

Props, costuming, and make-up

Wigs, make-up, and costuming are essential components in an actor's portrayal of a stylized *kabuki* character. All performers wear white cotton *tabi* socks on stage, unless the role requires special shoes. Domestic play costuming references the clothing of townspeople, and everyday objects such as umbrellas, lanterns, and fans are used as props. Costuming for the historical plays is more fanciful, resulting in the oversized outfit of an *aragoto* player, which tends to be twice as large as normal costuming and requires stage attendants to keep it straight as the actor moves. More exaggerated props such as giant swords and oversized cudgels complement the voluminous wigs, headpieces, and outlandish make-up.[19]

As in *noh*, character transformation is a thematic element in *kabuki*. Shedding a costume and revealing one's true nature is called *jitsu wa*, "in reality." While transformations happen backstage in *noh*, they are executed directly in front of a *kabuki* audience by attendants called *koken* who maintain an "invisible" presence on stage. *Bukkaeri*, or "sudden change," is a beloved *kabuki* costuming trick in which the quick alteration of a wig and *kimono* demonstrates a lead character's profound emotional or physical change. For instance, a man may be instantly transformed into a spider by three *koken*, who unobtrusively help peel back a layer of the outer *kimono* to reveal a differently patterned one beneath and release clips fastening his wig that allow the hair to fall slack. During an *onnagata's* dance scene, *koken* will remove basting stitches holding the panels of a *kimono* together so that they fall open to magically present another robe of an entirely different color and pattern. As many as seven *kimono* transformations might occur within a dance sequence.[20]

In *noh* theater, masks are famously used, but in *kabuki*, actors wear elaborate make-up. They begin by painting

Figure 4.11
Japanese Living National Treasure Shoroku as the Earth Spider in the *kabuki* version of *Tsuchigomo* with the Grand *Kabuki* of Japan.
Image: Jack Vartoogian, Front Row Photos.

a white base onto their faces with a wide brush. An *onnagata* adds pink shading to the eyes, and draws on eyebrows and lips. *Aragoto* characters wear *kumadori* facial make-up, which features thick lines of red, black, brown, or blue, painted in patterns that appear as blood vessels, distended due to violent or victorious feelings. Blue lines indicate an evil character, while red ones can imply that the character is a heavy drinker. Opponents of *aragoto* warriors have *kumadori* make-up lines painted on their arms, chests, and legs to emphasize their musculature. More common characters such as farmers have a darker skin color, emphasizing the fact that they are manual laborers. All characters wear wigs, which are extremely varied. *Aragoto* characters appear in voluminous wigs and headpieces; *onnagata* wear large smooth wigs typical of seventeenth-century courtesans; and ghosts have long manes. A wig-cap painted blue on the top of the forehead indicates a shaved scalp – a convention of *samurai*, who shaved the top of their foreheads and wore topknots due to the heat of their helmets.

The *kabuki* stage

The elaborate *kabuki* stage differs greatly from its origins as impromptu riverbank theater. Today, the largest theater is the Kabuki-za in Tokyo, which seats 2,600 and features both matinee and evening shows lasting four hours. A typical *kabuki* stage has an extremely wide proscenium, set within a "frame." The audience facing the front of the stage is seated in a pit, while on the right and left sides there are three levels of tiered seating. The *hanamichi*, or "flower walk," is an elevated ramp for entrances and exits that extends from the back of the theater onto the stage through the left side of the audience. As a character enters, the audience engages in a long-held tradition of shouting a sort of verbal applause for the actor. The *hanamichi* also has a lift at a point called *shichi-san*, three-tenths of the way from the stage, that allows for a supernatural, ghostly character to mysteriously emerge from below. This zone is an important place where an actor will stop and pose, revealing something about their character, or an intimate dance sequence might occur on this prime vantage point.

The enormous *kabuki* stage is full of devices that enable spectacular theatrical feats. The revolving stage allows scene changes to occur without the use of the curtain, and can be split into two concentric circles that move independently. The ceiling has rigging for *chunori*, enabling actors harnessed with wires to "fly," while the floor is studded with numerous trap doors that allow an actor to drop instantly into to the basement. This "underworld" of the *kabuki* stage is called *naraku* (literally meaning "hell") and houses the skillfully engineered stage machinery. An actor can disappear through a trap, make a fast costume change, run under the *hanamichi* ramp, and then magically resurface, transformed. The massive Kabuzi-za in Tokyo has three traps that are capable of raising or lowering an entire set.

Kabuki music

Originally, Okuni offered simple song-like melodies and rhythms played on a small gong. Today, an onstage chorus chants the traditional story, but the musicians play within the *geza*, a screened area on stage right. Although they are concealed from the audience, they can see the action of the performers, whose gestures they accompany. A *kabuki* orchestra includes many of the same instruments used in *noh*: flutes, stick drums, small hand drums, and shoulder drums, and several musicians play the *shamisen*, a three-stringed wooden instrument. *Nagauta* (long song) is the most popular form of *shamisen* music and accompanies *kabuki buyo*, or classical dance. During a dance scene, an onstage *nagauta* musical ensemble plays drums, flutes, and *shamisen* as the dancer portrays the sung text with movements and gestures. Wooden clappers called *hyoshigi* are struck repeatedly against the stage to cue the opening of the curtain, or to mark the end of a play, intensifying as the curtain closes. A more dramatic percussive devise is *tsuke uchi*, or "accompanied beating," in which a wooden board is beaten with sticks, producing beats that are timed to match combative movements or to punctuate a *mie*.

Current trends

In postwar Japan, avant-garde theater directors and *kabuki* actors began exploring new approaches to dance and drama in contemporary productions. In particular, s*ho-gekijo* (little theater), an underground theater movement that began in the 1960s, has yielded several generations of artists. Experimental theater director Tadashi Suzuki (b. 1939) blends elements of *noh* and *kabuki* with Western realism into both his productions and his eponymous actor training system. In Suzuki's play *Nastasya* (adapted from Dostoevsky's *The Idiot*), legendary *onnagata* actor Bando Tamasaburo played both the fiancée and the prince. Noda Hideki, director of the Tokyo Metropolitan Theater and a prolific playwright, adapted and contemporized a 1920s *kabuki* play, *Togitatsu no Utare* (*Tatsuji the Sword Sharpener*), which was also made into a film in 2001. Over the last two decades, renowned experimental director Yukio Ninagawa has presented his *kabuki* versions of Greek tragedies and Shakespeare, with the most recent being *Ninagawa Juniya (Twelfth Night)* and *Ninagawa Macbeth*. Contemporary playwright Mitani Koki, founder of the *sho-gekijo* troupe Tokyo Sunshine Boys, wrote *Ketto! Takadanobaba* (*Duel in Takadanobaba*), a play about an errant *samurai* that toured internationally beginning in 2006. The highly popular Gekidan Shinkansen, a contemporary *sho-gekijo* theater troupe in Osaka directed by Inoue Hidenori, finds inspiration in traditional *kabuki*, but is infamous for its punk nature and flamboyant acting, as seen in his recent production of *Vamp Bamboo Burn* (2016).

Discussion questions: *kabuki*

1 *Kabuki* catered to the tastes of the middle class that was not admitted to aristocratic *noh* theater. Yet *kabuki* playwrights enjoyed subversively portraying the exploits of the upper class, which was forbidden, and reveled in tales of star-crossed lovers from two different worlds, doomed to commit suicide together. How does catering to the lower classes as opposed to nobility affect theater in subject matter, acting style, and innovation?

2 How much credence do you give to the long-standing idea, held by *kabuki* professionals and aficionados, that no woman could ever play an *onnagata* as well as a man?

3 Early *kabuki* plays featured irreverent exploits of *kabuki mono* rebels, who defied social order by flaunting outlandish outfits and hairdos. In the 1960s during the era of student protests, the underground theater movement s*ho-gekijo* (little theater) arose, which pushed *kabuki* in a new direction. How and why does *kabuki* lend itself towards rebellious theater, regardless of the century?

4.4 *Butoh*: Japan's dance of darkness

Key points: *butoh*

1 *Butoh* arose as a subversive dance genre in the 1950s in postwar Japan. Its cofounders, Tatsumi Hijikata and Kazuo Ohno, initially found inspiration in German Expressionist dance and elements from *noh* and *kabuki*, but they broke the boundaries of dance in radical ways.

2 Hijikata made provocative *ankoku butoh* works that were seen as shocking and sexually perverse in their displays of homosexual themes, cross-dressing, and movements depicting human deformity, but his work attracted progressive-minded audiences to the gritty cabaret-style performances at Asbestos Hall. His early death made him a mythic figure.

3 Unlike Hijikata, who never left Japan, Ohno embarked on an international performing career. His dances drew inspiration from female figures such as the flamenco dancer known as La Argentina, Divine, the tragic transvestite from Genet's *Our Lady of the Flowers*, and his own mother. Ohno enjoyed performing and teaching well into his nineties.

4 Today, *butoh* is a global form, and many versions exist. Nudity, bodies
   painted in white, exaggerated facial expression, contortions of the body,
   hyper-controlled motion, inward rotated legs, grotesque imagery, and taboo yet
   universal topics such as eroticism, sex, and death are all associated with butoh.
5 All the different forms of *butoh* have some elements in common, including
   moving in slow motion and lengthy squatting. *Hokotai* is the basic butoh walk:
   the knees bend, the torso drops down, and the body seems to float as the feet
   slide lightly along the floor. The concept of *ma*, which translates as "the space
   between," is also important, as is the idea of "shedding the skin."

> **Hijikata and Ohno represent two opposites of a yin and yang magnetic
> polarity. While Hijikata celebrates the negative in his themes of death and
> sacrifice, in ugly beauty, and in mud, Ohno also spirals downward, but with
> a fluid spirituality. For Ohno, the sacred is dynamic and organic, belonging
> to the embryo in the mother's womb, and to the dance.[21]**
> **– Sondra Fraleigh and Tamah Nakamura**

In the chaotic wake of World War II in Japan – the aftermath of the atomic bombs
dropped on Hiroshima and Nagasaki, the Emperor's concession speech, and the
subsequent American occupation of Japan – *butoh* arose as a subversive dance
genre. The physical and environmental devastation and fierce resistance against
the pervasive Westernization of a defeated Japan all led to a loss of social order. Yet
amidst this turmoil, a fertile arena for unprecedented artistic departures emerged.
Tatsumi Hijikata and Kazuo Ohno, the future cofounders of *butoh*, were two dancers
from northern Japan whose paths crossed in Tokyo during the 1950s. As each
began working experimentally as a choreographer, inspiration sprang from European
artistic movements such as Expressionism and Surrealism, and *neue tanz* – German
Expressionist dance founded by Rudolph Laban and Mary Wigman in the early
twentieth century. As Hijikata and Ohno began tearing down the boundaries of dance
in radical ways, elements from traditional Japanese forms such as *noh* and *kabuki*
entered their works, but any archetypically aesthetic features of perfection and
beauty were thrown to the winds.

Tatsumi Hijikata (1928–1986)

> *I demand a sense of crisis. I am not visited by a sense of crisis, rather I am
> demanding it.*[22]
>
> —Tatsumi Hijikata

Born as Kunio Yoneyama, Hijikata was one of eleven children who grew up in
the harsh farmland of Tohoku in northern Japan. Nature was a playmate of sorts:
he later claimed that wallowing in mud during winter thaws taught him to dance.
Many times he witnessed his father – an unrestrained drinker – beating his mother,
never forgetting the dreadful sound of the slow, measured footsteps taken before
striking her.[23] When the boy was 13, the war began. Although he was too young to
be conscripted, he was assigned to a weapons factory, where he sustained severe
burns from molten steel. He also lost three of his older brothers in the war. By the
time Hijikata left for Tokyo in 1952, he was no stranger to hardship. Tohoku, with its
primordial mud, its peasants, and its cruel beauty, would remain a preoccupation
throughout his life.

While living in squalid poverty in still-devastated Tokyo, Hijikata found work as a
longshoreman, a junk dealer, and as a self-declared petty thief. Amidst the ruins of
the bombed-out landscape, however, for many like Hijikata, the freedom to rebel
against past conventions of a strict Japanese society and the imposition of Western
values on an eroding Japanese culture created an environment of unprecedented
artistic freedom. Hijikata began taking classes in *neue tanz* with Ando Mitsuko. In
1956, he met Akiki Motofuji, a dancer who had received a large studio as a gift from
her father, an asbestos magnate. Hijikata irreverently named it "Asbestos Hall."

Although he was married and a father, Hijikata moved in with Motofuji, who was also married. Asbestos Hall supplied them with a studio and performance space, a cinema, and a drinking hole called "Bar Gibbon." The couple eventually wed in 1968.[24]

Taking "Tatsumi Hijikata" as his stage name, he began creating his own work at Asbestos Hall. Literature became a potent source of inspiration. In the company of other experimental Toyko artists, Hijikata delved into Dadaism and Surrealism through French writers such as Jean Genet, Antoine Artaud, Henri Michaux, and Georges Bataille. The aberrational worlds these writers conjured up, full of rebels, indigents, erotic deviance, death, and obfuscations of reality, resonated immensely with Hijikata. He would come to call his own dance *ankoku butoh*, or "dance of darkness." (*Ankoku* means pitch black, and *butoh* comprises two characters – *bu*, or ancient dance, and *toh*, to stamp the ground.) His first *butoh* offering was *Kinjiki* (*Forbidden Colors*), an adaptation of the novel by avant-garde writer Yukio Mishima that explored the societal taboo of homosexuality. In 1959, *Kinjiki* was thrust squarely in front of the All-Japan Art Dance Association, many of whose members never fully recovered from Hijikata's blow.

The debut of *Kinjiki* has taken on mythic status.[25] This was a duet, performed by Hijikata and the angelic 21-year-old Yoshito Ohno, Kazuo Ohno's son. Under dark lights, a predatory Hijikata, with shaven head and dressed only in black trousers, loomed toward the bare-chested Ohno, clad in tight white shorts. He presented a live chicken to the young man as a gesture of love. Clutching it between his thighs, Ohno's character began to squeeze it as he danced – an act that some perceived as choking, and others, as sodomy. The lack of any musical score added to the tense atmosphere: there was no masking the sounds of Hijikata's footsteps as he chased the young boy, the sexual gasps, or the protestations of the bird.[26] The outraged presenters managed to cut the lights off before *Kinjiki* was finished. What also came to an end was Hijikata's affiliation with the Association, and theirs with him: *ankoku butoh* cleaved the modern dance scene, forming a rift between outraged conventionalists and the future avant-garde, who would now follow Hijikata's path. For the next decade, using primarily male performers including Kazuo Ohno, Hijikata made highly provocative *ankoku butoh* works that were seen by many as shocking and sexually perverse in their displays of homosexual themes, cross-dressing, and movements depicting human deformity, but his work attracted progressive-minded audiences to the gritty cabaret-style performances at Asbestos Hall.

Hijikata's Rebellion of the Body (1968)

1968 was a turbulent yet catalytic time of counter-cultures and student demonstrations in the United States and Japan, among other countries. At the height of these protests, Hijikata presented *Hijikata Tatsumi to nihonjin: Nikutai no hanran* (*Hijikata Tatsumi and the Japanese: Rebellion of the Body*). The performance began with the entrance of a flying model airplane that circled ominously over the audience and then crashed into a tremendous suspended metal sheet. Hijikata was carried in on a golden palanquin from the back of the hall upon which he moved spastically, wearing only a thin *kimono* and clutching a large golden phallus in his hand.[27] Short grainy film clips alternating with photographic stills from *Rebellion of the Body* reveal Hijikata in a long frilly skirt, dancing wildly to *flamenco* music. In another scene, he disturbingly contorts his face and writhes disjointedly. Wearing nothing but the phallus, he slams his body into the hanging steel sheet, which sways dangerously. A photograph sears into our brains the image of a demonic, open-mouthed Hijikata, ruthlessly tossing a sacrificial chicken into the air. In the last bit of footage, he is bound up by ropes and ascends horizontally over the heads of the audience as "Amazing Grace" is played on the bagpipes. Perhaps thrusting his body into extreme situations liberated Hijikata from complacency, from conventionality, from the mundane. *Rebellion of the Body* had an emotional impact on audience members such as Ko Murobushi, who was compelled to join Hijikata's company at once. Mishima purportedly wept at the performance, saying, "It's terrifying – this is time dancing."[28]

In the 1970s, Hijikata began to withdraw from performing. One of his last solos was *Hosotan* (*A Story of Small Pox*). In an excerpt from a 1972 film, Hijikata is on the floor, writhing feebly on his back in a fetal-like position dressed in a loincloth and a disheveled *kabuki onnagata* wig. He is covered in white make-up that incorporates a scab-like effect of skin hanging off his body, as if he were a bomb survivor. He is in the abject state of a dying man who is trying to rise, but can't. *Hosotan* demonstrated Hijikata's continued obsession with death: "I may not know death, but it knows me," he once said. He claimed his dead sister had come to inhabit his body, and began wearing a *kimono*, his hair tied in women's fashion, and speaking in a woman's language.[29] When Hijikata stopped dancing at the age of 45, women had begun to participate in his work, such as Ashikawa Yoko, Natsu Nakajima, and his wife, Akiko Motofuji. He embarked on an intense collaboration with Ashikawa, who became his muse, and taught the material they created to the other dancers in a new group they formed at Asbestos Hall.

Although Hijikata had ceased performing, he continued to choreograph. In 1984 Hijikata choreographed *Ren-Ai Butoh-ha* (*Love Butoh Sect*) for dancer Min Tanaka. Tanaka, who found truth in Hijikata's provocative performances, said, "Since Hijikata stung my eyes, I became his son."[30] Hijikata also maintained his longtime collaboration with Kazuo Ohno, working as a dramaturgical director on all of his dances. By this time, Ohno had an international career, unlike Hijikata, who had never left Japan. Hijikata had just been invited on his first tour abroad when he died of liver cancer in 1986, due to years of hard drinking. He was 57 years old.

> *Think about*:
> Could Hijikata's obsession with death tie into Japanese themes of death, ghosts, and ancestors inherent in *noh* theater?

Kazuo Ohno (1906–2010)

Like Hijikata, Kazuo Ohno was also from northern Japan, but unlike Hijikata, he remembered his childhood fondly. After college, he became a physical education teacher at a Christian school, where he was baptized. When Ohno began dancing at age thirty, an influential teacher was Eguchi Takaya, who had studied in Germany with Mary Wigman. The war then intervened; Ohno was in the service for seven years and held as a prisoner of war.[31] When released, he taught physical education in Yokohama and established an experimental dance school on his own property in 1961. Ohno was 43 when he performed for the first time in a concert in 1949, which Hijikata saw in Tokyo. Despite his late start, Ohno embarked on a performing career. After Hijikata and Ohno formally met in 1952, Hijikata helped direct Ohno's choreographic visions, and the two began performing together in pieces such as *Rose-Colored Dance* (1965).

Although Hijikata and Ohno shared a deep bond, they had a contentious relationship as well. In *Hijikata, Revolt of the Body*, Stephen Barber discusses their long-term disagreement on whether a gesture should be pre-determined or improvised:

> Hijikata knew exactly what intensively physical and perceptual demands he wanted to subject the audience to; he disregarded improvisation and prepared his works with exhaustive discipline . . . Ohno believed that dance is eternal and finite, and that it is imbued with death as a liberatory force; his position was that dance should not have any fixed, inflexible form . . . Those disputes had no solution.[32]

Hijikata and Ohno parted ways for a decade. They reunited in 1977, when Ohno decided to pay choreographic homage to his idol Antonia Mercé, the Argentinian *flamenco* dancer known as La Argentina, who he had seen perform in 1928. The result was *Admiring La Argentina*, a *tour de force* solo for Ohno,

Figure 4.12
Legendary *butoh* dancer Kazuo Ohno, at age 93 in 1999, performing his *Dance of Jellyfish: There is a Universe in a Single Flower*.
Image: Jack Vartoogian, Front Row Photos.

choreographed by both men. Ohno made onstage costume changes, gradually transforming from the glamorous female star to his male self. The success of *Admiring La Argentina* led to performances in the United States and Europe, and catapulted Ohno into international stardom. A later successful collaboration between the two was *My Mother* (1981). Ohno claimed, "The movement motifs of *My Mother* came from what I thought I was doing in my mother's womb. I was in her – what was I doing in there?"[33] While situating himself in a fetal position, Ohno was dressed just as he imagined his mother would have been.

After Hijikata's death in 1986, Yoshito Ohno, who had performed in the scandalous *Kinjiki* in 1959, became his father's choreographer. Kazuo Ohno continued performing abroad and also taught in his Yokohama studio; the atmosphere there was diametrically opposed to the volatile environment at Asbestos Hall. Instead of telling students what to do, Ohno would perform for them and try to activate their own memories and instincts in finding their dance. Sondra Fraleigh, who studied with Ohno, observed, "As a non-violent revolutionary, he teaches, like Mahatma Gandhi, the importance of making 'the whole world' your friend."[34] Unlike Hijikata, who never left Japan, and whose early death made him a mythic figure, Ohno enjoyed an international career well into his nineties. At the end of his life, he kept on dancing – albeit with only one good arm, and from a wheelchair.

Figure 4.13
Japanese *butoh* troupe Dai Rakuda Kan (The Great Camel Battleship) perform *Universe of Darah – Return of the Jar Odyssey.*
Image: Jack Vartoogian, Front Row Photos.

Second generation

In Japan, an artist or company is unlikely to be recognized in Japan until they get an international stamp of approval. This concept, known as *gyaku-yunyu*, means "to go out and come back." Ironically, when Hijikata retreated from the public eye, *butoh* began to receive attention when two of his former students, Akaji Maro (b. 1943) and Ushio Amagatsu (b. 1949), founded companies and began to tour abroad. In 1972 Maro's company, Dai Rakuda Kan (The Great Camel Battleship) was first invited to perform in America in 1982. Maro's highly theatrical work often conveys hallucinatory, nightmarish images such as nude bodies, seemingly pierced by arrows, bobbing up and down to jarring music, or contorted faces, drooling mouths, and upwardly rolled eyes. After performing with Dai Rakuda Kan, Amagatsu started Sankai Juku (School of Mountain and Sea) in 1975. In Amagatsu's work, he and his elegant male dancers – with shaven heads, and painted white bodies – often employ extremely slow motions in creating exquisite choreographic images. True to the concept of *gyaku-yunyu*, Western recognition of Dai Rakuda Kan and Sankai Juku garnered Japanese respect for *butoh*. In 1985, the first *butoh* festival occurred in Tokyo – a two-week event whose participants included Kazuo Ohno (directed by Hijikata); Min Tanaka and his group, Maijuku; Dai Rakuda Kan; Biyakko-sha; and Natsu Nakajima of Muteki-sha. Two Japanese dancers not present were the duo now known simply as Eiko and Koma, who had worked with both Hijikata and, more profoundly, with Kazuo Ohno. They had moved to New York City in 1976, where they began their prolific career as international artists.

Butoh technique

Butoh has grown exponentially into a global form. Unlike other dance forms, which have been codified and made "classical," it is almost impossible to pin down exactly what *butoh* entails, since there are so many versions. Nudity, bodies painted in white or mud, exaggerated facial expression, contortions of the body, hyper-controlled motion, inwardly rotated legs, grotesque imagery, and taboo yet universal topics such as eroticism, sex, and death are all associated with *butoh*. However, Bonnie Sue Stein, who studied *butoh* in Japan, thinks the strength of commitment is at the heart of the form. She offers this perspective, common in Japanese art forms and even in the tenacious nature of the *samurai*:

> Working beyond one's threshold of endurance increases human potential, thereby increasing emotional and physical strength in reaching *satori* [awakening]. When the body and mind are exhausted, self-control is abandoned, and there is nothing to fear with spontaneous learning. Room, and time, would disappear.[35]

By pushing one's limits past self-imposed boundaries, one enters unchartered terrain, in which the body and mind make new discoveries. Through practicing exercises repeatedly, dancers are trained to manipulate their bodies physiologically and psychologically. *Butoh* scholar Kurihara Nanako writes, "As a result, *butoh* dancers can transform themselves into everything from a wet rug to a sky and can even embody the universe, theoretically speaking."[36] In workshops with Kazuo Ohno, students explored being a stone.

Some commonalities in *butoh* include moving in slow motion and lengthy squatting. *Hokotai* is the basic *butoh* walk: the knees bend, the torso drops down, and the body seems to float lightly as the feet slide lightly along the floor. The concept of *ma*, which translates as "the space between," is also important. Sondra Fraleigh claims there is no equivalent for this experiential concept in the West, but offers this explanation:

> Ma, the space between, is the global connective tissue of butoh, allowing the permeable passage of images in butoh alchemy. Moving through ma,

Figure 4.14 (p. 119)
Ushio Amagatsu, founder and choreographer of Sankai Juku, performs in *Umusuna: Memories Before History*.
Image: Jack Vartoogian, Front Row Photos.

Figure 4.15
Eiko and Koma in *Raven*.
Image: Anna Lee Campbell.

butoh-ka (practitioners) awaken self-reflexive moments in themselves and their audiences. Ma is not merely a perceptual and spatial concept; it is also an expansive state of mind.[37]

In considering *butoh*'s myriad approaches in training and performance and its widespread popularity today, the origins of the form seem very distant. However, perhaps the *butoh* concepts of pushing past boundaries and self-reflexive awakenings – also popular in somatic dance practices today – can be directly traced to the inchoate and rebellious days of *ankoku butoh* at Asbestos Hall. By daring to show an audience the raw, the disconcerting, and the unthinkable, Hijikata, Ohno, and their followers unleashed a liberating movement whose time had come.

Think about:
How can the global embrace and popularity of *butoh* be explained?

Current trends

In Japan, *butoh* continues to thrive. Dai Rakuda Kan gives weekly classes in Tokyo, as do Natsu Nakajima and Kasai Akira, and Yoshito Ohno gives workshops twice weekly at the Ohno studio in Yokohama. Outside of Japan, many dancers practice, teach, and perform. Based in the United Kingdom, Marie-Gabrielle Rotie (*Mythic*; 2010), a former collaborator with the late Ko Murobushi, teaches at Roehampton University. SU-EN (*Fragrant;* 2005) danced in Japan with Hakutobo (founded by Hijikata) and later with Ashikawa's group, Grunt. She teaches workshops in Sweden and performs worldwide. Ephia Gburek and Maura Balocchi both studied with Min Tanaka and Kazuo Ohno in Japan. Gburek founded Djalma Primordial Science in 1998 near Lyon, France, where she choreographs and runs *butoh* workshops, while in Brazil, Balocchi has made works inspired by Artaud and Samuel Beckett for her Taanteatro Companhia in Sao Paolo.

Figure 4.16
Eiko Otake performs her project, *A Body in Places*, in Fukushima after the *tsunami* and the ensuing nuclear disaster.
Image: William Johnston.

In the United States, Eiko Otake, of the duo Eiko and Koma, teaches her unique
style of existential exploration through movement in universities in the New
York metropolitan area. She performs her ongoing project, *A Body in Places*,
in diverse venues ranging from the streets and churches of New York City to
post-tsunami Fukushima. Other artists and teachers in the United States include
Maureen Fleming, Tanya Calamoneri, and LEIMAY, directed by Shige Moriya
and Ximena Garnica (*boarders*; 2015). In the San Francisco area, two disciples
of Hijikata, Hiroko and Koichi Tamano, founded Harupin Ha Butoh Company in
1979 (*Fur Out*, 2011). Canadian choreographer Denise Fujiwara, a solo artist and
former student of both Kazuo and Yoshito Ohno, runs Fujiwara Dance Inventions.
Natsu Nakajima, who worked closely with Hijikata, choreographed *Sumida River*
(2010) for Fujiwara, which sensitively blended *butoh* with elements of *noh* theater.

4.4 Exploration: excerpt from "Selections from the Prose of Kazuo Ohno" by Noriko Maehata[38]

More than 50 years ago I saw Argentina dance for the first time. I was a student in
a gymnastics school then . . . I saw the dance of Argentina from the top seat of the
third floor of the Imperial Theater [in Tokyo]. At the first glance of her dance I was so
impressed, it was a shock, I was totally killed by her charm. This is the encounter I can
never forget.

Fifty years have passed since then. I have had a long journey both in dance and life. Through these years I sometimes thought of Argentina. She lived deep in my soul never actually showing her incredible being in front of me.

It was when I saw a painting that I clearly saw Argentina for the second time. In 1976 I went to Natsuyuki Nakanishi's one-man show. I walked in, looked around, and was just about to leave when I was nailed in front of a painting that was hung near the exit. I unconsciously exclaimed inside, "Oh, this is Argentina!" This reunion with Argentina gave me the determination to dance on stage in order to express my admiration for her . . . I thought, no matter even if I were cremated and become ashes, I will never stop chasing her.

I went home still excited and had another surprise that day. On my desk were some materials about Argentina sent from New York by one of my students. I saw her photograph on a performance brochure. Argentina smiled at me and whispered.

"Now, shall we dance?" I nodded my head in assent. She gently asked me again. She cheered me up. "Shall we dance, Ohno? Now, with me!"

All my warm thoughts for her were evoked and integrated into the dance I made in 1977 to praise Argentina. This dance is called "Admiring La Argentina."

I received a book called Argentina before my departure for Paris. It made me so happy I thought I would die for joy. I cried out, "It's a miracle!" And this first miracle was followed by another. . .

A spectator at Nancy gave me the information that Argentina is buried in Paris . . . I immediately visited her grave located in Nouille [Neuilly], a suburb of Paris. I felt like I was visiting my bride. When Argentina broke down in 1936 her family was in Spain. But they couldn't come to see her because of the Civil War. There in the book was her photograph: standing in a wasteland in a fur coat . . . That noble and most beautiful creature, Argentina, had to die physically, although she must have longed for the eternity of her beautiful being. These painful thoughts came to my mind as I stood in front of her grave. I touched the gravestone and stood there not wanting to leave.

The third miracle, such a wonderful one. On the first day of my performance in Paris I danced to music composed by de Falla – music which Argentina also danced to. In the audience was a niece and nephew of Argentina. They were both in their 60s, and the niece is said to have the strongest resemblance to Argentina. When I saw her I cried out, "Oh, Argentina!" . . . The next day she invited me to her home and gave me a book which contained everything about Argentina. Photographs, autographs, letters, etc. It still puzzles me: when did they prepare this beautiful gift for me? It could have been ready when I first saw her at the Imperial Theater. It must be, I believe so.

Discussion questions: *butoh*

1 *Butoh* arose in the fractious environment of postwar Japan. Discuss why Japanese artists were driven to rebel in reaction to their surroundings, and if it is logical that disaster can lead to innovation.
2 It has been said that if Hijikata is the devil, then Ohno is an angel. Discuss the nature of their collaboration, and of artistic collaboration itself: do opposite views hinder or help a process?
3 *Butoh* is a worldwide practice today, yet unlike *bharatanatyam* or ballet, it is not a codified technique. Would *butoh* be *butoh* if it were?

Notes

1 Takahashi, Mutsuo, *Noh,* 261.
2 Sorgenfrei, Carol Fisher. "What Is Nō?," 164–165.

3 Bowers, Faubion, *Japanese Theater*, 22.

4 Komparu, 24.

5 Takahashi, 244.

6 Komparu, 220.

7 Ibid., 217.

8 Sorgenfrei, 161.

9 Komparu, Kunio, *The Noh Theater*, xxiii–xxiv.

10 Bowers, 42.

11 Ortolani, Benito, *The Japanese Theater*, 164–165.

12 Nakamura, Matazo. *Kabuki, Backstage, Onstage: An Actor's Life*, 23.

13 Ibid., 26–27.

14 Scott, A. C. *The Kabuki Theater of Japan,* 107.

15 Shively, Donald. "Social Environment of Kabuki," 41; personal communication, Karina Ikezoe, January 2, 2017.

16 Brandon, James R. "Form in Kabuki Acting," 84.

17 Nakamura, 27.

18 Ibid., 96.

19 Ortolani, 197.

20 Brandon, 81.

21 Fraleigh, Sondra, and Tamah Nakamura. *Hijikata Tatsumi and Ohno Kazuo*, 24.

22 Senda Akihiko, Hijikata Tatsumi and Suzuki Tadashi. "Fragments of Glass: A Conversation between Hijikata Tatsumi and Suzuki Tadashi," 64.

23 Hijikata, Tatsumi. "Plucking off the Darkness of the Flesh," 50.

24 Barber, Stephen. *Hijikata: Revolt of the Body*, 19–21.

25 This account draws from three sources: Stein, 337; Fraleigh, 23; Barber, 24; Nana, 18.

26 Sondra Fraleigh was told by Yoshito Ohno that the chicken was not harmed in any way. In *Butoh: Metamorphic Dance and Global Alchemy,* 174.

27 Ibid., 20.

28 Stein, Bonnie Sue. "Twenty Years Ago We Were Crazy, Dirty, and Mad," 116.

29 Barber, 9; Nanako, 20.

30 Tanaka, Min. "I Am an Avant-Garde Who Crawls the Earth," 155.

31 Fraleigh and Nakamura, 25.

32 Barber, 44–45.

33 Schechner, Richard, and Kazuo Ohno. "Kazuo Ohno Doesn't Commute: An Interview," 164.

34 Fraleigh, 3.

35 Stein, 116.

36 Nanako, 16.

37 Fraleigh, 6.

38 Maehata, Noriko. "Selections from the Prose of Kazuo Ohno," 159–160.

Notes Bibliography

Visual sources

YouTube

Noh

"National Noh Theater (Sumida-gawa)," YouTube video, 6:38, posted by "Tokyo Stock Footage Channel," October 27, 2011, www.youtube.com/watch?v=lc_7fNy_t_8

Kabuki

"Kabuki: Sumidagawa (歌舞伎 雙生隅田川)," YouTube video, 13:02, posted by "mei629," May 18, 2012, www.youtube.com/watch?v=r4y_k9qoB2w

Butoh

"Wallow (1984)," Vimeo video, 19:21, posted by "Eiko and Koma," http://eikoandkoma.org/wallow

Written sources

Barber, Stephen. *Hijikata: Revolt of the Body*. Chicago: Solar Books, 2010.

Barrault, Jean-Louis. *Souvenirs Pour Demain*. Paris: Editions du Seuil, 1972.

Bowers, Faubion. *Japanese Theater*. London: Peter Owen Ltd., 1954.

Brandon, James R. "Form in Kabuki Acting." In *Studies in Kabuki*, edited by Brandon, James R., William P. Malm, and Donald H. Shively, 1–60. Honolulu: University Press of Hawaii, 1978.

Fraleigh, Sondra. *Butoh: Metamorphic Dance and Global Alchemy*. Chicago: University of Illinois Press, 2010.

Fraleigh, Sondra, and Tamah Nakamura. *Hijikata Tatsumi and Ohno Kazuo*. New York: Routledge Press, 2006.

Gillespie, John K. "Interior Action: The Impact of Noh on Jean-Louis Barrault." *Comparative Drama*, Vol. 16, No. 4 (Winter 1982–83): 325–344, Published by: Comparative Drama Stable. Accessed January 8, 2016, 17:01 UTC URL: www.jstor.org/stable/41153035.

Hijikata, Tatsumi. "Wind Daruma." *The Drama Review*, Vol. 44, No. 1 (Spring 2000): 71–81. Stable URL: www.jstor.org/stable/1146810.

Holborn, Mark. *Butoh: Dance of the Dark Soul*. New York: Aperture, 1987.

Komparu, Kunio. *The Noh Theater*. Translation: Jane Corddry. New York: Weatherhill, 1983.

Kuniyoshi, Kazuko. "Butoh Chronology: 1959–1984." *The Drama Review*, Vol. 30, No. 2 (Summer 1986): 127–141. Stable URL: www.jstor.org/stable/1145732.

Kustow, Michael. *Peter Brook: A Biography*. New York: St. Martin's Press, 2005. Maehata, Noriko. "Selections from the Prose of Kazuo Ohno." *The Drama Review*, Vol. 30, No. 2 (Summer 1986): 156–162.

Mezur, Katherine. *Beautiful Boys/Outlaw Bodies: Devising Kabuki Female-Likeness*. New York: Palgrave Macmillan, 2005.

Nakamura, Matazo. *Kabuki, Backstage, Onstage: An Actor's Life*. Tokyo and New York: Kodansha International, 1990.

Nanako, Kurihara, "Hijikata Tatsumi: The Words of Butoh." *The Drama Review*, Vol. 44, No. 1 (Spring 2000): 10–28. Stable URL: www.jstor.org/stable/1146810.

Ortolani, Benito. *The Japanese Theater*. Princeton: Princeton University Press, 1995.

Pronko, Leonard. *Theater East and West: Perspectives Toward a Total Theater*. Berkeley: University of California Press, 1967.

Rothfuss, Joan, Ed. *Time Is Not Even, Space Is Not Empty: Eiko and Koma*. Minneapolis: The Walker Art Center, 2011.

Schechner, Richard, and Kazuo Ohno. "Kazuo Ohno Doesn't Commute: An Interview." *The Drama Review*, Vol. 30, No. 2 (Summer, 1986): 163–169. Stable URL: www.jstor.org/stable/1145737.

Scott, A. C. *The Kabuki Theater of Japan*. London: George Allen and Unwin Ltd., 1956.

Senda, Akihiko, Hijikata Tatsumi, and Suzuki Tadashi. "Fragments of Glass: A Conversation Between Hijikata Tatsumi and Suzuki Tadashi." *The Drama Review*, Vol. 44, No. 1 (Spring, 2000): 62–70. Stable URL: www.jstor.org/stable/1146817.

Shibusawa, Tatsuhiko, and Tatsumi Hijikata. "Hijikata Tatsumi: Plucking Off the Darkness of the Flesh – An Interview." *The Drama Review*, Vol. 44, No. 1 (Spring 2000): 49–55. Stable URL: www.jstor.org/stable/1146814.

Shively, Donald H. "Social Environment of *Kabuki*." In *Studies in Kabuki*, edited by James R. Brandon, William P. Malm, and Donald H. Shively, 63–131. Honolulu: University Press of Hawaii, 1978.

Sorgenfrei, Carol Fisher. "What Is Nō?" In *Theater Histories*, edited by Gary Jay Williams, 157–167. New York and London: Routledge Press, 2010.

Stein, Bonnie Sue. "Twenty Years Ago We Were Crazy, Dirty, and Mad." *The Drama Review*, Vol. 30, No. 2 (Summer 1986): 107–126. Stable URL: www.jstor.org/stable/1145731

Stein, Bonnie Sue, and Min Tanaka. "Farmer/Dancer or Dancer/Farmer: An Interview." *The Drama Review*, Vol. 30, No. 2 (Summer, 1986): 142–151. Stable URL: www.jstor.org/stable/1145733

Takahashi, Mutsuo. *Noh*. Tokyo: Pie Books, 2010.

Tanaka, Min. "From 'I am an Avant-Garde Who Crawls the Earth: Homage to Tatsumi Hijikata.'" *The Drama Review*, Vol. 30, No. 2 (Summer, 1986): 153–155. Stable URL: www.jstor.org/stable/1145735.

Toshio, Kawatake. *Japan on Stage: Japanese Concepts of Beauty as Shown in the Traditional Theater*. Translation: Patrick G. O'Neill. Tokyo: 3A Corporation, 1990.

Tsubaki, Andrew. "The Performing Arts of Sixteenth-Century Japan: A Prelude to *Kabuki*." In *A Kabuki Reader*, edited by Samuel L. Leiter, 3–15. Armonk, NY: M.E. Sharpe, 2002.

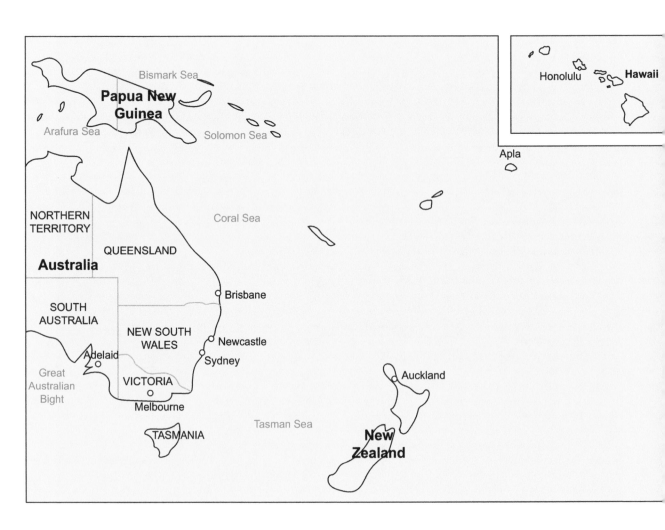

Hawai'i, Aotearoa/ New Zealand, and Papua New Guinea
Guardians of culture

5.1 Overview

Hawaiians, the Māori of Aotearoa (New Zealand), and the Bosavi people of Papua New Guinea share deep cultural connections to nature, chant, and dance – and all have been subjugated to intrusion from those outside their own cultures. When Christian missionaries arrived in Hawai'i and Aotearoa in the nineteenth century, they eradicated the worship of numerous gods in local polytheistic religions along with other aspects they regarded as heathen, such as dance. In Hawai'i, the *hula* had long been patronized by royal courts and had deep religious significance. Yet missionaries were highly successful in converting the nobility, who then banned *hula*. The Māori, who were prohibited from practicing the *haka* and its sacred chants, battled fiercely yet unsuccessfully against British colonization in the nineteenth century. Due to their extremely remote mountain habitat, the Bosavi did not experience contact with Europeans until the 1930s. But arriving missionaries did try to convert many, and government officials interfered with the use of fire in traditional cathartic dances such as the *gisalo*, in which an audience, moved by a performer's emotional song and dance, burns them in retaliation for making them grieve.

Of all three forms, the *gisalo* has experienced the least disturbance. But the cultural practices of *haka* and *hula* have suffered tremendous upheavals over the past two centuries. Ironically, these dances, once considered pagan, were eventually appropriated and commercialized in numerous ways to serve the needs of the oppressors themselves. One example includes the Hollywood film industry, which sold "paradise" through stereotypical images of Pacific Islanders in grass skirts and coconut bras. But perhaps the cruelest irony is found in the presence of the *hula* in Christian church services today. In the name of Christianity, the wanton dance was once banned; yet *hula* – formerly a part of temple worship – is again being danced in front of an altar.[1]

Currently, Pacific peoples are finding new modes of defining and representing themselves. A cultural resurgence beginning in the 1960s and 1970 in both Aotearoa and Hawai'i has led to the revivification of once-forbidden and forgotten indigenous practices and languages. Even though what has been recovered could never replicate what was practiced before pre-European times, many embrace the emergence of innovation from tradition.

5.2 *Hula kahiko*: from Hawaiian royal courts to the global stage

Key points: *hula*

1 *Hula* evolved from a sacred ritual known as *ha'a*. At temples called *heiau* under the auspices of a *kahuna* (priest), the major *akua* (gods) in the Hawaiian polytheistic pantheon were worshiped through *mele* (chanted poetry) and *hula* (dance), both repositories for Hawaiian mythology and history.

2 *Hula* performers trained in a *hula hālau* under a *kumu hula*, an expert teacher. If a troupe from a talented *hālau* found patronage in a royal court, they were paid and gained social prestige as well. Performances of *hula* were to honor the gods and to praise the chiefs and their ancestors in this highly stratified society.

3 After the arrival of European missionaries in 1820, many Hawaiians converted to Christianity, and rulers embracing the new religion banned *hula*. The *hula* went underground, but during King Kalākaua's reign (1874–1891), he revived the tradition of *hula* and made many innovative changes. *Hula* began to flourish again under the "Merrie Monarch."

4 The poetry of *mele* is communicated in *hula* through the use of a vocabulary of symbolic hand gestures representing both tangible and abstract ideas. As the dancer enacts the story of the accompanying *mele*, one or two hands can form a symbol for a specific object – a flower, a tree, a house – or convey an emotion such as love.

5 In the twentieth century, *hula* was divided into two major categories. Comprising the many varieties of traditional forms is *hula kahiko*, or "ancient" *hula*, which is accompanied by traditional Hawaiian instruments and performed to chant known as *mele*. *'Auana* means "drifting," and *hula 'auana* has come to define all modern *hula* and is popular with tourists.

Can these be human beings? How dark and comfortless their state of mind and heart. How imminent the danger to the immortal soul, shrouded in this deep pagan gloom. Can such beings be civilized? Can they be Christianized? Can we throw ourselves upon these rude shores, and take up our abode, for life, among such a people, for the purpose of training them for heaven? Yes.[2]
—Hiram Bingham, Hawai'i's first Christian missionary

The *hula* before European intrusion

At least five centuries ago, sea-faring Polynesians sailed their canoes to the archipelago of Hawai'i. Native Hawaiians trace their ancestry back to these original Polynesian settlers. Despite the distance between the eight major islands, Hawaiians developed a common language, ethos, and religion. Their religion was polytheistic, in which major gods (*akua*) were worshiped along with more minor and ancestral types. At the core of this culture were *mele* (chanted poetry) and *hula* (dance), both repositories for Hawaiian mythology and history. The origins of *hula* are considered to have evolved from a sacred ritual of music and dance known as *ha'a*. At outdoor temples called *heiau* under the auspices of a *kahuna* (priest), the major *akua* in the Hawaiian pantheon were worshiped by the performance of dances accompanied by *mele* chant and the *pahu*, a sharkskin drum. These dances were dedicated to the deities with the intent of pleasing them so that the people's prayers would be answered.

Hawaiian society was ruled by *ali'i*, a noble class. At the top was a king (*mō''ī*) followed by ruling chiefs, then the common people (*maka'āinana*), and at the bottom, the outcasts, or *kauwā*. It was believed that *mana*, a spiritual life force, extended from the gods to the king. The sacred power of a ruler's *mana* determined his military success and the fertility of his lands and his people, while any defeat, drought, pestilence, or barrenness indicated his weakness.[3] To demonstrate their prestige and power, *ali'i* maintained troupes of highly trained dancers. Through chanted poetry, music, and dance, *hula* performers honored the gods, celebrated the births and war triumphs of *ali'i*, and relayed Hawaiian myths. *Hula* practice was sacred, and governed by strict rules. Dancers were taught under the protection of Laka, goddess of the *hula*, in a *hula hālau* – a consecrated training ground run by a master teacher called a *kumu hula*. Despite the stratified society of Hawai'i, men or women of any class could receive training in the *hālau*. After their education, they were presented in a formal debut called the *'ūniki*. A troupe from a particularly talented *hula hālau* could find lucrative patronage and prestige in a royal court.

Captain Cook and the advent of Christian missionaries

In 1778, Captain James Cook landed on the Hawaiian island of Kauai. Cook's men soon found that the Hawaiians coveted metal, and serious bartering began. While Cook traded chisels for hogs to take on provisions, his sailors discovered that they could buy the favors of a beautiful native woman for the price of a nail. Allegedly, by the time the ship headed out on its search for the Northwest Passage, the majority of the crew could no longer hang their hammocks, and the ship was literally creaking from a lack of hardware. Officers wrote that the men would have pulled the ship apart if not stopped.[4]

On the same voyage a year later in 1779, Cook returned. He sailed into Kealakekua Bay as the Hawaiians were celebrating *makahiki*, a religious festival dedicated to Lono, the god of fertility. It was a legendary belief that one day Lono would manifest himself on earth, and when the people saw Cook's massive ship with its lofty masts and sails, they thought it was a floating *heiau*. Hiram Bingham, an early American missionary, wrote a historical recount about Cook's arrival:

> Some of the people scanning the wondrous strangers, who had fire and smoke about their mouths in pipes or cigars, pronounced them gods . . . and applied to the commander the name of a Polynesian deity, and rendered him the homage which they supposed would please him.[5]

The Hawaiians called these strange white men *haole*. Cook was pronounced to be Lono himself, and his men were hailed as gods until a crewman's death exposed them as mere mortals. With relations now strained, Cook sailed away from Hawai'i, but was forced to return due to a broken mast. The now-unfriendly Hawaiians hurled rocks at the *haole* and, after the Europeans shot and killed some men, a mob formed. In the melee, Cook was murdered. Although Cook's men and other European travelers left behind devastating diseases which decimated scores of Hawaiians such as syphilis, measles, and smallpox, the cultural fabric and the traditional pantheistic religion of Hawai'i was left intact. But when Christian missionaries began to arrive in 1820, their targeted and successful attack on Hawaiian culture was profound and widespread.

Christian missionaries encountering *hula* did not attempt to understand its religious, cultural, and aesthetic significance, and quickly condemned it for its "heathen" nature, half-clad dancers, and provocative pelvic movements. Bingham and others were successful in converting several *ali'i* chiefs to Christianity and pressured them to prohibit the *hula* on the grounds that it was pagan worship. When Queen Ka'ahumanu, the powerful wife of Kamehameha I converted in 1823, she banned *hula* dancing.[6] After Hawaii nobility withdrew their patronage and formal *hula hālau* training ceased, this abandonment of *hula* effectively eliminated a keystone of Hawaiian religious culture. Yet a cultural *coup* against encroaching Western domination occurred during King Kalākaua's reign (1874–1891) when he reinstituted the *ali'i* court custom of maintaining resident *hula* performers. His motto was *Ho'oulu Lāhui* (Increase the Nation), and he fostered the resurgence of indigenous practices such as healing and surfing to strengthen Hawaiian cultural identity.

King Kalākaua and the revival of *hula*

When King Kalākaua assumed the throne in 1874, *hula* was in a precarious state. A great number of Hawaiians had lost both their religion and their language due to conversion to Christianity and missionary schooling. Consequently, the two basic underlying principles of *mele* chant – religion and poetic language – had been severely undermined, and most Hawaiians were no longer capable of appreciating their textual richness. Yet there were performers and *kumu hula* who had continued practicing *hula* in private, especially in rural areas. Kalākaua invited elderly *kumu hula* and dancers who still retained their knowledge to court and encouraged the preservation of old chants. *Hula* began to flourish again under the "Merrie Monarch," and in addition to recovering at least three hundred forms of ancient *hula*, his court became an incubator for experimentation and the implementation of new influences, many of them Western. *Hula ku'i* (to join old and new) became the term for this new genre, and major innovations occurred, especially in music.[7] European stringed instruments such as the guitar and the *'ukelele* (introduced by the Portuguese) replaced indigenous Hawaiian percussion instruments; the melodious style of Christian hymn singing replaced chanting; and new *mele* were composed by court artists including Kalākaua himself, and his sister, Lili'uokalani, who composed many *mele* to Western music.[8]

A Trip to Hawaii.   *Forbes Co., Boston.*

HULA GIRLS.

Throughout Kalākaua's reign, large *hula* festivals were staged. Although some converted Hawaiians and missionaries had pronounced Kalākaua's *hula* renaissance "a retrograde step of heathenism and a disgrace to the age," by the 1880s, professional troupes had reappeared, presaging the emergence of commercialized touristic forms.[9] In 1893, two years after his death, and six months after the monarchy was overthrown by the United States, *haole* (white) settlers encouraging tourism arranged for Kalākaua's Hui Lei Mamo court dancers to perform at the World's Columbian Exposition in Chicago. The exhibit featured a cyclorama of Pele's crater at Kilauea and had a twenty-five-foot statue of the fire goddess amidst a simulated lava flow.[10] The exotic "hula hula" was met with great acclaim and the huge appeal of *hula* as entertainment for spectators was made manifest.

> *Think about:*
> Considering *hula's* sacredness and strict rules, would the experimentation embraced by King Kalākaua's court have been accepted if *hula* hadn't been in a state of near extinction?

Case study: The overthrow of the Hawaiian Kingdom

As Hawaiian culture became increasingly subjugated by Western influences, Hawaiians struggled to protect their cultural identity as well as to maintain their sovereignty. Queen Lili'uokalani, who inherited the throne in 1891, also inherited much political dissent over tariffs and the sugar trade. A group of *haole* Hawaiians, Americans, and Europeans with business interests in Hawai'i formed a committee to oust the queen. With the help of the US Navy, this was achieved in 1893 and was followed by the US annexation of Hawai'i in 1898. This cultural domination went in tandem with the emergence of a tourism industry, which effectively promoted the idyllic image of "Island Life" through *hula 'auana* and Hawaiian music.

Despite Kalākaua's commitment to the revitalization of the cultural traditions such as *hula*, the Hawaiian language was officially banned in 1896. Yet missionaries and their elite, Hawaiian-born *haole* children recognized that certain aspects of Hawaiian culture could become commodities. By 1910, *hula* had become an integral part of tourist entertainment in the islands, and developing the form into a marketable commodity brought further changes. As tourism grew, *hula 'auana* developed. *'Auana* means "drifting" and this genre of dance, which often to the uninitiated represents the "native" dancing of Hawai'i, is sometimes pejoratively called "airport

> *Think about:*
> Why is the banning of a people's language by those in power the ultimate *coup* to the subordinate culture?

hula" because of its use in welcoming tourists. To differentiate between the more modern *hula 'auana*, with its Western-influenced songs, and that of pre-European *mele* and *hula*, the term *hula kahiko* (ancient) was coined in the twentieth century.

Training in the *hula hālau*

Although court patronage of *hula* is no more, today, there are *hula hālau* throughout Hawai'i, and one can train seriously while maintaining a job or attending school. Originally, *hula* students (*haumana*) would live within the confines of the *hālau* under the strict guidance of their *kumu hula*. An account of nineteenth-century training is found in Nathanial Emerson's 1909 book, *Unwritten History of Hawai'i*. According to his research, throughout their training *haumana* sought the protection of Laka, goddess of *hula*, until their *'ūniki* graduation, since any mistakes in interpreting the auspicious words of the *mele* chants could bring on disastrous results from the deities. They worshiped the goddess at the *kuahu*, an altar in the *hālau* decorated with greenery such as *maile* and ferns that represented the spiritual power of gods and demi-gods.[11] While training in chant and dance, they followed strict dietary and sexual restrictions and the rules of the *hālau*, known as *kapu*. Emerson discusses these constraints:

Figure 5.2
Members of Hālau Hulu Ka No'eau perform *hula kahiko*.
Image: Jack Vartoogian, Front Row Photos.

> The members of the company were required to maintain the greatest propriety of demeanor, to suppress all rudeness of speech and manner, to abstain from all carnal indulgence, to deny themselves specified articles of food, and above all to avoid contact with a corpse. If anyone, even by accident, suffered such defilement, before being received again into the fellowship or permitted to enter the *hālau* and take part in the exercises he must have ceremonial cleansing (*huikala*). The *kumu* offered up prayers, sprinkled the offender with salt water and turmeric, commanded him to bathe in the ocean, and he was clean.[12]

The students were careful to not break the *kapu*; if they did, a fine of a pig was imposed. *Kapu* upheld the authority of the *kumu hula* and maintained discipline within the group, thereby pleasing the deities.

Emerson recorded that the *kumu hula* decided when *haumana* were ready for their *'ūniki* graduation. The night before the *'ūniki* was devoted to dance and chant, and after midnight, all students bathed in the ocean to purify themselves and returned naked. The *kumu* met the procession at the *hālau* door and sprinkled each student with *pikai*, blessed water. At dawn the *haumana* prayed before the altar. Marking their official entrance into the guild of *hula* performers was the *'ailolo* ceremony, in which a pig was sacrificed, cooked, and eaten. The students would then costume themselves carefully for their *'ūniki* debut at a noble court.

Kumu hula and *hula hālau* today

Before the advent of Christianity in Hawai'i, the existing belief was that the *kumu* was a spiritual person, inspired by the gods. Many *kumu* today run their *hālau* much like a sacred order, functioning as artistic director, manager, and spiritual leader. The aim of a *kumu* is to guide *haumana* into a state of physical and mental grace through discipline and the sharing of his or her wisdom. *Haumana* learn how to make costumes, adornments, and musical instruments, and become knowledgeable about plants used for costuming and decorating the *kuahu*. When a *kumu hula* calls for a *'ūniki*, preparations are made. Although this varies from *hālau* to *hālau*, in general, *haumana* fast, take a ceremonial bath in the ocean, and partake in a ritual *'ailolo* feast – all elements Emerson recorded in his research. Once they complete their *'ūniki* they earn the title of *'ōlapa* (agile). When a higher degree of training and maturity has been obtained, they may become assistants to the *kumu hula*, eventually earn the title of *hula ho'opa'a* (steadfast), and will perform *mele* chants and/or play instruments.

Diverse movement styles, aims, and varying interpretations of *mele* exist between *hula hālau*. In fact, the saying *aohe pau ka ike I kau hālau* translates as "think not that all wisdom resides in your *hālau*."[13] *Hula kahiko* is practiced by all genders, can be performed individually or in a group as large as two hundred, and there are many forms of *hula* danced while standing or while kneeling (*hula noho*). In some instances, the style of a *hālau* is influenced by its location. For instance, Hālau O Kekuhi, run by the respected Kanaka'ole family, is on the Big Island, proximal to the Halema'uma'u Crater on the summit of Kilauea – the legendary domain of the fire goddess, Pele. To honor her creative forces, dancers are taught in the energetic *aiha'a* style: in the low *aiha'a* stance, a dancer draws energy from Pele's earth by keeping their knees bent, their back straight, and their feet flat.[14]

Figure 5.3
The Kanaka'ole sisters, Nalani (left) and Pualani of Hālao O Kekuhi, chant and play the *ipu*.
Image: Jack Vartoogian, Front Row Photos.

Case study: The myth of Pele, Hi'iaka, and Lohiau

Of the many myths involving Pele – goddess of fire, lightning, wind, and volcanoes – one involves a rivalry with her sister, the beautiful Hi'iaka. While in her spirit form during a dream lasting nine days, Pele embarked on a tryst with the handsome chief Lohiau. Concerned over Pele's slumbering state, Hi'iaka chanted to bring her sister back. Once Pele returned to her body, she was driven by a desire to consummate her love with Lohiau, but this time in the physical realm. Protecting Hi'iaka with supernatural powers, Pele sent her to Kauai with instructions to deliver him in forty days and not to fall in love with him. Hi'iaka agreed, but on the grounds that her forest grove, and her best friend Hopoe, would be guarded by Pele during her absence. When Hi'iaka arrived on Kauai, she discovered that Lohiau had died of heartbreak over his separation from Pele. After days of her sacred chanting, Lohiau was revived, but due to his infirmity, Hi'iaka could not meet Pele's deadline. The raging, jealous goddess set Hi'iaka's forest afire and sacrificed Hopoe. Once Hi'iaka and Lohiau arrived on Hawai'i, Hi'iaka retaliated by taking the handsome chief as her lover. Livid, Pele launched a torrent of lava toward the couple. Hi'iaka was untouched, but Lohiau turned into a pillar of rock and his spirit left his body as a bird. Eventually he was brought back to life and reunited with Hi'iaka.

The basic steps of *hula kahiko* are performed with the knees flexed and the feet close to the ground, and there is very little airborne work. In a *kaholo*, a dancer steps sideways: right, left, right, and then taps the floor with the ball of the left foot, and repeats this to the other side. This step is paired with *ami*, the rotation of hips (perhaps the most defining feature of *hula*), while the rhythmic sway side to side is called *lewa*. In the basic *hela* step, one foot extends diagonally front, and is placed flat on the ground, turned out at a forty-five-degree angle. The weight sinks into the opposite hip as the knee bends; the extended foot returns, and then the movement is repeated on the other side. In *'uwehe*, one foot lifts up and, as it is lowered, the dancer rises onto the balls of feet and pulses the knees. On top of the footwork, the story of the accompanying *mele* is enacted through a vocabulary of symbolic arm and hand gestures representing both tangible and abstract ideas. The arms can be held out in front, parallel to the floor, extended horizontally at either chest level with one arm bending to meet the sternum, or hands can be held on the hips. "Where the hands are, let the eyes follow" is an ancient rule of *hula* in presenting the meaning of *mele*. One or two hands can form a symbol for a specific object, such as a flower, a tree, or a house, while both hands can describe locomotion, such as the movement of water, rain, or paddling a canoe. Concepts such as love, jealousy, sorrow, or power are expressed as well through gestures that are both understatedly mimetic but also metaphoric. In general, the demeanor of a performer is serious in nature.

Figure 5.4
Members of San Francisco-based Hālau o Keikiali'i perform *hula kahiko*.
Image: Jack Vartoogian, Front Row Photos.

Mele chant and *hula* music

Until missionaries developed a Hawaiian alphabet in the nineteenth century, *mele* chants were scrupulously memorized in an oral tradition to preserve historical facts and legends. This is especially true for *mele* that accompany *hula pahu*, which evolved from ancient *ha'a* temple worship and whose lyrics are not open to interpretation or change.[15] Hawaiian genealogical history is passed through *mele inoa* (name chants), compositions that honor a specific *ail'i* or deity by recounting stories about his or her life. *Mele inoa* celebrate various legendary battles, exploits, love affairs, and births of gods and chiefs, while *mele ho'oipoipo* are songs about people, places, or historical events.

An informed audience might perceive how a dancer skillfully reveals the double entendre inherent within the poetry of *mele*. Scholar Joann Kealiinohomoku states that the images in chants are not just simplistic reactions to nature – gestures about fish and palm trees might not really *be* about fish and palm trees, but are metaphoric images that at once couch and imply an idea. She explains:

Figure 5.5
Dancers from Hālao O Keikiali play the feathered gourd rattle.
Image: Jack Vartoogian, Front Row Photos.

> Linked metaphors within a well-written Hawaiian chant seem often to be disconnected or illogical in English . . . the choice of abstruse words presents an intellectual challenge to the listener to decode the ingenious play on words as presented by a master poet and a master dancer. Few . . . were privy to all the meanings.[16]

These layered meanings were often cleverly incorporated in *mele ma'i*, chants that honored the genitals of an *ali'i* and his procreative *mana*.

In *hula kahiko*, *mele* are always in a 2/4 rhythm, and accompanied by indigenous Hawaiian instruments. These include the sharkskin *pahu* drum; the *ipu*, a double calabash gourd that is alternately thumped on the ground and struck with the hand; the *'uli'uli*, a feathered gourd rattle; *'ili'ili*, lava rock castanets; *ka la'au*, rhythm sticks; *pu'ili*, slit bamboo rattle; *ohe*, nose flute; and the body itself – striking the chest and the legs is called *pa'i umauma*.

Hula costuming

Traditional *hula* costuming was made of *kapa*, a material made from pounded mulberry bark, decorated, and fashioned into wrap-around skirts (*pa'u*). Men wore their *pa'u* over their *malo*, a loincloth. Further adornments included *lei* (garlands of vines or leaves worn on the head, shoulders, anklets, and wrists) and *kupe'e* (wristlets and anklets of whale teeth, bone, or shells). Both men and women performed bare chested until missionaries insisted women wear a modest *holoku*, a loose cotton gown covering the dancer from the neck to the ankles. Less than a decade after the advent of missionaries, Captain Beechey observed a *hula* performance in 1827 and expressed his opinion:

> The dance of the females was spoiled by a mistaken refinement, which prevented their appearing, as formerly, with no other dress than a covering to the hips, and a simple garland of flowers upon the head; instead of this they were provided with frilled chemises, which so far from taking away the appearance of indecency, produced an opposite effect, and at once gave the performance a stamp of indecency.[17]

By the 1880s, King Kalākaua's dancers wore Western-style pantaloons and long calf-length pleated cotton dresses.[18] Today, costuming varies as much as *hula hālau* do. In general, *hula kahiko* is still danced barefoot, women's hair hangs loose, and all wear *lei*, head wreaths, and *kupe'e*. Women wear colorful sleeveless bodices and full calf-length skirts, while men are often bare chested and wear loincloths, or skirts.

Current trends

A Hawaiian renaissance in the early 1970s stimulated serious research on indigenous cultural traditions, and many Hawaiians pursued *hula kahiko*. Several *hula* festivals emerged; the oldest and most spectacular is the annual Merrie Monarch Festival. Since 1971, the Festival has invited prestigious *hālau* to compete in both *kahiko* and *'auana* styles. Judges weigh in on the dancers' entrance, interpretation of *mele*, precision of footwork and hand gestures, and costuming, as well as their exit. These competitive performances often spark passionate debates about authenticity and legitimacy: some *hālau* present chant and *hula* as ancient and sacred legacies that must be preserved and protected, while others controversially use tradition as a springboard for contemporary creativity.

The following *kumu hula* are examples of those who are rooted in tradition but continue to offer innovative approaches to choreography and music. Robert Cazimero, Māpuana de Silva, Vicky Holt Takamine, and Michael Pili Pang all studied with Maiki Aiu Lake. In 1975, Cazimero founded Hālau Na Kamale, the first all-male *hālau*. They compete only every ten years, and were the overall winners of the 2005 and 2015 Merrie Monarch Festival. Māpuana de Silva runs the Hālao Mōhala 'Ilima, Takamine is *kumu hula* of Pua Ali'i 'Ilima, while Michael Pili Pang opened his Hālao Hula Ka No'eau on the Big Island and a second *halau* in Honolulu in 2002. In addition to their perpetuation of the ancient traditions of *hula*, Hālao O Kekuhi in Hilo is famous for its groundbreaking stage productions. Their *Holo Mai Pele* (1995) toured widely and was hailed by some as being the first "*hula* opera." *Hanau Ka Moku* ("An Island is Born"), a 2003 co-production with Peter Rockfort Espiritu's Tau Dance Company, included *hula* and contemporary dances performed to ancient and newly composed chants about the emergence of a future Hawaiian island beneath the sea. Espiritu, currently the director of the Oceania Dance Company in Fiji, founded Tau Dance Company in 1996. His hybrid choreography integrates his deep knowledge of *hula* with Western and other Pacific dance forms. In *Naupaka* (2006), based on a legendary romance between a chief and a lowly *kauwā*, the choreography included *tango*, and pointe shoes were worn.

Outside of Hawai'i, *hula* has exploded into a global form. There are an estimated forty *hālau* in Holland, over six hundred in Mexico, and at least a thousand in Japan. In Oakland, California, Mark Keali'i Ho'omalu runs the Academy of Hawaiian Arts, which pushes forward new expressions in *hula* and music. Patrick Makuakane, who trained at Robert Cazimero's *hālau*, opened his school Na Lei Hulu I Ka Weklu in San Francisco in 1985. His large dance company has earned awards for its productions such as *Ka Leo Kanaka* (2012), a tribute to Hawaiian-language newspapers. Their newest, *The Natives are Restless*, opened in 2016. All of these choreographers, whether based in Hawai'i or elsewhere, regard tradition to be the bedrock of their creativity. Kekuhi Keali'ikanaka'oleohaililiani of Hālao O Kekuhi declares:

> Whether you're changing with the world or not can determine whether your practice lives or dies. We choose to live, and we choose to evolve, based on the principles and philosophies of our grandparents and their grandparents . . . we don't compromise those things, ever.[19]

Discussion questions: *hula*

1 *Hula* has gone from being a sacred ritual to commercialized entertainment. In looking at tradition versus innovation, how can a contemporary artist today best honor both, and create cultural meaning from ritual or classical dance traditions transferred to the stage?
2 To Hawaiians, corpulence is auspicious. Yet in the dance world, this is often not the case. Discuss the differences between body type in *hula* and that of other dances, which value a thin physique. Does the form of the dancing body enhance the aesthetics of the dance?
3 The *kapu* system in *hula* enforces order in a *hālau*. In some aspect of your training, have you experienced similar restrictions, and if so, have these enhanced your commitment to your practice, and to your teacher?

5.3 The Māori *haka*: a dance of defiance, a dance of welcome

Key points: *haka*

1 In the thirteenth century, Māori ancestors sailed from Polynesia in large canoes, and settled on the two islands of Aotearoa. Māori ceremonial gatherings called *hui* occurred in a sacred open meeting area known as the *marae* and in the *whare tapere*, the community meetinghouse.
2 In Māori ideology, ancestral power is manifested in *mana* – a spiritual essence from the gods; *tapu* is a spiritual restriction from an activity; and *utu* is the concept of compensation in terms of reciprocating friendly gestures, as well as seeking compensation for offensive acts – hence their war-like nature. The Māori traditionally passed down their history via songs called *waiata*. Both *waiata* and *haka* are integral in *pōwhiri*, a welcoming ritual reflecting the tenets of *mana* and *tapu*.
3 Traditionally upon meeting, Māori groups tested the thin line between cordiality and hostility with a demonstration by each party of their fierce nature through an intimidating *haka*. With quivering hands, stamping feet, bent legs, highly active movements of the eyes and tongue along with facial grimaces, the *haka* could be a dance of welcome, or a true war dance – a prelude to battle that served to warn their opponents of their fate.
4 Early European explorers were met by Māori, who performed their "war dance" while brandishing weapons. Because the Europeans had trouble deciphering whether the *haka* was bellicose or cordial, this resulted in confusion that led to violence and death on both sides. Nineteenth-century missionaries discouraged the *haka* and other cultural traditions such as *moko* (tattooing) and speaking their own language.
5 Redefinitions and reclamations of Māori culture began in the 1960s, when protests against their subordination increased. Tribal rights that had long been ignored in the Treaty of Waitangi were recognized and a resurgence of interest in reviving Māori culture resulted in the revival of Te Reo Māori, their language.

Little by little, their bodies are thrown back, their knees strike together and look like convulsions, their eyes turn up so that with horrible effect, their pupils are absolutely hidden under their eyelids, while at the same time they twist their hands with outspread fingers rapidly before their faces . . . Was it a battle song they performed for us? Whatever their intention, be it victory or love, they have a music of an overwhelming force.[20]

—Louis Auguste de Sainson, 1827

The above description, written long ago by a baffled yet awed Frenchman, is of a *haka* – the dance of the Māori people living in Aotearoa, or "Land of the Long White Cloud." For early European explorers attempting to land in Aotearoa (called New Zealand by settlers), the *haka* was often their first impression of the Māori, and they were struck by its ferocity and appalled by its unfamiliar movements. Brandishing their weapons and directing their dance toward the strangers, the elaborately tattooed men sang, shouted, and grunted while trembling their fingers and slapping their thighs as they stamped their feet in strict rhythmic unison. In addition to the threat of weapons, the menacing facial distortions – protruding tongues, bulging eyes, and grimaces – accompanying their dance were especially disconcerting to the Europeans. Was this a show of their might, a decree of war, or a form of welcome? In fact, the *haka* could, and did, serve all these purposes. Traditionally, Māori groups who met on friendly terms knew there was a thin line between cordiality and hostility, and by performing this mock war dance, each party demonstrated their fierce nature as a means of declaring their potency. However, because Europeans had trouble deciphering their intent, initial contact between the explorers and the Māori resulted in confusion that led to violence and death on both sides. What Europeans perceived to be a "dance of war" was probably a ritualized process of welcome.

In Aotearoa/New Zealand today, many *haka* are grouped under the term *kapa haka*. *Kapa* translates as "to stand in row or rank," while *haka* means dance and the song that accompanies it. *Haka* exposes many facets of life: it can welcome esteemed guests, belittle an enemy before a battle, or be performed ritually at tribal gatherings or at funerals. More recently composed *haka* address contemporary concerns of individual *iwi* (clans) in competitive festivals like Te Matatini. New Zealand rugby teams perform *haka* before games as an assertion of their *mana* (authority and power) and the Royal New Zealand Navy's *haka* groups are greatly esteemed. The expressive, characteristic *haka* gestures demonstrate the passion behind the singing and dancing, and are a vigorous activation of pride. To the Māori, it is a *taonga* – a cultural treasure.

Early Māori history and *haka* legends

Thirteenth-century genealogical stories tell of Māori whose ancestors sailed from Polynesia in large canoes and settled on the two larger islands of Aotearoa. Initially, they lived in small settlements on the coast, but as inter-tribal warfare became more frequent, fortified settlements on hilltops called *pa* were constructed on the North Island. Māori ceremonial gatherings occurred in a *marae*, a sacred meeting area, and the *wharenui*, a community meetinghouse. The Māori greatly valued amusement and would gather here in the summertime to play games, sing, and dance.[21]

Māori oral history was passed down through generations via chants and mythological storytelling. The origin of the *haka* involves Tamanuiterā, the sun god, and his wife, Hine-raumati – the personification of summer – whose presence was revealed by a wavering radiance in the hot summertime air. Tamanuiterā and Hine-raumati had a son called Tāne-rore. The motions of the child's restless hands reflected his mother's shimmering presence and were incorporated into the *wiri* – the distinctive, quivering

Figure 5.6
The Māori Chief Tarra, also known as "George," at a war dance.
Image: Dr. Florance Augustus, 1812–1879. Reprinted with permission of the Alexander Turnbull Library, Wellington, New Zealand.

movements of a *haka* performer's hands. It is Māori belief that when it is so hot that the air shimmers, Tāne-rore is dancing a *haka* for his mother.[22]

In 1820, a chief of the Ngāti Toa *iwi* named Te Rauparaha composed the lyrics for the *ka mate* – perhaps the most widely recognized *haka* song. It tells the tale of fleeing from a clan who intended to kill him in revenge for a bloody raid he had led on them years ago. He sought sanctuary from a local chief named Wharerangi and his wife Te Rangikoaea, who hid Te Rauparaha in a *kumara* (sweet potato) storage pit. In hot pursuit, the warriors chanted magical incantations to enable them to find Te Rauparaha. Protecting him, the wife dispelled these chants by straddling her legs widely over the pit, since it was a Māori belief that female genitalia had the power to neutralize the divinatory power of incantations.[23] As they approached, Te Rauparaha lamented to himself, *Ka mate! Ka mate!* (I die! I die!); as they retreated, he rejoiced, *Ka ora! Ka ora!* (I live! I live!). Te Rauparaha's composition encompassed myriad emotions: his fear of being captured, his exhilaration over surviving, his thanks to his hosts, and his joy of exiting into daylight from the depths of the pit.

European arrival

The disruption of Māori culture by *Pākehā* – those of European descent – first began in 1642, when Dutch seafarer Abel Tasman sighted Aotearoa. Soon after his vessel's smaller boats headed to shore, they were surrounded by large canoes manned by tattooed, weapon-wielding Māori. A bloody encounter between Māori and *Pākehā* changed Tasman's notions about landing. He departed without planting the Dutch flag, but not before renaming the area "Murderers' Bay" (Moordenaar's Bay).

More than a century later in 1769, Captain James Cook and his English expedition arrived in Aotearoa aboard the *Endeavour*. A smaller boat with some of his men set out for shore, which was followed by Māori in canoes. After the two parties landed on opposite banks, one sailor recounted seeing the *haka*: "We call'd to them in the George Island Language, but they answered us by flourishing their weapons over their heads and dancing as we supposed the war dance."[24] This was the first of many *haka* that met Cook's expedition throughout their time in Aotearoa. Māori behavior, which they perceived as ranging from bellicose to cordial, was unpredictable to them. Joseph Banks, a botanist on the expedition, described his perceptions of erratic behavior:

> Their words were almost universally the same, *haromai haromai hare uta a patoo pattoe oge* – come to us, come to us, come but ashore with us and we will kill you with our *patoo patoo* [weapons]. In this manner they continued to threaten us, venturing by degrees nearer and nearer until they were close alongside, at intervals talking very civilly and answering any questions we ask'd them but quickly renewing their threats till they had by our nonresistance gain'd courage enough to begin their war song and dance.[25]

Cook and Banks said that although the "war dance" was done on peaceful occasions, they believe that the Māori never omitted it in their real wars and that it stoked their ferocity before attacking their opponents.[26]

By the nineteenth century, Christian missionaries had established schools and churches. Missionaries found the "war dance" to be in conflict with Christian beliefs and

Figure 5.7
Māori chief with full facial *moko*, or tattoos, in 1784. When missionaries arrived in 1814, they deemed *moko* to be "heathen".
Image: watercolor by Sydney Parkinson. Reprinted with permission of the Alexander Turnbull Library.

were affronted because men performed the *haka* naked, wearing only a rope around the waist from which their weapons could be hung. Samuel Marsden, the first missionary to the Māori in 1814, posed this question in 1819: "Have they in any degree laid aside their ferocious habits, such as shouting, dancing naked, and sham fighting to inflame their passions and their warlike ardor?"[27] The Reverend Henry Williams prohibited the *haka* and its sacred chants, and discouraged tattooing. The Māori, with their aptitude for singing, learned to harmonize hymns as part of their conversion to Christianity.

Think about:
How should we
distinguish cultural
change from cultural
annihilation?

Case study: The tradition of tattoos: *moko*

The Polynesian tradition of tattoos, or *moko*, has existed for 2,000 years. *Moko* indicate one's genealogy, occupation, and social rank. *Moko* masters carefully followed an untainted lifestyle in order not to offend their patron god, whom they credited for their talent. Held in high esteem, they decided what designs were appropriate for whom, and on what occasion. During the early years of colonization, many Māori signed legal documents using a unique pattern within their *moko*, which was recognized by colonial authorities as proof of identity.

Counterbalancing this missionary zeal in Aotearoa was the growing market for prostitution due to the increase of American and European whalers. In an attempt to control the increasing lawlessness, "New Zealand" officially became a British colony in 1840, when Māori chiefs and British Crown representative Captain William Hobson signed the Treaty of Waitangi. The Māori unwittingly ceded their governance in exchange for the possession of their lands, forests, and fisheries. Altercations between Māori and Europeans became increasingly hostile, and eventually erupted into a war in 1860. Following a series of battles, 1.25 million acres of land were confiscated from the Māori by the colonial government in 1864. By the end of the nineteenth century, most Māori people were dispossessed of their land – a violation of the Treaty of Waitangi.[28]

Mana, tapu, utu: Māori ideology and its relevance to the *haka*

In Māori ideology, all living things descend from *atua* – gods and goddesses – and their ancestral power is manifested in *mana* – a spiritual essence that also translates as authority or power. Because *mana* is considered to exist in certain mountains, rivers, and lakes, Māori have sustained strong spiritual ties and reverence for their land. Those who descended most directly from the founding ancestors were considered to be extremely *tapu*, or sacred, and regarded to have the strongest *mana*. This presence of godly *mana*, manifested in the earthly realm by respected *tapu* individuals, grounded early Māori society by fostering an effective system of social control. *Tapu* is also defined as spiritual restriction and is a strong force: imposed rules must be followed or the wrath of the gods could be invoked.

Utu is the concept of compensation, or balance. *Utu*, in tandem with the authority of *mana*, requires reciprocating friendly gestures as well as seeking compensation for offensive acts. The dual aspects of *utu* could be either peaceful offerings or violent acts of vengeance such as cannibalism, previously practiced by the Māori, whose *mana*, or authority, impelled them to eat their vanquished enemies.

Māori songs and the *pōwhiri* welcoming ceremony

Māori passed down their ancestral knowledge and history via traditional songs called *waiata*. These poetic songs, rich with imagery and metaphor, could be sung *a capella* (with no musical accompaniment) to express a range of emotions.[29] Some honorary *waiata*

Figure 5.8 (p. 139)
Tukukino, a land activist and leader of the Ngāti Tamaterā, with elaborate facial tattoos.
Image: painted by Gottfried Lindauer in 1878. Auckland Art Galleries (public domain).

are sung for funerals, while laments and love *waiata* are often sung in welcoming guests. Traditional *waiata* continue to be sung today, but new ones are also composed that reflect current social and political concerns within *Māoritanga* – the ideals of Māori culture.

Both *waiata* and *haka* are integral in *pōwhiri*, the Māori welcoming ceremony. It continues a cultural imperative from earlier times when an *iwi* needed to insure that visitors harbored no ill intentions. When the host party, known as the *tengata whenua* (people of the land), meets their *manuhiri* (guests) on the communal meeting ground, an evolved protocol that continues today is followed between both parties. The test of the *te wero* (cast a spear) begins the *pōwhiri*: as a challenge, one of the hosts places a *taiaha* (spear) and a leaf or feather on the ground. As long as the spear is not chosen, they have come in peace. Selected women in each group trade a *karanga*, a call and response of welcome. Everyone respectfully enters the meetinghouse, where the guests are entertained with sung laments honoring the spirits of the dead. The hosts then begin the *whaikorero* (speeches), which honor ancestors of both *iwi* and is concluded by the women chanting a *waiata*.[30] The visitors reciprocate by performing their own *waiata* and *haka*. One by one, the hosts and guests shake hands, and touch their noses and foreheads together in *hong*, mingling their breath in a show of unity. A feast follows and the *manuhiri* are accepted as *tengata whenua* for the remainder of their visit.

Technique and styles of *haka*

The expressive and passionate gestures of *kapa haka* demonstrate the vigorous zeal behind Māori singing and dancing. *Pukana* is the rolling of the eyes; *pukari*, wild

Figure 5.9
Haka performers show their fierce demeanors.
Image: Tom Iclan.

staring; and the rapid vibrations of the hands are called *wiri*. *Whatero* – the protrusion of the tongue, symbolic of the phallus – is the domain of men only. Originally, women performed in the front ranks of the *haka* and carried weapons. Today, females equally perform *haka* and, though the domain of girls and women has traditionally been the *haka poi*, a gentler dance, often to a *waiata*, which is a lullaby. However, it is significant to note that male warriors once trained the suppleness of their wrists for combat with *poi* – a ball attached to a long string that is twirled rapidly.

Although many *haka* from pre-*Pākehā* times have disappeared, several practiced today fulfill particular functions in social situations. *Haka taparahi* is a ceremonial dance that can express joy or contemporary grievances, such as unjust government actions, domestic violence, health concerns, etc.[31] The defiant *haka ngeri* rouses a group to achieve its aims, using free-style movement. Normally, men lead, while women provide vocal support from the rear. These two forms are not all uniformly enacted – they both involve a good deal of spontaneity and creativity as the power of the *haka* moves the performers to give their own meaning and force to the words. This freedom is not an option in a *haka* in preparation for combat.

War *haka*

In anticipation of a battle, *haka ngārahu* was a means of inspection by elders and experienced warriors who judged if the participants were emotionally and physically ready for fighting. They also made sure it was danced in regimented unison, since any disharmony could be a disastrous omen.[32] The *haka peruperu* – the true war dance – was a prelude to battle that served to warn their opponents head-on of their

Figure 5.10
A Māori battalion in Egypt during World War II performing a *haka*.
Image: Reprinted with permission of the Alexander Turnbull Library, Wellington, New Zealand.

fate. *Peru* means anger, which was stoked through fierce facial expressions and the waving of weapons to invoke Tuumatauenga, the *atua*, or god of war. In both World War I and II, Māori soldiers performed the *haka peruperu* before battles. Awateri Arapeta (1910–1976), a brave leader in the Māori battalion in World War II, was an avid *haka* performer. Claiming that hard conditioning made the warriors physically and mentally fit to perform *haka peruperu*, he described its power:

> This dance . . . has the psychological purpose of demoralizing the enemy by controlled chanting, by conditioning to look ugly . . . to roll the fiery eye, to spew the defiant tongue, to distort, to snort, to stamp furiously, to yell hideous, blood-curdling sounds, to carry the anger of the ugly-faced war-god throughout the battle.[33]

Facing their enemy head on, the dancers did their utmost to intimidate their adversaries and concluded their threatening dance by jumping high with their legs folded underneath as they held their weapons high. For the Māori, the *haka* was a demonstration of their invincibility and authority, and steeled them for battle.

Think about:
Why do ancient, indigenous cultures such as the Māori and Native American peoples value dance as a means of preparing for war?

Māori culture: reclaiming or claiming?

After the wars with the British in the nineteenth century, the Māori unjustly lost much of their land through confiscations, compromising their traditional way of life. Many migrated to newly built cities in order to find employment and opportunity; at present, only fifteen percent of the Māori still live in a rural environment. Compared to the *Pākehā* population today, statistics show high unemployment rates, low income, poor education, ill health, and high crime rates, and these circumstances have led Māori activists to fight for the preservation of their culture and self-esteem. To this end, *marae* community meeting spaces were built in urban communities. In the sanctuary of the *marae*, Māori are able to engage in practices that enhance their worldview. In *pōwhiri*, funerals, and other ceremonial gatherings occurring there, *kapa haka* are integral to these events.

Redefinitions and reclamations of their culture began in earnest in the 1960s, when Māori protests against their subordination increased. Tribal rights that had long been ignored in the Treaty of Waitangi were recognized, and a resurgence of interest in reviving Māori culture resulted in the revival of Te Reo Māori, the Māori language. The government officially recognized Te Reo in 1988 and Māori Television was created as part of the Waitangi Tribunal Settlement. *Kapa haka* has received more international exposure due to pre-game demonstrations by sports teams such as the All Blacks and performances by the Royal New Zealand Navy. But as crowds are roused, is Māori culture given the respect and credit that it is due? Cases of cultural misappropriation, such as a the recent controversial commercial by the Italian car company, Fiat, raise many issues. Whether the *haka* has been a victim of appropriation in its transformation into an emblem representing an entire society is a question worthy of debate. But *kapa haka* plays a role in preserving tradition, gives opportunity for artistic expression and the nurturing of tribal identity, and for provides a social voice for the Māori. Choreographer Jack Gray states:

> As with all aspects of Māori worldview, *haka* is a living embodiment of these complex values and symbolic of an approach towards guardianship and territorial power. It is one of the many reasons that Māori are empowered as indigenous peoples today.[34]

Current trends

Today in Aotearoa/New Zealand, competitions of *kapa haka* teams contribute to the preservation of Māori traditional culture – and also benefit tourism. Te Matatini is the bi-annual Māori performing arts festival, in which approximately forty *kapa haka* teams from competitions compete. The winners travel the world as cultural ambassadors for two years. *Kapa haka* continues to be enjoyed both nationally and internationally through its customary performances by the All Blacks and the Black

Ferns, New Zealand's female rugby team. In schools, Te Reo and *Tikanga* Māori (language and culture) are taught through *kapa haka*, *pōwhiri* welcoming rituals, and *whaikorero* speeches; they also impart Māori social values such as kinship, hospitality, and compassion. The establishment of Te Reo as a national language has also led to new compositions and innovations in *kapa haka* and *waiata*. One innovator is Bub Wehi, the founder of several *kapa haka* groups including Te Waka Huia. In collaboration with his late wife, Nen, Wehi has composed new *haka* and *waiata* addressing Māori male violence, treaty settlements, and health issues, and has stated that his contemporary, politically charged *haka* are the equivalent of the war-like challenges of pre-*Pākehā* times.

In the contemporary dance realm, Atamira Dance Company is a platform for Māori dancers and choreographers. Atamira founder Jack Gray's work often offsets the theater as a place of belonging. Through community performance, ceremony, and ritual, his current project, *I Moving Lab*, functions through site-specific installation to create a type of *papakainga* (homestead) for indigenous artists who have actually lost their familial links to ancestral land. Māori choreographer and dancer Louise Potiki Bryant has an ongoing collaboration with scholar Charles Royal, with whom she created *TE KĀROHIROHI: The Light Dances* (2014), an indigenous project on the *whare tapere* amusement traditions that incorporated Māori puppets and instruments. Choreographer Charles Koroneho explores Māori cosmology, rituals, and incantations of *tohunga* shamans in his solo, *Pure* (2013). Choreographer Lemi Ponifasio, of Samoan descent, founded his company, MAU, in Aotearoa in 1995. His work, *Stones in Her Mouth* (2013), featured Māori women's stories of oppression and abusive power, and used ancient *waiata* chants. Founded by Neil Ieremia in 1995, Black Grace Dance Company offers highly physical contemporary dancing with storytelling and dance traditions of the Pacific Islands, as seen in his 2015 work, *Siva*. Ieremia stated, "Siva explodes from the collision of the past and future, capturing our common beauty, our shared history and divine difference. It is more than a celebration of the past . . . it is about rushing headlong into the future."[35]

5.3 Exploration: excerpt from "Ko Mitimiti Ahau, I am (of) the Place, Mitimiti" by Jack Gray[36]

Mitimiti is the tribal homeland of Māori choreographer Jack Gray, and the inspiration for a series of research iterations that brought many artists and disciplines into creative exploration around legacy, heritage, dispersal, removal, and restoration. Gray recently performed his dance "Ruatepupuke" in front of his father's meetinghouse—which is now displayed in the collection of Chicago's Field Museum.

I grew up in Auckland, Aotearoa (New Zealand)'s most populated city. Compare Mitimiti's population of sixty (on a good day) to Auckland's 1.4 million, and it's understandable to see the distance between them. The name for Auckland (Auckland was named after a British Governor General to India in 1840) is "Tamaki Makaurau," isthmus of a thousand lovers. A Matariki (Māori New Year) event I attended included stories about this area's famed voyagers who remind us now of our customary relationships to bird migrations, changing seasons and landscapes, recounting the ways we fished, hunted, fought wars, arranged marriages, hid in caves, carried large canoes overland.

As a child I was drawn toward learning Māori language through songs and dances, and as a young adult, captivated by the beautiful black voids of artist Ralph Hotere's paintings, where my imaginative expression surfaced through the use of contemporary dance. I founded Atamira Dance Collective as a platform for Māori Contemporary Dance artists to create new work in 2000. Ten years later, I reconnected with my tribal genealogy (after my Grandmother's death) only to discover Ralph Hotere was from Mitimiti too.

Looking back at my practice making in dance, I can say that my research is continually about the same things – Manaakitanga – the artful practice of relational making. Through my dance research with Atamira, I have explored different ways of relating to Mitimiti the place over the past five years. I develop choreographic portraits with different dancers and visit my tribal lands at least once a year. I travel abroad yearly to North America to exchange Indigenous knowledge as a writer, teacher, performer and facilitator, and return to New Zealand to cultivate this process, deepening the work we might do and increasing impacts it might have. It is by no coincidence that the godwit's flight from New Zealand to Alaska is the longest non-stop flight of any bird.

Coming from a strong culture of self-determination, Māori vehemently hold onto traditional protocols, claiming ancestral right to land and practices of being. For us, knowing and speaking pepeha (naming places of origin) and respecting ancestral paths always guarantees us turangawaewae, someplace to stand. Fragmented by urban drift, not having access to my pepeha till later in life, caused invisible rupture to my cultural sense of belonging. I witness disconnection around me on multiple levels, made worse by prevailing Western cultural attitudes that ancestry and land is, for the most part, unnecessary to personal wellbeing. Going into someone else's lands without powhiri (ceremonial process meant to show respect), I should enact (or at least do parts of) protocols to respect our welcoming (or being welcomed). In many of the places, the Indigenous people, who would have been tangata whenua (people of the land), had literally been removed for centuries. Those who remained were either disempowered or treated tokenistically. Others simply didn't know how to do their rituals anymore . . . Complex because of oppressive colonial histories, it is now the reason why global Indigenous artists are so invested in meeting diverse needs.

In Aotearoa, we gather to share intimacy, knowledge and to connect on deeper levels. We call this ritual wananga, meaning time/space, a specific intention of gathering for shared and common goals. Māori unconsciously shift away from Western modalities, in the same way Native Americans might go to ceremony. We sing, dance, pray, speak, eat, sleep and remind ourselves of our beliefs and value systems to continue on into our daily contemporary lives. My wairua (spirit) leaps off Te Reinga, the departure point, towards Turtle Island. I have whakapapa links there, to Ruatepupuke II (my father's wharenui at the Field Museum in Chicago) and Paikea (the Whale Rider, a carved ancestral tekoteko) stored privately at the American Museum of Natural History in New York. Though my ancestors reside in other lands, I am living proof that their children, and their children's, children's children, have not forgotten. We will return.

Discussion questions: *haka*

1 Discuss the use of *kapa haka* pre-game performances of the All Blacks, the national rugby team of New Zealand, and those of Royal New Zealand Navy. Do you see this as a preservation of tradition, an opportunity for artistic expression, or as an act of appropriation?

2 Compared to aristocratic dance in other cultures such as *hula* in royal Hawaiian court, the characteristic stamping, zealous singing, and use of unbridled facial gestures in *kapa haka* could be perceived as lacking in "refinement." Is the *kapa haka* "anti-court" dance, or do its characteristics distinctively reflect the *mana* of a Māori chief?

3 *Kapa* translates as "to stand in row or rank." The *kapa haka* is performed in lines, which is culturally parallel to the formations used by military troops in other cultures. What does the use of horizontal line formations say about human nature, human order, one's own community, and the nature of confrontation in meeting the unknown?

5.4 The *gisalo*: pathos and pain of the Bosavi-Kaluli of Papua New Guinea

Key points: *gisalo*

1 The *gisalo* ceremony involves an invited group of guests from another longhouse community, who perform for the benefit of their hosts from dusk until dawn. In preparation, the hosts cook food and decorate themselves with paint, feathers, and shell jewelry.
2 The guests prepare by composing and rehearsing songs that explicitly evoke the relationship between the hosts and their environment that refer to familiar landmarks. These lyrics are metaphorically tied to the hosts' relationship with deceased community members, and their purpose is to make the hosts nostalgic, reflective, and able to mourn.
3 The guests recruit a chorus and four young men who will dance and sing solos in elaborate costumes. The men, who know that they will be burned, regard this to be a sign of their bravery, and their scars become a source of pride.
4 The sadness evoked by a performer's singing and dancing moves some in the audience to tears. In retribution for making them feel such grief, members of the host party are compelled to ritualistically burn the backs of the performers, who continue their performance while stoically bearing the pain.
5 The *gisalo* is considered to be most successful if the songs are moving, the weeping of the hosts is uncontrolled, and the dancers severely burned. Six weeks later, the two parties hold another *gisalo*, with the former host party as the guests, and vice versa.

> **The Kaluli regard the gisalo with enthusiasm. The dancer is full of splendor and pathos, because the beauty and sadness that he projects causes the people to burn him. The point is for the dancers to make the hosts burst into tears. The hosts burn them in revenge, angry for the suffering they have been made to feel.**
>
> **—Edward Schieffelin[37]**

The Bosavi-Kaluli

The rugged Southern Highlands Province of Papua New Guinea is a remote home to over four hundred ethnic groups, many of whom live in isolation from one another. The Kaluli and the Kosua, both subgroups of the Bosavi people, dwell in the verdant tropical rainforest of the Papuan Plateau on the slopes of Mt. Bosavi. Their first exposure to outsiders occurred in the 1930s when Australian explorers first entered the Highlands. In 1936, an airplane carrying anthropologists landed on the Plateau. It was the first time the Bosavi had ever heard an engine's roar and, in terror, they fled into the bush. Later, they learned from another clan that the mysterious buzzing had actually been airborne. Alarmed by the possibility of its return, their reaction was to prepare food and hold a big dance, just as they would do for a celebration. Edward Schieffelin, an anthropologist who lived with the Kaluli for two years in the 1960s, observed that when faced with illness or the arrival of the unknown, they customarily reacted by conducting *sing-sings* – ceremonies of singing and dancing.[38]

In Bosavi society, leadership is egalitarian; there is no chief, and decisions are made on a consensual basis. Elders are respected and arrange marriages. To compensate for the loss of a daughter's labor, "bride wealth" is paid, usually in the form of shells. Her husband then brings her to live in his longhouse, a communal living space that houses as many as fifteen families. The raised structure is built on posts as a deterrent to raids and pigs sleep under the house at night, keeping guard. Women and men share equal roles in finding food, which contributes to the egalitarian nature of their society. The self-sufficient clan participates together in cultivating gardens of bananas, sweet potatoes, breadfruit, and green vegetables, and in foraging for wild palm trees from which sago, a starch paste, is made. Fishing and hunting provide important sources of protein. Reciprocity and sharing food is crucial in Bosavi life. *Wi aledo* is a term for those who have shared meat, an important social obligation and a fundamental way of showing friendship and affection.[39] Girls are expected to take care of their younger siblings, especially by sharing food. Children are taught early on how to participate in social exchanges and learn to equate hunger with loneliness and abandonment. Reciprocity is a fundamental part of Bosavi ethos, especially in their *gisalo*, an all-night *sing-sing* between two clans involving singing, dancing, and cathartic inducement of deep grief and violent pathos.

The importance of music, birds, and water

In Oceania, fish, birds, and water are frequent inspirations for song lyrics. Songs may link a clan to their land by referencing geological locations associated with sacred "place spirits" that are believed to inhabit streams or large stones.[40] Many Bosavi melodic compositions are derived from bird songs that abound in the forest. Birdcalls are significant to the perception of time: those heard at certain times initiate specific daily activities, and their migration measures seasonal changes. There is a belief that some birds house the spirits of the dead and their songs are the voices of those spirits who have gone to the treetops. *Gisalo* songs – aural representations of loss and loneliness – use familiar ascending and descending melodic sound patterns that are found in birdcalls as well as in the movement of water. The names for the intervals between certain notes are inspired by the flow of a waterfall or a swirling pool at the bottom. The Bosavi cry in a melodic fashion and, at funerals, women improvise sung laments as they weep.[41]

Figure 5.11
A Bosavi girl helps her mother prepare *mumu*, a roasted pig feast. Girls learn how to keep their younger siblings fed and happy.
Image: Blake Everson.

Case study: The Bosavi myth of the *muni* bird

The societal importance of weeping is expressed in the myth of the *muni* bird, a dove with a high falsetto call. In the story, a sister takes her little brother fishing for crayfish. Although she was more successful in catching them, she refused to share any with him. His sadness at this breach in the normal behavior of a big sister left him lost and abandoned, causing his transformation into a *muni* bird. Whenever the call of the *muni* is heard, it is equated with the sad tears of the abandoned boy, who was denied food by his sister.

The *gisalo*

Some Bosavi *sing-sings* are cathartic rituals. The *gisalo* of the Kaluli, and the *balo* and *koluba* of the neighboring Kosua – sister tribe to the Kaluli – are especially similar in their use of song and dance to evoke grieving that results in ritually burning the performers. In the *gisalo* ceremony, a host group invites guests from another longhouse to their own for a *sing-sing*. In anticipation, the hosts cook food and elaborately decorate themselves with paint, feathers, and shell jewelry. It is the guests who take on much more preparation, since it is they who will perform from dusk until dawn for the benefit of their hosts. In advance, the guests recruit four male volunteers who will dance and sing solos, as well as a chorus, which composes several songs designed to elicit sadness in their hosts. The impact of a song depends upon surprise: the hosts must not know the music or the identity of the dancers until they arrive.[42]

Since the purpose of *gisalo* songs is to move a person to tears, the music and the singing have a plaintive quality, evocative of bird songs and water sounds. The term *gesema*, or "one feels sorrow or pity," should be heard in the singer's

Figure 5.12
A longhouse can house several families, and is made from durable rainforest wood that lasts fifty years.
Image: Blake Everson.

clear, unrestrained voice. The opening parts are sung alone and then the group joins as the soloist's voice "lifts over" the chorus. In his fieldwork in the 1980s, ethnomusicologist Steven Feld found that the Kaluli knew what singing in unison was because missionaries had tried to make them sing hymns that way. Yet they never sang in unison and no term existed for it. Instead, they contended that the song must flow like water, or be layered, like the sounds of birds in the forest.[43]

The lyrics of *gisalo* songs are composed to evoke the relationship between the hosts and their forest environment and refer to familiar landmarks such as boulders, trees, waterfalls, streams, and past natural disasters such as storms. Often the lyrics are metaphoric references to the hosts' relationship with deceased family. These poetic memories and associations evoke feelings of loneliness, grief, and nostalgia in the host audience, who begin to wail and weep. In retribution for generating such painful feelings of sorrow, the bereaved hosts become violent and vent their anger by thrusting flaming resin torches into the shoulders of the dancer singing the song. The dancer must continue his performance, seemingly oblivious to the commotion, and numb to the pain of the torch attacks that will continue throughout the night. The *gisalo* is considered to be most successful if the songs are moving, the hosts' weeping is uncontrolled, and the dancers are severely burned.[44]

The day of the *gisalo*, the guest drummers lead the procession as it emerges from the forest and goes toward the longhouse. As the two groups meet, an antagonistic move occurs on both sides: the hosts, decorated in paint and brandishing axes, charge down the ladder of the longhouse towards them, while the guests splash them with poison used for killing fish. Once this scuffle is over, the drummers go into the longhouse to play. The *gisalo* dancers and the chorus sit outside and inure themselves to repetitive crude scatological or sexual jokes made by the hosts in the attempt to make them laugh. (Schieffelin was told that if they did, the ceremony would turn out badly, but he never saw the dancers succumb to this temptation.)[45] When the evening descends, the torches in the longhouse are lit. As the chorus and dancers enter, the hosts continue to taunt them with jokes. Schieffelin's informant told him, "They act like that so they won't cry too soon."[46]

The four *gisalo* dancers trade off performing solo throughout the night. They dress identically and are trained to hide their personality so that, during the ceremony, their hosts might see in them the faces of their own now dead, who danced in past ceremonies.[47] The elaborate costuming is heavy, causing the dancer to move slowly

Figure 5.13
The solemn entry of the *gisalo* performers.
Image: Blake Everson.

and to be pitched forward, as if carrying a symbolic burden. Red ochre paint covers his face and body, and his eyes are outlined in a black mask with a thin white border. He wears a crown of black plumes, red bird of paradise feathers emerge from his armbands, red and yellow beads crisscross his chest, and his hips are encircled with a short cloth wrap. Another more practical part of his costume involves a long "cape" of fresh yellow palm leaves, which act as a sort of flame retardant. As further protection, his back is anointed with an aromatic salve of fermented vegetable resins. Women may be taken by his beauty as he dances and sings with his feathers and streamers swaying. One Kaluli bachelor confided to Feld that he wanted to sing a song so powerful "that if he sang it well a woman would follow him home from the ceremony, i.e., consent to elope," a social *coup* lending prestige to the visiting group.[48] Coupling between members of the two tribes can occur at *sing-sings*, and the burns a young man receives in the *gisalo* are regarded as a badge of credibility and manhood.[49]

As a dancer sings mournfully, he bounces slowly in place with his knees bent and his torso tilted forward. His arms stay fully extended at his sides, and he holds a long string attached to a mussel shell rattle called a *sob*. With every bend of the knee, the *sob* resounds lightly on the longhouse floor. The Kaluli claim that this bobbing movement of a dancer imitates that of the *wokwele*, a giant cuckoo dove that nests near waterfalls. As the dancer moves up and down, the rustling sounds from the palm streamers of his cape add to those of the singing and the rattle, creating an effect that the Kaluli say is "like a waterfall."[50] Like the bird of paradise, whose males are colorful while the females are inconspicuous, the plainly dressed Kaluli women add another layer to the soundscape with rhythmically hooting birdcalls inspiring the intricately costumed men to perform better.

Figure 5.14
Resting between dancing, singing, and being burned for his poignant performance.
Image: Blake Everson.

In his field notes from the 1960s, Schieffelin remarked that at "good" *gisalo*, when the ceremony reached its highest pitch as chain reactions of weeping occurred, the hosts would take leave of their senses.[51] A wailing host who was particularly moved by a song would not only try to extinguish a torch on the shoulders of the singer, but would burn the chorus as well. When these attacks became particularly violent, another less-agitated host member would not stop his fellow clan member, but instead would pour water onto the dancer's back, or shield him with leaves to mitigate the burns. While a dancer was being burned, the cadence of his song and the rhythm of his dance would stay constant.

According to Schieffelin, the ceremony ended as soon as the sounds of birdcalls were heard at dawn. As the guests filed out, they gave their hosts gifts of *su*, or compensation – mirrors, paint, knives, shell necklaces – to assuage the emotions of anger and sorrow and to insure the continuation of their friendship. Schieffelin noted that as some entered the forest towards home, they empathetically wailed to release their own sorrow over the emotional pain their singing and dancing had inflicted on their guests, despite their own injuries.[52]

To many outside the Kaluli culture, this purposeful burning of another human being may seem utterly barbaric and illogical. The Australian government certainly did and was concerned over a ritual that induced third-degree burns that took three to six weeks to heal. Edward Schieffelin was present when the government tried to ban the practice of burning in the 1960s. Afraid that they could not revenge their induced sadness by not being allowed to burn the dancers, the Bosavi brokered a deal in which they could use the torches, but only would touch them to the palm capes. At this chaperoned *gisalo*, Schieffelin witnessed the frustration that arose over being forbidden to perform their ritualistic actions. This resulted in a brawl in which the

Think about:
What explanation can be made for how a Bosavi-Kaluli man stoically endures being burned so severely?

Figure 5.15 (p. 150)
The burning of a performer.
Image: Blake Everson.

hosts brutally punched the dancers and threw gigantic flaming logs at them. Schieffelin observes:

> To move a person deeply with songs and then deny him the right to retaliate is to make him suffer helplessly, unable to return his pain . . . The grief and anger generate a tension during the performances that requires some sort of periodic release. Burning the skin was apparently how this happens.[53]

Once the administrator departed the area, the Kaluli were able to return to their regular practice.

An effective *gisalo* is in itself emblematic of the reciprocity inherent in Kaluli culture. The songs and dancing by the guests incite the weeping and violence of the hosts, and if this emotional crescendo is not reached, the ceremony is considered to be unsuccessful. By being burned, the guests take pride in the potency of their songs and dancing, and the grief of the hosts motivates them to reciprocate by staging an equally affecting *gisalo* for their guests. Schieffelin explains:

> Kaluli do not regard their ceremonies as expressing hostility. They see them as grand and exciting, deeply affecting, beautiful and sad, but not antagonistic. The songs are not presented as taunts or mockery of the listeners. Nevertheless, they are clearly experienced as provocative by Kaluli as they incite them to rage and violence. But the point is, it is a provocation among friends.[54]

Although the *gisalo* dancers endure painful burns, the performers are volunteers who are willing to play a potent role in evoking such profound sentiments of pathos, sorrow, and desire in the hearts of others. What makes it worth the ordeal is the prospect that, next time, they will be the ones to receive this cathartic release.

Figure 5.16
The scars of a seasoned Bosavi are badges of honor.
Image: Blake Everson.

Current trends

In Papua New Guinea today, the Bosavi-Kaluli still live in the remote Highlands region, where their relative isolation has enabled their *sing-sings* to continue.[55] These ceremonial gatherings continue to provide opportunities for trading, sharing resources, and encourage marriages between different groups. But the Bosavi, along with many indigenous groups in Papua New Guinea today, also perform their dances and music in large festivals. Every September, over a hundred groups have gathered at the Goroka *sing-sing* in the Eastern Highlands Province since 1957. At the Mount Hagen Cultural Show held every August in the Western Highlands Province, numerous regional groups converge to celebrate their cultural heritage. The music, dancing, and colorful costuming of the groups participating in these large *sing-sings* has become a huge draw for tourists. These national festivals are competitive and are an opportunity for performers to win prize money.

5.4 Exploration: excerpt from *The Sorrow of the Lonely and the Burning of the Dancers* by Edward Schieffelin[56]

Reprinted with kind permission from Palgrave Macmillan

Anthropologist Edward Schieffelin spent two years with the Kaluli, from 1966 to 1968. In this excerpt from his book, The Sorrow of the Lonely and the Burning of the Dancers, *he describes the entrance of the gisalo dancers and chorus into the torch-lit longhouse of their hosts, and the events that followed.*

A group of about twenty-five men came in, their faces downcast. They moved in a body quietly up the hall to the middle of the house. There they drew apart to reveal the resplendent figures of the four *gisalo* dancers in their midst. After a moment, all whispered "shhhh" and sat down, leaving one dancer standing alone. His body was painted in red ocher with black markings, his head crowned with feathery black cassowary plumes tipped with white cockatoo feathers. His chest was hung with shell necklaces; his wrists, arms, and legs decorated with bracelets . . . His whole figure was outlined against waving streamers of stripped yellow palm leaf, which shot up to shoulder height from below his belt and fell down past his feet: "breaking like a waterfall," as the Kaluli say. The dancer was slowly bouncing up and down in place, his eyes downcast, his manner withdrawn. A rattle made of mussel shells suspended from a string from his hand was clashing softly on the floor in time with his motion. As the house became quieter, his voice became audible, singing softly in a minor key.

Throughout the night, one by one the four dancers took turns dancing in place or moving up and down the small space in the middle of the hall, singing songs in company with the choruses seated at each end . . . As dancer followed dancer, the songs began to refer to specific places on the host's clan lands and recalled to the listeners' former houses and gardens and close relatives, now dead, who lived there. One dancer sang a song that alluded to the dead son of a senior man of the host community. The youth had died at a small house near a creek called Abo, and his soul was believed to have gone to the treetops in the form of a bird. The dancer sang:

> There is a *Kalo* bird calling by the Abo waterfall, juu-juu-juu.
> Do I hear my son's voice near the Abo spring?
> Perched, singing in a *dona* tree, is that bird my son?

The senior man, who was sitting with the crowd at the sidelines, brooding and withdrawn, suddenly became overcome with grief and burst into loud wails of anguish. Enraged, he jumped up, grabbed a torch from a bystander and jammed the burning end forcefully into the dancer's bare shoulder. With a tremendous noise, all the youths and young men of the host community jumped into the dancing space, stamping and yelling and brandishing axes. The dancer was momentarily lost in a frightening pandemonium of shadowy figures, torches, and showers of sparks. Showing no sign of pain, he moved slowly across the dancing space; the chorus burst into song. The senior man broke away from the crowd and ran out the back door of the house to wail on the veranda. This scene was repeated over and over from dancer to dancer during the course of the night.

Discussion questions: *gisalo*

1 The Bosavi have not experienced much interference by outside influences due to the isolated nature of their mountain home. Do you see remoteness as something that serves and protects a culture, and if so, how long do you think this phenomenon can last in a world that has become so globalized?
2 Pain is something many people avoid, yet in the *gisalo* of the Kaluli, it is integral to a cathartic and emotional exchange between two communities and serves as a badge of honor. How does this presence of pain, which is endured in a non-trance state, compare with anything similar in gaining valor in your society?
3 When the Bosavi were met with unfamiliar, unsettling circumstances – such as witnessing the arrival of the first airplane to their area – their reaction was to hold a ceremonial dance. What does this say about their relationship between emotion and physicality?

Notes

1 Buck, Elizabeth, *Paradise Remade*, 105.
2 Bingham, Hiram, *A Residence of Twenty-One Years in the Sandwich Islands*, 81.
3 Buck, 35.
4 Campbell, Jeff Logan, and Glenda Bendure, *Hawai'i, the Big Island*, 236.
5 Bingham, 32.
6 Imada, Adria L. "Hawaiians on Tour: Hula Circuits through the American Empire," 117.
7 Buck, 113.
8 Kaeppler, Adrienne L. "Music in Hawaii in the Nineteenth Century," 114.
9 Buck, 108.
10 Kamehiro, Stacy L. "Hawai'i at the World Fairs, 1867–1893," 1.
11 Barrère, Dorothy B. "The Hula in Retrospect," 58.
12 Emerson, Nathan Bright, *Unwritten Language of Hawaii*, 15.
13 Ibid., 38–39.
14 Mugge, Robert. "*Kumu Hula*: Keepers of a Culture," Film.
15 Kaeppler, Adrienne L. "The Beholder's Share: Viewing Music and Dance in a Globalized World," 191–192.
16 Ibid., 12.
17 Beechey, Captain F. W., *Narrative of a Voyage to the Pacific*, Vol. II, 424.
18 Pollenz, 226.
19 Lang, Leslie. "Making Hula History," 2.
20 Mitchell, Hillary, and Maui John Mitchell. *History of Māori*, 216–217.
21 Best, Elsdon. "The Diversions of the Whare Tapere," 36.
22 Ibid., 40.
23 Awatere, Arapeta. *Awatere: A Soldier's Story*, 144–145.
24 Beaglehole, J. C. *The Endeavour Journal of Joseph Banks, 1768–1771*, Vol. II, 169.
25 Beaglehole, Vol. II, 29.
26 Youngerman, Suzanne. "Māori Dancing Since the Eighteenth Century," 79.
27 McNab, Robert, Ed. *Historical Records of New Zealand*, 440.
28 Van Meijl, Toon. "To Sing Is to Be Happy," 279.
29 Van Meijl, 284.
30 Ibid., 277–278.
31 Smith, Valance. "*Kapa haka* in the 21st Century," 5.
32 Arapeta, Awatere. "Review of Barry Mitcalf, 'Maori Poetry: The Singing Word,'" 513.
33 Ibid., 514.
34 Personal communication with author, December 12, 2016.
35 www.blackgrace.co.nz/
36 Gray, Jack. "Ko Mitimiti Ahau: I am (of) the Place, Mitimiti," 33–36.
37 Schieffelin, Edward. *The Sorrow of the Lonely*, 24.
38 Ibid., 163.
39 Ibid., 65.
40 Wolffram, Paul. "The Pacific Islands," 249.
41 Feld, Steven. "Flow like a Waterfall," 22–23.
42 Schieffelin, 165.
43 Feld, 34–36.
44 Knauft, Bruce M. "Ritual Form and Permutation in New Guinea," 324.
45 Schieffelin, 169.
46 Ibid., 174.
47 Ibid., 175–176.
48 Feld, 29.
49 Personal Communication, Blake Everson.
50 Feld, 32–33.
51 Schieffelin, 166–167.
52 Ibid., 193–194.
53 Ibid., 204.
54 Ibid., 202.
55 Expert guide Blake Everson hiked three days to get to a Bosavi community, where he witnessed the *sing-sings* seen in these photographs.
56 Schieffelin, Edward. *The Sorrow of the Lonely and the Burning of the Dancers*, 23–23.

Bibliography

Visual sources

YouTube

"Hula Hālau O Kekuhi at the 2011 Merrie Monarch," YouTube video, 6:07, posted by
    "Local Kine Tracks," July 30, 2015, www.youtube.com/watch?v=5JWUWdKB2Jk
"Papua New Guinea Sing-Sing," YouTube video, 5:10, posted by "Origin Papua New
    Guinea," March 4, 2015, www.youtube.com/watch?v=wELoh23JLV0
"Te Waka Huia Haka 86," YouTube video, 4:02, posted by "RAKZ 05," February 14,
    2014, www.youtube.com/watch?v=pVnMmOnRjqY

Film

Mugge, Robert. "Kumu Hula": Keepers of a Culture. Film, 85 minutes. Honolulu:
    Mug-Shot Productions, distributed by Winstar Entertainment, 1989.

Written sources

Arapeta, Awatere. "Review of Mitcalf, Barry. 'Māori Poetry: The Singing Word.'"
    Journal of the Polynesian Society, 84, No. 4 (1975): 513–514.
Awatere, Arapeta. Awatere: A Soldier's Story. Wellington: Huia Publishers, 2003.
Balme, Christopher B. "Dressing the Hula: Iconography, Performance and Cultural
    Identity Formation in Late Nineteenth Century Hawaii." Paideuma: Mitteilungen zur
    Kulturkunde, Frobenius Institute. Bd. 45 (1999): 233–255. Stable URL: www.jstor.
    org/stable/40341772.
Barrère, Dorothy B., Mary Kawena Pukui, and Marion Kelly. "The Hula in Retrospect."
    In Hula: Historical Perspectives, edited by Bonnie T. Clause, 1-66. Honolulu:
    Department of Anthropology, Bernice Pauahi Bishop Museum, 1980.
Beaglehole, J. C. The Endeavour Journal of Joseph Banks, 1768–1771, Vol. I and II.
    Sydney: Angus and Robertson, 1962.
Beckwith, Martha W. "The Hawaiian Hula-Dance." The Journal of American Folklore,
    Vol. 29, No. 113 (July–September, 1916): 409–412. Stable URL: www.jstor.org/
    stable/534686
Beechey, Captain F. W. Narrative of a Voyage to the Pacific, Vol. 1 and 11. London:
    Henry Colburn and Richard Bentley, 1831.
Best, Elsdon. "The Diversions of the Whare Tapere: Some Account of the Various
    Games, Amusements, and Trials of Skill Practiced by the Māori in Former
    Times." Transactions and Proceedings of the Royal Society of New Zealand,
    1868–1961, Vol. 34 (1901): 34–69. http://rsnz.natlib.govt.nz/volume/rsnz_34/
    rsnz_34_00_000540.html.
Bingham, Hiram. A Residence of Twenty-One Years in the Sandwich Islands.
    Canadaigua, NY: H.D. Goodwin, 1855.
Buck, Elizabeth. Paradise Remade: The Politics of Culture and History in Hawaii.
    Philadelphia: Temple University Press, 1994.
Campbell, Jeff Logan, and Glenda Bendure. Hawai'i, the Big Island. New York:
    Lonely Planet, 2009.
Emerson, Nathan Bright. Unwritten Language of Hawaii: The Sacred Songs of Hula.
    Washington, DC: Smithsonian Institution, Bureau of American Ethnology, Bulletin
    38, 1909.
Everson, Blake. May 28, 2016. Personal Interview.
Feld, Steven. "Flow like a Waterfall: The Metaphors of Kaluli Music Theory."
    Yearbook for Traditional Music, Vol. 13 (1981): 22–47, Stable URL: www.jstor.org/
    stable/768356.
Gardiner, Wira. Haka: A Living Tradition. Auckland: Hodder Moa, 2007.
Gray, Jack. "Ko Mitimiti Ahau: I am (of) the Place, Mitimiti." Dance Research Journal,
    Vol. 48, No. 1 (April 2016): 33–36, Copyright © Congress on Research in Dance
    2016. DOI: http://dx.doi.org/10.1017/S0149767716000085.
Imada, Adria L. "Hawaiians on Tour: Hula Circuits Through the American Empire."
    American Quarterly, Vol. 56, No. 1 (March, 2004): 111–149. Stable URL: www.
    jstor.org/stable/40068217.

Kaeppler, Adrienne L. "Acculturation in Hawaiian Dance." *Yearbook of the International Folk Music Council*, Vol. 4, 25th Anniversary Issue (1972): 38–46, Stable URL: www.jstor.org/stable/767671.

Kaeppler, Adrienne L. "The Beholder's Share: Viewing Music and Dance in a Globalized World." *Ethnomusicology*, Vol. 54, No. 2 (2010): 185–201. Stable URL: www.jstor.org/stable/10.5406/ethnomusicology.54.2.0185

Kaeppler, Adrienne L. "Music in Hawaii in the Nineteenth Century." In *Dance in Africa, Asia, and the Pacific: Selected Readings*, edited by Judy Van Zile, 97–121. New York: MSS Information Company, 1976.

Kamehiro, Stacy L. "Hawai'i at the World Fairs, 1867–1893." October, 2011. http://worldhistoryconnected.press.illinois.edu/8.3/forum_kamehiro.html

Kealiinohomoku, Joann W. "Hula Space and Its Transmutations." In *Dance as a Cultural Heritage*, edited by Betty True Jones, 11–21. Honolulu: Congress for Research on Dance Proceedings, 1978.

Knauft, Bruce M. "Ritual Form and Permutation in New Guinea: Implications of Symbolic Process for Socio-Political Evolution." *American Ethnologist*, Vol. 12, No. 2 (May, 1985): 321–340. Stable URL: www.jstor.org/stable/644223.

Lang, Leslie. "Making Hula History." *Hana Hou!* Vol. 4, No. 4 (August/September 2003). http://www.hanahou.com/pages/magazine.asp?Action=DrawArticle&ArticleID=238&MagazineID=13

McNab, Robert. *Historical Records of New Zealand, Vol. I*. Wellington: John Makay, Pub., 1908.

Mitchell, Hillary, and Maui John Mitchell. *History of Māori of Nelson and Marlborough*. Wellington: Huia Publishers, 2004.

Pollenz, Philippa. "Changes in the Form and Function of Hawaiian Hulas." *American Anthropologist, New Series*, Vol. 52, No. 2 (April–June, 1950): 225–234. URL: www.jstor.org/stable/664924.

Reiny, Samson. "Performing Arts." *Hana Hou*! Vol. 14, No. 2 (May 2011). http://www.hanahou.com/pages/magazine.asp?Action=DrawArticle&ArticleID=970&MagazineID=61

Rowe, Sharon Māhealani. "We Dance for Knowledge." *Dance Research Journal*, Vol. 40, No. 1 (Summer, 2008): 31–44. Stable URL: www.jstor.org/stable/20527591.

Sakamoto, Hiromi. "Kapa Haka and Its Educational Meanings Today in Aotearoa New Zealand." In *Proceedings of the International Indigenous Development Research Conference, 2012*, edited by Daniel Hikuroa, 95–101. Auckland: Ngä Pae o te Märamatanga, 2012.

Schieffelin, Edward. *The Sorrow of the Lonely and the Burning of the Dancers*. New York: Palgrave Macmillan, 1976; 2nd ed., 2005.

Smith, Valance. "Kapa haka in the 21st Century." *Te Ara* – the Encyclopedia of New Zealand, updated 20-Oct-14. URL: www.TeAra.govt.nz/en/kapa-haka-Māori-performing-arts/page-5.

Stillman, Amy Ku'uleialoha. "Globalizing Hula." *Yearbook for Traditional Music*, Vol. 31 (1999): 57–66. Stable URL: www.jstor.org/stable/767973.

Turner, Stephen. "A History Lesson: Captain Cook Finds Himself in a State of Nature." In *Voyages and Beaches, Pacific Encounters 1769–1840*, edited by Alex Calder, Jonathan Lamb, and Bridget Orr, 89–99. Honolulu: University of Hawai'i Press, 1999, Stable URL: www.jstor.org/stable/j.ctt6wr2c5.8.

Van Meijl, Toon. "To Sing Is to Be Happy: The Dynamics of Contemporary Māori Musical Practices." In *Austronesian Soundscapes: Performing Arts in Oceania and Southeast Asia*, edited by Birgit Abels, 278–294. Amsterdam: Amsterdam University Press, 2011. Stable URL: www.jstor.org/stable/j.ctt46mvnd.19.

Wolffram, Paul. "The Pacific Islands." *Music and Dance Performance*, (2013): 248–259. Published by: University of Hawai'i Press. Stable URL: www.jstor.org/stable/j.ctt6wqh08.25.

Youngerman, Suzanne. "Māori Dancing Since the Eighteenth Century." *Ethnomusicology*, Vol. 18, No 1 (January 1974): 75–100. www.jstor.org/stable/850061.

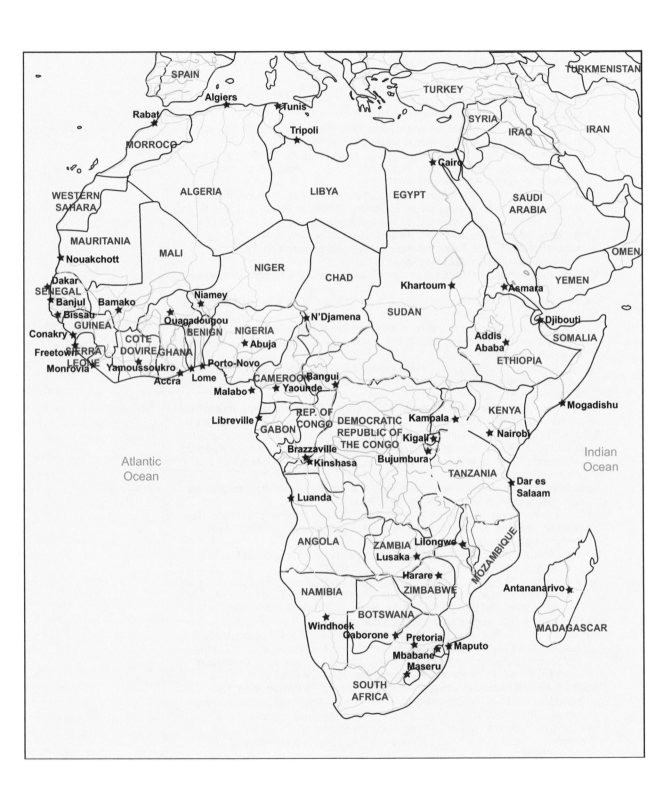

Africa
Fertility festivals, death ceremonies, and ancestor worship

There is always something new coming out of Africa.

—Pliny the Elder

6.1 Overview

In numerous African societies, life cycles – from birth, to death, to the afterlife – are all significant rites of passage. This chapter examines the courtship rituals of the Wodaabe, the masked funeral traditions of the Dogon and the Mossi, and Yoruba ancestor worship.

The nomadic Wodaabe converge annually for the *Geerewol* Festival, a sort of beauty contest in which young male dancers are judged for their good looks and charm by young women. Regardless if one wins or not, dancing at this gathering creates an atmosphere conducive to sexual union, and hopefully, to more babies. On the other side of the spectrum, funeral ceremonies are enormously crucial to the Dogon and the Mossi. To insure balance in the community, the Dogon *dama* is a collective send-off for important men in the community, in which descendants honor the departed through masked dances to appease any wandering spirits. Similarly, in Mossi ideology, after a person dies, spiritually charged masks, dancing, and drumming at funerals are essential in pointing the soul of the deceased toward the route to the afterworld. This sacred pathway, which the Mossi believe was taken by their ancestors when they descended from the sky to the earth, is called *yaaba sooré*.

For the Yoruba, the departed who have attained ancestor status descend to visit the living, manifesting themselves as *Egungun* in magnificent masks. As they dance in front of their descendants at colorful festivals in their honor, they are at once revered and feared. *Egungun* are conduits between heaven and earth, and give advice, grant blessings, or punish wrongdoers. In their elaborate costumes, *Egungun* demonstrate the power of ancestors to their descendants through dance.

6.2 The *Geerewol* Festival of the Wodaabe: judging male charm and beauty

Key points: the *Geerewol* festival

1 The nomadic Wodaabe, a sub-set of the large Fulani tribe, are known as "people of the taboos" because of the strict tribal codes in their daily lives that govern seasonal activities and behavior toward family members.

2 The Wodaabe are devoted to their herds of cattle and are great healers of both livestock and humans. Although they are derided by those who call them "cattle Fulani," they cherish their way of life.

3 To the Wodaabe, physical beauty, charm, patience, and fortitude are signs of potency and power, and are exceedingly valued. They are admittedly vain and consider themselves to be "the most beautiful people in the world."

4 Fertility is a crucial to the Wodaabe, and having more babies is fundamental to the tribe's survival. Several opportunities are offered for this even before an arranged marriage occurs.

5 As many as 1,000 Wodaabe converge at the annual *Geerewol* Festival, a beauty contest in which male dancers are the objects of desire, and are judged for their beauty and charm by young women. Amorous assignations occur, wife-swapping is rife, and marriages are made.

I wandered about to watch dancers putting on their elaborate makeup . . . I found this scene quite miraculous: men applying rouge and lipstick under an almost full moon, in preparation for a contest to decide which one of them was most nearly perfect.[1]
—Robert Gardner, filmmaker of *Deep Hearts*

The Wodaabe – nomadic shepherds who travel with their families and *zebu* cattle throughout the Sahel steppe in southern Niger – are known as "people of the taboos." This label refers to the strict codes that govern their seasonal activities, location of camp, care of animals, and social conduct. They are a sub-tribe of extensive Fulani, which is one of the largest in Africa, and was the first to convert to Islam in the sixteenth century. Although the Wodaabe are not as devoutly Muslim as the Fulani, the two groups speak the Fulfulde language, do not marry outside of the parent tribe, and follow the same moral tenets. Ideal behavior should incorporate patience and fortitude: *munyal*; self-control and reserve: *semtuudum*; and intelligence: *hakkilo*. Courage, hospitality, and confidence are all desirable traits as well, and keeping one's emotions hidden is especially important. Physical beauty and charm – exceedingly valued by the Wodaabe – is a sign of potency, life force, and power. They proudly declare themselves to be the most beautiful people in the world.

What some might perceive as vanity is a duty in Wodaabe life. After checking his herds in the morning, a young man takes out his hand mirror and inspects his appearance. An application of black make-up around the eyes is required, followed by black lipstick. Traditionally, men attend to their own beautification and adornment more than women do, and are expected to keep up their appearances. Self-grooming begins in early childhood. Despite their healthy self-esteem, non-nomadic Fulani often call these herders Wodaabe-Bororo – a derogatory term meaning "cattle Fulani." As herdsmen, they are expert in creating medicines from herbs and tree bark to heal their livestock, as well as to craft love potions for people. Fertility is valued in Wodaabe society, since more babies increase their population.

After a child is born, an arranged marriage called a *koobgal* is brokered between cousins of the same lineage. However, before marriage, teenagers have considerable sexual freedom and follow a convention called *waldeebe*, which translates as "cousin." A young woman who has not yet had her *koobgal* is free to simultaneously court two of her male cousins – one who is her betrothed and one whom she finds appealing. After the *koobgal* wedding, if the wife is willing, whenever the cousin visits their camp his host will invite his *waldeebe* to sleep with her. Instead of arousing feelings of jealousy between male cousins, this arrangement generates sentiments of generosity and rapport.

In a *koobgal* marriage, the wife is given a dowry of cattle by her husband's family and then moves to their camp. After the *koobgal* obligations are met, the practice of polygamy in Wodaabe society permits men to have as many as four wives. "Wife-stealing" is a frequent occurrence, especially during tribal gatherings between two lineages. While a wife has the freedom to leave her marriage, she will not be

Think about:
Why would the nomadic lifestyle of some be looked down upon by others who have chosen to "settle"?

Figure 6.1
A Wodaabe man attending the *Geerewol* Festival.
Image: Alfred Weidinger.

taken back into her lineage. When "love marriages" called *teegal* are formed, they are usually between different lineages and are a looser agreement. If a woman gets pregnant and is not yet married, she will immediately marry her intended *koobgal* husband. The child will live with them, but is considered to be of the other man's lineage. Any jealousies that occur between wife-stealers or multiple wives in this seemingly wide and complex net of situations are carefully hidden within what the Wodaabe call a "deep heart."

Because the Wodaabe are frequently in migration and travel in smaller family units, two lineages converge in large numbers to celebrate the annual *Geerewol* Festival. Occurring at the end of the rainy season, usually in September, this weeklong gathering of dancing brings together as many as a thousand Wodaabe in a beauty contest. Young men performing in the three dances – *ruume*, *yaake*, and the *geerewol* itself – will be judged for their attractiveness and charm by young women from the other lineage. Regardless if one wins or not, this atmosphere is conducive to sexual union. Amorous assignations occur, wife-swapping is rife, and marriages are made. Women in a *koobgal* marriage who have remained childless may be with any man they choose, in hopes of getting pregnant. Carrying a child overrides any marital fidelity and is condoned by the community.

The large amount of cosmetic and sartorial preening by the men for the dances in the *Geerewol* Festival is time-consuming, exacting, and emphatically aimed at making themselves devastatingly irresistible. Using personal hand mirrors, men spend hours together making up their faces. For both the *ruume* and the *yaake*, the facial make-up is saffron yellow – the color of magic. Mixed with butter from special clay called *makkara*, it is then applied as a base. A contrasting tone is then drawn vertically down the nose, accentuating the length of their lean faces. To obtain the black make-up for their mouths, roasted egret's bones are ground into a black powder and mixed with butter. Only this concoction allows for the undulating vibrations of their lips in the dances, which is so appealing to the judges. Those who "cheat" by using another substance – such as the toxic black residue found inside burnt-out double AA batteries – won't get the same winning results as those who use only the burnt-bone lipstick. Wodaabe contestants say that the ability to finesse the vibrations of their lips comes from the supernatural magic of the mixture.

The opening of the *Geerewol* Festival begins with men parading their camels, which are akin to sports cars, connoting

Figure 6.2
Men gathering in the circular *ruume* dance, surrounded by curious women who closely observe them.
Image: Alfred Weidinger.

wealth and flash. Women are great judges of the attractiveness of these beasts as well and will sing songs about their grace and swiftness as they pet them. The first dance of the festival, the *ruume* ("spending the rainy season"), is a dance of welcome by day and ardor by night. Facing inward in a large circle, the men dance and sing call-and-respond chants that wax poetically about love and the beauty of women, as well as broadcast their own masculine charms. They clap continuously in a duple meter, weaving diverse rhythms together as they dance, shuffling in a counterclockwise circle. The young women surround them in a larger circle, dancing the same steps but at a slower pace, which allows them a chance to view the men. When the *ruume* occurs in the evening, if a woman wants to get to know one of them better, she approaches his back and slowly draws her fingers down his spine. In turn, he gives her a sign and they will later meet for a tryst beneath the night sky.

The *yaake* ("ancient dance") is a contest in which a man's charm is judged by three women. Charm is different than beauty – it is *personality*. The Wodaabe believe that having no charm is worse than being ugly. A man who is physically imperfect can make up for this with charm, especially if he is a great dancer. *Yaake* contestants have yellow faces as in the *ruume*, but geometrical designs and dots are drawn on with white paint, made from bird guano. The men's long, intricate braids cascade down their shoulders from beneath white turbans, each topped with a vertical ostrich feather, and elaborately embroidered tunics cover their tall, lean bodies. Leather amulets worn around their necks contain inspiring words from the Quran, as well as love potions and scents to entice the female judges.

In the *yaake*, men of one lineage dance together in one line shoulder to shoulder and rock up and down on the balls of their feet, trying to appear as tall as possible. Rhythmically turning their heads from right to left as they dance, the contestants exude their beauty, energy, and charm to three unmarried women from the opposite lineage. The Wodaabe say that a good marriage is made through the eyes, and in

Think about:
Is it possible that Wodaabe men feel the same pressure of societal norms to exude charm and take pains over their appearance that many women in Western societies do?

Figure 6.3 (p. 161)
Wodaabe man in yellow *yaake* make-up.
Image: Alfred Weidinger.

Figure 6.4
Men are judged for their charm as they dance in the *yaake*.
Image: Alfred Weidinger.

the *yaake*, certain desired eye movements must be proffered. If a man can show off the whites of his eyes, focusing straight ahead with one while the other eye rolls around in its socket, the female judges will find him most alluring. Continuous broad smiling and showing one's white teeth is another way to attract attention. Although the men have been well reviewed in advance, the three female judges cannot look directly at the object of their desire, so with downcast eyes, they slowly approach the man they have collectively picked to be the winner. When they stop in front of him, their choice is made clear to the audience, who cheers for the young man's win in this very tough competition of charm.

The culmination of the *Geerewol* Festival is the eponymous *geerewol* itself, a dance for as many as fifty in which only the most confident and handsome men from two lineages compete. Three unmarried women, picked for their own beauty, will judge the beauty of the men from the opposite lineage. Out of the finalists, only three men will be picked as "a bull," a prestigious status. The red facial make-up for the *geerewol* symbolizes war, aggression, and power. Even though no violence occurs, this is a fierce competition and rates as the most important dance in Wodaabe culture. One lineage is host to the other and they alternate from year to year. When they converge, competing men from the other clan don't eat food from the hosts, fearing that they could be poisoned – and the herbal magic they carry wards off any bad spells that could be cast by their hosts. The guest clan performs by day and the hosts at night.

In the *geerewol* men wear colorful long fabric wrapped tightly around their lower body, topped by a white apron. Strands of long white beads crisscross their bare chest, and ankle bracelets of bells are worn. White turbans are adorned with vertical ostrich plumes and black leather headbands decorated with cowrie shells, and

Figure 6.5
When performing the *geerewol*, the men face into the sun so that their beauty may be better seen.
Image: Liba Taylor/Alarmy Stock Photos.

beaded strands frame their red faces. Side by side in a long horizontal line, the dancers face the sun in order to show off their beauty, despite the heat. For hours, they smile relentlessly, displaying their milk-white teeth as they tread up and down in a line. Elder women from the opposite lineage approach them, admonishing them to dance better while older men straighten their lines. Gradually, some drop out of the ranks and the final contestants remove their ostrich plumes, replacing them with a white ox tail. The horizontal dancing line forms again, but this time it is much more energetic and the percussion from their ankle bells intensifies. Jumping repeatedly in unison, they propel the line forward while rhythmically swinging a *jalel*, a ceremonial axe. When the time comes for each of the three women to pick her bull, the men stand in line, bobbing up and down, as they puff out their cheeks, pucker their lips, and roll their eyes independently from one another. As each judge approaches the line with downcast eyes and her hand demurely framing her face, they energetically send her air kisses while rocking

Figure 6.6
Wodaabe female judges pick the most beautiful men.
Image: Alfred Weidinger.

back and forth onto their tiptoes. Once close to the object of her desire, her right arm begins to sway slowly. In a graceful gesture, she swings her arm up toward one and picks her "bull." Those men chosen for their beauty will be held in high esteem for the rest of their lives.

Current trends

Nomadic life for the Wodaabe is a treasured existence, but challenging. Two decades of severe droughts beginning in the 1970s resulted in catastrophic losses of *zebu* cattle and the subsequent cancellation of several *geerewol* gatherings for years at a time. Consequentially, many Wodaabe men have been forced to abandon life in the bush for the city in an attempt to earn money to replace their cattle. There is also the inevitable draw of urban life for the younger generations of Wodaabe. While some have had to resort to more menial labor, other Wodaabe have depended upon their handiwork in embroidered tunics and jewelry, and dance to make a living outside the bush. In urban areas, public Wodaabe dances are held, and at *Geerewol* Festivals, foreign photographers or filmmakers may record them, but for a fee. Ironically, those opting for city life who disappointed their parents by abandoning life in the bush are often able to give support by replacing their cattle when drought hits. In the face of these hardships, life for the Wodaabe is fragile. But for those who are able to maintain their traditions of beauty and adornment, as well as populate their tribe through the rituals of charm, the "people of the taboo" live a unique nomadic life, full of beauty.

6.2 Exploration: excerpt from *Nomads Who Cultivate Beauty* by Mette Bovin

Anthropologist Mette Bovin, who has studied the Wodaabe for over three decades, gives her explanations of why the Wodaabe are more vain than other peoples of the region, and why male beauty is predominantly cultivated.

The males show their feathers to impress others: "the peacock spreads his fan." The females are less colorful than the males among birds, so too within the human group: Wodaabe men are even more colorful than Wodaabe women. They show their beauty in the impressive dance performances that are also competitions for the most beautiful girls and for offspring – children to perpetuate the family.

When you live surrounded by such an impressive natural environment as the Sahel . . . there is always a danger of confusion between human beings and animals. It is very important to "stamp" culture on your body, in the form of tattoos, paints, embroidered clothes, jewelry, etc. so as to not be mistaken for an animal. All the fine cultural items of the Wodaabe nomads serve the triple purpose of (1) providing aesthetic satisfaction, (2) being a defense against nature, and (3) protecting against the animal quality in oneself. Self-control and self-discipline add to this.

Why do nomads put on more jewelry and adornments than peasant farmers of the same country? Nomads walk and ride animals in open landscapes . . . in an upright position. These human beings are very "vertical" in an enormous open environment with very few people. The *yaake* dance and the *jeerewol* dance are both extreme examples of male "vertical posture." Farmers of the same country work with bent backs, hoeing the fields. This V-shaped body position makes it harder to wear jewelry or to care about vanity.

The Wodaabe are a "Fourth World People," a small and threatened ethnic minority, numbering only some two to three percent of all the Fulani in Africa. Wodaabe extravagance is part of their *cultural resistance*. Dances, songs, and beauty parades are cultural weapons against the increasing marginalization of nomads everywhere in the world. The pressures on nomads to "settle down and become civilized . . ." are heavy and very real . . . Others wish them to stay in real villages or cities, with fixed addresses and easy access for government officials. In order to avoid the unfavorable power relation between cultivators and nomads, the Wodaabe stress their own old "nobleness," their purity and their aristocratic non-slave background. Being red-skinned, slim, and handsome is part of that identity.

In order to win an extra woman/wife, a man is forced to be beautiful. He must be handsome, pretty, attractive, well-proportioned, slim, long-limbed, charming, symmetrical, perfect in body and appearance in the movements of the body and in "performance" – in short, have style. He should have elegance, wakefulness, a gentleman-like quality and be generous, unselfish . . . and a woman who wishes to change partners is obliged to be beautiful, slim, charming, etc. So that is one way of understanding male vanity.

Discussion questions: the *Geerewol* Festival

1 In the Wodaabe tribe, physical beauty is valued more in men than in women, and male self-grooming begins in early childhood. How does this contrast with behavior in Western society?
2 How do values of virginity differ among cultures? Discuss the sociological, moral, and traditional tropes that exist in terms of this issue.
3 Discuss Mette Bovin's observation that Wodaabe extravagance—make-up, jewelry, etc. is actually a form of cultural resistance. Can you equate this concept to the adornment of other cultures?

6.3 The Dogon *dama* ceremony: a collective funeral ritual

Key points: the *dama*

1 The Dogon live high up in the Bandigiara Cliffs (Mali), where they fled centuries ago to escape aggressive slave traders on horseback. The remoteness of the cliffs allowed the Dogon to resist conversion to Islam, as well as French colonizers and missionaries during the nineteenth century.
2 Important personages in Dogon communities are Hogons, elder spiritual leaders presiding over Dogon agricultural and religious services, and blacksmiths, who make tools and also carve the unique Dogon masks essential in funeral ceremonies.
3 Three main gods exist in Dogon cosmology: Amma, the sky god; Nommo, the water god; and Lebe, the serpent god. All three deities are accessed by the living via one's ancestors, who act as intermediaries in negotiating the welfare of their descendants.
4 Funeral ceremonies are crucial to the Dogon, who believe that *nyama* – the soul, or life force – is released at the moment of death and must be contained so that no harm comes to the living. The *dama* is a collective masked funeral celebration occurring approximately every twelve years. The departed are honored through masked dances that appease any wandering spirits and mitigate the negative effects of the release of *nyama*. The ritual of the *dama* allows the souls to be freed to the afterworld.
5 Preparations for the *dama* are secret and enacted by members of *awa* – an exclusive male masking society. The mask-wearers are called *èmna*, who dance for the public for several days during the *dama*. Women and children watch from a distance. After a *dama* crops should be plentiful, women fertile, and the society in perfect harmony.

All men shall climb the ladder of death.

—African proverb

The Dogon are an ancient people living in the Bandigiara Cliff region, located in the Republic of Mali. This sandstone escarpment, roughly 125 miles wide and ranging as high as 1,500 feet, is studded with natural caverns, ravines, and topped by a vast plateau. Its geographic isolation made it a perfect place of refuge for the Dogon, who fled to this elevated region in the fourteenth century to escape from aggressive Muslim slave traders on horseback. They found protection in caves and dwellings hewn into the rock by the Tellem, earlier settlers who were displaced by the Dogon. The remote nature of the cliffs allowed the Dogon to resist conversion to Islam and later helped curtail their contact with French colonialists and missionaries during the nineteenth century. The French were surprised by the fierce resistance of the Dogon, who were steeled by years of avoiding Islamization, and led punitive expeditions, including massacres, to break their fierce resistance. They were one of the last peoples to lose their independence to French rule.[2] Today, 600,000 Dogon live in approximately 700 villages scattered high on the plateau, or the rocky region at the foot of the cliff.

Case study: The "Scramble for Africa"

In 1884, the African continent was divided up among the rival European powers at the Berlin Conference, otherwise known as the "Scramble for Africa." Without regard for tribal lands or affiliations, and with not even one African present, the "dark continent" was partitioned and colonialized by various European countries, save for Liberia and Ethiopia. Africans were forced to labor in the diamond, rubber, copper, cocoa, and cotton industries. In the process of clearing land for settlements, thousands of native people, such as the Herero and the Congolese, were slaughtered.[3] Joseph Conrad's *Heart of Darkness* (1889) was one way that Europeans learned about colonial injustice and, in an effort to mitigate growing public concern, Colonial Expositions showed off the wonders of wild animals and indigenous people to curious Europeans. Many African nations finally gained their independence in the 1950s and 1960s.

Dogon ideology and cosmology

As a means of maintaining order and balance, Dogon philosophy and religion are reflected in many aspects of daily life. An important philosophy is dualism: the concept that all things come in pairs. Twins are indicators of fertility, so mothers bearing them are highly honored, as are the twins themselves. Twin-ship is associated with harmony, as is the existence of opposite forces. Perpetual alternation of opposing forces in the universe – wet/dry, hot/cold, east/west, male/female – is dualism in perfect balance. The alternation of these pairs is represented by decorative zigzag or serpentine motifs called *ozu tonnolo* that are prominently displayed on religious altars and in weavings, carvings, and choreography.[4]

Three main gods exist in Dogon cosmology. Amma, the sky god, is the supreme creator. The first being created by Amma was Nommo, the water god, who the Dogon call upon in times of drought. Lebe, the serpent god, is an underworld deity, representing fertility and the earth.[5] A Dogon myth tells the tale of Lebe, one of the eight original Dogon ancestors who lived in a time before death existed. Lebe was the first to die and be buried. When his family decided to migrate, they dug up his grave to take his bones with them. Instead of a finding a human skeleton, they discovered a live snake in its place, which they interpreted as evidence of Lebe's magical regenerative powers. Therefore, an altar to Lebe is found in every village.

The Dogon are animists, who adhere to the belief that animals have souls and that other entities such as rocks, plants, and trees possess spirits. They respect the clairvoyant knowledge that animals possess and consequently their hunters are respected men of great mystical powers, capable of transforming themselves into bats, bees, snakes, or lions while in the bush that stretches out below the cliffs. Any success in hunting depends on using magic, since normally any prey would have an acute awareness of human presence and intention.

Case study: Dogon diviners

The job of a diviner is to keep people and the society in equilibrium, as well as to interpret the will of the gods. The Dogon divination system involves drawing a series of small boxes in the sand with a stick during daylight. Within each partition, small sticks and markings that pose various questions are placed, and poetic invocations are made asking a fox (*yurugu*) to please come and reveal truths to them. The fox visits by night, picking up peanuts and other treats left behind as enticement. The marks of his tiny footprints leave answers that are read by the diviner. People who have misfortune, fall ill, or have sick livestock consult the diviner, who, with the help of the fox, gives advice. A diviner can also advise people when a mourning period should end.[6]

Hogons are elder, revered spiritual leaders in Dogon communities, who preside over all agricultural and religious services. The Hogon lives alone, save for a large tortoise, an animal the Dogon associate with longevity, protection, and leadership. Ancestor spirits give advice and warnings to the Hogon through his tortoise.[7] The Hogon is priest of the Lebe cult. The Dogon believe the Hogon is visited and licked clean by the snake god nightly, gaining *nyama* from Lebe's purifying saliva. Because of this, the Hogon never washes himself and must avoid sweating.

A Dogon family compound is called a *ginnu*, and carvings decorating its wooden doors relate each family's history. The husband and each wife have their own respective hut within the *ginnu*, as well as a personal granary that has a distinctive pointed roof. Also within the compound is an altar for sacrifices and prayers to the gods and to one's ancestors. Housed in the altar are wooden statuaries of ancestors called *dege*. The Dogon believe that *nyama* – the soul, or life force – is released at the moment of death, and must be contained so that no harm comes to the living. In order to maintain a peaceful environment, the *nyama* of the deceased is channeled into the *dege*, making these statues powerfully spiritual magnets in petitioning one's ancestors.[8]

Funeral ceremonies are enormously crucial to the Dogon because of the belief that after death, the release of *nyama* – the soul or life force of the disembodied spirit – has the power to disrupt the realm of the living if it is not properly guided to the next world. To insure balance in the community, Dogon funerals have three phases: the cliff burial; the *nyû yana* – a yearly rite honoring all who died; and the *dama*, a final send-off for important men in the community, which occurs in the village approximately every twelve years. In these rituals, the descendants honor the departed through masked dances to appease any wandering spirits. The use of the masks mitigates the negative effects of the release of *nyama* at death.

When a person passes away, the men of the family announce the death to the community by shooting bullets into the air from the rooftop of their *ginnu*, which also scares off evil spirits. The corpse is washed and covered with a blue and white death blanket, and tied to a wooden bier. The whole village gathers at the house of the deceased to accompany the cortege along the path to the collective burial cave, high in the steep cliffs. As women weep and men continue to fire intermittent shots, the body is held aloft and carried by members of the family to the burial site. The young, sturdy males of the family climb up to the cave and send down a rope, which is lashed around the corpse. As it is hoisted upward and then carried into the cave, people respectfully watch from below. Once in the cavern, the men retrieve the death blanket, place the bones of other ancestors on the body, and return to the village.[9]

Figure 6.7
Èmna of the *awa* masking society prepare *dama* costumes and masks in secret.
Image: Dennis H. Miller.

The *dama*

The *dama* is a collective funeral ceremony held approximately every twelve years for esteemed men such as Hogons or important elders. The function of the *dama* is to shepherd the souls of the deceased to the spirit world, where they will then attain the rank of ancestor and become conduits between Amma, the creator, and the living. Men who have been spiritually important to the village are communally honored in this ritual, but a wealthier family might sponsor a *dama* for an individual. Essential in this final farewell are numerous masked dances, which are believed to be powerful means of containing *nyama*. Known as *èmna*, masks are associated with the realm of death, and are therefore a threat to fecundity. To avoid becoming infertile or miscarrying, women must have nothing to do with *èmna* and can only regard masked ceremonies from a distance. Therefore, the masking society – called the *awa* – is exclusively for initiated men of the village. When *awa* members are completely costumed and masked, they are also called *èmna*.

Preparations for the *dama* are held in secret, far from the eyes of women and children. The Hogon makes animal sacrifices daily to guarantee the spiritual potency of the ritual, and blacksmiths – also high-ranking members of Dogon society – carve new *dama* masks from wood selected from the bush. *Awa* members repaint older masks in colors of black, red, yellow, and white. The numerous masks feature a variety of humans, reptiles, bush animals, and birds that represent intrinsic aspects of the Dogon cosmos. In the 1930s, when French anthropologist Marcel Griaule first encountered a *dama*, he counted seventy-eight different masks, and over the years new ones have emerged, including as the French commandant, Muslim scholar, European tourist, and ethnographer.[10]

Figure 6.8
Masked *dama* dances honor the deceased, appease wandering spirits, and mitigate the negative effects of *nyama* – the soul, or life force.
Image: Dennis H. Miller.

Case study: Marcel Griaule (1898–1956)

Marcel Griaule first studied the Dogon in his long expedition from Dakar to Djibouti in the early 1930s, and returned repeatedly to visit and to research. In 1946, he conducted interviews with a blind elder, Ogotemmêli, who claimed to share knowledge having never been imparted to any non-Dogon that included deep insights on creation myths and astronomical space travel. Hoping this knowledge would revolutionize Western understanding of Africa, Griaule astounded the anthropological world when he published *Dieu d'eau* in 1948 (later translated into English as *Conversations with Ogotemmêli*). Although taken as gospel at the time, Ogotemmêli's veracity has recently been refuted, causing contention in anthropological circles. Regardless, Griaule's huge body of research on the Dogon was a great contribution to the fields of anthropology and ethnography. In 1956, Griaule passed away in France. When the news of his death reached the Dogon town of Sanga, they held a *dama* for him befitting a Hogon. Because his body was in Europe, they created an effigy of the ethnographer and entombed it in their ceremonial cave, just as they would have for one of their own.

Another more recent mask – a long human face marred by a large goiter protruding from below the chin – is a humorous view of the very real problem stemming from a lack of iodine in the diet that exists in the region.[11] Unlike the diverse masks of the *dama*, the general costuming for the body is fairly uniform. A woven hood covers the back of the head and neck, and a bra-like covering embroidered with white cowry shells surrounds the chest. Hibiscus fibers are dyed bright colors for costuming and mask framing. Bright fiber skirts are worn, loose indigo cotton trousers worn below, and colorful fiber armbands cover the wrists and biceps. Many rehearsals between dancers and drummers are undertaken in the cliffs in as much secrecy as the carving and costume making.

Once the private preparations for the *dama* are finished, a dancing pole (*dani*) is placed in the middle of the public square. In an initial, semi-private preview, the *èmna* gather at sunset, and follow their elders and drummers down to the village via a traditional route. Nothing must allow this zigzag path to deviate from that of the last *dama*; in some cases, trees have been felled and, in one occasion in the town of Tireli, a new wall was torn down. Because the magic of the masks is so potent in the beginning of the *dama*, only the men from the village are allowed to attend this preview and the drums warn women and children to stay away. As the *èmna* make their approach, they are given praise and thanks in *sigi so*, a secret language to address the *èmna*. *Sigi so* must be shouted, not spoken, so the air reverberates with loud, high-pitched utterances as the *èmna* are hailed. Since normal speech is forbidden while masked, *èmna* can only respond with this falsetto refrain: *hee hee hee!*

The first day of the public performances in the *dama* is a highlight, due to the grand entrance of as many as forty *èmna*. Visitors from other villages attend, and women and children are permitted to watch from afar. Costumed in full regalia, and charged with the powerful *nyama* contained in the masks, the dancers radiate this vital energy as they make their energetic entrance into the square, dancing to the rhythms of the drums and the cowbells. After revolving around the *dani* three times in a counterclockwise direction, they disperse, and sit around the arena with others of their mask type until it is their turn to dance.

In the village of Tireli, famous for its masked dances, the *tingetange* is often the first group of *èmna* to appear.[12] This difficult dance on tall stilts requires years of practice. *Tingetange èmna* represent water birds, albeit with female human attributes: they wear a brassiere with two protruding "breasts" of dried baobab fruits. Their faces are covered with a black cloth flap embroidered with white cowry shells rather than wooden masks. Dogon dualism is evident in the merging of woman and bird: the crested headpiece imitates the distinctive hairstyles of Fulani women and pokes fun at the vain nature of a rival tribe, while the stilts evoke the *tingetange*, a bird believed to keep away evil spirits as it flies over sleeping villages at night. In their regal dance, each magical step of the *tingetange* looks like a towering bird commandeering its way through water.

Figure 6.9
Èmna bounding into the performing space.
Image: Alfred Weidinger.

They come together as a flock, weaving in and out as their elongated legs pump high in the air, then probe the ground in a commanding way. Shaking flywhisks in time to the drumbeats, their faces repeatedly turn right then left in a seemingly vain display of beauty, half bird, half human, all female. As they take their haughty exit, spectators are left with the image of a sassy yet elegant gaggle of dancing storks.

Kanaga èmna represent birds, but carry a deeper mythological meaning as well. The headpiece of this mask is a vertical piece of wood, crossed horizontally by an upper and lower blade parallel to each other. On the upper one, two small wooden pieces at each end point up, and on the lower, two point down, symbolically connecting the spiritual world above with the physical world below. The energetic torso movements of the *kanaga* evoke this union: circling the upper body backward, the head, neck, and spine gather momentum, and suddenly, the dancer's whole torso lurches forward as he fiercely swipes the headpiece against the ground and returns to a vertical position with lightning speed. As a large group slashes the ground in unison, stirring up the dust, the repetitive sound of an army of swords swooping through the air in perfect unison is both mesmerizing and unsettling. With this circular action – a metaphoric journey between the upper and lower realms of heaven and earth – the *kanaga* drives the disembodied spirits of the dead toward the spirit world.

The magnificent *lebe* mask (called *sirige* in some villages) represents Lebe, the snake god. This mask is a large rectangular box, divided by a vertical ridge with

Figure 6.10 (p. 171)
Tingetange èmna represent birds, and is one of the most difficult *dama* dances.
Image: Alfred Weidinger.

two carved eyes, topped by a towering plank decorated with geometrical patterns. Only the most experienced men are able to manipulate this *èmna*. To support the heavy, unwieldy headpiece, a dancer bites a wooden mouth-grip hidden inside and ties the back of it to a belt. As he sets the *lebe* mask whirling in a horizontal motion, suggesting the revolution of the earth around the sun, this repeated gyration causes it to snake dangerously one way then the other. A *lebe* genuflects to each of the four cardinal points, touching the long blade to the earth, then arches back deeply, touching the ground behind him. This remarkably difficult feat, a symbolic bowing to all those who have passed away, is impressive the first time, but becomes almost superhuman by the fourth and epitomizes a link between the spiritual and mortal worlds.

The *satimbe* mask represents the importance of women's presence in society. The wooden superstructure of the *satimbe* (superior lady) is a seated naked woman with jutting breasts, whose bent elbows are held tightly to her ribcage, with forearms raised.[13] She holds a flywhisk in her right hand, and a calabash – the Dogon receptacle in which women brew and serve beloved millet beer – in her left. The movement of the *satimbe* is a tight, lady-like march. The knees do not lift high, yet great energy emanates from the dancers' bent elbows flapping in and out sideways as they parade around the square.

Figure 6.11
Two *èmna* in hunter masks.
Image: Dennis H. Miller.

The *walu* is the antelope, a rectangle mask with two small horns at the top. With two sticks in hand, the *èmna* bow forward as they dance energetically, magically creating the illusion of a four-legged creature who plows, struts, and prances – and is also capable of "crowd-control." Able to dart around the square at any time, *walu* are in charge of prodding any unruly audience members who may come too close as other *èmna* perform. Another popular mask is the hunter, which takes on both animal and human aspects: foreboding sharp teeth protrude from a crude mouth sunk into a long male face. Sometimes these *èmna* perform in pairs, intently stalking around the square with sharp spears in their hands. In some villages, they enact a mock chase of a *gou* – a rabbit *èmna*, who is far shrewder in out-witting the hunter, bringing levity to the crowd.

For the next five days, *èmna* will perform in the dancing square and on the roofs of the houses of the deceased. In a gesture of hospitality, copious quantities of millet beer are provided for spectators and performers. At the end of the *dama*, the *èmna* gather all together in one massive spectacle of a dance: the *tingetange* strut in the center while the other masks – *kanaga*, *lebe*, *satimbe*, *walu*, and others – fan out into a spiral. This kaleidoscopic effect makes one imagine that the souls of the dead, now honored, can effectively launch themselves toward the afterlife where they will attain the revered status of ancestor.[14] In the meantime, the community revels in drinking together and looks forward to the beneficial effects emanating from this communal call to order in a cosmos disrupted by death. After the *dama* – the bridge that shepherds the souls of the departed to the afterlife – crops should be plentiful, women fertile, and the society in perfect harmony.

Think about:
How are the animist beliefs of the Dogon reflected in *dama* masks?

Current trends

Many changes have occurred in Dogon culture due to circumstances interfering with their traditional systems of thought, ritual ceremonies, and lifestyle. The advent of Islam, Christianity, and the era of European colonial rule have inevitably damaged Dogon culture. In some regions, Hogon leaders are no longer permitted by the government, and in Songho, now a Muslim village, masked dances have not been performed since the 1960s. Unfortunately, many young people are becoming unaware of the place of the *awa* society in Dogon tradition.

In the face of devastating droughts that severely affected West Africa in the last decades of the twentieth century, many Dogon began to leave their region in search of seasonal migrant work in countries such as Côte d'Ivoire and Burkina Faso, leading to more loss of culture. Many choosing to stay have found it necessary to abandon their tradition of farming in favor of tourism, which has boomed since the construction of roads that allow easier access to the Bandigiara Cliffs. Tourists are especially eager to see èmna perform traditional dances of the *dama*, but the infrequent nature of the funeral ceremony, as well as its expense, has given rise to its dances being performed out of context for tourists. Non-Islamic villages that still have *awa* societies offer performances for a fee, such as in Tireli. In creating masks for tourist entertainment, blacksmiths no longer need to go through sacred rituals in cutting special wood, and frequently craft imitations of sacred *dege* ancestor sculptures and *ginnu* doors to sell to tourists. However, the recent Ebola epidemic in Africa also grounded tourism all over Africa to a halt. Moise Sagara, a guide in Dogon country, surmised the situation:

> We're under pressure from modern religion, education, tourism, as well as a migration from the villages, commerce . . . the Hogons no longer exist in many villages, and other things in our culture are disappearing . . . But tourism does contribute an income for us, and our mask dancers, and that's positive.[15]

As in many cases, the commodification and modification of a dance or ritual is sometimes a necessity means for surviving in modern society. One can only hope that the uniqueness of Dogon ideology and the beauty of their masked traditions will still maintain a place in their tradition of shepherding souls to the ancestral realm.

Discussion questions: the *dama*

1 The Dogon highly value the ideas of twin-ship and opposing forces in their culture. How does this cultural ideal manifest in the *dama*?
2 Controlling powerful *nyama* – the soul or life force of the body – is central to Dogon funeral rituals. Is channeling this entity addressed in funerals in Western culture?
3 Although a gender binary is present in Dogon society, men portray women in the *dama* masks. Discuss how females are represented in the *dama* masks, and what this indicates about their society.

6.4 The Mossi: *yaaba sooré* – the path of the ancestors

Key points: the Mossi

1 In the fifteenth century, horsemen from the south invaded present-day Burkina Faso and became the ruling class of powerful Mossi states. Today, Mossi society is divided into two clans: the *nakomsé* ("people of power") are descendants of the victors and still act as political chiefs. The second group is the *tengabisi* ("people of the earth"), whose relatives were originally conquered by the *nakomsé*.
2 The *tengabisi* group includes farmers called *nyonyosé* who perform the spiritual masking traditions used in funeral rites, during which ancestors and spirit beings are made manifest through the dancing masks. Mossi masks (*wando*) are owned by lineages and clans, passed down through the generations, and worn by the young men of the family.
3 After a burial, the masks, dancing, and drumming at their funeral celebration point the soul of the deceased toward the route to the afterworld. The Mossi call this sacred pathway *yaaba sooré*.
4 Ancestor spirits, if properly venerated, have enormous power to help as long as their descendants follow the aforementioned *yaaba sooré*, which also serves as a moral pathway for the living.
5 A result of rural Mossi resistance to Islam and Christianity has been the survival of masking traditions that have stayed remarkably intact.

It is the ancestors who kill their descendants. When they are not happy with them, they strike them: they fall ill, and die. As for others, their grandfathers let them live longer, but they will always finish by coming to collect them.[16]
—Louis Tauxier

Invaders do not readily understand the people they have conquered. But the above words of Monsieur Tauxier, a French colonial administrator in Haute Volta in the early twentieth century, demonstrate a very pointed understanding of the importance of the ancestors to the people. Like the Dogon and many other African peoples, Mossi habitually propitiate ancestor spirits in order to receive their blessings, advice, and help, and lead virtuous lives so that their chances of achieving the venerable status of ancestor are high. After a person dies, spiritually charged masks, dancing, and drumming at funerals are essential in pointing the soul of the deceased toward the route to the afterworld. This sacred pathway, which the Mossi believe was taken by their ancestors when they descended from the sky to the earth, is called *yaaba sooré*.[17]

Mossi history

The Mossi are located in Burkina Faso in sub-Saharan Africa, which is home to over sixty distinct ethnic populations.[18] This diversity reflects their history: in the fifteenth century, invading horsemen from the south established themselves on the Mossi plateau. This band of cavalry, called the *nakomsé* ("people of power"), formed powerful Mossi states and became the ruling class. They were strong enough to successfully fight the Muslim empires and were the only society in the region to successfully resist the spread of Islam.[19] The *nakomsé* merged with the many indigenous ethnic groups, who ultimately became "Mossi" by default. Not all succumbed, however – many of the Dogon people escaped north, taking refuge high in the Bandigiara escarpment, where they still live today.[20]

The Mossi *nakomsé* frequently raided the southwest of their kingdom for slaves, then sold them to traders.[21] In the late 1890s, the French curbed this aggression, although they inflicted their own violence in their attempts to colonize the area. The Mossi fiercely resisted, but by 1904 French military might had prevailed and the region became part of French West Africa (Haute Volta). During French occupation, the power of the *nakomsé* diminished greatly and the people were subjugated to forced labor and mandatory recruitment into the French army. France granted independence to the region in 1960 and, in 1983, Haute Volta became the Republic of Burkina Faso: "land of upright and honest men."

Mossi society is divided into two clans. The *nakomsé* are descendants of the victors and still act as political chiefs. The second group is the *tengabisi* ("people of the earth"), whose relatives were originally conquered by the *nakomsé*. The *tengabisi* include classes of blacksmiths, weavers, merchants, and the *nyonyosé* – farmers whose relatives had lived there for centuries before *nakomsé* occupation.[22] Although intermarriage occurs, there is still a wide class divide and considerable friction between the two groups. While the *nakomsé* function politically, it is the *nyonyosé* who perform the spiritual masking traditions used in initiations and funeral rites, during which ancestors and spirit beings are made manifest through the dancing masks.

Traditional Mossi religion and ancestor worship

Unlike other groups in Africa whose traditional religions have been supplanted by Islam and Christianity, only twenty-five percent of Mossi are Muslim and five percent are Christian.[23] Seventy percent follow their traditional religion. Wendé is their creator god, who positively or negatively controls the supernatural forces affecting their environment. The intermediaries between the living and Wendé are ancestor spirits, who have enormous power to help as long as their descendants follow the moral pathway of *yaaba sooré*. Scholar Christopher Roy notes that rejection of traditional religion occurred less amongst rural Mossi and, as a result, their cultural

Think about:
Is it surprising that colonialism, and the subsequent establishment of Burkina Faso, could not level the existence of these two classes in Mossi society?

practices – especially those involving masks – have stayed intact. He observes, "To stray from the *yaaba sooré* – the way of the ancestors – is to risk arousing their anger; the ancestors may punish any important transgression with a disease, especially smallpox, with some physical infirmity, especially blindness, or with infertility."[24] To this end, the Mossi give offerings of libations and animal sacrifices to their ancestors at family shrines and follow proper protocols of masked dancing in funeral ceremonies.

Masking and drumming traditions

Mossi masks are not owned by secret societies, but by lineages and clans. They are passed down through generations and worn by the young men of the family, who learn the significance of the masks as well as the traditional dances complementing them. If ancestors are the conduit between the living and the creator god, masks are conduits that enable the living to communicate with their spiritual forbearers – in other words, the masks make the supernatural come alive. The masks also function as reincarnations of an animal totem such as an antelope or hawk, the spirit of an important elder who has passed away, or the collective ancestor spirits of a family.

Blacksmiths carve masks from lightweight wood and mix abstract physical characteristics of different animals into one mask. They are painted in combinations of white, black, and red: white represents inexperience and death; black signifies wisdom and health; and red, danger and the spirit world. Just as the masks are abstracted, a masker's costume – made from hibiscus fibers dyed red or black – is designed to conceal and alter the human form of the dancer. In this same vein of abstraction, the steps of the dances emulating animal spirits are also performed in a stylized manner.[25] The percussion ensemble accompanying masks in funereal ceremonies includes the *bendre*, the *lunga*, and the *kiema*. The *bendre* is made from a rotund calabash, and covered by a goatskin. The *lunga* is a cylindrical tension drum whose pitch can be changed by squeezing the gut strings on the side. The *kiema* is an iron bell that keeps a steady rhythm.[26]

Mossi burials and funerals

Mossi burials and funerals differ from one another. Masks are present at the burial of a family elder, and accompany the body to the grave. They do not dance during this period of mourning, but their presence informs the ancestor spirits that the elder was an important figure to the community. In contrast, a funeral is a joyous celebration that can be held months or even years later. Because the *nyonyosé* are farmers, funeral season takes place after the harvest beginning in February so there will be plenty for guests to eat, and lasts until May, when planting begins. This momentous occasion enables the soul of the deceased to finally be released to the afterworld. To insure their ascent into the rank of ancestor, sacrifices of chickens and offerings of millet beer are made. In funeral celebrations, spirits become manifest through the masks, who interact with the people by dancing, and escort the soul of the deceased to the *yaaba sooré* – the path of ancestors.[27]

In his ethnographic film, *Masks of the Mossi People*, Christopher Roy documents a three-day funeral celebration honoring a *nyonyosé* male elder in the northern Yatenga region.[28] Family, friends, drummers, and maskers gather in a procession that revolves three times in counterclockwise direction around the man's house. A male relative of the

Figure 6.12
The arrival of *gur-wando* masks at a Mossi funeral.
Image: Christopher Roy.

deceased wearing a *karanga* – a towering vertical plank mask – begins to dance on the threshold, a symbolic act to send the soul off to the afterworld. The oval, concave face of the *karanga* mask, bisected by a raised ridge, has two triangular eyeholes on either side, and represents an antelope, while the plank represents the *yaaba sooré* path. Two elegant carved horns emerge from the forehead, backed by the tall plank painted with red and white geometrical designs of diamonds, triangles, circles, and zigzags that all carry meanings. The zigzag motif is especially significant, and represents the *yaaba sooré* pathway of the ancestors.

Case study: Masks in Burkina Faso

Throughout Burkina Faso, masks are a rich and varied tradition. They play crucial roles in purification, initiation rituals, and funeral ceremonies not only of the Mossi, but of the Dogon, Bwa, Bobo, Nuna, and Winiama peoples. More on masks and the peoples of Burkina Faso can be found at http://africa.uima.uiowa.edu/.

The lofty *karanga* ties at the back of the wearer's head and, for stability, he bites down on a wooden dowel inserted in the mask from cheek to cheek. He wears a long black hemp fiber wig and skirt, and his legs are covered in loose pants, but the sturdy arms of a strong young man are clearly on display. His athletic dancing emulates the swiftness and sudden movements of the antelope: as he prances, his legs lift high in a rhythmic in-place run. His head impulsively darts from side to side in feral fashion, as if he senses danger in the bush. Suddenly, turns of his head catapult his body in a fast rotation in one direction and then in the other, causing the tendrils of his costume to flare out horizontally. In a difficult counter-rhythmic move, his shoulders and hips shimmy at breakneck speed as his bent arms flap in and out to the beat of the *bendre* drum. Although this dance on the threshold dance stays in one place, it electrifies the surrounding crowd, who, grateful for his role in sending their relative to the realm of the ancestors, cheer and clap for this beloved antelope spirit.

Think about: How are both the present and the past addressed in *gur-wando* masks, which manifest ancestral spirits?

For funerals in eastern Mossi country, bush spirits masks that represent a family of a father, mother, and child are called *gur-wando*. They are completely concealed by shaggy masses of dark red hemp fibers, and hold a reed in their mouths that allows them to whistle high and low birdlike tones. The smallest is the *yali* mask – a dwarf bush spirit – worn by a boy less than five feet tall. His wooden white mask has two horns that jut upward. His innocent dance is filled with little hops, wiggles, and rhythmic shuffles which cause the costume fibers to sway playfully. The male *wan-zega*, the most common *gur-wando*, is anything but innocent. His imposing figure is quite intimidating, a feeling that grows as the numbers of these masks increase at a funeral. As in the *yali*, the face of a *wan-zega* is white and the body is covered in long dark red fibers, but a long, thin pole towers up from the center of the headpiece, covered by two-tiered sets of fibers that swing out in a dome-like umbrella shape as the masker sways and twirls. The *wan-zega* takes short, jerky steps in time to the drums, then suddenly twirls repeatedly in one direction while bobbing up and down. Another unexpected movement occurs when he bends forward at the waist so the top of the mask hits the ground, followed by a quick return to the vertical. The impetuousness of his dancing causes the audience to give him a large berth, as does his penchant to suddenly charge toward spectators in a violent manner. Both *yali* and *wan-zega* carry whips called *sabaga*; normally, *yali* chase after any children while *wan-zega* menace adult spectators.[29]

The third mask type is the female *wan-sablaga* mask, which is equally impressive but much more serene. The exquisite mask face is studded with cowrie shells, and intricate patterns of red seeds and beads are imbedded in beeswax. A jug-like handle protrudes from the forehead to the chin, and four round mirrors are embedded in vertical pairs on the eyes and

Figure 6.13
The face of a *karanga* mask represents an antelope, while the plank represents the *yaabe sooba*, the pathway of the ancestors.
Image: Christopher Roy.

the cheeks. *Wan-sablaga* maskers wear a tight black skirt typical of Mossi women so that their walking, as well as their dancing, is restricted. These more peaceful spirits, who tend to walk in a bobbing fashion and twirl gently as they dance, do not carry whips. In addition to funerals, these three masks are also used in annual ancestor celebrations that purify the community and honor the harvest.

Current trends

An important result of the resistance of the rural Mossi to Islam and Christianity has been the survival of the use of masking traditions, which have stayed remarkably intact in contrast to other groups in Africa. Photographs of the same masks taken in the early 1900s by the German ethnographer and anthropologist Leo Frobenius show little or no change in comparison to those of today, despite the yearly refurbishing of costumes and the creation of new ones. Masking traditions from Burkina Faso merge with those of other African nations in FESTIMA, which occurs in Dédougou for two weeks in February. Dances from rituals such as the Dogon *dama* are taken out of a spiritual context and adapted to serve the purpose of entertainment for a wide audience. But when weighing the threats modernity imposes, such as the exodus of younger people from rural areas to urban centers, and the rejection of traditional religion, it is better for people to keep up their cultural practices, albeit in a commercial setting, than having them die out. Although the original context for the dances is removed, the joy of performing them still allows for a sense of cultural pride.

Another trend in Burkina Faso is the secularization of the *warba*, a dance formerly performed for enthronements and funerals of *nakomsé* rulers.[30] Today, *warba* dancers perform for weddings, and troupes compete in public festivals. The movements in twerking – a popular dance today – seem to have antecedents in the *warba*, which entails the rapid shaking of the hips and buttocks. Men dance in a circle and take turns in impressive, virtuosic solos. In one instance, a *warba* dancer falls to the ground horizontally, taking weight in his palms, lifts his buttocks, and executes an athletic, polyrhythmic combination, simultaneously gyrating and vibrating his gluteal muscles with rapid-fire speed. The popular *Warba* Festival in Burkina Faso occurs biannually in Ganzourgou.

6.4 Exploration: excerpt from *Land of the Flying Masks* by Christopher Roy

African art historian and author Christopher Roy is a professor at the University of Iowa. His first visit to Burkina Faso was in 1966, and he later served there in the Peace Corps for two years. His research centers on the art of Burkina Faso and West Africa.

Of the diverse Mossi people, those who are descendants of the ancient conquered farmers use masks in the dry season for initiations and funerals. Initiations are secret, and in the southwest Mossi country they are impenetrable. Funerals, however, are public . . . Funerals for members of the *nyonyosé* community are very different from those for *nakomsé*, because, among the *nyonyosé*, masks appear to honor the deceased and to free his or her spirit to travel to the land of ancestors. Masks may appear briefly at interments, within three days of death, alerting the ancestors that the deceased was an honored member of the community. The funerals are comparable to memorial services, occurring during the dry season, anytime from a couple of months to a year or two years after the burial. The celebration invites large numbers of friends and relatives of the deceased, who travel through the bush for the celebration, bringing large quantities of food and drink, especially millet beer. The masks appear twice each day, in the morning and the evening, when the sun is low enough so it is not too hot. Each mask has a particular performance that communicates the character of the spirit being it represents. Young male escorts accompany each mask, wielding whips made of thin branches from *neem* trees to

Figure 6.14 (p. 178)
A *wan-zega* and a *yali* arrive at a funeral ceremony, whips in hand.
Image: Christopher Roy.

keep the crowd back. They represent the family that owns the mask. The masks are aggressive, and the audience flees before them if they approach. The masks also tend not to like white people in the audience, and I have received a few welts across the back when, on several occasions, I stepped too close. The function of the performance of the masks is to reenact the encounters between the ancestors and the spiritual beings, many generations ago when the families first settled on the land they now farm. Their appearances honor the spirit of the deceased, so that it is free to leave the world of the living to dwell forever in the realm of spirits. There are numerous sacrifices of chickens and goats. They smash weapons and tools of the deceased on the threshold of the dead. The mask performance ends within an hour of sunset, and the masks makes their way back to their home villages . . .
I never saw another white person at any of these funerals. The *nakomsé* in the region never attended either, fearing that the spiritual power of the masks would threaten their health, let alone their political power. Someone told me that if, by some accident, a *Naba* (chief) ever arrived at a *nyonyosé* funeral, there would be a cataclysm of an irresistible force meeting an immovable object.

Figure 6.15
A *wan-zega* dances.
Image: Christopher Roy.

Discussion questions: the *Mossi*

1 In Mossi society, there is a distinction between the ruling *nakomsé* class and the *tengabisi* workers. As stated in the chapter, it is the farmer class that perpetuates and performs the sacred masking traditions. How does this cultural divide impact your perceptions about the respective natures of politicians and artists?
2 In the traditional religion, ancestor spirits affect the Mossi people by inflicting both positive and negative elements on their lives. They can be aggressive, unleashing famine and disease, or gentle and generous, aiding in growth and reproduction. How are these positive and negative actions of the ancestors reflected in Mossi funeral ceremonies?
3 When a society is more isolated, such as in rural areas, we see that traditions are less affected by change. Is this an asset or a detriment to the culture in this day and age?

6.5 The *Egungun* of Yorubaland: the ancestors descend

Key points: the *Egungun*

1 For the Yoruba, ancestor worship stems from the belief that a person's spirit never dies and can be deeply involved in the lives of their relatives. If ritually honored on earth, these ancestral spirits, called *Egungun*, can be invoked to aid the living by giving advice, granting blessings, or punishing wrongdoers.
2 Ancestor spirits physically manifest themselves by descending into the bodies of *Egungun* maskers, who, in colorfully elaborate and varied costumes, demonstrate the power of the *Egungun* to their descendants through dance.

3 The *Egungun* cult is a secret society of men who perform in the "masks" – a term for the whole costume. When an *Egungun* cult dancer dresses in a mask, his identity is erased, and he becomes the channel through which an ancestor spirit emerges. The identity and the body of the masker must be hidden at all costs.
4 Although it is good luck to catch wind from an *Egungun* costume, it is commonly believed that the touch of an *Egungun* is fatal. Men in the *Egungun's* entourage, and sometimes the *Egungun* himself, use whips to keep spectators away from his path.
5 Although the presence of the ancestors is especially powerful during festivals, *Egungun* are capable of returning to earth at any time to hear the needs of the people, or to execute dreaded control by exposing any who violate the high moral codes valued in Yorubaland.

Even a Prince cannot go near an Egungun with impunity.
—Yoruba proverb

Ancestor worship – a cornerstone in Yoruba traditional religion – stems from the belief that a person's spirit never dies. Although the dead no longer dwell with the living, the *ara orun*, or "beings from beyond," are keenly involved in the lives of their relatives.[31] In exchange for being ritually honored on earth, ancestral spirits called *Egungun* are conduits between heaven and earth. They can be invoked collectively or individually to help the living by giving advice, granting blessings, or punishing wrongdoers.[32] These ancestor spirits physically manifest themselves by descending into the bodies of *Egungun* maskers, who, in their finery, demonstrate the power of the *Egungun* to their descendants through dance. *Egungun* are formally celebrated in annual and biennial masquerade festivals throughout Nigeria and Benin that last from a week to three weeks, with the dates set by divination.[33] The *Egungun* cult is a secret male society that performs in the masks, a term that also encompasses the costume that covers them from head to foot. Although preparations are private, people of any age or gender can attend these masquerades honoring the spirits of the ancestors.

Although the presence of the ancestors is especially powerful during festivals, *Egungun* are capable of returning to earth at any time to hear the needs of the people or to execute dreaded control by exposing any who violate the high moral codes valued in Yorubaland. An early anthropologist who studied the Yoruba was William Bascom, who catalogued these offensive traits:

> A wicked person loves no one but himself . . . he injures others and destroys their property without cause. Still worse is the criminal, the sinner, including the liar, the murderer, the thief, one who commits incest . . . Prostitutes, witches, wizards, ugly persons, busybodies, slanderers, and other treacherous people fall into other undesirable categories.[34]

Correct social behavior is monitored by the ancestors, whose omniscient powers enable them to control the living from beyond. One may think of *Egungun* as a supernatural, moral police force that generates stability in a community where evil actions have dire consequences.

The legend of the *Egungun* masquerade

The *Egungun* masquerade dates back to the fourteenth century. Its origins are couched in a myth about a hunchbacked king who did not receive burial rites befitting his stature. Because his three sons had no money, they abandoned his body in the bush. Years later, the eldest son became king, but his wife was barren. A diviner revealed that his father's inadequate funeral was the cause, but since time had decomposed his father's remains long ago, reversing this was futile. His wife unfortunately was raped by a gorilla and she gave birth to a child – part monkey, part human – whom she promptly abandoned in the bush. Returning home, she reported her ordeal to the king. Anthropologist Margaret Thompson Drewal recounts:

He went to consult a diviner who revealed that the child did not in fact
die in the bush and that it would grow up to be Amu'ludun (literally,
'One-Who-Brings-Sweetness' to the community). The diviner advised the king
to return to the place of his father's unfinished burial and perform the proper
rites, where his father would "materialize in a costume."[35]

After the rescue of the hybrid baby, he was mounted on the back of a masker to
represent the hunchback of the deceased king. This first "costume" initiated the
tradition of the *Egungun* masquerade, in which an ancestor, or "*egun*," descends into
a masker and makes his or her appearance to the community. Because of this legend,
Egungun costumes featuring monkey skulls are a formidable display of power.[36]

The Yoruba concept of lineage

The lineage of a family is called *idile*. When children are born, they are said to
possess physical or intellectual aspects of an ancestor. This idea is also perpetuated
in the naming of children: a first-born son is called Babatunde, which means "father
comes back." Keeping an ancestor's memory alive is important, and *Egungun* masks
help people to do so by representing a lineage, a particular person of either gender,
or by embodying a wider concept of the ancestors or *orisa* (gods).[37] Wealthy families
may commission and create a shrine for their own *Egungun*, who represents their *idile*.
Although they are worn by initiated *Egungun* maskers who parade around the town in
a grand fashion symbolizing the eminence of a lineage, the families are considered to
be the owners.[38] Every year, they add new elements to the costume, or further adorn it
with more embroidery or beadwork to broadcast their status and wealth.

Egungun costuming

When an *Egungun* dancer dresses in a mask, his own identity is erased and he
becomes the channel through which an ancestor spirit emerges. It is unlikely to ever
find two identical *Egungun*, since their costumes are unique. This diversity in role-
playing and costuming allows an audience to experience a wide array of personalities
and modes of behavior. However, the identity of any masker must be disguised at
all costs and, consequently, he communicates in either a high-pitched tone or a low
frog-like voice, and makes certain that no part of his body is exposed. To insure that
no skin is seen during the athletic dancing, the masker first covers himself in a white
burial cloth, his leggings are sewn to his shoes, and gloves cover his hands. Once his
face is concealed by netting, the elaborate layering of exquisite fabric begins.

A typical *Egungun* costume consists of colorfully patterned cloth strips that are tied
on a belt and on a collar around his neck, which whirl sensationally as he spins
and careens. An *Egungun* headpiece may be crowned by a carved face towering
above the wearer's own head, or decorated with shells, feathers, animal bone, and
skulls. These imposing costumes can be very heavy and are extremely effective in
rendering a dancer unrecognizable to spectators. The Reverend Stephen Farrow
stressed this mandatory disguising of the performer in a 1926 account:

> It is absolutely essential that not a single particle of the human form should be
> visible; for, if this rule is broken, the man wearing the dress must die . . . and
> every woman present must likewise die . . . On one occasion an Egun who
> was dancing in Abeokuta in the presence of a crowd, which contained a large
> number of women, had the misfortune to tear his clothes. He was killed, and
> every woman present was taken and put to death. The horror produced by
> this event was so great that Egun-worship was never again permitted in the
> particular township where it occurred.[39]

The inherent danger in an *Egungun* masquerade does not stop at what we refer to
today as "costume failure." Although it is considered good luck to catch the wind
from an *Egungun* costume, it is commonly believed that the touch of an *Egungun*
is fatal. People watch the spectacle with caution, and there have been instances in
which a person touched by an *Egungun* has collapsed into trance, overcome with

Think about:
Can an *Egungun*
representing an *idile* be
a sort of status symbol
for the family?

Figure 6.16
Three *Egungun* take a break.
Image: Dietmar Temps.

fear.[40] This is why the men in the *Egungun's* entourage act as mediators between the masker and the crowd by using whips to keep spectators away from his path. The *Egungun* himself may also a carry whip or cudgel, which he is not shy about wielding.

Performance of *Egungun*

In preparing for an *Egungun* festival, priests, chiefs, and the members of masking societies retreat to conduct secret rituals in the *igbo*, their sacred forest grove. People deliver gifts of palm wine, kola, and other foods, leaving them at the edge of the forest. After the dancers have partaken of the offerings, they painstakingly dress in the elaborate *Egungun* costumes and exit from the *igbo* with their entourage.[41] Often an *Egungun* will first visit family graves and then proceed to the homes of their relatives to give blessings and receive gifts of thanks in exchange. He then continues on to the festival in the marketplace, where all *Egungun* will cajole, tease, terrify, and delight the public through their antics and dancing.

Case study: *Bata* talking drums

A *bata* ensemble contains talking drums, which approximate the tones of the speech and vocal pitch of the Yoruba language. It consists of four drums, three of which are double-headed and hang horizontally from the drummers' necks. The large head is played with the right hand, while the small head is beaten with a leather thong held in the left hand. The ones that "talk" are the lead and largest drum, the *iyalu* (mother drum), together with the *omelet abo* (female pitch). The *omelet ako* (male pitch) keeps the rhythm but does not speak. The *kudi*, a small, single-headed drum, provides a rapid baseline beat and is played by a younger drummer with two long sticks.

As the entrance of an *Egungun* masker draws near, the talking *bata* drum ensemble plays and invokes the spirits by chanting their names. The women begin to sing *oriki* (praise songs) as the music grows louder and louder. The *bata* drums give an *Egungun* basic directional instructions on where to travel, but it is the masker who is in charge of dancing in a way that reveals the personality of the spirit to the spectators. A lineage *Egungun* dances gracefully, bobbing up and down while taking gentle, wide turns, allowing the costume to move elegantly as well. But many are far more energetic, such as *elewe* maskers of the Igbomina Yoruba, which represent an ancestral lineage of chiefs. The virtuosic dances of the *elewe* are highly athletic and require great technical skill. Their costume allows them to have one arm and both feet free, affording them greater mobility than other maskers. While his dancing keeps pace with the furious drumming, an *elewe* masker might bend a leg, hold it with the opposite hand, and jump through the "hole" with the other leg. Flips, wild spins, dervish-like turning, sudden lurches from side to side, and other unpredictable, improvised movements result in a risky performance for the crowd, who, while avoiding contact with him, marvel in the gyrating spectacle of vivid colors, patterns, and trinkets adorning the imposing *Egungun*.

In contrast to their altruistic acts, *Egungun* have been known to use their might against one another. Anthropologist John Pemberton III witnessed two embroiled in a contest of power, in which they hurled powders toward one another, cast spells, and danced violently while threatening each other with menacing gestures. When one finally relented, he was put in the lowly position of forever having to follow the victor at a distance, thereby lowering his own authority and demonstrating how *Egungun* exercise control not only over the community, but also within their own structural hierarchy.[42]

Figure 6.17
An aggressive *Egungun* tears through an awed yet apprehensive crowd.
Image: Dietmar Temps.

At the end of an *Egungun* festival, all the maskers convene for final prayers. Having cleansed the community and resolved any concerns or needs of the people, they will return to Kutome, the afterworld. Farmers will harvest their crops, bolstered by the agricultural advice the *Egungun* have bestowed upon them, and the people give offerings of thanks at *Egungun* shrines and Yoruba temples. The dualistic nature of the *Egungun* causes them to be revered, yet dreaded at the same time. One might ask why these honored ancestor spirits – who are consulted by the living in times of trouble – would chase their relatives with a whip while admonishing them in a disguised voice that sounds like a croaking toad? The answer is simple: by instilling fear, *Egungun* maintain order and stability in the community.

Current trends

Political, religious, and economic factors all have the potential to impact traditions such as *Egungun* worship. During the 1970s oil boom, exportation of Nigerian oil brought great wealth to the country. Margaret Drewal noticed an increase of urban rituals in which the *Egungun* masks became more intricate and sumptuous due to the use of imported damask, brocade, and velvet fabrics. Observing the playful way contemporary items such as plastic dolls or a World War II gas mask were

Think about:
Since *Egungun* dancers' identities are erased while masked, do you imagine that the acrimony described here would persist when one is unmasked?

incorporated into costumes, Drewal commented, "Unfixed and unstable, Yoruba ritual is more modern than modernism itself."[43] These changes, improvisations, and artistic flexibility allow room for innovation within tradition, an adaptation to changing times or an increasingly urban environment. Today, cities such as Ibadan, Ilesha, and Lagos all host *Egungun* festivals annually.

Traditional Yoruba religion has been encroached upon by Islam and Christianity for centuries. More recently, the increase of Pentecostal churches in the 1990s in West Africa presented challenges to *Egungun* worship as churches demonized the indigenous practice. Dr. Charles Gore, a Nigerian anthropologist, observes that those following the *Egungun* tradition have been proactive, stating "Egungun has responded in elaborating a counter-narrative of localized Yoruba memories, personalized histories, and ritual through performance that upholds the ethical values of the community."[44] An example of this counter-narrative is evinced in the recent work of Leonce Raphael Agbodjelou, a Yoruba photographer from Benin whose *Egungun Project* has been exhibited in galleries throughout Europe. *Egungun* sit for these regal portraits, draped and enshrouded in layers of bejeweled cloth, feathers, bones of animals, and snakeskins. Their magnificent appearance stands in sharpest contrast to that of the living, and the power that they exude is palpable. While shooting the *Egungun* in Nigeria, politics intervened; Agbodjelou was sent home to Benin by police, who were threatened by the presence of his camera. Despite the obstacles that politics and religion pose, these ancestor spirits continue to provide a thread of stability in ever-changing Yoruba society by hovering between the spirit world and that of the living. Separated from yet powerfully present in human affairs, the *Egungun* tradition presents a living link to the ancestral legacy of the Yoruba.

Discussion questions: the *Egungun*

1 How does the *Egungun* tradition insure that ancestors will maintain authority over the whole community?
2 Is there a way that you, or your family, keep your own lineage alive – religiously or artistically?
3 Can you think of traditions in which a performer's identity must be completely erased to be effective?

Notes

1 Gardner, Robert. *Envisioning Dance on Film and Video*, 269.
2 Griaule, Marcel. *Conversations with Ogotêmmelli*, 3. Consequently, many Dogon, under pressure to abandon their own "pagan" religion by both Christian and Muslim converts, adapt to Islam instead.
3 Josephy, Alvin. *The Horizon History of Africa*, 452.
4 Azuonye, Chukwuma. *Dogon: The Heritage Library of African Peoples*, 39.
5 Van Beek and Hollyman. *Dogon: Africa's People of the Cliffs*, 104–109.
6 Ibid., 77.
7 Ibid., 147.
8 Ezra, Kate. *Art of the Dogon*, 18.
9 Van Beek and Hollyman, 142–134.
10 Ibid., 24. Consequently, many Dogon, under pressure to abandon their own "pagan" religion by both Christian and Muslim converts, to adapt to Islam instead.
11 Van Beek and Hollyman, 157.
12 "Dogon Mask Dance," Vimeo video, 22:16, posted by Dennis Miller, May 15, 2010, https://vimeo.com/24962330
13 Dieterlen, Germaine. "Masks and Mythology Among the Dogon," 40.
14 Van Beek and Hollyman, 161.
15 Moise Sagara, personal communication, September 16, 2015.
16 Tauxier, Louis. *Le Noir du Yatenga*, 385.
17 Wheelock, Thomas G.B., and Christopher D. Roy. *Land of the Flying Masks: Art and Culture in Burkina Faso*, 55.

18 Ibid., 11.
19 Finnegan, Gregory. "Mossi." *Encyclopedia of World Cultures*
20 Wheelock, Thomas G. B., and Christopher D. Roy, 55.
21 Finnegan, Gregory.
22 Wheelock, Thomas G. B., and Christopher D. Roy, 34.
23 Roy, Christopher D. "The Art of Burkina Faso," 6.
24 Ibid., 6.
25 Wheelock, Thomas G. B., and Christopher D. Roy, 41–42.
26 Mason, Katrina and James Knight. *Burkina Faso*, 17.
27 Wheelock, Thomas G. B., and Christopher D. Roy, 30.
28 "Masks of the Mossi People: Yatenga (Northern) Style," YouTube video,
    5:04, posted by Christopher D. Roy, April 21, 2011, www.youtube.com/
    watch?v=idLqJw9J40A
29 Roy, Christopher D. "The Art of Burkina Faso," 13.
30 Wheelock, Thomas G. B., and Christopher D. Roy, 441.
31 Drewal, H. John. "The Arts of Egungun Among Yoruba Peoples," 18.
32 Beckwith and Fisher, *African Ceremonies*, 239.
33 Drewal, H. John. *Yoruba Ritual: Performers, Play, and Agency*, 90–91.
34 Bascom, 494.
35 Ibid., 92.
36 Jonas, *Dancing*, 55.
37 Drewal, 18.
38 Ibid., 22.
39 Farrow, *Faith, Fancies and Fetish or Yoruba Paganism*, 76–78.
40 Beckwith and Fisher, *African Ceremonies*, 317.
41 Pemberton III, John. "Egungun Masquerades of the Igbomina Yoruba," 45.
42 Pemberton, 42.
43 Drewal, 43.
44 Reade, Orlando. "The Afterlife of African Studio Photography," www.
    africaisacountry.com

Bibliography

Visual sources

YouTube

"African Kings and Tribal Leaders," YouTube video, 5:18, posted by "Alfred
    Weidinger," May 3, 2014, www.youtube.com/watch?v=jOlGYUX5utQ
"Alfred Weidinger, Dogon Country," YouTube video, 9:13, posted by "Alfred
    Weidinger," June 15, 2015, www.youtube.com/watch?v=GequphFNW9g
"Dogon Art and Life," YouTube video, 60:32, posted by "Christopher Roy," June 21,
    2015, www.youtube.com/watch?v=qCP9Dsbl9pA
"Dogon Mask Dance," Vimeo video, 22:16, posted by "Dennis Miller," May 15, 2010,
    https://vimeo.com/24962330
"Masks of the Mossi People: Yatenga (Northern) Style," YouTube video, 5:04, posted
    by "Christopher D. Roy," April 21, 2011, www.youtube.com/watch?v=idLqJw9J40A
"Warba de Bango," YouTube video, 10:22, posted by "Bernie Ouedraogo," April 9,
    2009, www.youtube.com/watch?v=bg3UZeCAOcs
"West African Dogon Masks: BBC Hidden Treasures," YouTube video,
    58:57, televised by the "BBC," March 14, 2011, www.youtube.com/
    watch?v=aBmPota4tpU
"Wodaabe, Herdsmen of the Sun," YouTube video, 49:48, film by Werner Herzog,
    1989, posted by "gertrudemcmillian," March 19, 2012, www.youtube.com/
    watch?v=MlnO1QDqpaQ

Written sources

Azuonye, Chukwuma. *Dogon: The Heritage Library of African Peoples*. New York:
    The Rosen Publishing Group, 1996.
Babayemi, S. O. *Egungun Among the Oyo Yoruba*. Oyo, Nigeria: Oyo State Council
    for Arts and Culture, 1980.

Bascom, William. "Social Status, Wealth, and Individual Differences Among the Yoruba." *American Anthropologist*, Vol. 53, No. 4 (October 2009): 490–505. DOI: 10.1525/aa.1951.53.4.02a00040.

Beckwith, Carol, and Fisher, Angela. *African Ceremonies*. New York: Harry N. Abrams, 1999

Bovin, Mette. *Nomads Who Cultivate Beauty: Wodaabe Dances and Visual Arts in Niger*. Uppsala, Sweden: Nordiska Afrikainstitutet, 2001.

Dieterlen, Germaine. "Masks and Mythology Among the Dogon." *African Arts*, Vol. 22, No. 3 (1989): 34–43.

Drewal, Henry John. "The Arts of Egungun among Yoruba Peoples." Source: *African Arts*, Vol. 11, No. 3 (April, 1978), pp. 18–19 and 97–98. Published by: UCLA James S. Coleman African Studies Center. Accessed June 1, 2015, 15:03 UTC, Stable URL: www.jstor.org/stable/3335409.

Drewal, Margaret Thompson. *Yoruba Ritual: Performers, Play, and Agency*. Bloomington and Indianapolis: Indiana University Press, 2001.

Ezra, Kate. *Art of the Dogon*. New York: Harry N. Abrams, Inc., 1988.

Farrow, Stephen S. *Faith, Fancies and Fetish or Yoruba Paganism: Being Some Account of the Religious Beliefs of the West African Blacks, Particularly of the Yoruba Tribes of Southern Nigeria*. Brooklyn: Athelia Henrietta Press, Inc. 1996 (Originally published in 1926 for the Society for Promoting Christian Knowledge)

Finnegan, Gregory. "Mossi." *Encyclopedia of World Cultures*, 1996. *Encyclopedia. com*. Accessed June 14, 2015. www.encyclopedia.com/doc/1G2-3458001536. html.

Gore, Charles. "Burn the 'Mmonwu' Contradictions and Contestations in Masquerade Performance in Uga, Anambra State in Southeastern Nigeria." *African Arts*, Vol. 41, No. 4 (2008): 60–73.

Griaule, Marcel. *Conversations with Ogotêmmelli*. London: University of Oxford Press, 1965. Reprint 1970.

Houlberg, Marilyn Hammersley. "Egungun Masquerades of the Remo Yoruba." *African Arts*, Vol. 11, No. 3 (April, 1978), pp. 20–27 and 100. Published by: UCLA James S. Coleman African Studies Center. Accessed June 1, 2015, 14:13 UTC. Stable URL: www.jstor.org/stable/3335410

Jonas, Gerald. *Dancing*. New York: The Metropolitan Museum of Art. Distributor: Harry N. Abrams, Inc. 2001.

Karade, Baba Ifa. *The Handbook of Yoruba Religious Concepts*. York Beach, ME: Red Wheel/Weiser, LLC., 1994.

Mason, Katrina, and James Knight. *Burkina Faso*. Guilford, CT: The Globe Pequod Press Inc., 2011.

McKissack, Patricia, and Fredrick McKissack. *The Royal Kingdoms of Ghana, Mali, and Songhai: Life in Medieval Africa*. New York: Henry Holt and Company, 1995.

Pemberton III, John. "Egungun Masquerades of the Igbomina Yoruba." *African Arts*, Vol. 11, No. 3 (April, 1978), pp. 40–47 and 99–100. Published by: UCLA James S. Coleman African Studies Center. Accessed June 1, 2015, 14:28 UTC. Stable URL: www.jstor.org/stable/3335412.

Reade, Orlando. "The Afterlife of African Studio Photography." *Africaisacountry. com*, November 28, 2011. http://africasacountry.com/the-afterlife-of-africa n-studio-photography/.

Roy, Christian. *Traditional Festivals: A Multicultural Encyclopedia*. Santa Barbara: ABC-CLIO Inc., 2005.

Roy, Christopher D. "The Art of Burkina Faso." *Art and Life in Africa*, 1–113. http:// africa.uima.uiowa.edu/topic-essays/show/37?start=5.

Tauxier, Louis. *Le Noir du Yatenga*. Paris: Larose, 1917.

Van Beek, Walter E. A. "Haunting Griaule: Experiences from the Restudy of the Dogon." *History in Africa*, Vol. 31 (2004): 43–68. Published by African Studies Association. Accessed June 26, 2015. Stable URL: www.jstor.org/stable/4128581.

Van Beek, Walter E. A., and Stephanie Hollyman. *Dogon: Africa's People of the Cliffs*. New York: Harry N. Abrams, Inc., 2001.

Wheelock, Thomas G. B., and Christopher D. Roy. *Land of the Flying Masks: Art and Culture in Burkina Faso*. Munich: Prestel, 2007.

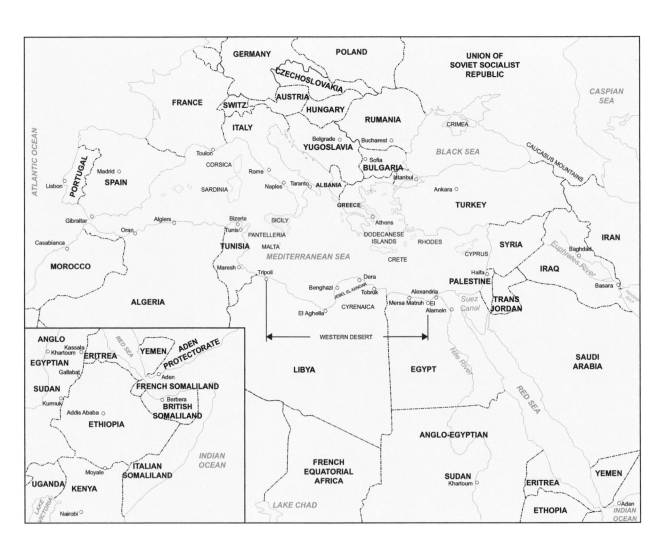

North Africa, Turkey, and Spain
Healing, worship, and expression

7.1 Overview

This chapter examines how dance functions as a healing ceremony, as a form of worship, and as a vehicle for personal expression. Practiced in North African Muslim and non-Muslim communities, the *zār* is a healing rite which aims to cure maladies caused by possession of "*zār*" spirits, who are placated with music, dancing, and sacrificial feasts. In Turkey, Mevlevi dervishes of the Sufi Islamic order seek divine truth and unite with God through the ritual of *sema*, a whirling dance that induces a state of religious ecstasy in its performers. *Flamenco* is not only a cultural treasure of Spain, but is now a global phenomenon. Its long and varied roots tap into the music, song, and dance of Arabs, Jews, Africans, and North Indian Gypsies who coexisted for several centuries in Andalusia, and converged into a *Gitano* manifestation of protest against fanatical government persecution. *Zār*, *sema*, and *flamenco* have all been plagued by various factors that include royal decrees, governmental bans, appropriation, and commercialization. But each has survived, perhaps for reasons that are best attributed to the humanistic and universal desires and needs for health, spirituality, and passion.

7.2 The *zār* ritual: ridding women of troublesome *jinn*

Key points: *zār*

1 Practiced in North African Muslim and non-Muslim communities in the Nile region, the *zār* is a healing rite in which maladies caused by possession by "*zār*" spirits are cured through music, dancing, and sacrificial feasts.
2 *Zār* ceremonies are predominantly sought after by women and are presided over by a female spiritual medium known as a *shaykha*. By entering a trance state, she consults her own spirits for advice and communicates with those possessing her clients. The *shaykha* brokers an agreement with the spirits troubling an afflicted woman, who is called an *'ayāna*.
3 The large pantheon of *zār* spirits are "stock characters" of all ages and professions, and recognizable by their costuming, speech, behavior, and demands that reflect the many different cultural, religious, and historical influences that have impacted the cultural history of the Nile Valley.
4 Once an *'ayāna* is diagnosed as possessed, her *zār* spirit(s) are never exorcised, but just placated. She will enter a symbolic marriage with her *asyād*, or spirit. In Egypt, this initial *zār* is called *farah ma'a al-asyād*, or "wedding with the masters." The symbolism inherent in weddings is present in a *zār* ceremony and the *'ayāna* follows the typical preparations of a bride.

5 Today, *zār* ceremonies are often criticized as being an unorthodox mode of
  healing, and at times have been banned by religious and political authorities,
  yet they are regularly practiced by women who adhere to the belief that
  dissatisfied *zār* spirits are the cause of illness and infertility.

**When people enter the ceremonial place, the atmosphere is
charged, the mood is set, and participants approach in a mood of
exhilaration . . . Therapeutic activities take place from which orthodox
religion and God are excluded, in which social rules are suspended, and
where the partially unpredictable forces of evil are in evidence.[1]**
—John Kennedy

The *zār* is a healing rite practiced in Muslim and non-Muslim communities in the Nile
River regions of Sudan, Egypt, and Ethiopia. Although customs vary depending upon
geographical location, the overall mission of a *zār* ceremony is to cure physical or
psychological maladies caused by possession of one or more "*zār*" spirits – powerful
and demanding supernatural beings that are appeased through music, songs,
dancing, and sacrificial feasts. Although men may seek help or be healers, *zār*
ceremonies are predominantly sought after by women, and are presided over by a
female spiritual medium known as a *shaykha* – an expert who acts as a powerful go-
between between the mortal and spiritual world. Her role in a *zār* ritual is to broker
an agreement with the spirits troubling an *'ayāna* – an afflicted woman. Once *zār*
spirits possess someone, they remain an ever-present force and therefore exorcism
is not possible. However, if the agreed-upon terms are respected, the benevolence
of the spirits is secured, and they will cease inflicting the *'ayāna* with sickness and
misfortune. Through a symbolic "wedding" inherent in the *zār* ritual, the *'ayāna*
and the spirit/s forge a symbiotic, life-long bond.[2] Today, *zār* ceremonies are often
ridiculed and criticized as being an unorthodox mode of healing, and at times have
been banned by religious and political authorities – yet they are regularly practiced
by women who adhere to the belief that dissatisfied *zār* spirits are the cause of
illness and infertility, as well as the source of hardships in the community.

Followers of *zār* believe that the world is inhabited by a host of invisible, mobile
spirits.[3] People attempt to drive them away by reciting the first line of the Quran,
the primary religious text of Islam. However, possession by *zār* spirits – who can
be both good and bad – may happen before this
incantation occurs. The more important spirits,
known as *asyād* in Egypt, and as *zayran* in Sudan,
are generally considered to be benevolent, but will
cause trouble when their demands are ignored.
Jinn are considered to be less powerful, yet are
annoying and malevolent. The large pantheon of
zār spirits are "stock characters" of all ages and
professions, and recognizable by their costuming,
speech, behavior, and demands that reflect the
many different cultural, religious, and historical
influences that have impacted the cultural history of
the Nile Valley. They include the *derewish*, a variant
of a Sufi dervish teacher and a revered spirit; the
khawajāt, or pale-skinned foreigner; the *pashwat*,
administrators from the Turco-Egyptian era; and
although spirits are predominately male, the *sittat*
are female, and include the Virgin Mary, mother
of Jesus. A Christian, Ethiopian, or Turkish *asyād*
might make demands through the possessed
person, who will voice these in a foreign tongue.[4]

Although the exact origins of the *zār* are
inconclusive, one theory on its beginnings comes

Figure 7.1
The Central Sudan village of Sennar is an important center
for *zār*.
Image: Susan Kenyon.

from John Kennedy, a professor of anthropology and psychology, who in the 1960s began to study *zār* in the ancient African kingdom of Nubia (bordering Egypt and Sudan). Kennedy claims that in Nubian society, *zār* ceremonies emerged as a means of coping with social stresses caused by the 1920 construction of the Great Dam at Aswan. Subsequently, Lake Nassar emerged and the ancestral land of one of the oldest civilizations in the world was permanently submerged. 100,000 Nubian people were removed en masse and forced to resettle elsewhere in 1963. Many men, formerly farmers, sought work in cities. Nubian women left behind in strange new settlements ostensibly found relief from their worries through *zār* practice.[5]

Women, the *zār*, and Islam

In Islamic countries, there is a marked separation between the sexes both publicly and privately, and a great distinction between gender roles. In the female-dominated *zār*, the profession of a *shaykha* is one of the few in which a woman can hold leadership and financial independence within a male-dominated society. A *shaykha* is highly valued by her female followers for her substantial knowledge and powers as a medium to the spirit world. Essential to her profession – often inherited from a female relative – is her ability to enter an altered state of consciousness. While in trance, a *shaykha* gains access to her own personal spirits for advice and is able to communicate and negotiate with those possessing her clients.

A sick woman who is experiencing spirit possession for the first time is considered to be in a vulnerable and dangerous state, since she has not yet discovered what spirit or spirits are troubling her. Often visiting a *shaykha* is a last attempt when all other methods, such as bloodletting, herbs, charms, and Western medicine, have failed. When an afflicted *'ayāna* consults a *shaykha*, a ritual divination ascertains if her client is indeed possessed and, if so, the identity and demands of the *zār* spirits are revealed. In her fieldwork during the 1980s in the village of Sennar in Sudan, Susan Kenyon noted that consulting an expert was not an easy decision: "It is often a last resort, one which people are loath to accept, mainly because they recognize that this brings a permanent commitment. *Zār* spirits are never exorcised, but simply pacified."[6] She witnessed that when women accepted their relationship with their *zār* spirits, they seemed to benefit positively.

In possession illness, spirits rarely disturb pre-pubescent females. Instead, fertile, married women are targeted and can be rendered infertile as a result. Not surprisingly, fertility problems are frequently treated through a *zār*. Anthropologist Richard Natvig conducted his research on the *zār* cult in rural village societies in Egypt's Sharkiya province. He observed that women were under tremendous pressure to bear male children, especially in a polygamous household, in which fertility increased a wife's status, while a barren one risked being rejected.[7] Cases abound when a husband neglects his wife for the favors of another, since when one is distressed, she is most vulnerable to becoming possessed by spirits who will torment her with emotional or psychological disturbances manifested in stomach aches, migraines, miscarriages, epilepsy, semi-paralysis, weight loss, anxiety, or nervousness. Other instances that might ignite the ire of a *zār* spirit and induce it to possess a woman have to do with her vanity. Some *asyād* are known to covet luxury items such as jewels, henna, perfumes, and new clothes, so one might descend into a woman who obsessively admires herself and her jewelry in front of a mirror.[8] Being near water makes a woman more susceptible to possession, so rivers, wells, or even toilets are vulnerable places, as are liminal crossroads such as a threshold of a door or a staircase. All these venues are rendered even more dangerous during the darkness of night.

A private *zār* or "wedding with the masters"

If an *'ayāna* is diagnosed as being possessed, the problems plaguing her are brought under control by the *shaykha* organizing a private *zār* for the sick woman that might last anywhere from three to seven days. This must be held, regardless of cost, in an attempt to ameliorate her infirmity.[9] In Egypt, this initial *zār* is called *farah* ma'a al-asyād, or "wedding with the masters," since she and the asyād enter a union of sorts. The 'ayāna is sometimes referred to as an arūsat al-zār, or "zār bride." Traditionally, wedlock leads to bearing children, and procreative powers guarantee a woman's security in marriage and, subsequently, her good fortune. Therefore, the symbolism inherent in weddings is present within numerous ritual elements in a zār ceremony. The 'ayāna follows the typical preparations of a bride – ornate henna designs are painted on her feet and hands, and for the ceremony, she wears a long white shift and is adorned with gold jewelry. As in a wedding, a zaffa procession with candles and music announces the commencement of a private zār, followed by dancing, music, and a celebratory meal.

At a private zār, the immediate family of the 'ayāna is usually present on her behalf. A shaykha presides with her female assistants and the musicians, who may be male. They make invocations to Muslim saints and prophets, and chant incantations of the first verses of the Quran. As the ritual unfolds, the lively percussion is a crucial catalyst for summoning spirits, who each are attracted to the rhythm of a certain beat, or daaq. As chief drummer, the shaykha guides the musicians through a variety of speeds and rhythms to invoke those spirits possessing her client, and also calls forward her personal asyād masters, who help guide her as she coaxes and argues with those troubling the 'ayāna.[10] Drawn by their respective daaq, the zār spirits descend into the bodies of the 'ayāna and the shaykha, who both enter a disassociated state of consciousness. As the 'ayāna encounters her possessing zār spirit/s for the first time, she becomes "host" to them, and enters a state of ecstatic trance, during which she dances as well as emulates their speech and mannerisms. The shaykha hears their demands and propitiates them with promises of gifts and other offerings. To suit the tastes of the asyād, assistants to the shaykha dress the 'ayāna in different costumes and supply her with various ritualistic accessories, such as swords engraved with Koranic inscriptions. Throughout the course of a zār the 'ayāna may be possessed by several spirits. The stock behavioral traits of the asyād are recognized by the expert zār musicians, who then sing honorific songs addressed to that particular spirit.[11]

While under the command of an asyād, undignified behavior prevails. Janice Boddy, who conducted her ethnographic work in rural Sudan, saw women engaging in unnatural behavior such as smoking and dancing in a wanton manner, which countered their normally dignified demeanor. An 'ayāna might drench her own body with water, or a Christian spirit may induce her to guzzle forbidden alcohol or even blood as she dances in an un-ladylike fashion. Possession by a forceful male spirit can provoke the 'ayāna to exhibit uncharacteristic dominance over her husband. Channeling his voice through hers, a spirit will forcefully demand that the husband provide him – via her – with expensive jewelry, fancy clothing, and other luxury items, and even brandish a sword to underline his demands.[12] Anne Cloudsley, who lived in Sudan during the 1960s, observed that women under the influence of a possessing zār spirit were considered to be malbusa (clothed) or ma'zura (excused). Her infirmity was perceived as a "veil" that obscured her normal self, and therefore she was communally forgiven for any health issues or familial tensions that the possessing spirit caused.[13] While under the shroud of possession, a woman holds no fear of repercussion and is not faulted for exhibiting socially unacceptable behavior that is permissible only within the parameters of the zār.

Sacrificial zār feast

After a "zār bride" has made the acquaintance of her personal spirits through a private ceremony, a great wedding feast follows. Delicacies such

Think about:
The ultimate "cure" for a woman in the female-driven ritual of zār is a wedding ceremony. What does this fact reveal about cultural norms in Nile Valley societies?

Figure 7.2
Drum rhythms are essential in drawing zār spirits.
Image: Susan Kenyon.

as oranges, bananas, guava, and watermelon are served, along with milk, fish, rice, white flour, goat cheese, and eggs. These white foods are offered to spirits because they are deemed to be "clean" and thought to benefit a woman's fertility and health. Meat, rice, bread, and spicy broth are prepared for all to eat, along with any specific demands of the spirits according to their native cuisines. Animal sacrifice is common practice at a wedding ceremony; therefore it is an integral part of a private *zār*. While in trance, the *'ayāna* will either ride the animal, lead it by hand, or carry it as she makes a processional circle around a table of offerings.

After the sacrifice, the animal's blood is poured over the possessed *'ayāna*, who lets it soak into her clothes and rubs it into her skin. Since the spirits are ritually possessing her, it is actually they who are directly partaking of the sacrifice, and they choose what portions of the animal the *'ayāna* should eat. By virtue of this act, the disease of the person is transferred to the animal and thus is returned to the spirits. At the conclusion of *zār*, the *'ayāna* eats the brains and sensory organs, while the rest is shared between the *shaykha*, her assistants, the musicians, and any guests.[14] In Natvig's observations of *zār* practice in rural Egyptian villages, after the sacrifice the "*zār* bride" was bloody, like a woman having given birth. During a "confinement" period, she could not wash herself or change clothes, and avoided contact with her husband. The remains of the sacrificial meal were disposed of either in the Nile or in the ground beneath the house, just as a placenta is often disposed of in rural communities in North Sudan and Egypt.[15]

The weekly *hadra* – a public *zār*

After an *'ayāna* has met, appeased, and entered into an ongoing "marriage" with her possessing spirits through her private *zār*, she is not believed to remain in a state of constant possession. It is now considered that she "has a spirit" and, although she initially struggled, her possessor/s now will act in her best interest.[16] To perpetually maintain harmonious relations with her personal spirits, she hones her ability to access them through an altered state in a weekly *zār*. Members of this ritual gather to reconnect and dance with their respective possessors.

In Egypt, this weekly *zār* is called a *hadra*. In the 1980s, ethnographer Laurie Eisler attended several and noted that women of a lower income status called "*baladī*" were the most common attendees. A *hadra* was usually held in an economically depressed part of town, often at the home of a *shaykha*. A woman would pay a small entrance fee, remove her shoes, be purified with incense, and then consult the *shaykha*, who instructed her to wait until she found herself physically moved by the music. When a woman fell into trance, she was considered to be successfully responding to the beat, or *daaq*, of her possessing spirit. Eisler observed that women who had grown familiar with the particular *daaq* of their spirits would slip a small "bribe" to the musicians in order for those rhythms to be played sooner than later. One woman quipped, "Give me the red *jinn*, the mermaid, the doctor, and make it quick, because I have to get home."[17] Despite the fact that the majority of the educated population scorned the *zār*, Eisler also witnessed the presence of young, middle-class women who claimed they did not believe in spirits, but had not benefitted from Western medicine.

In Sudan, informal *zār* gatherings are held in private homes in the form of small "coffee parties" called *jabana*. For a nominal fee, *zār* followers can bring their concerns, or ask for advice to the *zār* spirits directly, and share refreshments with them. During her decade living in Sudan, Kenyon observed that these routine *zār* rituals increased from three to four days a week due to need after the institution of Shari'a law, followed by a *coup* in which a fundamentalist

Figure 7.3
A woman possessed by her *zār* spirit.
Image: Susan Kenyon.

military regime took power. She also noted that some spirits would descend on certain days, such as the Christian spirit, Bashir, who made his appearance on Sundays.[18]

Disapproval of *zār* practice

Zār is practiced in largely Islamic cultures. Although the Quran acknowledges the existence of *jinn* and spirit possession, many *imams* in the mosques and civic officials publicly denounce the *zār* as pagan devil worship and, despite the function of a *shaykha* in a therapeutic practice valued by many women, she has low social status within society.[19] Since Islam allows the worship of only one god – Allah – devoted Muslims regard the practice of summoning *zār* spirits as being contrary to the Islamic faith. From this monotheistic perspective, pacifying one's personal demons through dancing and ritual offerings is deemed blasphemous, and from a cultural standpoint, non-participants often dismiss the *zār* as a superstitious ritual sought after by mentally unstable women. On a more personal level, husbands who are suspicious of the *zār* claim that such demands are a means of extortion by women and provide a means of acquiring desired items from reluctant spouses.[20]

*Think about:
If more men in male-dominated North African societies sought out zār, would it be such a target of opposition?*

Benefits of *zār* practice

In his studies on the *zār*, John Kennedy noted that Nubians are peaceful people who believe that malevolent spirits are attracted to those who deviate from their customary, nonviolent societal behavior. Therefore, *zār* ceremonies were an essential tool used to preserve their peaceful society. He also observed that Nubian healers could usually distinguish between neurotic symptoms, such as hysteria, and major psychoses, such as schizophrenia. Kennedy recounted an incident involving a young woman from the village of Qustal, who had recently lost her mother and had developed what he considered to be schizophrenia:

> One morning shortly after the death . . . Sa'diyya . . . awoke screaming and ran from the house. Her father caught her and beat her, but to no avail . . . her speech was meaningless and jumbled, and she would run frantically through the village laughing wildly. She remained in this hopelessly incapacitated condition for several months.[21]

The father arranged for a seven-day *zār* for Sa'diyya, and her malady went into complete remission. She eventually married, bore two children, and was considered mentally sound by the village.

One might well ask how the *zār* can provide therapeutic relief from infertility, symptoms of anxiety, or more seriously, hysteria, which can manifest itself in mental illness and semi-paralysis. Kennedy observed that the introspection and "working through" of a person's trauma that occurs in Western psychotherapy were absent in the *zār* and, instead, emotional factors such as faith, catharsis, and group support all led to the creation of an emotional, dramatic, and ritually charged atmosphere in which societal restraints were abandoned and repressed impulses were allowed to run free.[22]

A *zār* provides a place of refuge for its followers, who are bolstered by a strong social network within the entertaining club-like atmosphere of the ritual. As it is culturally taboo for a woman in male-dominated Islamic society to express frustration over her circumstances, the *zār* is an accepted "safe haven" in which she can express her troubles and relieve psychological, social, and physical stresses on a regular basis. A parallel could be drawn between the Western practice of psychotherapy and the *zār*, which both draw individuals weekly. But while therapy may result in a patient being prescribed psychotropic drugs to alleviate depression or anxiety, the *zār*, with its exuberant music, dancing, costumes, and spirit possession, can be viewed as being an alternative, communal, and drug-free method of coping with social, familial, and personal anxieties. *Zār* ritual provides a socially sanctioned arena in which a woman, in tandem with her spirits and members of her community, can voice her unhappiness, assert her needs or her own power, and feel exuberant afterward. Spiritually refreshed, women emerge from the *zār* ready to face their problems with confidence.

Current trends

The escalation of Islamic fundamentalism has affected secular society in numerous ways, especially in Sudan, which has experienced tremendous political, economic, and religious disturbances since the 1980s. As the Sudanese economy faltered and a tense political climate ensued, Susan Kenyon anticipated a decline in *zār* ceremonies due to fear of civil and religious authorities that regarded the practice as anti-Islamic. But despite societal disapproval, *zār* has continued to provide welcome relief to women, especially from the stresses that the harsher laws imposed. Kenyon observed that *zār* practice actually increased overall in Sudan in the latter part of the twentieth century, and stated, "Officially, *zār* has been banned since 1992 . . . but unofficially, the drums are still beating loudly."[23] When Kenyon returned in 2000, she was surprised that it was being practiced quite openly.[24] Boddy feels that *zār* is resurfacing in other forms: its dances are currently performed as part of affluent weddings. A bride undergoes several changes of clothing over one or two afternoons, each time wearing the costume of an ethnic group different from her own, and dances to *zār* spirit rhythms, played on the *daluka*, the typical *zār* drum.[25]

In Egypt, a *fatwa* issued from Al-Azhar, a Muslim institution sometimes described as "the Vatican of Islam," decreed that "formal Islam condemns the *zār* for being a cult which violates numerous sacred prohibitions."[26] A way around this has been to separate the music from the ritual, but this has had its consequences. For almost two decades, Ahmen al-Maghraby has endeavored to preserve *zār* music at Makan, the only public venue for the *zār* in Egypt. Makan also sponsors *zār* groups such as the Mazaher Ensemble, led by female members who are purportedly among the last *zār* practitioners in Egypt. Madiha, a popular performer at Makan, learned *zār* ceremony from her mother and a long line of women who practiced the tradition, but claims that no one new is learning it.[27] Although perhaps *zār* ceremonies still occur behind closed doors in Egypt, Sudan, and Ethiopia, apparently the tradition is experiencing a transition from being a therapeutic, social ritual for women into mystical concert music, performed in Cairo on a theatrical stage.

7.2 Exploration: excerpt from *Wombs and Alien Spirits: Women, Men, and the Zār Cult in Northern Sudan*[28] by Janice Boddy

A piercing cry – a uniformed schoolgirl nine or ten years old has sprawled forward into the *mīdān* . . . [her] body jerking rapidly up and down from the shoulders. Immediately, she is led off by some older women, told that it is not proper for a child to behave this way at a *zār*. But she does not stop. Outside the *mīdān* the women try to calm her. Now she is sobbing and has gone quite limp. When efforts to revive her fail she is dragged, resisting, back into the center. She balks at attempts to bring her to the *shaykha* and is deposited before the drums. The *shaykha* approaches; the girl cringes. The *shaykha* censes her, covers with a white *tōb*, and asks, "What do you want? Who are you?" No response.

Onlookers taunt the intrusive *zār*, trying vainly to garner its sympathy: "Ah, her father is poor! Her mother is blind! Her brother is ill!" The *shaykha* sends for the girl's father. He is brought into the *mīdān* and made to give his daughter's spirit ten piasters (about twenty-five cents). Still there is no word from the *zār* . . . the girl remains limp, appearing deeply entranced. More drumming and dancing are called for. The *shaykha* requests certain [musical] threads to test for various species of *zayran*, hoping the presumptuous spirit will be drawn to identify itself. She blows into the schoolgirl's ears and behind her neck; she pulls at her limbs, whips her softy with a length of rope, beats her slightly with an iron spear . . . She takes the girl in her arms and dances to and fro, blowing a whistle to the incessant beat. She leads the girl around the *mīdān* and is twice successful in getting her to move briefly of her own accord. At last the girl jogs back and forth through the open space, one arm pumping like the wheel of a locomotive, the other raised and crooked at the elbow, sounding an imagined alarm. The *shaykha* blows her pipe whistle in accompaniment. The troublesome spirit is identified: Basha-t-'Adil, the Kawāja railway engineer . . . Still the episode continues. For over an hour the *shaykha* tries every technique in her repertoire to try to persuade the implacable *zār* to abandon its newfound host and refrain from bothering her again until she is a woman and married. Finally the *shaykha* guides the girl out of the *mīdān* and out of the *hōsh*. They cross the threshold backwards, facing the assembly . . . the girl, now calmed and weeping softly, is brought to sit . . . but placed with her back to the ritual.

Discussion questions: *zār*

1 Why is the profession of a *shaykha* one of the few in which a woman can hold leadership positions and have financial independence within a male-dominated society?
2 In Islamic countries, there is a marked separation between the sexes both publicly and privately, and a great distinction between gender roles. How does the female-dominated *zār* level the playing field?
3 Many women – regardless of region or culture – face the same worries and issues, and have the same symptoms. Discuss the use of psychotropic drugs in Western countries versus the weekly *zārs* women attend in North African communities.

7.3 The *sema*: mystical dance of the Sufi Mevlevi dervish

Key points: *sema*

1 In Turkey, Mevlevi dervishes of the Sufi Islamic order seek divine truth and unite with God through the ritual of *sema*, a whirling dance that induces a state of religious ecstasy in its followers, who are called *semazen*. The Mevlevi order was founded by the sons of the poet Mevlana Jalalu'ddin Rumi (1207–1273).
2 Dervishes were known for their asceticism and for their practice of *zikr*, or remembrance of God through frequent repetition of phrases. A dervish's initiation lasted 1,001 days, and took place in a *tekke*, a spiritual conservatory.
3 The music, action, and costuming of a *sema* is filled with symbolism. A *semazen* wears a long black overcoat with wide sleeves, representing the grave, or death itself. Underneath is a long white robe symbolizing the funeral shroud of the ego, while the tall cylindrical hat, made of camel's hair, recalls the tombstone.
4 The *sema* has four periods of dancing and music known as *selams*, or salutations. The incessant spinning enables a *semazen* to enter a state of disassociation that allows his soul to elevate and experience a union with God. Each dancer represents a planet rotating on its axis, while the *sheikh* turns alone in the center, symbolizing the sun.
5 After the overthrow of the Ottoman Empire, the Republic of Turkey was established in 1923. Its new leader, Kemal Ataturk, passed a law that forbade Sufi practices of worship in his attempt to secularize and modernize Turkey. Thirty years later, the government began to allow secular performances of sema and its music.

There are many roads which lead to god. I have chosen the one of dance, and music.[29]

—Mevlana Jalalu'ddin Rumi

The Mevlevi dervishes are members of a Sufi order founded in the thirteenth century in Konya, Turkey. Sufism, an esoteric form of Islam, is a belief and practice in which Muslims seek to find divine truth and knowledge through their union with God. Dervishes were known for their asceticism, and for their practice of *zikr*, or remembrance of God through frequent repetition of phrases, such *la'illaha il'Allahu* – "there is only God." In their worship, the Mevlevi practice *zikr* through the ritual of *sema*, a whirling dance that induces a state of ecstasy in followers that unites them with God.

The Persian word *darwish* (sill of the door) is written in Arabic and Turkish as *dervish*, and metaphorically depicts one who seeks the door of enlightenment. Dervishes lived in a *tekke*, a spiritual lodge and conservatory for philosophical teaching and training master performers of Turkish music and *sema*. These lodges served as an important part of spiritual and intellectual life in Turkey and other parts of the former Ottoman Empire. However, after the overthrow of the Empire, the Republic of Turkey was established in 1923. Its new leader, Kemal Ataturk, passed a law that forbade Sufi practices of worship in his attempt to secularize and modernize Turkey. Thirty years later, the Turkish government began to allow performances of *sema* and its music, but only publicly, in a secular context.

Case study: The Ottoman Empire

The Ottoman Empire was an Islamic imperial monarchy that existed for over 600 years. At the height of its power in the sixteenth and seventeenth centuries, it encompassed three continents and served as the core of global interactions between the East and the West. The Empire was defeated and broken up by the victors after World War I and was dissolved in 1920. In 1923, Turkey was proclaimed a republic and led by Mustafa Kemal Ataturk, who set about doing away with many Islamic traditions in order to modernize the country. In 1925, he outlawed mystical orders, and whirling was officially banned.

The inspiration behind the organization of the Mevlevi order was Mevlana Jalalu'ddin Rumi (also spelled Mevlana Celaddin-i Rumi), who was born into a Sufi family in Afghanistan in 1207. Through his father, Bahauddin Walad, a renowned scholar and theologian, Mevlana learned Turkish, Arabic, Persian, and Greek, and studied other religions in addition to Islam. Fleeing a Mongol invasion in 1215, the family migrated to Konya, where Rumi eventually married, and began to teach in theological universities. A turning point in Rumi's spiritual life occurred in 1244, when he met Shams-i Tabrizi, a wandering Sufi master. An intense, all-consuming friendship arose between the two men, who sequestered themselves for months while engaging in religious discussions. Tabrizi's presence caused great jealousy in Rumi's students, who missed their teacher, and their damaging rumors caused Tabrizi to leave abruptly for Damascus. The absence of his spiritual soul mate caused Rumi such profound grief that his son, Sultan Veled, was forced to travel to Damascus to retrieve him. Their joyous reunion was short lived; Tabrizi disappeared again – and purportedly was murdered. Rumi's great love and admiration for his friend inspired him to compose *Divan-i Shams-i Tabrizi*, a masterpiece in Persian poetry, and he remains one of the most beloved and widely read poets.

Rumi's other writings – poetry, letters, and lectures inspired by the teachings of the Quran – speak about maintaining inner peace and harmony, being appreciative of god's blessings, and how to be tolerant and loving. When Rumi died on December 17, 1273, he was buried next to his father in a mausoleum that has become a shrine for pilgrims who venerate his teachings and mystical poetry. Mevlevi disciples celebrate this date, which they call his *Seb-i Arus* – wedding night, or night of unity with God. Rumi's son, Sultan Veled, founded the Mevlevi (followers of Mevlana) order in his memory, espousing a doctrine that advocates tolerance, positive reasoning, goodness, charity, and awareness through love. The Mevlevi order spread throughout the Ottoman Empire, but the *tekke* in Konya, attached to

Think about:
Why is religion – and often dance – so threatening to those newly in power?

the Mevlana Mausoleum, remained the largest, and thrived as an institute of art and culture for generations.

Ataturk outlawed Sufism in 1925, but was conflicted over closing the Mevlevi order. He said to Abdulahalim Chalabi, Rumi's descendant, "You, the Mevlevis, have made a great difference by combatting ignorance and religious fundamentalism for centuries, as well as making contributions to science and the arts. However we are obliged not to make any exceptions and must include Mevlevi *tekkes*."[30] Further evidence of his conflict was apparent when, in 1927, Ataturk allowed Mevlana's *tekke* in Konya to become a museum and supported the translation of the poet's books from Persian into Turkish.

Mevlevi dervish training

Prior to 1925, a boy's initiation into a Mevlevi order was an educational process that occurred in a *tekke*. Recommendation by a member was necessary for entry, and parental permission was required for anyone below the age of 18. There were two paths of choice: one could opt for a *chille* – a retreat which would last for 1,001 days and result in the granting of the title of *dede*; the other was to study daily at the *tekke*, but not reside there. If the initiate chose the sequestered retreat, he would be brought to the *ahchi dede* (chief of the kitchen) and given his first test. The word *ahchi* not only was connected to the preparation of food, but is a metaphor for the preparation of the soul of a follower, an idea reflected in Rumi's words: "I was raw, then cooked, and now I am burnt."[31] In the kitchen, or *matbah*, a new initiate would sit for three days on his knees on a thick sheepskin, and observe the comings and goings of the *tekke*. He was not allowed to speak or sleep, and could only leave his post in order to pray five times a day. During this ordeal, he would be closely observed to see if he was fit to be a *chille* initiate. If so, the initiate was required to make a promise of allegiance to the *sheikh* – the leader of the *tekke*, who would then present him with a *sikke*, a conical dervish hat, and a *chille tennuresi*, a long black dress worn throughout the 1,001 days of his education.

Case study: Female dervishes

Although the Mevlevi order is typically composed of men, there have been instances in which women have held the position of a *sheikh*. Sefer Hatun, Sultan Veled's daughter and Mevlana's granddaughter, was a renowned teacher. The most famous was Destine Hatun, the daughter of Sheikh Sultan Divani of the Afyon *tekke*. In Afyonkarahisar, Kucuk Meahmed Chalabi's daughter Gunes Han held positions of both *sheikh* and caliph. Women there would perform together in an all-female *sema*.

During the reclusive training, an initiate became literate in Arabic in order to read the Quran, and studied Persian and Turkish to be versed in literature and poetry. He repeated Muslim prayers five times a day and learned about ethics and religious principles. His education included lessons with the *semazenbashi* (dance master) in order to become a *semazen* (whirler). Cooking and cleaning in the *tekke* was required, and the *ahchi dede* gave the initiate a *zikr* to repeat as he executed a multitude of daily chores. If at any time he disobeyed the rules, or failed to attend his evening class with the *sheikh*, his retreat was considered to have been broken and he had to begin his *chille* again.[32]

Initiates who successfully completed the 1,001 days were given the title of *dede*. Only a *chille* initiate could aspire to be a *sema* musician, a dance master, or a *sheikh*. If he chose to live an austere life in the *tekke*, he couldn't marry, since women were not permitted to live there. Those students who had chosen not to reside at the *tekke* during their training were allowed to marry and perform in the weekly *sema*. Until dervish practice was outlawed, *dede* functioned as teachers and performed the weekly *sema*. They were supported by the government and exempt from military service and paying taxes.

Symbolism within *sema*

A legendary story exists about the origins of the whirling *sema*. As Rumi was walking in the marketplace in Konya, he heard a gold beater hard at work, making vessels. In the rhythmic hammering, he heard the *zikr, Allah, Allah, Allah*, which inspired him to spin around in ecstasy with his arms wide open, embracing God. After his death, when his son, Sultan Veled, and others organized the Mevlevi order, this dancing was developed into a codified ritual and performed to music combining Persian and Turkish traditions, with lyrics incorporating poetry of Rumi and other thirteen-century poets.

The essential purpose of the *sema* is to attain the blissful, mystical state of *wajd*, where one sees God in everything.[33] A *semazen* enters a state of disassociation that allows his soul to elevate through induced exhaustion from the incessant spinning and the constant repetition of *zikr*. In this altered state, the metaphorical annihilation of the self brings on a state of ecstasy, and a *semazen* experiences a union with God. The *sema* is filled with symbolism, as its surroundings, music, action, and costuming all carry special meanings. The circular room of the *semahane* (dance hall) represents the universe, while the color red of the sheepskin post on which the *sheikh* sits symbolizes the sun. Death, which metaphorically symbolizes departure from the earth and ascension into spiritual life, is represented in the costuming. A *semazen* wears a *hirqa*, a long black overcoat with wide sleeves, representing the grave, or death itself. Underneath is a *tennure*, a long white robe symbolizing the funeral shroud of the ego, while the tall cylindrical *sikke* hat, made of camel's hair, recalls the tombstone. Supple leather ankle-boots are worn to facilitate turning.

In the counterclockwise rotations of the *sema*, the harmony of celestial bodies is manifested as each dancer represents a planet rotating on its axis, while the *sheikh*, who turns alone in the center of the hall, symbolizes the sun. To learn how to turn, a smooth, round-headed nail is nailed into a wooden board, which is placed on the floor. An initiate will kiss the nail and place his left foot so that his first and second toes are between it. He keeps his right arm crossed over the left, with palms hugging the shoulders, and uses his right foot to drive his body to the left. The eyes are open, but unfocused, which allows reality to become blurred during the rotation. Mastering this turning takes at least ninety days. Once an initiate is deemed ready to participate, he is considered to be a *semazen*, and prepares for a ceremony by fasting and ritually washing his body with cold water while repeating a *zikr* in the name of God.[34]

Figure 7.4
During the *sema*, the internal gaze of a *semazen* helps lead to his union with the divine.
Image: Linda Vartoogian, Front Row Photos.

Think about:
What does the symbolism inherent in the sema *tell us about the Mevelevi ethos?*

Performing the *sema*

When performing a *sema*, the dervishes enter the *semahane* led by the *semazenbashi*. With heads bowed, they proceed to line up on one side of the hall. The last to enter is the *sheikh*, who walks slowly to his post, a red sheepskin rug. The *semazen* and the *sheikh* kneel as the opening prayers and music begin. The musicians seated on the opposite end of the hall on a raised platform include the *hafiz*, who can recite the entire Quran by heart. He begins by chanting a *naat* – an opening prayer to Mevlana or to Mohammed. The strike of the *kudum* drum signifies the sound of "be," God's command when he created the cosmos. This is followed by a musical improvisation called the *taksim*, played on the *ney*, a reed flute. Its plaintive sound evokes the divine breath that brought life to the universe, as well as the sound of the human voice.

After opening prayers and music, the *semazen* rise to begin the Sultan Veled Walk, named in honor of Mevlana's son. Accompanied by music known as *peshrev*, this circular walk symbolizes the meeting of souls in a collective, spiritual journey. Following the *sheikh* in single file, they travel in a measured pace three times around the circumference of the room, which symbolizes the three stages that take one nearer to God: the path of science, the path of vision, and the path leading to union with God.[35] After the third circle, the *sheikh* returns to his sheepskin post. Arranged in a line, the *semazen* all bow, and simultaneously remove their black cloaks, kiss them, and drop them to the floor in an audible *whoosh*. Symbolically, they have left their ego behind and are now ready to unite with God through their turning. This is done in four periods of dancing and music known as *selams*, or salutations. At the beginning and end of each *selam*, a *semazen* holds his arms crosswise over the chest to represent the number one, and testifies to God's unity.

Dressed now in the white *tennure*, each *semazen* approaches the *sheikh* one by one. Bowing with crossed arms, he kisses the back of the *sheikh*'s hand, who in turn kisses the *semazen*'s hat, thereby giving permission to enter the dancing space and begin the first *selam*. With his left foot as the axis, the *semazen* slowly begins to turn counterclockwise, pedaling with his right foot. Gradually, his head inclines toward his right shoulder as his crossed arms unfurl into the whirling posture. His right arm lifts above his head with the palm turned upward, while his left arm remains horizontal, with the palm facing down. As he spins in place, free of unworthy attachments and passions, a *semazen* become a conduit for divine energy, which passes through the right hand, through the heart, and is distributed through the left hand to the earth. With downcast eyes and an expressionless face, the *semazen* all silently repeat an inaudible *zikr* in Allah's name as they turn. The *semazenbashi* wanders among the

Figure 7.5
Mevelvi dervishes from Konya performing *sema*.
Image: Jack Vartoogian, Front Row Photos.

dancers, correcting their position, posture, or speed. After about fifteen minutes, the music and the chanting chorus in the first *selam* stops. The *semazen* halt so quickly that their skirts, which flare widely in a bell shape as they whirl, snap abruptly in a spiral around their legs. Bowing toward the *sheikh*, they step back in line and begin the next *selam* with the musicians.

In the fourth and last *selam*, the *sheikh* joins them. As he slowly revolves in the center of the *semahane*, he represents the sun, while the dervishes symbolize the planets revolving around him. At the end of the fourth *selam*, a solo *ney* sounds a long note that leads the *sheikh* back to his post, where he bows, then sits and kisses the floor. The *semazen* put their black cloaks back on, signaling a symbolic return to their tombs, but now in a more perfect state. The *sheikh* concludes the *sema* with a reading from the Quran and a prayer for the repose of souls. The *semazen* then kiss the floor, rise, and all chant the sound "Hu," which represents all the names of God in one. In a stately finish, the *sheikh* silently leads the dervishes from the *semahane*.

For the Mevlevi, the *sema* is a mystical pursuit of the elevation of the mind so that one may leave his soul, unite spiritually with god, and return in a more purified state in order to be of service to the world. Even the youngest of *semazen*, who are taught to never go to extremes in behavior or speech, seem to view the world more maturely after participating in *sema*. Twelve-year-old Fahiri Ozcakir attested, "Sometimes, during the *sema*, it feels as if Mevlana is holding my hand. I begin to smile inside, and my heart is warm and later it is as if what my eyes see is different from before."[36]

Figure 7.6
In *sema*, the *sheikh* represents the sun, the center of the universe.
Image: Jack Vartoogian, Front Row Photos.

Figure 7.7 (p. 202)
The Akram Khan Company in *Vertical Road*, a 2010 work inspired by the Sufi tradition and the Persian poet, Rumi.
Image: Richard Haughton.

Current trends

Although the *tekkes* have never been re-opened as places of worship in Turkey, concerts of Mevlevi music began to be permitted in the 1940s, but the *sema* was still forbidden. Today, *sema* is performed at the Mevlevi Museum in Konya for the public twice a month. Every December, on the anniversary of Rumi's reunion with God, over 25,000 tourists descend upon the city to see a *sema* in his honor. Today, *sema* performances in Turkey are deprived of their religious significance in that they are no longer performed in traditional context, but in front of tourist audiences. The Mevlevi order still functions, and is led by Rumi's descendant, Faruk Herndem Celebi. Outside of Turkey, Mevlevi orders exist in places including Damascus, Tripoli, Cairo, Cyprus, and Jerusalem, and some, such as those in the United Kingdom or the United States, offer courses on learning *sema* and its music, as well as on Rumi's writings.

British choreographer Akram Khan's work *Vertical Road* (2010) was inspired by the Sufi tradition behind the Mevlevi dervish and the poetry and philosophies of Rumi. Khan incorporated the winding arms of *kathak* into the ecstatic turns seen in both *kathak* and *sema*. Two Turkish choreographers using whirling of the *sema* in their contemporary works are Nejla Yatkin and Ziya Azazi. While Yatkin uses spinning as an abstract element in her dances, Azazi incorporates authentic *sema* turning for long periods in his work "Dervish in Progress."

7.3 Exploration: excerpt from *The City of the Sultan* by Julia Pardoe[37]

Miss Julia Pardoe was a nineteenth-century Englishwoman who wrote travelogues throughout her journeys abroad.

One by one, the Dervishes entered the chapel, bowing profoundly at the little gate of the enclosure, took their places on the mat, and, bending down, reverently kissed the ground; and then, folding their arms meekly on their breasts, remained buried in prayer, with their eyes closed and their bodies swinging slowly to and fro. They were all enveloped in wide cloaks of dark colored cloth with pendent sleeves; and wore their *geulafs* [hats] . . . The service commenced with an extemporaneous prayer from the chief priest to which the attendant Dervishes listened with arms folded upon their breasts, and their eyes fixed on the ground. At its conclusion, all bowed their foreheads to the earth, and the orchestra struck into one of those peculiarly wild and melancholy Turkish airs which are unlike any other music that I have ever heard. Instantly, the full voices of the brethren joined in chorus, and the effect was thrilling; now the sounds died away like the exhausted breath of a departing spirit, and suddenly they swelled once more into a deep and powerful diapason that seemed scarce earthy . . . The Dervishes, slowly rising from the earth, followed their superior three times around the enclosure; bowing down twice under the name of their Founder, suspended above the seat of the high priest. This reverence was performed without removing their folded arms from their breasts . . . I am no means prepared, nor even inclined, to attempt a Quixotic defense of the very extraordinary and *bizarre* ceremonial to which I was next a witness; but I cannot, nevertheless, agree with a modern traveller in describing it as "an absurdity." I should imagine that no one could feel other than respect for men of irreproachable character, serving God according to their means of judgment. An interval of prayer followed; and the same ceremony was performed three times; at the termination of which they all fell prostrate on the earth, while those who had remained spectators flung their cloaks over them, and the one who knelt on the left of the Chief Priest rose, and delivered a long prayer divided into sections, with a rapid and solemn voice, prolong the last word of each sentence by the utterance of "ha-ha-ha" with a rich depth of octave . . . the superior, rising to his knees while the others continued prostrate, in his turn prayed for a few instants; and then, taking his stand upon the crimson rug, they approached him one by one, and clasping his hand, pressed it to their lips and forehead. This was the final act of the exhibition; and the superior having slowly and silently traversed the enclosure, in five seconds the chapel was empty, and the congregation busied at the portal in reclaiming their boots, shoes, and slippers. I had never hitherto seen such picturesque groups as those which thronged the Dervishes' chapel . . . nor did I ever witness a more perfect order in any public assembly. A deep stillness reigned throughout the whole ceremony, only broken by the sobs of a middle-aged Turk who stood near me, and who was so overcome by the saddening wail of the orchestra that he could not restrain his tears; a circumstance by no means uncommon in this country, where all ranks are peculiarly susceptible to the influence of music.

Discussion questions: *sema*

1 *Semazen* attain a trance state when they perform a *sema*, yet how they enter this state is far more structured and organized in its approach than in other dance forms. What does this say about the culture and training of the Mevlevi dervishes?
2 In terms of an initiate's training, discuss the significance of Rumi's words, "I was raw, then cooked, and now I am burnt."
3 Thirty years after being banned in 1925, at first only the music of the Mevlevi *sema* was allowed to be performed – not the dance. Discuss why dance – something that is seen – would be more problematic than music, which is listened to, for an audience.

7.4 *Flamenco*: a manifestation of cultures and passions

Key points: *flamenco*

1 *Flamenco* music, song, and dance is an amalgam that arose due to convergences of various cultural and religious influences in Andalusia reaching back to the fifteenth century. Jews, Arabs, Indians from Rajasthan, and Spanish folk traditions all contributed to its development. Spaniards called the Indians "*Gitanos*" – a distortion of the word for Egiptanos, or Egyptians. *Gitanos* were repeatedly persecuted by royal decrees until 1783.
2 Arabic rule in Spain began in 711 A.D. and lasted seven hundred years, during which Muslims, Christians, Sephardic Jews, and Gitanos lived together in a peaceful era known as *La Convivencia*. In 1480, Ferdinand and Isabella launched *La Reconquista*, a crusade aimed at establishing Catholicism throughout the country. The Spanish Inquisition was launched in 1480, targeting anyone not of the Catholic faith.
3 A *flamenco* singer, called a *cantaor/a*, sings in a style known as *cante jondo*, or deep song. The *flamenco* guitar is played by a *tocaor/a*. Instrumentalists also play a cajón, a wooden box that is struck while sitting upon it. Adding to the percussion are *pitos* – finger snapping – and hand clapping called *palmas*. Dancers use heeled shoes that are studded with nails to enhance the sound of their *zapeteado*, or footwork.
4 *Gitano* dancing, in the form before its commercialization in the nineteenth century, is known today as *flamenco puro*. In the nineteenth century, *flamenco* performers emerged from the *barrios* to work professionally in *cafés cantantes*, and the commercialization of *flamenco* began.
5 After the Spanish Civil War (1936–1939), Generalissimo Francisco Franco ruled as a dictator for the next thirty-six years. In the 1950s, Franco used dance to bolster Spanish nationalism. Despite his antagonism toward *Gitanos*, he recognized *flamenco's* tourist appeal, and a repackaged version was forged into a propaganda tool known as *nacionalflamenquismo* – a joyous symbol of Spanish identity.

The duende works on the body of the dancer as the wind works on sand. With magical power, he changes a girl into a lunar paralytic, or brings an adolescent blush to the broken old man begging in the wine shop, or the odor of a nocturnal port to a woman's hair, and he works continuously on the arms with expressions that give birth to the dances of every age.[38]
—Federico García Lorca

The word *duende*, above, translates as "goblin-like spirit." The eloquent Spanish poet Federico García Lorca famously addressed this elusive, dark quality in his 1933 lecture, "Theory and Play of the Duende," declaring, "The great artists of Spain . . . whether they sing, dance, or play, know that no emotion is possible unless the *duende* comes."[39] This term embraces the ineffable charisma, soul, and fiery passion that remarkable *flamenco* singers, musicians, and dancers possess. This "passion" inherent in *flamenco* makes it one of the most recognizable and popular forms of global dance and is also a phenomenon that may be added to the numerous clichés that have mythologized Spain in popular culture as a romantic land of matadors, exotic Gypsy dancers, and colorful *fiestas*. While *flamenco* is regularly presented in concert halls in cities and in high-profile festivals around the world, many people might not be aware that part of the origins of its dance, music, and singing arose due to convergences of political injustice; social marginalization; vibrant music, dance, and singing; and various religions in Andalusia, Spain's southernmost province. Although its influences reach back to the fifteenth century, it was during the nineteenth century that the music, dance, and singing crystalized into the distinct form of *flamenco*.

In the fifteenth century, peoples from Rajasthan in northern India migrated to Spain and came to Andalusia. Spaniards called them *Gitanos* – a distortion of the word for *Egiptanos*, or Egyptians. (Although Gypsies elsewhere in Europe identify as *Rom*, or *Roma*, in Spain they continue to call themselves *Gitanos*.) Because of their nomadic lifestyle, *Gitanos* were repeatedly persecuted under Spanish laws, and often branded as vagabonds, sorcerers, beggars, and horse thieves by the populace. Forced to engage in gainful work, many became blacksmiths and horse-trainers, settling in their own *barrios* (neighborhoods) in Seville, Jerez, Cádiz, and Granada.

Case study: *Gitano* harassment

Apprehension about the nomadic nature of *Gitanos* caused them to be repeatedly persecuted by royal decrees, such as this one issued in 1499, pressuring them to settle: "The gypsies . . . will in the future be forbidden to wander around in the kingdom. Within sixty days after the public announcement of the law they may emigrate from the country and never return. If he does not comply with the provisions of this law, each offender shall receive one hundred lashes the first time he is caught. The second time his ears shall be cut off, and he shall receive sixty days imprisonment. The third time he shall be imprisoned for life."[40]

In another decree issued in 1539 by Charles V, *Gitanos* faced potential enslavement in galleys of warships, propelling the boats for six-year terms. In 1586, Phillip III decreed that *Gitanos* could not settle in cities of less than one thousand families, and forced them to abandon their traditional dress, language, and names. *Gitano* harassment continued until Charles III granted them citizenship in 1783.

Some theorize that the term *flamenco* derives from two Arabic words: *felag* and *mengu*, which together mean "wandering peasant."[41] Although the *Gitanos* were not Arabic, *flamenco* became the name of their music, song, and dance. Scholar Ninotchka Bennaham comments on their ongoing status as foreigners:

Although gypsies had wandered into Europe between the ninth and the fourteenth centuries, exiled from Rajasthan by Muslim invaders, they are considered as outsiders to this day, just like the Moors and the Jews. Gypsy customs – their dancing, singing, clothing – were considered strange and inferior to those of the white European, even after their incorporation into the European tradition over the centuries, with their forced conversion to Catholicism from the early fifteenth to the early nineteenth centuries.[42]

Not surprisingly, this unwelcoming atmosphere dovetailed with the tendency of *Gitanos* to isolate themselves. They performed their dance and music in the Sacromonte caves of Granada, and later, in the seclusion of urban *barrios*. The *Gitano* style of dancing and singing before its commercialization is known today as *flamenco puro* – an expression of protest, discontent, and sometimes joy that can be considered analogous to Blues music sung by impoverished African Americans in the rural south. In the mid-nineteenth century, the exodus of *flamenco puro* out of the *barrios* and into the highly visible realm of *cafés cantantes* in Spanish cities resulted in professionalization and codification of the form.

A history of imported cultural influences

The Iberian Peninsula was invaded numerous times by populations that include the Phoenicians, Jews, Greeks, Romans, and the Visigoths. Although each group made their respective cultural and artistic imprints, the Moorish invasion in 711 A.D. ushered in an era that was particularly rich both intellectually and artistically. Entering through northern Africa, the Moors took over the whole peninsula except for the northern province of Asturia. The center of Islamic Spain was established in Al-Andalus (the Arabic name for Andalusia), with Cordobá as its capital. This sophisticated city of converging races, cultures, religions, and languages became an educational center for science, literature, poetry, and music.[43] During the seven centuries of Arab rule in Spain, Muslims, Christians, Sephardic Jews, and *Gitanos* lived together in a mostly peaceful and prosperous era known as *La Convivencia*. This came to an end with the advent of the Catholic monarchy of Ferdinand and Isabella, who were married in 1469. Due to their policies of aggressive exploration, colonization, and ethnic purging, Spain became one of Europe's most wealthy and feared countries for two centuries.

In an attempt to unify Spain, Ferdinand and Isabella launched *La Reconquista*, a crusade aimed at establishing Catholicism throughout the entire Iberian Peninsula and ridding Andalusia of Muslim rule. To this end, the brutally cruel Spanish Inquisition was launched in 1478, targeting heretics and anyone not of the Catholic faith. Tribunals were established and presided over by Tomás de Torquemada, the "architect" of this reign of terror. A method of torture implemented was *auto-da-fé* (act of faith), in which people were burned at the stake. Until the official termination of the Inquisition in 1834, these public (and highly popular) immolations were practiced in all Spanish territories, including those in the New World.

In 1492, after a decade of regaining Arabic territory, *Reconquista* troops finally conquered Granada – the last stronghold of Moorish Spain. Three months later, Ferdinand and Isabella issued the Alhambra Decree, which started the *Expulsión*: all practicing Jews had to convert or be exiled. Jews who complied were called *conversos*, but those accused of covertly practicing their original faith were victims of *auto-da-fé*. *Moriscos* (converted Moors) were tolerated in Spain until Philip III issued a royal decree expelling them in 1609. Although thousands of Jews and Moors chose exile, there is speculation that many of them in Andalusia sought refuge in the *barrios* of the *Gitanos*, casting their fates with that of an abject population subjected to poverty, hunger, and social stigmas.

Development of *flamenco*

Some historians posit that *flamenco's* origins are rooted in the North Indian dance form of *kathak*. Dance scholar Miriam Phillips observes that although both share characteristics such as percussive footwork, precise spins, and circuitous arm gestures, their respective origins are completely antithetical.[44] *Kathak* synthesized into lavish court entertainment from Rajasthan, Persia, and Turkey, while *flamenco* evolved from an amalgam of influences originating in an impoverished environment. Its song, or *el cante*, became infused with the rhythms and vocalizations of Arab and Jewish music, and was accompanied by *el toque*, or guitar playing – an instrument of Arab origin. Dance – *el baile* – reflected the percussive footwork of Indian dance and the serpentine arms seen in that of the Middle East. Scholar Meira Goldberg notes African contributions as well, such as winding hips, sudden stops, and percussive rhythms, due to Seville becoming a huge redistribution center of West African slaves in the sixteenth century.[45] In Andalusia, these cultural elements contributed to the emergence of *flamenco* – a powerful artistic vehicle for pouring out one's emotions.

In the eighteenth century, *escuela bolera* (*bolero* school) evolved into the classic school of Spanish dance during the Napoleonic occupation. Often accompanied by castanets, popular folk dances such as *fandangos*, *malagueñas*, and *la cachucha* were synthesized with French ballet.[46] Unlike *escuela bolera*, *flamenco's* nascence in *Gitano* caves and urban *barrios* of Andalusia made it much less visible. Soon, however, the Andalusian aristocracy and wealthy classes discovered this untamed, unrehearsed entertainment, and frequently hired *Gitanos* to entertain at their raucous

Figure 7.8
Ursula Lopez (in white) and Elena Algado as two sides of Carmen Amaya in *La Leyenda*, performed by the Compania Andaluza de Danza.
Image: Jack Vartoogian, Front Row Photos.

parties. In Goya's eighteenth-century tapestry cartoons, Spanish aristocrats parade in the fashions of the urban lower classes and are spellbound by Gypsy songs and dances. Members of the aristocracy became patrons of Gypsy families, and some gave them their prestigious surnames, such as Flores or Amaya.[47] However, *Gitanos* were still shunned by society and persecuted by repressive royal edicts until Charles III granted *Gitanos* citizenship in 1783, officially recognizing them as Spaniards.

Dance style and costuming

In traditional *flamenco* dance, or *baile*, there is differentiation between the style of *bailaores* – male dancers – and *bailaoras* – female dancers – and the costuming for each often dictates what movements are possible. Both men and women use heeled shoes studded with nails to enhance the sound of their *zapeteado*, or footwork. In the male style, *de cintura para abajo* – from the waist down – refers to the dancing and the sound of their *zapeteado*, while *de cintura para arriba* concerns female *baile*, in which the majority of the movements are from the waist up.[48] The motions of a *bailaora's* torso, arms, and hands are typically serpentine, circuitous, and sensuously executed, and she sometimes manipulates a fringed shawl or a fan. A colorful *bata de cola* dress hugs her torso closely and extends into a long, ruffled train that she manipulates as she dances. As a *bailaora* arches to the side in a series of *cambrés*, or takes a *vueltas de pecho*, turning while bent at the waist as her upper body rotates backward, the costume simultaneously accentuates her torso's twisting movement while restricting the mobility of her legs. In the *Escuela Sevillana* (Seville School) of classical *flamenco*, developed by Pastora Imperio and Matilde

Figure 7.9
Bailaora Belén Maya deftly manipulates her magnificent *bata de cola* train.
Image: Jack Vartoogian, Front Row Photos.

Coral, a *bailaora* emphasizes her musicality in silent marking steps called *marcaje* and small runs known as *carretillas* instead of executing percussive *zapateado*. Purists who advocate for a strict division between gender norms in *flamenco* deplore the use of pronounced *zapateado* by women.[49] However, female *flamenco* artists such as Carmen Amaya (1913–1963) shattered these norms as far back as the 1940s by dressing in a tight matador's *traje corto* suit and performing the fierce, lightning-speed *zapateado* reserved for the male dancer. Today, female dancers – Manuela Carrasco, Belén López, and Rocío Molina being prime examples – regularly perform impressive footwork, and some, such as Molina, have followed Amaya's trajectory by performing the *farruca* – traditionally a man's dance – in men's costuming.

Unlike the curvaceous sensuality of the women's style, male *baile* is very upright and requires a show of strength. Rather than making articulate spirals, the austere hands of a male dancer either make fists or display open palms, and are held at shoulder height, in front of the chest, or symmetrically overhead. *Zapateado* is powerfully executed in time to numerous rhythms and includes *golpe*, a striking step against the floor, *vueltas de tacón* (turns on the heel), and *redoble*, rapid stamping. Men often perform percussion on their own bodies while performing footwork. Unlike the women's costuming, the tight, high-waist pants of the *traje corto* suit allow them to take deep lunges and jumps, and a short jacket or vest is worn on top. However, some experimental artists reject this traditional costume today. Dancer/choreographer Rafaela Carrasco first began choreographing with the *bata de cola* dress on men, and Manuel Liñan wore a woman's *bata de cola* dress and manipulated a shawl in his 2014 work, *Nómada*.

Flamenco styles, music, and singing

Palos are *flamenco* styles classified by *compás*, rhythmic patterns that predominantly fall into two categories: *grande* (big, heavy) and *chico* (light). *Alegrías*, *tangos*, and *bulerías* are examples of the happier dances of *flamenco chico*, while those in the *flamenco grande* category, such as *siguiriya* and *soleá*, are much more somber. The complex rhythmic phrases within *compás* range from four beats, such as in *tangos* and *farrucas*, or can include as many as twelve beats such as in the *palos* of *alegrías*, *soléa*, and *bulerías*, with the emphasis placed on 3, 6, 8, 10, and 12: 1, 2, **3**, 4 5, **6**, 7, **8**, 9, **10**, 11, **12**. The guitar is played by a *tocaor/a*, and instrumentalists also play a *cajón*, a wooden box that is struck while sitting upon it, which was introduced by guitarist Paco de Lucía. Adding to the percussion are *pitos* – finger snapping – and hand clapping called *palmas*. Three middle fingers strike an open palm to make a sharp sound of *palmas claras*, while clapping two cupped palms together creates the muted sound of *palmas sordas*. Castanets may be played and have become a principle element in the female style, as seen in the rapid-fire playing by dancers such as Carmen Amaya.

At the heart of all *flamenco* is the *cante*, or song, and a *flamenco* singer is called a *cantaor/a*. Many possess the capability to sing in a style known as *cante jondo*, or deep song, which is often described as raspy or harsh. The influence of Islamic chants and Jewish religious singing is heard in the tonal modulations and athletic vocal *melismas*, in which one syllable is catapulted into a range of notes by the singer. A singer improvises to lyrics that may address themes of sacrifice, undying love, fate, a mother figure, or death, while the guitarist follows the singer's tempo, melody, and mood. Lorca, who claimed that no emotion is possible unless the *duende* comes, noted the potency of *cante jondo* lyrics: "In these poems, Pain is made flesh, takes human form, acquires a sharp profile. She is a dark woman wanting to catch birds in nets of wind."[50] Two examples of *cante jondo* expressing great melancholy are *siguiriya* and *soleá* (derived from *soledad*, or loneliness). The pain inherent in *siguiriya* is manifested by a singer's improvisation of the syllable *Ay!*, which can endure for almost a minute. Legendary *Gitano cantaor* Manuel Torres (1878–1933) excelled in *siguiriya*, and his *duende* was recalled by guitarist Diego del Gastor:

> I have seen Manuel transformed three times, when the veins stood out on his face and he tore at his clothing, as if that helped him release his torrent

Figure 7.10
Carmen Cortés, an innovative *bailaora*, executes a fusillage of *zapateado* footwork in *Duende Flamenco*.
Image: Jack Vartoogian, Front Row Photos.

of passion. His face and eyes would become wild and crazy, and his ***cante***
absolutely unbearable, until you found yourself also ripping off your shirt and
shouting or weeping uncontrollably.[51]

El duende may be evoked in a dancer performing slow-paced deep bends, rotations
of the torso, and languorous arm movements in response to the somberness and
anguish inherent in *cante jondo*.

In *flamenco*, the sensitive relationship between a dancer and the musicians
involves a great deal of unspoken communication. After the musicians have begun,
the dancer makes his or her *salida* (entrance), taking *marcajes* (marking steps)
while executing *palmas* or *pitos*. During a lull in the music, a phrase of footwork
is executed in a certain speed to signal a desired tempo to the musicians. This
unspoken message, known as a *llamada*, or call, is also used throughout a dancer's
improvisation to signal a transition. What makes *flamenco* such a communal form is
that the dancers are also musicians. After taking a solo, a dancer will retreat upstage
and perform *palmas*, or join in the singing as another dances. The performers, along
with the audience, also give *jaleos* – spontaneous shouts of encouragement or
praise.

Cafés cantantes **and** ópera flamenco

In the second half of the nineteenth century, *flamenco* performers emerged from the
barrios to work professionally in *cafés cantantes* – intimate venues for working-class

audiences. Café Silverio in Seville was seminal in establishing this commercialization of *flamenco*. Its *patrón* (owner) was Silverio Franconetti, an Italian who had learned singing from *Gitanos*. During the nascent days of *cafés cantantes*, the *cantaores* were usually men, accompanied by male guitarists; women were the *bailaoras*; and the audiences were all male. *Flamenco* was presented in *cuadros*, in which the female dancer performed a solo in the midst of a half-circle of male musicians and singers. As men began to dance in *cafés cantantes*, the technique of both men and women became stronger, but differences between them emerged. New dances evolved, such as the *farruca*, in which men performed rapid-fire *zapateado* footwork while keeping their bodies relatively still. Female dancers, considered *mujeres de arte*, used very little *zapateado* and instead emphasized the movements of their arms, hands, and upper torso in a highly sensual manner. By performing in *cafés cantantes*, many singers and dancers discovered their professional paths.

In the 1920s, *café cantantes* were overshadowed by the growing popularity of *ópera flamenco*, a larger, more theatrical form, accompanied by an orchestra. Narratives were crafted into spectacles and group choreography was set to *flamenco* songs that had never accompanied dance. Castanets were also used, and women adopted male *zapateado*.[52] Although dominated by non-*Gitano*, *escuela bolera* dancers such as La Argentina (Antonia Mercé), Vicente Escudero, La Argentinita (Encarnación López), and her sister, Pilar López, the popularity and lucrative pay of *ópera flamenco* also lured *Gitano* performers, such as renowned singer La Niña de los Peines (Pastora Pavón Cruz) and dancer Pastora Imperio.[53]

Think about:
Can the emergence of non-Gitano flamenco stars be seen as an invasion into a Gitano tradition, or just as a part of inevitable change in the evolution of the form?

Federico García Lorca (1898–1936) and the Spanish Civil War (1936–1939)

Andalusia-born Federico García Lorca was a poet, playwright, avant-garde theater director, and a key figure in Generation of '27 – a group of experimental Spanish artists who were largely left-wing intellectuals that formed in 1927. Both Lorca and his friend, modernist composer Manuel de Falla, were ardent aficionados of *flamenco* who lamented the loss of the *flamenco puro* due to its commercialization. In an effort to present *flamenco* as a uniquely Andalusian cultural artifact, in 1922 Lorca and de Falla organized the *Concurso de Cante Jondo* in Granada, a contest that awarded unknown singers. Lorca, whose potent, eloquent poetry was incorporated into *flamenco* lyrics, used recording technology to capture the voices of *cantaores* from the 1920s and 1930s. Lorca's many contributions to the worlds of poetry, *flamenco*, and avant-garde Spanish culture were cut short when he was executed in 1936 by a right-wing firing squad in the first month of the Spanish Civil War, due to his leftist politics and homosexuality. He was buried in an unmarked grave, and his remains have never been found.

The Spanish Civil War

In the early 1930s, a Democratic Republic replaced a repressive administration in Spain, and upset many conservatives with its liberal policies such as women's rights and the separation of church from the state and schools. By 1936, a vicious fight had ensued between the leftist Republican Party – whose members tended to be poor, exploited, anti-clerical, and Marxist – and the right-wing Nationalist Falange Party, whose conservative members espoused Catholicism, nationalism, and mirrored the Fascist regimes in Germany and Italy. Both these countries aided the Nationalists by supplying troops, weapons, tanks, and aircraft. Because of the experience German and Italian soldiers gained during this war, many consider the Spanish Civil War to have been a "rehearsal" for World War II. Bombs from German and Italian air strikes – an unprecedented mode of warfare – rained down on Republican troops, and Guernica, a small Basque town, became a military target, with the relentless bombing of hundreds of innocent civilians. Pablo Picasso responded to the massacre by painting *Guernica*, a 1937 mural depicting torturous images of the powerless victims – dying animals, burning buildings, and a weeping mother with her dead child. *Guernica* raised awareness of the Spanish conflict when it was featured at the International Exposition in Paris in 1937, and the painting was further exhibited outside of Spain throughout the duration of the conflict. The international community also learned more about the crisis through the gripping images of war photographer Robert Capa and the journalism of Martha Gellhorn and George Orwell, who all supported the Republican Loyalists. Despite the outpouring of foreign support, Republican troops couldn't deflect the power of German and Italian air strikes and the heavily armed Nationalist troops. In 1939, Generalissimo Francisco Franco's Nationalist army was the victor. For the next thirty-six years that Franco ruled as dictator, Spain regressed to a state reminiscent of the Inquisition as firing squads executed an estimated 500,000 people. The government enforced labor camps, imposed censorship, repressed women's rights, and persecuted *Gitanos* and other ethnic minorities. Many intellectuals were killed, while others, including *flamenco* artists Carmen Amaya, La Argentinita, and Vicente Escuerdo, went into exile.

Franco and *nacionalflamenquismo*

In the 1950s, Franco turned to dance in an effort to bolster Spanish nationalism. Despite his antagonism toward *Gitanos*, he recognized *flamenco's* tourist appeal. A repackaged version of *flamenco* was forged into a propaganda tool known as *nacionalflamenquismo* – a joyous symbol of Spanish identity that displayed no trace of its *Gitano* origins.[54] Discouraged from being singers and instrumentalists, women were spotlighted as attractive *bailaoras*, and in many cases, emulated stereotypical representations of Carmen – the Andalusian sexual bombshell – while men were presented as virile and forceful. Scholar and dancer Ryan Rockmore notes the link between Fascism in Nazi Germany and Franco's philosophy, which both espoused an idealized image of manhood:

> In order to define masculinity, both Fascism and Falangism regulated non-masculine behavior in an attempt to extinguish homosexuality from society . . . Under these conditions, perhaps the masculine style of flamenco became more pronounced and exaggerated because of the lack of acceptance regarding male displays of femininity.[55]

Male dancers during the Franco era adopted a more ferocious and aggressive style of dancing that was featured in touristic *ópera flamenca*. In the late 1960s, a more traditional form of *flamenco* emerged in the work of the trio of *Los Bolecos*, which featured Matilde Coral, Rafael *el Negro*, and *El Farruco* (Antonio Montoya), a *Gitano* from a renowned *flamenco* lineage known for his ferocity and bursts of explosive frenzy. Franco condoned this aggressive style of male dancing, which reaffirmed patriarchy in Spanish society.[56] Yet it is highly doubtful that *El Farruco* intended his style to align with Franco's ideology: at age seven, he witnessed his father dying in his mother's arms after being shot in the doorway of their home during the Spanish Civil War.[57]

Throughout Franco's regime, *flamenco* remained tightly regulated. In the 1950s and 1960s, *tablaos flamencos* – reminiscent of *café cantantes*, and geared for tourists – became popular, especially in Madrid. Virtuoso dancers such as Pilar López, Antonio Ruiz Soler, and Carmen Amaya performing in *tablaos* raised the level of technical skill in both male and female dancing. Because these intimate nightclubs allowed for more experimentation and improvisation, dress rehearsals and performances were subject to inspection by local officials.[58] Franco's officials kept close watch on *flamenco* performers, who had become valuable "cultural treasures." Very few *flamenco* performers were allowed to leave the country, with Pilar López and Carmen Amaya being among the exceptions.

When Franco died in 1975, Spain experienced a cultural efflorescence. After decades of censorship, *flamenco* artists were finally free to

Figure 7.11
Since El Farruca's death in 1997, his grandson Farruquito is the heir to the Farruca *Gitano* dynasty in Seville.
Image: Jack Vartoogian, Front Row Photos.

experiment in innovative ways. Paco de Lucía collaborated with jazz musicians and brought in non-traditional instruments to *flamenco*. *Gitano* dancer Mario Maya (1937–2008) paired with a *kathak* performer, and his 1977 dance drama, *Ay Jondo*, portrayed *Gitano* repression. Like Maya, Antonio Gades trained under Pilar López. In the 1980s he formed his own company and collaborated with filmmaker Carlos Saura on a dance film trilogy that included *El Amor Brujo* and featured *bailaora* Cristina Hoyos. Manuela Carrasco – still an active performer – began her *flamenco* career in the 1970s. She toured internationally in the 1980s with *Flamenco Puro*, which included stars such as *El Farruco* and singer *El Chocolate*. The next generation of dancers taught or influenced by the artists above includes Joaquín Cortés, Antonio Canales, Sara Baras, Carmen Cortés, Javier Barón, Carmen Ledesma, María Pagés, Eva Yerbabuena, Antonio el Pipa, Belén Maya, Farruquito, *La Farruca*, Joaquín Grilo, Manuel Liñán, and Israel Galván. Some of these artists are more traditional, while others venturing into experimental *flamenco* have expanded its boundaries in myriad directions.

Think about:
What must the resentment have been like for *Gitano flamenco* families, whose history and contributions to *flamenco* were at once both appropriated and yet ignored during the time of *nacionalflamenquismo*?

Current trends

In Spain today, *flamenco* is extremely popular in urban *tablaos* and theatrical shows that cater to tourists. In Andalusia, more intimate performances by *Gitano* groups – although just as touristy as the *tablaos* – occur in the caves of Sacromonte in Granada. Although *flamenco* has long been commercialized, an exception is found in *peñas* – small inconspicuous *flamenco* social clubs in which local *aficionados* socialize and perform. These are mostly private, although sometime tourists are

Figure 7.12
Akram Khan and Israel Galván merge traditions of Indian *kathak* and *flamenco* in their collaboration, *Torobaka*.
Image: Jean-Louis Fernandez.

permitted for a fee. However, Spanish festivals, such as *Bienal de Flamenco de Sevillla*, *Festival de Jerez*, *Concurso Nacional de arte Flamenco de Cordoba*, *El Potaje Gitano de Utrera*, and *Los Veranos del Corral* give the public an opportunity to see less commercialized versions of *flamenco* and newer artists.

Israel Galván has been called a "deconstructivist" of *flamenco* because of his reinterpretation of traditional form, including his abstraction of typical gestures and postures. Galván first electrified *flamenco* audiences in 1998 with his *Mira Los Zapatos Rojos*, and reminded many of the masculinity of Vicente Escudero. The intensity Galván delivers on stage is also manifested in his social concerns, such as in his 2013 work, *Lo Real*, which addressed the extermination of Gypsies in the Nazi Holocaust. In 2014, Akram Khan and Galván brought their respective backgrounds in *kathak* and *flamenco* to their collaboration, *Torobaka*.

Other *flamenco* artists collaborating with non-*flamenco* performers include María Pagés with Sidi Larbi Cherkaoui, a contemporary choreographer from Belgium, while Eva Yerbabuena recently collaborated with Patrick de Bana, a former dancer with Pina Bausch. Other artists pushing *flamenco* in new directions are Rocío Molina, Manuel Liñán, Olga Pericet, Marco Flores, and Pastora Galván. In 2008, Molina, a riveting dancer, was the youngest in *Mujeres*, a work by the late Mario Maya that featured three generations of dancers: the seasoned Merche Esmerelde; his daughter, Belén; and Molina. Both Molina and Pericet won awards at prestigious Max Awards for the Performing Arts: Pericet for best dancer in her work, *Pisadas: Fin y Principio de Mujeres*, while Molina won for her choreography for *Bosque Ardora* (2014). Pastora Galván has performed in much of her brother Israel's work, but is also a choreographer, and recently choreographed *flamenco* flash mobs in protest of violence against women at the 2016 *La Bienal de Flamenco Sevilla*.

Since the onset of Spain's economic crisis in 2008, Flo6x8, a guerilla-style collective, has used *flamenco* as a form of social activism by performing flash mobs in public spaces. These anti-capitalist artists have been protesting the impact of the crisis on working-class people by showing up in bank lobbies and performing *baile* in dark glasses while singing taunting lyrics condemning the injustices of the Spanish banking system and the failing economy.[59] Flo6x8's newest work, *Doñato y el Tulipán Africano*, lambasts CaixaBank for supporting a pipeline affecting Andalusia. It is fitting that *flamenco* – originally a *Gitano* expression of social protest that transmuted into enticing entertainment for aristocrats, a dictator's political tool, a tourist draw, and a cultural artifact of Spain – comes full circle in the works of Flo6x8 and other *flamenco* artists engaging in social activism.

Discussion questions: *flamenco*

1 Discuss *flamenco's* trajectory from being the personal expression of an ethnic group that was politically hounded to its current status as a commercialized, global form. Can you equate this phenomenon to another dance or art form?
2 *El duende* is an ineffable, enthralling quality that a *flamenco* performer exudes. Have you ever experienced this, and can you identify dancers or musicians possessing this powerful magic?
3 Discuss Franco's political aims in using *flamenco* as a tool of propaganda. Could artists have taken more of a stand against the regime, and if so, how? Cite some examples of how artists today use music and dance as a form of protest.

Notes

1 Kennedy, John G. "Nubian *Zār* Ceremonies as Psychotherapy," 218–219.
2 Boddy, Janice. *Wombs and Alien Spirits: Women, Men, and the Zār Cult in Northern Sudan*, 133–134.
3 Kennedy, 205.
4 Eisler, Laurie A. "'Hurry Up and Play My Beat'–The *Zār* Ritual in Cairo," 26.

5 Kennedy, 61.

6 Kenyon, Susan M. "Zār as Modernization in Contemporary Sudan," 234.

7 Natvig, Richard. "Liminal Rites and Female Symbolism in the Egyptian *Zār* Possession Cult," 63.

8 Sengers, Gerda. *Women and Demons: Cult Healing in Islamic Egypt*, 97.

9 Boddy, 159.

10 Ibid., 160.

11 Natvig, Richard Johan. "*Zār* in Upper Egypt: Hans Alexander Winkler's Field Notes From 1932," 23.

12 Kennedy, 214; Boddy, 131.

13 Cloudsley, Anne. *Woman of Omdurman: Life, Love, and the Cult of Virginity*, 67.

14 Natvig, Richard. "Oromos, Slaves, and the Zār Spirits: A Contribution to the History of the Zār Cult," 682–683.

15 Ibid.

16 Boddy, 133.

17 Eisler, 26.

18 Kenyon, 247–248.

19 Boddy, 160.

20 Kennedy, 214.

21 Ibid., 204.

22 Ibid., 217.

23 Kenyon, 241–242.

24 Kenyon, *Spirits and Slaves in Central Sudan*, 9.

25 Personal communication with author, August 25, 2016.

26 El-Shamy, Hasan M. *Religion Among the Folk in Egypt,* 101.

27 Kasinov, Laura. "Egyptian Music: "*Zār*" Tradition Gives Women a Rare Moment on the Concert Stage."

28 Boddy, Janice. *Wombs and Alien Spirits: Women, Men, and the Zār Cult in Northern Sudan*, 130–131.

29 Vitray-Meyerovitch, Eva de. *Rumi and Sufism*, 43.

30 http://mevlana.net/sema.html

31 Quoted in Friedlander, Shems. *Rumi and the Whirling Dervishes,* 115.

32 Ibid., 116.

33 Ibid., 107.

34 Ibid., 116.

35 Vitray-Meyerovitch, 46.

36 Friedlander, 93.

37 Pardoe, Miss (Julia). *The City of the Sultan.*

38 Lorca, Federico Garcia. *In Search of Duende*, 69.

39 Ibid., 60.

40 Thiel-Cramér, Barbara. *Flamenco*, 29.

41 Edwards, Gwynne. *Flamenco!*, 19.

42 Bennahum, Ninotchka Devorah. *Antonia Mercé, "La Argentina": Flamenco and the Spanish Avant Garde*, 14.

43 Phillips, Miriam. "Hopeful Futures and Nostalgic Pasts," 48–49.

44 Ibid., 48.

45 Goldberg, K. Meira "Sonidos Negros: On the Blackness of Flamenco," 86.

46 Benítez, Marta Carrasco. "Three Centuries of Flamenco," 27.

47 Ibid., 27.

48 Cruces-Roldán, 215–216.

49 Ibid., 217–218.

50 Lorca, 17.

51 Woodall, James. *In Search of the Firedance*, 215–216.

52 Edwards, 99.

53 Benítez, 26.

54 Ibid., 28.

55 Rockmore, Ryan. "Dancing the Ideal Masculinity," 237.

56 Washabaugh, William. "Fashioning Masculinity in Flamenco Dance," 42.

57 Seibert, Brian. "Farruquito, Dance Career Interrupted, Makes His Return."

58 Rockmore, 240.

59 Hayes, Michelle Heffner. "Choreographing Contemporaneity," 286.

Bibliography

Visual sources

YouTube

"Israel Galván, *La Curva*, IV Dutch Flamenco Biennal Rotterdam," YouTube video, 9.25, posted on May 4, 2013, by "Erik Pezerro," 20 January 2013, www.youtube.com/watch?v=MkIp9zj4_HM

"Oasis – Everything You Wanted to Know About the Middle East But Were Afraid to Dance," YouTube Video, 1:55, posted by "Nejla Yatkin," September 6, 2012, www.youtube.com/watch?v=KlkzM8FI_Bw&feature=youtu.be

"Sema Ceremony-Whirling Dervishes," YouTube Video, 12:30, posted by "Mevlana Foundation", March 28, 2011, www.youtube.com/watch?v=Qdi-it43j30

"Zār Ritual – The Mazaher Ensemble," YouTube video, 4:02, posted by "Layne Redmond", July 16, 2012, www.youtube.com/watch?v=057A8oi7iQ8

"Ziya Azazi – Dervish in Progress, A.D.O.B. Gala, (29.09.12 Ankara)," YouTube Video, 12:31, posted by "Ziya Azazi," December 16, 2013, www.youtube.com/watch?v=VCSO-Qf0Yag

Film

Saura, Carlos. "Flamenco." New Directions Video, 1994; 2003. Film, 100 minutes.

"*Zār* Ritual" [Videorecording]. *The JVC & Smithsonian Folkways Video Anthology of Music and Dance, Dance of Africa*, Vol. 1, 1996. Directed by Hiroshi Yamamoto. Barre, VT: JVC; Victor Co. of Japan, Distributed by Multicultural Media.

Written sources

Barber, X. Theodore. "Four Interpretations of Mevlevi Dervish Dance, 1920–1929." *Dance Chronicle*, Vol. 9, No. 3 (1986): 328–355. Published by: Taylor & Francis, Ltd. Stable URL: www.jstor.org/stable/1567602.

Benítez, Marta Carrasco. "Three Centuries of Flamenco." Translation K. Meira Goldberg. From *Flamenco on the Global Stage: Historical, Critical, and Theoretical Perspectives*, edited by K. Meira Goldberg, Ninotchka Devorah Bennahum, and Michelle Heffner Hayes, 23–39. Jefferson, NC: McFarland and Company, Inc., 2015.

Bennahum, Ninotchka Devorah. *Antonia Mercé, "La Argentina": Flamenco and the Spanish Avant Garde*. Hanover, NH: Wesleyan University Press, 2000.

Boddy, Janice. *Wombs and Alien Spirits: Women, Men, and the Zār Cult in Northern Sudan*. Madison, WI: University of Wisconsin Press, 1989.

Bonta, Bruce. "Nubian Singing in Sudan." *Peaceful Societies*, August 27, 2015. https://cas.uab.edu/peacefulsocieties/2015/08/27/nubian-singing-in-sudan/.

Bonta, Bruce. "Nubian Zār Ceremony Is Changing." *Peaceful Societies*, April 8, 2010. https://cas.uab.edu/peacefulsocieties/2010/04/08/nubian-zār-ceremony-is-changing/.

Cloudsley, Anne. *Woman of Omdurman: Life, Love, and the Cult of Virginity*. New York: St. Martin's Press, Inc., 1984.

Cruces-Roldán, Cristina. "Normative Aesthetics and Cultural Constructions in Flamenco Dance: Female and Gitano Bodies as Legitimizers of Tradition." Translation: K. Meira Goldberg. In *Flamenco on the Global Stage: Historical, Critical, and Theoretical Perspectives*, edited by K. Meira Goldberg, Ninotchka Devorah Bennahum, and Michelle Heffner Hayes, 210–224. Jefferson, NC: McFarland and Company, Inc., 2015.

De Waal Malefyt, Timothy. "Gendering the Authentic in Spanish Flamenco." In *The Passion of Music and Dance: Body, Gender, and Sexuality*, edited by William Washabaugh, 51–66. Oxford; New York: Berg, 1998.

Edwards, Gwynne. *Flamenco!* New York: Thames and Hudson, 2000.

Eisler, Laurie A. "'Hurry Up and Play My Beat' – The *Zār* Ritual in Cairo." *UCLA Journal of Dance Ethnology*, Vol. 9 (1985): 23–26.

El-Shamy, Hasan M. *Religion Among the Folk in Egypt*. Westport, CT: Praeger Publishers, 2008.

Friedlander, Shems. *Rumi and the Whirling Dervishes*. New York: Parabola Books, 2003.

Goldberg, K. Meira "Sonidos Negros: On the Blackness of Flamenco." *Dance Chronicle*, Vol. 37, No.1 (2014): 85–113. DOI: 10.1080/01472526.2014.877316.

Hayes, Michelle Heffner. "Choreographing Contemporaneity." In *Flamenco on the Global Stage: Historical, Critical, and Theoretical Perspectives*, edited by K. Meira Goldberg, Ninotchka Devorah Bennahum, and Michelle Heffner Hayes, 280–292. Jefferson, NC: McFarland and Company, Inc., 2015.

Kasinov, Laura. "Egyptian Music: '*Zār*' Tradition Gives Women a Rare Moment on the Concert Stage." *Christian Science Monitor*, Global News Blog, March 26, 2010. www.csmonitor.com/World/Global-News/2010/0326/Egyptian-music-Zar-traditio n-gives-women-a-rare-moment-at-center-stage.

Kennedy, John G. "Nubian *Zār* Ceremonies as Psychotherapy." In *Nubian Ceremonial Life: Studies in Islamic Syncretism and Cultural Change*, edited by John G. Kennedy, 203–223. Berkeley: University of California Press, 1978.

Kenyon, Susan M. *Spirits and Slaves in Central Sudan: The Red Wind of Sennar*. New York: Palgrave Macmillan, 2012.

Kenyon, Susan M. "Zār as Modernization in Contemporary Sudan." In *Across Boundaries of Belief: Contemporary Issues in the Anthropology of Religion*, edited by Morton Klass and Maxine Weigrau, 227–248. Boulder, CO: Westview Press, 1999.

Kia, Mehrdad. *Daily Life in the Ottoman Empire*. Santa Barbara, CA: Greenwood, and imprint of ABC-CLIO, LLD, 2011.

Lorca, Federico Garcia. *In Search of Duende*. Translation: Christopher Maurer. New York: New Directions Publishing Company, 2010.

Machin-Autenrieth, Matthew. *Flamenco, Regionalism, and Musical Heritage in Southern Spain*. New York: Routledge, 2016.

Natvig, Richard. "Liminal Rites and Female Symbolism in the Egyptian *Zār* Possession Cult." Published by Brill, *Numen*, Vol. 35, No. 1 (July, 1988): 57–68. Accessed June 6, 2016, 19:53, UTL. Stable URL: www.jstor.org/stable/3270140.

Natvig, Richard Johan. "Oromos, Slaves, and the Zār Spirits: A Contribution to the History of the Zār Cult." *The International Journal of African Historical Studies*, Vol. 20, No. 4 (1987): 669–689. Accessed June 6, 2016, 19:55, UTL. Published by Boston University African Studies Center. Stable URL: www.jstor.org/ stable/219657.

Natvig, Richard Johan. "*Zār* in Upper Egypt: Hans Alexander Winkler's Field Notes From 1932." Published by Brill, *Islamic Africa*, Vol. 1, No. 1 (Spring 2010): 11–30. Stable URL: www.jstor.org/stable/42656313.

Pardoe, Miss (Julia). *The City of the Sultan*. London: Henry Colburn, Publisher, 1837. https://archive.org/details/cityofsultandome01parduoft. Uploaded by University of Toronto, 3/6/2008; Robards Library, Catalogue Record MARCXML

Phillips, Miriam. "Hopeful Futures and Nostalgic Pasts." In *Flamenco on the Global Stage: Historical, Critical, and Theoretical Perspectives*, edited by K. Meira Goldberg, Ninotchka Devorah Bennahum, and Michelle Heffner Hayes, 42–55. Jefferson, NC: McFarland and Company, Inc., 2015.

Rockmore, Ryan. "Dancing the Ideal Masculinity." In *Flamenco on the Global Stage: Historical, Critical, and Theoretical Perspectives*, edited by K. Meira Goldberg, Ninotchka Devorah Bennahum, and Michelle Heffner Hayes, 234–243. Jefferson, North Carolina: McFarland and Company, Inc., 2015.

Seibert, Brian. "Farruquito, Dance Career Interrupted, Makes His Return." *New York Times*, February 25, 2016. www.nytimes.com/2016/02/28/arts/dance/ farruquito-dance-career-interrupted-makes-his-return.html?_r=0.

Sengers, Gerda. *Women and Demons: Cult Healing in Islamic Egypt*. Boston: Brill, 2003.

Shepard, Richard F. "The Elusive Inspiration of Flamenco." *New York Times*, November 3, 1986. www.nytimes.com/1986/11/03/theater/ the-elusive-inspiration-of-flamenco.html.

Thiel-Cramér, Barbara. *Flamenco*. Lidingö, Sweden: REMARK AB, 1991.

Vitray-Meyerovitch, Eva de. *Rumi and Sufism*. Sausalito, CA: Post-Apollo Press, 1987.

Washabaugh, William. "Fashioning Masculinity in Flamenco Dance." In *The Passion of Music and Dance: Body, Gender, and Sexuality*, edited by William Washabaugh, 39–50. Oxford: New York: Berg, 1998.

Woodall, James. *In Search of the Firedance*. London: Sinclair-Stevens Limited, 1992.

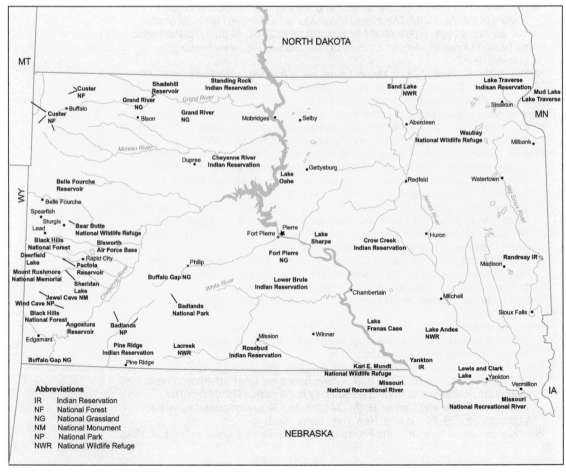

8 Native America, the Caribbean, and South America
Resistance, spirituality, and spectacle

8.1 Overview

This chapter looks at dance – and in two instances, religion – from three cultures in the Western hemisphere: the Ghost Dance religion of the Lakota Sioux, Haitian Vodou, and Argentinian *tango*. Although these three dance forms seem disparate, they all arose in communities that needed to unite and were used as a show of resistance, as a means of worship, or to dance out one's longings.

Although European colonialists called the Americas the "New World," it was a long-established domain of the Lakota Sioux and other First Nations people. After numerous wars over colonialist expansion were fought between the US Army and various tribes, treaties protecting Indian land were repeatedly broken by the government. These breaches led to deep distrust and, ultimately, to the establishment of the Ghost Dance religion, which was a reaction to ongoing injustices – poverty, disease, starvation, and the loss of their land and their fundamental freedom. Followers believed that by dancing the Ghost Dance, they could resume their indigenous ways: their ancestors and the buffalo would return, and white people would be obliterated. This movement ended brutally when hundreds of Lakota were massacred at Wounded Knee by the US government in 1890. Wounded Knee would again become a site of controversial resistance in 1973, when the activist American Indian Movement took possession of the village.

Haitian Vodou is a syncretic religion that evolved from the African religions of Vodun and Yoruba, and the Catholicism of French colonialists. Vodun followers (Vodouisants) worship ancestors and deities called *lwa*. In exchange for protection, a devotee cultivates a symbiotic relationship with a *lwa* by propitiating it with praise songs, dances, and by "feeding" it with animal sacrifices and other offerings. At a ceremony, if a *lwa* is particularly moved, it may "descend" and take possession of a devotee to impart advice to the community. Attaining this possession state is considered to be a sacred act, and is the highest aim of Vodou adepts.

In nineteenth-century Argentina, a confluence of the dance, music, and singing traditions of European immigrants and Afro-Argentinians in the predominately male migrant enclaves of Buenos Aires led to the emergence of *tango*. In the early twentieth century, Argentinians brought it to Paris, where it became a sensational form of entertainment that quickly spread to other countries. After World War I, when many Argentinian expatriates returned, *tango* eventually found acceptance by the upper classes.

8.2 Political resistance: the Lakota Ghost Dance and Wounded Knee, 1890 and 1973

Key points: the Ghost Dance

1 Because of the doctrine of "manifest destiny" justifying the expansion of white settlement, the US government decided that Native Americans should be contained on "Indian Territory." Through the 1868 Fort Laramie Treaty, the Great Sioux Reservation was established. This treaty was broken in 1876 after gold was discovered in their sacred Black Hills.

2 Reservation life suffocated Lakota traditions: the buffalo were exterminated, their religious dancing was banned, and children were being sent away to Christian boarding schools. Lakota Sioux, who once roamed freely were now weaponless, completely dependent on meager government rations, and facing starvation.

3 A Paiute named Wovoka began to preach his messianic vision: if Indians lived peacefully and performed the Ghost Dance, their ancestors would return, as would the buffalo, all whites would disappear, and their lifestyle would return. Wovoka's doctrine was adopted by thousands of suffering Native Americans, including the Lakota Sioux.

4 After failing to stop the Ghost Dance, the US Army ruthlessly massacred nearly three hundred Sioux men, women, and children at Wounded Knee Creek in 1890.

5 Although this massacre ended the Ghost Dance movement, Sioux resistance resurfaced through the activist American Indian Movement (AIM). In 1973, when AIM members occupied Wounded Knee village to protest grievances toward the US government, they declared the site to be the Independent Oglala Nation.

"Annihilation" was a word used frequently by the whites of that period . . . For those who think "annihilation" is too strong a word, consider that it has been estimated that there were 75 million Indians in the Americas, perhaps six million in the contiguous United States area, when Columbus arrived. By 1900, only 237,000 Indians in the United States remained.[1]
—James Welch and Paul Stekler

Mount Rushmore, located in the Black Hills of South Dakota, draws thousands of visitors every year. The carving of this massive monument featuring the faces of four white presidents began in 1927 to draw tourism. But to the Lakota Sioux, who regard the Paha Sapa (Black Hills) as the epicenter of their spiritual world, the onslaught of jackhammers and dynamite blasting was an utter desecration of a mountain they call "The Six Grandfathers." Mount Rushmore, created on sacred Lakota land illegally appropriated by the US government, is seen as an insulting monument commemorating *wasichu* (white) leaders who supported policies that ultimately decimated Native American populations. The Lakota term *wasichu* defines non-indigenous people, but it has taken on a pejorative connotation: "those who take the best meat." Greed was the government's motive for breaking a treaty that promised the area to the Lakota Sioux in perpetuity, but when gold was discovered there in the 1870s, that perpetuity vanished. They lost their most sacred hunting ground to *wasichu*, who indeed took the best meat. This greediness has a tumultuous history, and to understand how the Ghost Dance religion came to have special resonance for the Lakota, their mistreatment by the United States government – a century-long litany of lost land, imposed hunger, epidemics, banning of traditions, and broken treaties – must be considered.

Figure 8.1 (p. 221)
A member of the Lakota Sioux Indian Dance Theatre.
Image: Jack Vartoogian, Front Row Photos.

The Lakota, also known as the Teton Sioux, were an enormous band composed of seven sub-tribes and the richest of all the Plains Indians. They possessed horses, which enabled them to freely hunt the buffalo that roamed from Minnesota to the Rocky Mountains. By the 1850s the doctrine of "manifest destiny," which justified the expansion of white settlement westward, influenced the government to decide that Native Americans should be driven off certain lands permanently and contained on Indian Territory. Under the terms of the 1868 Fort Laramie Treaty, the Great Sioux Reservation was established – a sixty-million-acre tract encompassing all of South Dakota west of the Missouri River, including the Black Hills. In addition, a vast hunting area in Wyoming and Montana was declared their property, which no *wasichu* could enter. Hunting was permitted outside of the limits of the reservation "so long as the buffalo abounded," which to the Sioux meant forever. Although the land was "set apart for their absolute and undisturbed use and occupation," the agreement craftily brought the Lakota under governmental control.[2] If they gave up their weapons and horses, and allowed railroad routes and military posts to be built, they were promised rations. But the corruption amongst the suppliers was so unchecked that the people were starving. When *wasichu* hunters supplied with ammunition from reservation agents began to hunt down the buffalo from the safety of the new railroad traversing the Plains, this essential source of Lakota sustenance began to diminish. Next on the US government's agenda was assimilation: children were sent away to government boarding schools, where they were forced to adopt Christianity and Euro-American customs, and were punished if they spoke their native language.

US federal aggression

When General George Custer led an expedition of soldiers, geologists, and miners into the Black Hills in 1874, gold was discovered, and a rush of miners illegally raided the sacred Paha Sapa. After the Lakota flatly refused repeated government offers to buy the gold-laden Black Hills, an ultimatum was issued that all Plains Indians be confined to the Great Sioux Reservation within a year, or be considered "hostile." But some continued not to bend to the white man's ways, such as Sitting Bull, a Hunkpapa Sioux, and Crazy Horse, an Oglala Sioux. Both chiefs lived with their people off the reservation along the Powder River in Wyoming, and had refused to sign or recognize the 1868 treaty. Crazy Horse deplored the evolution of the "loafer" Indian dependent on government rations, and Sitting Bull warned his people to take nothing from *wasichu*, saying "You are fools to make yourselves slaves to a piece of fat bacon."[3] In 1876, these two "hostile" chiefs defended the Black Hills by leading thousands of warriors to victory against the US Army in the Battle of the Rosebud. A week later, despite Custer's "Indian killer" reputation, they crushed his Seventh Calvary in the Battle of the Little Bighorn – one of the worst defeats endured by the Army in Indian conflicts. Custer's death made him a legendary hero, and reinforced the trope that Indians were savages. Soon afterward, Crazy Horse surrendered and died after being bayoneted in the back while under government custody. Sitting Bull went into exile to Canada along with 2,000 of his people in resistance to reservation life.[4] In retaliation for Army losses, Congress instituted a "sell or starve" campaign on the reservation in order to annex the Black Hills. Eventually, some desperately hungry Lakota broke down and signed yet another agreement in 1876 that reduced the reservation by two-thirds. They lost the Black Hills and the hunting rights outside of their territory – all in violation of the 1868 Laramie treaty.[5]

The Lakota Sioux were now sequestered on a much smaller reservation and were forced to take up agriculture on the impossibly arid Plains. 1888 and 1889 were particularly devastating years in which viruses killed cattle, crops failed, and thousands died from sicknesses brought by white settlers. Further reductions of rations brought the starving people to their knees, and in 1889, when some desperate leaders signed an allotment agreement, the Great Sioux Reservation was further reduced into five agencies – most strategically separated from each other in an effort to "divide and conquer." In

Figure 8.2
Sitting Bull of the Hunkpapa Sioux refused all treaties. When asked how Indians felt about giving up their land, the exasperated holy man yelled, "Indians! There are no Indians left but me!" Circa 1885.
Image: David F. Barry. National Archives (public domain).

less than a century, Native American warriors who once roamed freely were now weaponless, demoralized, completely dependent on meager government rations, and facing starvation. Reservation life suffocated Lakota traditions, such as their annual religious Sun Dance, a rite that authorities perceived as barbaric and consequently banned in 1883. When word came from western tribes of a religion that promised annihilation of the white man and his ways, the people were hungry to know of it.

Case study: The Sun Dance

The Sun Dance of the Plains tribes, known as *wi-wanyang-wacipi*, was an annual religious ritual, held in the summer. A cottonwood tree, or "Mystery Pole," was carefully chosen and cut down by four virgins, painted, and ritually placed in the center of the Mystery Circle. After fasting, and ritually cleansing in the sweat lodge, men who had committed themselves as participants would offer "red blankets" – strips of flesh cut from their arms in an act of spiritual devotion. Another option was for their pectoral muscles to be pierced with eagle claws or wooden pegs attached to sinew ropes connecting to the Mystery Pole. While blowing through a hollow eagle bone to assuage their pain, the men would dance while leaning backwards, looking into the sun, until they finally broke free. Finding their mutilation barbaric, in 1883 the US government outlawed the Sun Dance, a keystone of Lakota life.

The Ghost Dance

Wovoka was a Paiute Indian in Nevada who worked as a rancher. In his youth, he had lived with a Christian family who taught him English, introduced him to Christianity, and named him Jack. As an adult, Wovoka experienced a mystical vision when he fell ill with a fever during a solar eclipse in 1888. James Mooney, a nineteenth-century ethnologist, visited Wovoka and documented his story. "When the sun died, I went up to heaven and saw God and all the people who had died a long time ago," Wovoka claimed. "God told me to come back and tell my people they must be good and love one another, and not fight, or steal, or lie. He gave me this dance to give to my people."[6] As Wovoka began to preach about his vision, surrounding tribes flocked to hear the words of this Paiute Messiah, and his doctrine was rapidly adopted by thousands of suffering Native Americans. Sitting Bull had returned from Canada and was living on the Standing Rock reservation. In 1889, Sitting Bull and Chief Red Cloud of Pine Ridge Reservation sent a delegation to Nevada to investigate Wovoka's religion.

When the delegation returned in the spring of 1890, Short Bull and Kicking Bear gave the Lakota an enthusiastic report about the spiritual dance and moral code of Wovoka's religion. If they lived peacefully and frequently performed the circular dance for four to five consecutive days, their ancestors would return, as would the buffalo – and all *wasichu* would be swallowed up by new fertile soil. Wovoka predicted that this apocalyptic event would occur in the spring of 1891. Knowing that his people had nothing to look forward to but inevitable starvation on government rations, Sitting Bull invited Kicking Bear to inaugurate the Ghost Dance at Standing Rock. Local federal agent James McLaughlin sent officers to arrest Kicking Bear, but the men returned empty-handed, dazed, and overcome by what they called his "medicine."[7] Sitting Bull informed the officers that his people would continue the dance, since they had received a direct message through Kicking Bear from the spirit world that they must do so to survive. Continually annoyed by Sitting Bull's influence and resistance, McLaughlin began to advocate for his removal to a military prison. Soon the majority of Lakota Sioux began dancing in earnest at the Standing Rock and Pine Ridge reservations in hopes of hastening the apocalypse. Because many fell into trance while dancing and had visions of their ancestors, the Sioux called it the "spirit, or ghost" dance: *wana'ghi wa'chipi*.[8]

Although the Ghost Dance was an inherently peaceful movement, the Lakota Sioux iteration demonstrated their deep distrust of the US government. In anticipation of *wasichu* aggression, the Sioux made "ghost shirts" which they believed would be impenetrable to bullets or weapons of any sort. Made of muslin, sewn with sinew, and ornamented in Indian fashion with fringing and eagle feathers, they were uniquely painted with mythological emblems such as totem animals. No glass beads or metal adornments were used, since these came from *wasichu*. Though they served as costuming, they were regularly worn as undershirts to insure physical protection against violence. Other preparations for the dance included ritual purification by fasting for twenty-four hours. Medicine men prayed at sunrise in the sweat lodge, while the dancers immersed themselves in a creek and then rubbed their bodies with sweet grass. Each dancer's face was painted with colorful designs that were frequently determined by visions one had seen while in trance – circles, crescents, crosses, stars, the sun, or the moon. Elements from the now-banned Sun Dance, such as a tree placed in the center of the dancing arena, were implemented in the Ghost Dance. To prove that this was not a war dance, an American flag emerged from the top of the tree and no weapons of any sort were carried, although the Lakota still tied on a sacred bow and arrow.[9]

Figure 8.3
Arapaho Ghost Dance, circa 1890
Image: Mary Irving Wright, after a photo by James Mooney. National Archives (public domain).

Lakota Ghost Dances typically lasted for four days and began at noon on Sundays – the "medicine day" of *wasichu*. *Wikasa wakan* (sacred medicine men) were seated underneath the tree, while men, women, and children joined hands in a large circle around them and began to sing. They circled in a counterclockwise direction, following the pathway of the sun, with the left foot stepping sideways as the right dragged behind. During the four days, the non-stop dancing, singing, and lack of food or water led to a state of exhaustion, in which Ghost Dancers fell backwards to the ground in deep trance. Upon awakening, they shared the visions they received from their dead ancestors.

In his research, Mooney included an 1890 account from Mrs. Z. A. Parker, a teacher from Pine Ridge Reservation who described seeing over three hundred people in a Ghost Dance:

> After walking about . . . chanting, "Father, I come," they . . . remained in the circle, and sent up the most fearful, heart-piercing wails I ever heard . . . shrieking out their grief, and naming their departed friends and relatives, at the same time taking up handfuls of dust . . . and throwing it over their heads. Finally, they raised their eyes to heaven, their hands clasped high . . . invoking the power of the Great Spirit to allow them to see and talk with the people who had died . . . and now the most intense excitement began. They would go as fast as they could . . . with hands gripped tightly in their neighbors', swinging back and forth with all their might. If one, more weak and frail, came near falling, he would be jerked up into position until tired nature gave way . . . they chanted . . . *Father, I come, Mother, I come, Brother, I come, Father, give us back our arrows* . . . until first one and then another would break from the ring and stagger away and fall down. One woman fell . . . I stepped up to her as she lay there motionless, but with every muscle twitching and quivering . . . They kept up dancing until fully 100 persons were unconscious. Then they stopped . . . each told his story to the medicine man, who shouted it to the crowd . . . After resting for a time they would go through the same performance, perhaps three times a day.[10]

To the Lakota Sioux, the Ghost Dance was not just a new religious movement – it was a reaction to the ongoing injustices of broken treaties, the extermination of the buffalo, the banning of religious customs, and systematic starvation. In hope of hastening the promise of the white apocalypse, the frequency and size of Ghost Dances grew. By August, crowds as big as 2,000 descended onto Pine Ridge Reservation for Ghost Dances. Police ventured out to stop the dancing, to no avail. By October, a new agent at Pine Ridge reported to Washington that 3,000 were dancing and begged for military aid.

Government reaction on Standing Rock reservation

Federal agent James McLaughlin had a contentious relationship with Sitting Bull. When this victorious leader of the humiliating Battle of the Little Bighorn had returned from Canada in 1881, he had been incarcerated for two years as a prisoner of war before being transferred to Standing Rock. Sitting Bull was granted permission to join Buffalo Bill Cody's Wild West Show for a two-year European tour, but after the chief returned in 1887, the agent kept a close watch on this influential "troublemaker," who continued to be a spiritual touchstone for the Lakota Sioux. As the Ghost Dance religion took hold, McLaughlin castigated Sitting Bull for letting his people follow what he considered to be an absurd doctrine. The fervor over the Ghost Dance led reservation agents to become more and more fearful of an "Indian outbreak," and they were unsuccessful in halting the dance. By November 1890, it was so prevalent that no children were attending school, the trading posts were empty, and farms went untended.[11] Panicked local agents declared the situation to be out of control, and 3,000 troops were dispatched to Sioux country, followed by newspaper reporters from miles around. Alarmed by the increasing troops, Kicking Bull, Short Bull, and approximately 3,000 Indians from the Rosebud and Pine Ridge Reservations fled to the sanctity of the Stronghold, a butte in the Badlands.

As tensions arose, McLaughlin ordered tribal police to arrest Sitting Bull in an attempt to stop the Ghost Dance. In the early morning of December 15, 1890, a force of forty-three men led by Lieutenant Bull Head descended upon his cabin. As Sitting Bull was being forced to leave, his people began to surround the cabin in protest. One was Catch-the-Bear, who shot Bull Head. As he fell, he shot Sitting Bull. Red Tomahawk, an Indian policeman, sent a second shot through the Chief's head. Brutal fighting broke out between Indians and Indian police, who had more guns. In reaction to the shots, Sitting Bull's horse, which had been trained to "dance" at the sound of gunfire in the Wild West show, raised itself up onto two legs and began to perform.[12] Tribal police – many of whom had been in exile with Sitting Bull in Canada – had done the dirty work for McLaughlin and his white administration, killing their own chief, his son Crowfoot, and several of their own brethren.

Fearful after hearing of the murder of Sitting Bull, Big Foot's Minniconjou band of Ghost Dancers soon headed from the Cheyenne Reservation to meet Red Cloud at Pine Ridge. They had the misfortune of being intercepted by the Seventh Calvary – Custer's old outfit. Racked with pneumonia, Big Foot hung out a white flag of truce and agreed to be escorted to nearby Wounded Knee Creek. As his people set up their encampment of tipis, they were surrounded by almost five hundred armed soldiers and four Hotchkiss artillery cannons.[13] The next morning – December 29, 1890 – the Calvary attempted to disarm them. While their tipis were searched for guns, Yellow Bird, a *wikasa wakan*, began dancing, and reminded his people that their protective ghost shirts would guarantee their safety. As they began to be frisked, Black Coyote defiantly waived his rifle above his head. Just as two soldiers grabbed him, Yellow Bird threw a handful of dirt into the air, an act of grieving in the Ghost Dance that the troops interpreted as a signal for an attack.[14] Pandemonium broke out between the two groups: some Lakota leveled their concealed weapons at the soldiers, who in turn commenced to relentlessly shoot them with their guns and cannons. American Horse gave this account:

> Right near the flag of truce a mother was shot down with her infant . . . Little boys who were not wounded came out . . . and as soon as they came in sight a number of soldiers surrounded them and butchered them right there.[15]

Nearly three hundred Lakota – two-thirds of them women and children – were ruthlessly massacred on the spot. Those who tried to escape were hunted down

Think about:
What factors could ultimately make a Lakota turn against his own people to become a member of a tribal police force?

and their bodies were strewn along as far as two miles away. Those not left for dead were taken to a local church, where they were surrounded by Christmas decorations including a banner displaying the ironic message, "Peace on Earth, Good Will Towards Men."[16] Mooney writes:

> When one of the women shot . . . was approached . . . and told that she must let them remove her ghost shirt in order . . . to get at her wound, she replied, "Yes; take it off. They told me a bullet would not go through. Now I don't want it any more."[17]

Three days after on New Year's Day, 1891, troops dug a long trench, and the frozen bodies of the Lakota were unceremoniously thrown in and covered with dirt. The twenty-five dead soldiers, meanwhile, were taken to the Pine Ridge agency and given proper burials.[18]

The Wounded Knee massacre did not stop the killings associated with the Ghost Dance, whose doctrine, with its apocalyptic promise of annihilation of the white man, had given many hope. Gradually, the violence that persisted in Pine Ridge for the following months caused Lakota Ghost Dancers to surrender to army commanders. Kicking Bear, who had brought the Ghost Dance to Sitting Bull's people, was one of the last. Rather than go to prison, he and several others joined a Wild West show, leaving reservation life far behind.[19]

Figure 8.4
Big Foot's band of Minniconjou Sioux in costume for a dance in 1890. Most died in the Wounded Knee massacre.
Image: John C.D. Grabill. Y National Archives (public domain).

Although the Ghost Dance movement ended tragically at Wounded Knee in 1890, it was neither the end of Native American political resistance, nor that of violent confrontation on Pine Ridge Reservation. In 1973, when members of the American Indian Movement (AIM) launched the occupation of Wounded Knee village to protest grievances toward the US government, they declared Wounded Knee to be the Independent Oglala Nation.

The Wounded Knee occupation of 1973

AIM – an urban Indian activist organization – was founded in Minneapolis in 1968 and rapidly grew into a radical civil rights group. Early influential members included Dennis Banks, Hank Adams, Clyde Bellecourt, Richard Oakes, and John Trudell, who contributed to AIM's growing notoriety by staging militant occupations of Alcatraz prison, Mount Rushmore, Plymouth Rock, and the Bureau of Indian Affairs in Washington. In 1973, Banks and Russell Means, an Oglala Sioux who had been born on Pine Ridge, led two hundred AIM members and reservation Indians to Wounded Knee. They gathered to protest the lack of justice for the murders of Native Americans by whites who were going unpunished, as well as to bring attention to the constant violence on Pine Ridge generated by despotic tribal chairman Dick Wilson, who commanded his tribal police to cordon off protesters at Wounded Knee. Federal troops soon arrived, encircling protestors with Vietnam-style artillery that included infrared gun scopes for spotting and shooting the rebels at night.[20] As news of the takeover quickly spread, the government's actions caused the media to draw analogies to the 1890 massacre. Although AIM militants were woefully under-supplied in comparison to the troops, gunfire was frequently exchanged during the seventy-one-day siege.

Figure 8.5
Native American dancer Hanobi Smith performs a "Men's Fancy Dance" in *Cokata Upo!* (*Come to the Center*) by the Lakota Sioux Dance Theatre
Image: Linda Vartoogian, Front Row Photos

The bravery of AIM members was inspirational to Indians all over the United States, and some became radicalized by embracing former religious ceremonies involving dance. Although the Ghost Dance and the sacred Sun Dance had been outlawed, they had not been lost, due to the efforts of traditional medicine men like Leonard Crow Dog, who reinstituted an annual Sun Dance in 1971 on the Rosebud Reservation. To Mary Crow Dog, who later became his wife, it was an unforgettable event:

> Many of the AIM leaders came to Crow Dog's place to dance, to make flesh offerings, to endure the self-torture of this, our most sacred rite, gazing at the sun, blowing on their eagle-bone whistles, praying with the pipe. It was like a rebirth, like some of the prophesies of the Ghost Dancers coming true. The strange thing was seeing men from other tribes undergoing the ordeal of the Sun Dance who came from tribes that had never practiced the ritual. I felt it was their way of saying, "I am an Indian again."[21]

Crow Dog, whose wife described his chest as a "battlefield of scars," saw religious ceremonies like the Sun Dance as a means of unifying people.

During the Wounded Knee siege, Crow Dog was a spiritual guide and used his healing powers to tend to the wounded. As conditions worsened and hunger steadily increased, Crow Dog announced that he would lead a Ghost Dance in the ravine where Big Foot's people had been massacred. He said they would dance barefoot in the snow from dawn until nightfall for four days, and warned of the visions that might occur. In a show of unity, forty agreed to join him. Although resources at Wounded Knee were limited, women made ghost shirts from scavenged curtains and painted them with sacred designs. Some augmented these by draping upside-down American flags around themselves in an AIM sign of protest. Russell Means danced and shared his thoughts with the community at the end of the four days:

> The white man says that the 1890 massacre was the end of the wars with the Indian, that it was the end of the Indian, the end of the Ghost Dance. Yet here

we are at war, we're still Indians, and we're Ghost Dancing again. And the spirits of Big Foot and his people are all around.[22]

Just as the Ghost Dance had given hope to Indians in the nineteenth century, Crow Dog's revival of the ceremony was a prime example of the cultural transformation that began to empower many American Indians.

AIM activism sparked a renaissance amongst many Native Americans who had been sent to government boarding schools, and consequently never knew their language or their religion, or related to their heritage. One example was Mary Crow Dog, whose baby boy was delivered by Lakota women during the siege because she refused to give birth in a white hospital. After Wounded Knee, she participated in her first Sun Dance, a formative experience in which she felt no pain from the skin offerings she made in honor of loved ones she had lost, and received a powerfully euphoric vision in which she saw these dead friends. Afterwards, she stated, "It was at that moment that I, a white-educated half-blood, became wholly Indian."[23] As a result of Wounded Knee, Mary Crow Dog was one of many whose political activism with AIM led to a kind of spiritual revival. After the Wounded Knee siege ended, many AIM activists were put on trial and repeatedly jailed, and dissent among members weakened the movement. However, the strides AIM made in terms of national recognition for Native Americans were invaluable. As author Ian Frazier reflects, "AIM changed the way people regarded Indians in this country, and the way Indians regarded themselves; in an assimilationist America, they showed that a powerful Indian identity remained."[24]

> *Think about:*
> Why did the Ghost Dance retain its power as a symbol of cultural pride for AIM activists, and what could be its legacy today?

Current trends

Each year, the anniversary of the Wounded Knee massacre is commemorated by the Memorial Chief Big Foot Ride, in which participants begin on horseback at Standing Rock on December 15th (the date of Sitting Bull's death), follow the path taken by the Minniconjou Ghost Dancers, and arrive at the Wounded Knee site on December 29th. Annual Sun Dances, popular with tourists, occur on Pine Ridge and other Sioux reservations, as do at least a dozen powwows per year. Crow Dog's Sun Dance has continued yearly since 1971 on Crow Dog's Paradise, his family's land on the Rosebud Reservation. This ceremony has grown both in participants and in intensity. Harkening back to tradition, the piercing and cutting of flesh have become more severe than the early days of its revival in the 1970s. Crow Dog, who still presides, has reinstituted the old practice of dragging heavy buffalo skulls that are attached to the dancers' back muscles. Unlike in the nineteenth century, women today also partake in making vows, which they honor by cutting themselves.

Sioux activism has been manifested most recently in the 2016 protests at Standing Rock reservation, aimed at halting the federal government and the oil industry from allowing the 1,172-mile Dakota Access Pipeline to cross the Missouri River. The protesters, who refer to themselves as "water protectors," believe the pipeline has the potential to pollute the water supply and violate their sacred sites. At Standing Rock – the site of Sitting Bull's murder – the accumulated history of wars, broken treaties, tribal harassment, and poverty has led to distrust and cynicism among Native Americans. These feelings are not unfounded, as the militarized police response to the unarmed protestors has been to attack them with pepper spray, rubber bullets, Tasers, water cannons, and dogs. In solidarity, the Sioux have been joined by thousands of indigenous peoples and supporters from around the world, who either have journeyed to Standing Rock or given their support via the powerful tool of social media. Many Māori from Aotearoa/New Zealand have shown their solidarity by posting *hakas*, the war dance they traditionally performed to intimidate their enemies before going to battle. Sioux Round Dances, which echo the Ghost Dance, are performed by protesters, and thousands of Jingle Dress Dancers have emerged during standoffs with riot police. In the face of ecological disaster, the Standing Rock protest has emerged as the largest Indian gathering since the days of the Ghost Dances, and many Indians feel a revival of the surge of empowerment manifested in the early days of AIM, when smoldering resentments were forged into powerful tools of activism.

8.2 Exploration: excerpt from *Killing Custer: The Battle of the Little Bighorn and the Fate of the Plains Indians* by James Welch and Paul Stekler[25]

Shortly before the Battle of the Little Bighorn in 1876, when the Sioux and Cheyenne defeated Custer's Seventh Calvary in their fight to keep the Black Hills, Sitting Bull arranged for a Sun Dance and vowed to make a sacrifice to Wakan Tanka, the great spirit, to benefit his people. This was one of the last of this scale before the government banned the dance in 1883.

A few days later, the Sun Dance began. It must have been one of the largest in history, for there were many thousands of Sioux and Cheyenne present. The camp spread all across the valley floor and was probably a couple of miles in length. At the gathering's final camping place, several days later on the Little Bighorn, the village was said to be eight thousand strong and three miles long. Sitting Bull had prepared himself physically and spiritually for the sacrifice, one he had made many times before as a Lakota youth, then as a holy man. Now, naked to the waist, he walked to the medicine pole and sat down, his back leaning against it, his legs straight out. Jumping Bull approached with a finely ground knife and a steel awl. He knelt before the leader and with the steel awl lifted the skin of his arm away from the flesh beneath it. He worked his way up the arm until he had cut fifty pieces of skin from it. Then he started up the other arm cutting fifty more. Sitting Bull did not flinch as the blood poured from his wounds. He sang to Wakan Tanka, asking for mercy from himself and his people. The cutting of a hundred piece of flesh from his arms took half an hour.

Sitting Bull danced all day and all night and half the next day. The people gazed in awe at the stocky figure of their leader, his long hair loose and his arms covered with blood. At last he could no longer dance and appeared ready to faint. His good friend and fellow chief Black Moon caught him and laid him gently on the trampled earth. After a time, his head came back and he said something in a low voice to Black Moon.

Black Moon stood and turned to the people. "Sitting Bull wishes to announce that he just heard a voice from above saying, 'I give you these because they have no ears.' He looked up and saw soldiers and some Indians on horseback coming down like grasshoppers, with their heads down and their hats falling off. They were falling right into our camp."

The people were happy with this vision, for they knew what the words meant. The soldiers had no ears to listen to the truth that the Sioux and Cheyennes wanted to be left in peace to hunt and to be together on the ground of many gifts. The soldiers who wanted war were coming to their camp and would be killed there. The announcement was clear enough. The people rejoiced. Wakan Tanka would protect them.

Discussion questions: the Ghost Dance

1 Some of the terms of the Fort Laramie Treaty included provision of certain rations, tools, and education for the Sioux. Discuss how did the US government's aid actually led to the demise of Sioux life.

2 How and why were dances like the Sun Dance and the Ghost Dance so threatening to government officials who held positions of obviously greater power, as well as to missionaries, who were fervent in their own religious beliefs?

3 Members of the American Indian Movement were not shy about using radical tactics in their takeovers of famous monuments, and of the village of Wounded Knee in 1973. Is violence justified in certain situations, and if so, when and why?

8.3 Haitian Vodou: an Afro-Caribbean spiritual pathway

Key points: Vodou

1 Haitian Vodou, along with other Afro-Caribbean faiths, has antecedents in the ancient West African religions of Vodun and Yoruba. African slaves in the New World were forced to convert to Catholicism and forbidden from practicing their own religions.

2 Africans found discreet ways of retaining their indigenous beliefs under Catholicism, and this was facilitated by the many similarities between the two: a hierarchy of a supreme godhead and saints/spirits, belief in an afterlife, and the pursuit of protection from patron saints/spirits.

3 In adapting to their new environment, Africans incorporated other religious customs into their own and, consequently, new syncretic religions developed in the New World, such as Candomblé in Brazil, Santería in Cuba, Sango in Trinidad and Tobago, and Vodou in Haiti.

4 Aided by the guidance of a *houngan*, a Vodou priest, or a *manbo*, a priestess, at a ceremony Vodouisants (adepts) seek help from the *lwa* (spirits or deities), who act as intermediaries between a Supreme Being and humans. A devotee cultivates a symbiotic relationship with a *lwa* (pronounced Lo-wah) by propitiating it with songs, dances, and by "feeding" it with animal sacrifices.

5 At rituals, if a *lwa* is pleased, it will descend into a devotee. In this state of deep possession trance, the devotee becomes a *chwal* (horse), and is "mounted," or "ridden" by the *lwa*, who uses him or her as a medium to communicate with the community.

In Vodou, every dance, every song is a prayer; every word and every act becomes a lesson.

—Claudine Michel[26]

The Bight of Benin, which spans the West African shores of Benin, Togo, Ghana, and Nigeria, was once more infamously known as the "Slave Coast" due to the slave trade that began to flourish in 1670. In return for luxury items and weapons, local warring kings sold their captives to Europeans engaged in the Triangle Trade. In the Middle Passage leg of this enterprise, multitudes of slaves were transported from West Africa across the Atlantic to the New World and sold for a second time to plantation owners who made fortunes in the sugar, coffee, and cotton industries. This accumulation of wealth, resulting from the forced labor of millions of Africans, supported the world economy on both sides of the Atlantic for centuries.

Africans who survived the inhumane crossing arrived with nothing but their faith, language, songs, and dances, which they held onto overtly, or covertly. Caribbean slaveholders attempted to "civilize" their chattel by converting them to Catholicism. In adapting to their new environment, Africans incorporated other religious customs into their own and, consequently, New World syncretic religions developed, such as Candomblé in Brazil, Santería in Cuba, Sango in Trinidad and Tobago, and Vodou in Haiti. While Cuba is dominated by Yoruba influence, in Haiti, there are three discernable trajectories of African influence: the Fon people from Dahomey (now Benin); the Yoruba from Nigeria; and the Kongo people, from today's Angola and Bas-Zaire.

Haitian Vodou, along with other Afro-Caribbean faiths, has antecedents in the ancient West African religions of Vodun and Yoruba. Vodun, a Fon word meaning "spirits, or gods" is practiced by the Fon, Ewe, Mina, and Ga people, among others, while the Yoruba religion is practiced by the Yoruba. These two religions share many similarities, especially in their aims to heal individuals and maintain the well-being of a community. Both have complex mythologies that teach correct behavior, and respectful worship of the deities is taken seriously. A spiritual pantheon exists in

Figure 8.6
Every June, Vodouisants make a pilgrimage to the sacred grotto of Saint Francis d'Assisi to pray and make sacrifices to Vodou spirits.
Image: Les Stone.

both, with a Supreme Being at the top, while the numerous deities below are all manifestations of this androgynous presence. These spirits, known as *vodun* in Vodun, and *orisa* in Yoruba, might inhabit various areas such as rivers or oceans; be found in forces or elements of nature, such as thunder, or iron; or may be manifested in fetishes – inanimate objects of innate power such as a mound of earth, a tree stump, or a sculpture. Worshiping ancestors is a part of everyday life, and practitioners of both religions believe that reincarnation occurs through the birth of children. In these indigenous African faiths, it is dance and music, in tandem with gift giving and/or sacrifice, that provide one with a direct connection with the spirit world. If a *vodun/orisa* is pleased with the offerings, he or she will descend and communicate with followers by "riding the head" of a priest, priestess, or devotee, who falls into a deep spirit-possession trance. In this state, the follower may execute superhuman feats such as cutting him/herself or licking burning-hot knives. If the trance is real, no harm or pain occurs, due to the protection of the spirit. This altered state of possession is considered to be the most sacred and joyous submission a devotee can experience and is the highest aim of followers. Afro-Caribbean religions share all these commonalities, but variations exist on every level, since the practices are not standardized and there is no sacred text.

Haitian colonization

On Christopher Columbus's quest to find gold and new trade passageways for Spain in 1492, he landed on a large Caribbean island and was met by the indigenous Taíno-Arawak people, who cheerfully brought the sailors nourishment

Figure 8.7
During the annual Sucre ceremony, Vodouisaints bathe in a sacred pool on the river. A priest douses devotees with *klerin*, Haitian moonshine.
Image: Les Stone.

and gifts. Due to their dark skins, Columbus deduced that he had arrived in India and called them "Indians" – a misnomer that has plagued many in the Western hemisphere to this day. Columbus named the island Hispaniola, and reported on its marvels when asking to be dispatched on another voyage. Claiming that the natives "are so naïve and so free with those possessions. . . when you ask for something they have, they never say no." He promised the Spanish Monarchs "as much gold as they need, and as many slaves as they ask."[27] For Spain's benefit, Columbus enslaved the Taínos to mine for gold, and ruthlessly exploited them on colonial estates. By 1650, due to disease, exhaustion, murder, and suicide, the Arawak people were no more.[28] In 1697, the French gained possession of the colony and renamed it Saint Domingue. Because no Taínos remained, thousands of African slaves were imported to work in the sugar and coffee industries in what became France's richest colony.

In French colonies the *Code Noir*, a 1685 decree signed by Louis XIV, controlled slavery and religion.[29] Masters were obligated to feed, clothe, and look after their slaves – but corporal punishment was liberally sanctioned. Within eight days of arriving on an island, slaves were baptized and instructed in Catholicism. Although they were explicitly forbidden from practicing their religions, Africans found discreet ways of couching their beliefs under the cloak of Catholicism, which was facilitated by the many similarities between the two religions. These include a hierarchy of a supreme godhead and saints/spirits, belief in an afterlife, and the pursuit of protection from patron saints/spirits. Africans disguised their spirits as Catholic "saints." Erzulie Freda, the Vodou deity of motherhood, was equated with the Virgin Mary, while the snake spirit Damballah was linked with St. Patrick. Africans also incorporated Catholic-style altars into their services, complete with candles, bells, and incense. This amalgamation of cultures was also present in the development of Kreyòl, or Creole, the language of slaves that blended West African languages and French, and is predominant in Haiti today.

After a long and hard-fought slave rebellion against French rule was launched in 1791, Haiti became the first black independent republic to be established in the Western hemisphere. Between 1791 and 1804, secret Vodou societies played an important role in the resistance movement waged by the slaves against the French. The prelude to the revolution was a Vodou ceremony held at rural Bois Caïman (Alligator Woods), led by Dutty Boukman, a Vodou priest. A black pig was sacrificed in honor of Ezili Dantor, the deity of motherhood, and several hundred slaves anointed themselves with its blood in a show of solidarity to the cause. The revolution erupted a few days afterward. The struggle was waged on two fronts, with both regular as well as spiritually charged weapons, with the societies' priests calling upon the most aggressive forces. Terrified colonists lived in fear of poisonings and assaults, and many saw their plantations burn to the ground. Led by former slave Toussaint L'Ouverture, Saint Domingue became a battleground in which slaves waged violent guerilla warfare for over a decade.

Ultimately, slavery was overturned, the French were defeated and expelled, and, in 1804, revolutionary leader Jean-Jacques Dessalines declared independence for the island. He renamed it Haiti ("Land of the Mountains"), the indigenous Taíno name.[30] Following the revolution, Haiti was boycotted by the United States and Europe for nearly a century, and the Catholic Church refused sending priests there for more than fifty years.[31] Unlike the rest of the Caribbean, Haiti was liberated from outside influences after driving out the French and the inhabitants were free to follow their African cultural traditions. Ironically, Catholic influence in Vodou never disappeared.

Think about:
Would Haitians have been able to hide their own indigenous beliefs as easily if their colonizers had been Protestants – a religion with less emphasis on saints and symbolism?

Case study: Vodou secret societies

Although Vodou is a healing religion, there are more nefarious, secret societies in Haiti, such as the Bizango society, which originated during the slave revolt in the eighteenth century. Bizango figurines are fetishes that hold secret contents, rumored to be human bones. Their heads, modeled after real human skulls, are decorated with horns or wings, as well as with mirrored shards that deflect evil forces. Ropes and chains are wrapped around them to assuage the hidden forces inside. In the twentieth century, the dictatorial Duvalier family (Papa Doc and Baby Doc) took advantage of secret societies such as the Bizango in order to instill fear in anyone opposing their regime. As a result, Vodou was negatively viewed by many.

Haitian Vodou ideology

In the Haitian Vodou pantheon, the Supreme Being is called Bondyè (good god), while the lower level deities are called *lwa* (pronounced *Lo-wah*). Rather than petitioning to Bondyè, Vodouisant adepts seek help from the appropriate *lwa*, who acts as an intermediary between the Supreme Being and humans. In religious ceremonies, a *houngan*, a Vodou priest, or a *manbo*, a priestess, assist in both summoning the *lwa* and in helping them depart from a possessed adept. A devotee cultivates a symbiotic relationship with *lwa* by propitiating them with praise songs, dances, and by "feeding" them with animal sacrifices and offerings in exchange for protection. A *lwa* becomes more powerful by granting assistance, but the power of one who is not "fed" dies out. In Haiti, it is believed that hundreds exist in the trees and in the courtyard of *hounfort* – Vodou temples – but their permanent residence is a mythical place below the sea, *Ville-aux-Camps*.[32]

All Haitian *lwa* have antecedents in African Vodun and Yoruba religions, and their counterparts exist in other Afro-Caribbean denominations. Deities fall into various families, or *nasyons*, with the Rada, Gede, and Petro being the most prominent. Rada rituals are rooted in Africa, and its sweet, benevolent *lwa* are old-world spirits, associated with white. Damballah, one of the oldest and most venerated ancestral spirits, presides over this cult along with his wife, Aida Wedo. Other Rada *lwa* are Erzili Freda, the spirit of love, motherhood, and wealth (who loves perfume, rum, dancing, and Damballah, at times); and Legba, the spirit of the crossroads. Since they represent the realm between life and death, Gede *lwa* have faces painted half white and half black, and their color is black. This family includes Papa Gede, spirit of death and sexuality, and Baron Samedi, guardian of cemeteries. Gede spirits are flashy tricksters who wear sunglasses, dress in black top hats and tails, and are avid smokers, drinkers, and eaters. Petro *lwa* signify the evolution of African-based religions due to New World influences. They reflect the experience of violence and oppression to Africans in the New World and are associated with the color red. Petro spirits, such as Ogou, the *lwa* of iron and thunder, are "hot." Because "hot" spirits should be balanced, each person usually also propitiates two or three other "sweeter" Gede or Rada spirits for protection.

Figure 8.8
A devotee of the *lwa* Damballah at a Vodou festival in Jacmel, Haiti.
Image: Benjamin Eagle.

For many Vodouisants, the influence of the *lwa* permeates all aspects of their lives and their credo is *sèvi lwa yo*: "I serve the spirits."[33]

Vodouisants believe that when a baby is born, a *lwa* makes a choice to love and protect them, but this association is further cemented through divination by priests and priestesses. This protective deity, whose personality will be emulated in the devotee, is called *mèt tet* – "master of the head." For instance, the sweet nature of the snake spirit Damballah will be seen in an even-tempered person, whereas a person who carries Ogou as his or her *mèt tet* manifests the warrior spirit's fiery temper in everyday behavior.

Another Vodou belief is that one possesses a *gwo bonanj* – a "big guardian angel" that can travel from the body. At rituals, if a *lwa* is pleased, it will descend into a devotee who, most often, has it as his or her *mèt tet*. In this state of deep possession trance, the devotee becomes a *chwal* (horse), and is "mounted," or "ridden" by the *lwa*, who uses the devotee as a medium to communicate with the community. In order for this desired possession to occur, the *gwo bonanj* must depart from the body before the *lwa* enters it – a transition seen in the struggle that occurs in a devotee at the onset of trance. The absence of the *gwo bonanj* explains the loss of cognizance and the lack of recall in the devotee who has been ridden.[34]

Figure 8.9
A possessed man during the St. Jacques festival in Plaine du Nord. Vodouisants immerse themselves in sacred mud, believing that the *lwa* Ogou dwells within.
Image: Les Stone.

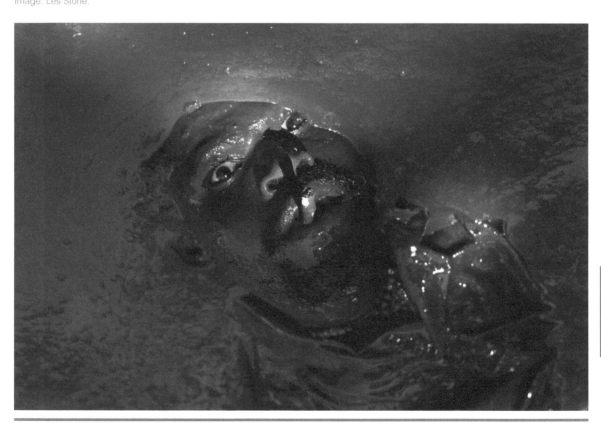

In the Vodou tradition, there is belief in the afterlife, which a person attains by becoming an ancestor. When a devotee dies, a *houngan* or *manbo* conducts a ceremony to remove his or her soul, which is believed to then retreat into dark water. At the end of a year and a day, the soul is retrieved through ritual prayers and singing, and housed in a clay jar called a *govi* which will then sit on the altar of the *houngan* or *manbo*. If these rituals are not conducted, the unsettled soul could roam, creating problems in the community, which many believed occurred when so many bodies went missing after Haiti's catastrophic 2010 earthquake.[35]

Clients and devotees

Vodouisants make daily offerings of prayers and small gifts to *lwa* at family altars. However, those who are grappling with deeper problems seek help through divination by *houngon* priests or *manbo* priestesses, who ascertain the nature of their client's problem. In a serious case, the *lwa*, if propitiated properly, will alleviate the problem and insure protection if the person commits hosting a costly ceremony with dancing, drumming, and animal sacrifice. Devotees may decide to make a deeper connection to their faith by becoming initiated as Vodou healers/diviners/leaders. An initiate, or *hounsi*, must master the phenomenon of possession trance to become skillful in controlling the arrivals and departures of *lwa* spirits.[36] Throughout Haiti, initiation processes vary, but common to all is seclusion in a Vodou *hounfour* (temple) from three days to three weeks with other initiates, with periods of fasting. In her initiation process in Port-au-Prince in the 1930s, American anthropologist and choreographer Katherine Dunham described three separate stages of initiation: the *lave tet*, the *kanzo*, and then the taking of the *asson*.[37] The *lave tet* (head washing) is a spiritual cleansing in which one's *mèt tet* (master of the head) is determined. In the more involved *kanzo* initiation, *hounsi* undergo a trial in which steaming dumplings are pressed into the sole of the initiate's left foot and the palm of the left hand. This process "cooks" them, strengthening them and rendering them impervious to harm by others. The *kouche* stage imitates rebirth. Initiates are blindfolded and led through an unsettling dance of spirals and turns before being taken to the small room where they will "*kouche*," or lie down. During this time, the *hounsi* are literally treated like infants – as they lie still, they are fed, cared for, and, for forty days, their heads stay wrapped like newborns, to protect the top of their heads. The final stage is a ceremony called "taking the *asson*," which gives them the license to heal. The *asson*, a tool of Vodou priesthood, is a small calabash gourd rattle covered with a net of beads and snake vertebrae. During a Vodou ceremony, its sound alerts the drummers to change their rhythms in case the *lwa* need to be sent away, such as when a *chwal* is inexperienced, and the violent struggle between the spirit and the guardian angel becomes too much for the "horse."[38] The initiation process of a *houngan* or *manbo* concludes in a life-long "marriage" with their *lwa*, a celebration in which rings are exchanged, a marriage license is drawn up, much dancing occurs, and wedding cake is eaten.

Food for all is inherent in all initiations and Vodou ceremonies. Because initiation rituals "feed the spirits in the head," every *hounsi* is bestowed with a *pò tet* (head pot) – a repository filled with secret contents that allows the *lwa* to reside outside of their head. Animal sacrifices are made to "*manje les anges*," or feed the spirits, so that the vitality from an animal is transferred to the spirit in order to restore its divine energy. During her time

Figure 8.10
Katherine Dunham's photo of Vodou possession, taken during her anthropologic fellowship in Haiti in the 1930s.
Image: Katherine Dunham Photograph Collection, Southern Illinois University, Carbondale.

in Haiti, Katherine Dunham struggled with these sacrifices. In her initiation as a
lave-tet hounsi, she received this explanation, which provided some solace:

> Facing our head pots, we were given the meaning of what was in them; why
> a sacrificed animal was considered fortunate to be allowed to take messages
> to the god to who this animal represented an approach; how the prayers
> that were said to this fowl or goat or pig or beef and their prayers for its safe
> conduct to the god made it indeed superior and privileged beside others of its
> kind who were butchered without care or rite.[39]

The initiation priest or priestess who performs the sacrifices remains as the spiritual
parent of the *hounsi*. From then on, initiates devote one day and night a week during
which they wear colors sacred to their *lwa*, and sleep alone so that the deity can
appear in their dreams.[40]

Vodou ceremonies

Vodou ceremonies at a *hounfort* temple take place in the *péristyle* or *tonnele*,
an outdoor courtyard that has a tall pole in the middle called a *poteau mitan*. In
sanctifying the space, a sword bearer makes salutations to the drums and prayers
are said, including the Lord's Prayer. The *houngan* emerges by walking backwards
out of the sanctity of the temple into the *péristyle*, and touches the *poteau mitan*
in a ritual gesture that beckons the *lwa*.[41] The *houngan* also attracts them by
passing a thin stream of cornmeal through his fingers onto the dirt, tracing *vèvè*
designs associated with various *lwa*. The ceremony begins with the striking of the
agogo iron bell, accompanied by drumming and singing by the chorus, led by a
female singer called an *oungenikon*.[42] Revolving in a counterclockwise direction
around the *poteau mitan*, the beginning dance is the *yanvalou* (meaning "I beg
of you") which attracts Legba. He is always summoned first, since he opens the
gates to *Ville-aux-Camps* that allow *lwa* to leave and then enter the *péristyle*
through the spiritually charged *poteau mitan*. Damballah and Aida Wedo also
dance the undulating *yanvalou*, while the warrior spirit Ogun prefers the martial
Petro dance, and Baron Samedi is drawn by the percussive and seductive *banda*.
Anthropologist Karen McCarthy Brown observes that *lwa* spirits do not descend
until the dancing, drumming, and singing has made the crowd *byen eshofe*, or
"well heated up." She writes:

> When the sweat is streaming down the bodies of the drummers . . . when their
> intricate polyrhythms drive the dancers to new heights . . . when . . . the leader
> of songs and the [*hounsi*] chorus challenge one another . . . that is when the
> ceremony is *byen eschofe* and that is when the *lwa* will mount their horses and
> ride.[43]

When the possessing *lwa* "arrives," he or she is soon identified by certain
stereotypical behaviors, as well as by the ritual implements they request. While a
devotee is being "ridden," the *lwa* goes through ritual salutations and embraces,
cures, or settles problems through blessings or reprimands, and dances with their
devotees. When a Rada *lwa*, a "sweet" spirit arrives, he or she is propitiated with
sweet food and drinks, and the ambiance of their possession performance is warm
and intimate. By contrast, the mood of a "hot" Petro possession dance is hostile.
Rum is a popular offering and the trance state is more frenetic rather than ecstatic.

Petro ceremonies differ from Rada in costume colors, music, and intensity. Petro
followers wear red – a color of deep emotion and of blood. Only two drums are used,
the *baka* and *tibaka*, and the rhythms are much more driving and complex. Petro
dances are fast and full of strong, combative movements: the knees are bent and the
torso rigidly pitches forward at a forty-five-degree angle while the shoulders shake
violently and the hands clench into fists and punch the air. The feet barely leave
the ground – a characteristic reminiscent of when slaves were in chains and were
unable to move their feet widely apart, or high off the ground.[44] In their possession

Figure 8.11
In the grotto of Saint Francis, three worshipers are "mounted" by Vodou spirits. Behind them are papers conveying prayers and wishes.
Image: Les Stone.

performances, Petro *lwa* call for whips. These reflect the days of the Middle Passage, when they were cracked to summon slaves on deck to dance as exercise, and were also commonly used by slaveholders. Dancer and scholar Yvonne Daniels writes:

> I believe the intensity of the Petro spirits takes hold in the idea that these are primarily new world spirits who were concerned with the needs and desires of the Vodou congregation of that era. People desperately wanted freedom from oppression and escape from enslavement in the colonial period. The newer *loas* were called upon to offer aid and strength for revolution."[45]

Daniels found the atmosphere of a Petro ceremony to be intimidating and that those "ridden" by a Petro *lwa* dance as if they were fighting.

Haitian scholar Claudine Michel writes, "Vodou followers are taught that a proverb, song, and musical rhythm takes life only when said recited, or cadenced in the movement of the dance."[46] This is especially evinced in the *yanvalou*, a dance associated with Damballah, the snake *lwa*. A dancer emulates his mesmerizing serpentine movements by drawing energy up from the ground through their extremely bent knees and undulating pelvis, which sends a rippling effect up through the back, chest, and neck and culminates in the graceful rolling articulations of the arms. Katherine Dunham, who was "married" to Rada spirit Damballah, described the complete submission and receptivity she felt when dancing this fluid dance: "For anyone interested in vaudun, the yonvalou becomes its signature. Its movement is prayer in its deepest sense."[47]

Think about:
How do the contrasting old-world Rada and new-world Petro spirits act as cultural repositories of history and also reflect the fluid nature of Vodou?

Current trends

In Haiti today, hardships have made the arts a luxury. The country is still reeling from the devastating 2010 earthquake, in which at least 250,000 Haitians died. Due to bacteria-infected water and other complications, a cholera epidemic killed thousands more during the next year. Because of potential contagion, many bodies were burned and others were never recovered. In the Vodou tradition, the inability to conduct proper death rituals leaves souls unsettled, which is considered extremely dangerous to the living. In solidarity, prayers were sent from Vodun communities in Benin, and in Haiti, traditional ceremonies were organized to appease spirits. But panic over the epidemic made some Haitians blame Vodou priests for spreading the disease and resulted in forty-five *houngan* being gruesomely murdered by mobs that believed they were responsible for the sickness. LBGT people were blamed as well for the earthquake because of their lifestyle. In response, Vodou devotee Marjorie Lafontant offers gay rights training and legal aid to the Vodou community in Port au Prince.[48]

Although six years have passed, much of Port au Prince is still in ruins and poverty abounds. But in the challenged city, respected teacher and choreographer Frantz Mètayer continues to teach at his school, carrying on the legacy from his teacher, Viviane Gauthier, who has trained many. Another important Haitian dance artist is Jeanguy Saintus, who runs a school called Artcho and Ayikodans, a professional troupe. Saintus is fostering a new aesthetic that blends tradition with modern Caribbean culture. Both Mètayer and Saintus acknowledge the difficulties for artists, especially in a depressed economy that has declined even further since the earthquake, but Mètayer persists with teaching and Saintus offers classes to children for free. "There are many things to be done in this country," states Saintus. "Some people are fighting to move on with their lives despite the catastrophic situation we are living in. My only wish is to be there for those who want to survive *dancing*."[49]

8.3 *Exploration*: excerpt from "Afro-Caribbean Spirituality: A Haitian Case Study" by Karen McCarthy Brown[50]

Reproduced with kind permission of Palgrave Macmillan

Karen McCarthy Brown was a respected scholar in the religion and politics of Haiti. In this essay, she notes that as much as a lwa *gives ritual blessings, they may also dole out punishment if the occasion warrants, as in this example.*

There was a *oungan* in Carrefour . . . who had a reputation for being a strict and dour disciplinarian in his Vodou family. Because she had angered him, he sent away a woman named Simone, the song leader in his temple, and told her never to return. At a ceremony not long after, this *oungan*, whose name was Cesaire, was possessed by the warrior spirit, Ogou. Ogou arrived in a rage and immediately began to berate Cesaire (the very horse he was riding). Who did Cesaire think he was, Ogou asked, that he could send Simone out of the temple? Simone was one of Ogou's favorites, and besides, it was he, Ogou, who was in charge of the temple, not Cesaire. The gathered faithful were instructed to convey this message to the ill-mannered *oungan* without fail, and then the spirit departed, leaving the body of Cesaire in a crumpled heap on the temple floor. When he had barely regained his senses, the reluctant Cesaire was carried along in a procession of all the temple dignitaries, complete with the brightly colored, sequined banners of the temple, right to the home of Simone. They stood outside and sang Vodou songs of invitation and reconciliation. After much coaxing, Simone agreed to come back to the temple, and, accompanied by the full parade, she was ritually reintegrated into the Vodou family. This example shows something of the complexity of the possession process in which a *lwa* can chastise, even humiliate, his own horse.

Yet, perhaps more significantly, it also shows the key role of the community in the interpretation and application of the wisdom of the spirits. Thus, the public airing of community problems and issues within the Vodou temple is a means of enforcing social sanctions, mobilizing the assistance of the community, and mending broken relationships. It is, in short, a way of healing.

Discussion questions: Vodou

1 Given the many similarities between West African religions and Catholicism/ Christianity in terms of spiritual hierarchy, and the symbolism of blood in ceremonies, how can one be considered to be pagan and the other civilized?
2 Discuss why possession trance occurs so readily in Vodou ceremonies as opposed to those of other religions. Is it culturally induced? How do dancing, drumming, and other contributing factors facilitate it?
3 How are forces of nature and animist beliefs manifested in Vodun dances?

8.4 *Tango*: from Argentinian dens of iniquity, to Parisian dance halls, and back

Key points: *tango*

1 In nineteenth-century Argentina, a confluence of the dance, music, and singing traditions of European immigrants, Argentinian *gauchos*, and Afro-Argentinians in the predominately male migrant *conventillos* enclaves of Buenos Aires led to the emergence of *tango*.
2 *Tango*, with its colloquial, sexually explicit lyrics, was restricted to red-light districts and performed in "*academias*," dance halls where men could hire waitresses as dancing partners and for other services as well. This led to *tango's* disreputable reputation in the eyes of wealthy Argentinians.
3 African music and dance traditions had the most significant impact on the development of dances in *criolla* (creole, or native) culture, such as the *candombe, milonga, cayengue*, and *tango*. This also partially explains why the upper classes viewed these dances with disdain.
4 In the early twentieth century, Argentinians brought *tango* to Paris, where it became a sensational form of entertainment that quickly spread to other countries. After World War I, when many expatriates returned, *tango* eventually found acceptance by the Argentinian upper classes. It is now a hugely popular global dance form.
5 *Tango* singers, dancers, and musicians faced challenges, censorship, and harassment during the twentieth century, especially during the 1946–1955 presidency of Juan Perón and during the years of the "Dirty War" (1976–1983).

In tango, intimate confessions are the occasion for spectacle.[51]
—Marta Savigliano

In the nineteenth century, Argentina's Buenos Aires was a cosmopolitan city, heralded as the "Paris of South America" and famous for its elegant architecture, tree-lined *avenidas*, theaters, and modern transit system. *Porteños*, the educated elite of this wealthy and culturally vibrant port city, wore the latest Parisian fashions as they danced European waltzes, mazurkas, and polkas. Just like certain *banlieues* outside Paris, the city's outlying areas were home to the socially disenfranchised immigrant laborers in this robust economy, and it is from this multicultural migrant underworld on the city's fringe that *tango* emerged. Like *flamenco* – also originally a diverse cultural expression of those low down on the social scale – this iconic form of music and dance has a complex and multiethnic history.

Settling of Argentina

When Spanish expeditions began arriving in Argentina in the early sixteenth century, colonialist settlers purchased tracts of *pampas* – a vast expanse of fertile plains – from the indigenous Araucanian inhabitants in order to establish cattle ranches and farms. By 1587, they were buying enslaved Africans from Portuguese slave traders in Buenos Aires. In addition to slave labor, immigrants worked as rural cowboys. Known as *gauchos*, these skilled horsemen dressed in baggy pants, wore *ponchos*, and settled scores with a *facón*, or knife. Although *gauchos* were considered to be outlaws by colonial society, they were also seen as valiant folkloric heroes and romanticized in works such as *Martín Fierro* (1872), an epic poem by José Hernández.

Throughout the tumultuous nineteenth century in Argentina, sweeping changes occurred. Independence from Spain, declared in 1816, was followed by raging civil wars until 1860. Slavery was abolished throughout Argentina in 1861. Two decades later, President Julio Argentino Roca pitilessly ordered the extermination of all the indigenous peoples of the *pampas* in order to accommodate colonialist expansion of ranches and farms.[52] To boost production, massive waves of migrants from Spain and Italy began arriving. With increasing exports of beef, wool, and wheat, by the 1920s Argentina was one of the most prosperous nations in the world. While *Porteños* were enjoying luxuries, the immigrants providing the labor were living in *conventillos* – squalid slum tenements in the south of the city. Due to the influx of settlers, *gauchos* lost their nomadic *pampas* livelihood and came to live in the *conventillos*. In this locale between the city and the *pampas*, the horseless, unsaddled *gaucho* became urbanized, and Italian and Spanish migrants settled alongside emancipated Afro-Argentinians. They mixed with young, poor Argentines known as *compadritos*, who emulated *gauchos* by wearing baggy pants and high-heeled boots, augmenting their outfits with jaunty fedora-style hats, long neckerchiefs, and the requisite knife. While *gauchos* were valiant fighters, *compadritos* were likewise skilled with their weapons, but were underworld thieves, brothel owners, and pimps. Out of the *conventillos* emerged *lunfardo*, a tough, working-class dialect that was a mix of Italian and Spanish. The staggeringly uneven proportion of men to women in this male-dominated enclave of migrants, *gauchos*, and *compadritos* was five to one. In the brothels that sprang up, most female workers were foreign and, unfortunately, there is evidence that many were victims of a white slave trade.[53] In the brothels, where lonely men far outnumbered women, a good male dancer stood a better chance at fighting for their attentions. In order to stay proficient, men practiced amongst themselves during the week on the streets and docks – an anomaly compared to other dance forms, which lack a male embrace. In this largely male migrant enclave, the blending of dance, music, and singing traditions led to the emergence of various dance forms and, ultimately, to *tango*.

Origins of *tango: candombe, habanera, milonga,* and *cayengue*

In the late nineteenth century, while *Porteños* were enjoying European ball dances, within the *conventillos* the traditions of European immigrants, Argentinian *gauchos*, and Afro-Argentinians were merging. *Gauchos* with roots in Andalusia – the home of *Gitano flamenco* – brought percussive heel stamping and finger snapping; Italian immigrants introduced compositional techniques influencing singers and composers; and former African slaves from Kongo and Angola contributed their own low, grounded movements and unrelenting rhythms. Scholar Robert Farris Thompson credits these particular African traditions as having the most significant impact on dances of *criolla* (native) culture in Buenos Aires, and points out that *candombe*, *milonga*, *cayengue*, and *tango* are all Kongo words.[54]

Candombe was a Kongo dance that became the foundation for the *milonga*, a predecessor of *tango*. The dancing was polyrhythmic, in which one part of the body, such as the shoulders, moves in one rhythm, while the legs follow another. The counterclockwise winding of the hips (*tienga*) followed the sun's pathway, and the fast twists and dips inherent in a Kongo warrior's training also appeared. Women and men danced in two separate lines but, at intervals, partners would invade each other's space by breaking from their lines and suddenly bump abdomens or other body parts together in a *bumbakana*.[55] *Compadritos* who witnessed Afro-Argentines dancing *candombe* incorporated these energetic moves and improvisations into the *milonga*.

Case study: *Candombe* at the Shimmy Club

Similar to Harlem's integrated Savoy Ballroom in New York City, the Shimmy Club in Buenos Aires was a popular venue for *tango* from the 1940s to the 1970s. But at midnight, all white patrons would be asked to leave its ballroom upstairs and, in the basement, *candombe* dancing would begin. Normally, this was a secular dance and not performed surreptitiously. But Robert Farris Thompson points out that when *candombe* was performed after midnight – the most advantageous time to commune with ones' ancestors in Kongo culture – that possession trance occurred. As a child, Facundo Posadas – a famous Afro-Argentinian *tanguero* – was told never to interfere with people in this state and was given the explanation that "a saint had grabbed them."[56]

Another African-based form, combined with Spanish and French influence, was the Afro-Cuban *habanera*, brought by black sailors from Havana in 1850 to Buenos Aires and neighboring Montevideo, Uruguay, on the other side of the Río de la Plata. This blending of cultures woven into the seductive bass rhythms of the *habanera* profoundly influenced nineteenth-century music and dance, such as jazz and the Brazilian *maxixe* (forerunner of *samba*), and inspired the beat of the *milonga* and the *tango*. Thompson states that *milonga* in Ki-Kongo means "moving lines of dancers" and in *gaucho* culture, it described a competition combining dueling guitar improvisations and stamping. In the *milonga*, *gaucho* folk traditions and *candombe* movements merged with speedier-paced *habanera* rhythms and the *abrazo* (embrace) of European ball dances.[57] Accompanied by improvisations on the flute, violin, harp, guitar, and clarinet, the *milonga* became the quintessential dance of the working class.

The *milonga* was followed by the *canyengue*, the nascent form of *tango*. In Ki-Kongo, *canyengue* means "melt to the music," and in Kongo culture, one honors another by bending low, with the knees pressed together. This stance asserts itself in the *canyengue*, a cheek-to-cheek couple dance in which the dancers "melt" by leaning into each other's chests while taking short steps with the knees bent, buttocks protruding, and the arms in a European ballroom embrace with clasped hands held down low.[58] *Canyengue* music was interspersed with break patterns in the rhythm, during which the hips twisted in motions called *quebradas*. With faces in profile, or cheek to cheek, their deadpan expressions harkened back to the African tradition of the "mask of black cool," as Thompson notes.[59] As they danced, the man's thigh would momentarily, assertively, and seductively press on the woman's in a move of restrained desire.

Outside the *conventillos*, *Porteño* rulers endeavoring to create an elite European society rejected these hybrid dance forms as primitive and hypersexual.[60] Yet Thompson refutes the idea that African-based dances lacked self-control:

Figure 8.12
Roberto and Guillermina performing at TangoFest '97.
Image: Jack Vartoogian, Front Row Photos.

Reason and control mastered the flow of sexual energy, shaping and diverting it with breaks, cuts, and flexions – equivalents to Kongo *bumbakana*. The intimacy was Continental. The control was sub-Saharan and exactly the opposite of what the elite of Buenos Aires assumed was going on.[61]

Think about:
In contrast to European ball dances, why would the absence of conversation between *tango* partners cause nervousness in the upper classes?

Another ironic point is that *tango's* characteristic *abrazo*, or embrace, was actually a European contribution, not an African one – yet how it differed from the waltz shocked many *Porteños*. Instead of dancing in an open embrace and facing one's partner, here, the gaze was inward, and couples danced cheek to cheek, and chest to chest, in a decidedly close embrace – without any polite conversing at all.

1895 to 1917: *tango's la guardia vieja* – the old guard

At the turn of the twentieth century, *tango* was thriving in the Buenos Aires *demimonde*, but was still distained by the upper class. During *la guardia vieja* – the early days of *tango*, when lyrics depicted men suffering over a deceitful woman or missing a mother figure, and were sexually explicit upon occasion – the dance was restricted to red-light districts, and performed in "*academias*" – dance halls where men could hire waitresses as dancing partners and for other services as well.[62] In this atmosphere of drunkenness, knife fights, and carnal pleasures, *tango's* disreputable reputation grew. Sons of *Porteños* gravitated to brothels and *academias* where they competed with *compadritos* in dancing with *milonguitas* – female *tango* dancers. Some brought *tango* uptown to *garçonnières*, their apartments reserved for romantic assignations. Continuing its upward trajectory, *tango* began entertaining the clientele of *clandestinos*, high-class bordellos in *Porteño* neighborhoods. Two famous establishments were María La Vasca's, and Laura's – frequented by the police chief, who ignored its illegal activities. Rosendo Mendizábal's popular *tango El entrerriano* was composed and performed at Laura's in 1897.[63]

By 1900, *tango* had begun to disentangle itself from its connections with prostitution and could be found in more respectable venues in Buenos Aires and Montevideo. Many former brothel workers became *tango* performers in dance halls such as the Stella de Italia.[64] Italians developed a style known as *tango liso* (smooth *tango*), adding mandolins to the instrumentation as well as the *bandoneón*, a German accordion that quickly became integral to the *tango* sound. Afro-Argentinian musicians added their sophistication, such as violinist El Negro Casimiro and *bandoneón* player "El Pardo" (Sebastián Ramos Mejía). While the still-marginalized *tango* was thriving and evolving in Buenos Aires, some Argentines brought it to Paris, where it would undergo a storybook "rags-to-riches" scenario – much to the embarrassment of *Porteños*, who were intent upon showcasing Argentina as a sophisticated and modern city to the rest of the world.

Tango's migration to Europe

Tango's transatlantic journey began in 1907, when musicians traveled to make recordings in France, which had the most advanced studios, and the most scintillating nightlife as well.[65] As rich Argentines began to travel on luxury ocean liners for extended vacations abroad, the French phrase *riche comme un Argentin* (rich as an Argentine) captured their lavish style. *Porteños* customarily sent their sons on European grand tours to "complete" their education, and some – who had surreptitiously frequented *clandestinos* and had become adept *tangueros* – electrified Parisian society with their dancing. One seminal instance was an impromptu performance in 1911 by Ricardo Güiraldes, a poet who had been raised in both Paris and Buenos Aires. He attended a Parisian salon in which the guests were asked to perform a dance best displaying the culture of a country. As a fellow Argentinian played *El entrerriano* on the piano, Güiraldes expertly guided an unwitting French woman through the twists, turns, walks, and dips of *tango* in front of a rapt audience. In noting how Parisian salons contributed to the visibility of the form, author Artemis Cooper suggests that Güiraldes's display was in part responsible for launching *tango* in Paris, and it quickly invaded French cabarets, dance halls, and high society venues.[66] Despite its staggering popularity, *tango* – with its close embrace, bold moves, and African/folk origins – remained a source of embarrassment for upper-class Argentinians and was banned at Argentinian Embassy dances in Paris. But its popularity was unstoppable: by 1913, "tangomania" had spread to London, Berlin, Barcelona, Tokyo, Helsinki, and bounced back across the Atlantic to New York and New Orleans.

As avid Parisians took up *tango*, changes occurred in form and in fashion. Languorous, extended postures and daring movements such as deep dips, backbends, and sways were introduced, punctuated by marching walks. Despite the accessibility of Argentinian recordings and sheet music, the compositions for these European iterations lacked the typical rhythms and the pace became much more leisurely.[67] Parisian fashion produced women's narrow *tango* skirts in shades of "*tango* orange," which were slit to allow mobility, and cut above the ankle to expose both footwork and the fashionable pointed-toe *tango* slippers. Eyeliner enhanced the eyes, hair was bobbed, and long cigarette holders became chic accessories. The elastic *tango* corset provided a shorter cut than a traditional one and liberated women from metal stays. Just as Coco Chanel was revolutionizing women's fashion by introducing disarmingly chic yet comfortable clothes, the rare combination of glamour and ease of *tango* fashion allowed women to exhibit a sense of independence, physicality, and sensuality on the dance floor. In the midst of this vibrant cosmopolitan era, the advent of World War I cast a pall on Europe. When the Germans invaded France in 1914, hordes of expatriates – including a large Argentine colony – embarked on luxury ocean liners and sailed home.

1917 to 1935: *tango*'s *epoca de oro:* the golden age

Tango – a sensation in European high society – was now not only associated with stylish elegance and glamour, but with Argentina itself. Wealthy *Porteños* were still slow to accept a hybrid dance that had emerged from the depths of *conventillos* as a symbol of their national identity, but since *tango* had gained validity abroad, they begrudgingly began to accept it. Due to the outlawing of prostitution in 1919, *tango* left the long-standing *academias* and bordellos in shady Buenos Aires neighborhoods and moved "uptown" to cabarets emulating Parisian venues, such as the Armenonville and the Nacional Café. Elegant dress became a must, and although the young women encouraging upper-class men to buy them drinks were still prostitutes, they had learned to speak French.[68]

Figure 8.13
Argentinian *tango* dancers Milena Plebs and Miguel Angel Zotto perform in *Tango X 2*.
Image: Jack Vartoogian. Front Row Photos.

Case study: *Tangueros* (tango dancers)

Many *tangueros* born in the *conventillos* rose to great fame and adopted glamorous personas in both their performances in *tango* venues and in the developing film industry. One example is José Ovidio Bianquet, known as "El Cachafaz." Born in 1897, he began dancing in the streets and eventually traveled abroad, performing *tango* in the Ziegfeld Follies in New York City and at the famed El Garrón in Paris in 1919. After returning to Buenos Aires, he opened a prestigious *tango* academy. In 1942, El Cachafaz died as he lived, suffering a heart attack while heading onto the ballroom floor to dance yet another *tango*. Famous *tango* duos of the following generation include Juan Carlos and María Nieves, Kely and Facundo Posadas, El Pibe Palermo and Norma, and Ester and Mingo Pugliese.

In 1919, World War I was over. As the world moved slowly from devastation toward normalcy, *tango* resurfaced in Europe. In ballrooms in Argentina and abroad, *tango* ensembles increased in size and innovative bandleaders such as Vicente Greco (1888–1924), Francisco Canaro (1888–1964), and Roberto Firpo (1884–1969)

Figure 8.14 (p. 245)
Tango dancers Nannim Timoyko and Nelida Rodrguez perform *Milongueras* from *Tango Argentino*.
Image: Jack Vartoogian, Front Row Photos.

expanded *tango* repertory. The era of the *tango-canción* had begun: *tango* lyricists were largely men and the narratives that they wove were sung from a male point of view that tended to reveal deep confessions, insecurities over women, or their dependence on a forgiving mother figure. It was so male-dominated that during the 1920s and 1930s, female singers had to assume male roles.[69] Azucena Maizani (1902–1970), who wrote music for numerous *tangos*, sang masculine songs to highlight her cross-dressing. Yet women's orchestras sprang up during the golden age and included *La Porteñita* and the sextet of Paquita Bernardo, the first professional female *bandoneón* player.[70]

A celebrated, innovative lyricist of this time was Celedonio Flores (1896–1947), an Afro-Argentine poet who incorporated *lunfardo* slang into *tango* lyrics that reflected plights of betrayed lovers, thieves, and the socially victimized. In his *Margot*, a man laments over his memories of a beloved young woman, who now has assignations with wealthier men in fancy circles while her poor mother toils in the *conventillos*. Music for Flores's songs was sometimes written by Carlos Gardel, who also sang on the recordings. Gardel, a romantic *tango-canción* singer, was to become the iconic and omnipresent face of *tango*. In 1917, when Gardel sang *Mi noche triste* (*My Sorrowful Night*), with lyrics by Pascual Contursi, he helped establish the trope of a jilted romantic drowning his sorrows in drink to forget his love, who is a heartless, opportunistic betrayer. In the same year, Firpo transformed a marching band song by Gerardo Hernán Matos Rodríguez into the most well-recognized *tango* tune of all time, *La cumparsita*. In the lyrics, a man finds himself not only abandoned by his woman, but by the dog she left behind. *La cumparsita* became another huge recorded hit for Gardel in Buenos Aires, and beyond.

Case study: Carlos Gardel

Like *tango* itself, Gardel himself came from poverty and grew into a sensation. Born in France in 1890, he immigrated with his single mother to Buenos Aires in 1893. Gardel began his career as a *payador*, or folk singer, but after finding fame in 1917 singing *tango-canción*, he became its chief interpreter. He was handsome, suave, and elegant, and his baritone voice reached many through his performances in Buenos Aires and abroad, as well as through his numerous recordings and *tango* films. In 1935, Gardel died in a plane crash at the age of 44. His death resulted in an international outpouring of grief, and his body was taken to New York City, Rio de Janeiro, and Montevideo, where it lay in state before returning to Argentina. In Buenos Aires, his funeral procession stretched for miles through the streets as people mourned for "Carlitos," their treasured national icon. Gardel's image – found on matchbooks, murals, and postcards – is ubiquitous throughout Argentina, and his fame – along with his music – endures.

Tango under oppression

Much of the twentieth century was a political challenge for many Argentines, as well as for their beloved *tango*. Pianist and bandleader Osvaldo Pugliese was always driven to help working people; in 1936, he founded an artist's union and later joined the Communist Party. Over the next two decades, Pugliese was repeatedly jailed for his activism, and he and his orchestra were banned from entering clubs and radio stations. But popular support for Pugliese was unconditional, and deep. Once, at a club when his band was in the midst of *La cumparsita*, the police entered. Claiming that Pugliese was barred, they ordered a halt to the dance, but the club's owner refused to interrupt his orchestra until the song was over. Knowing that when he stopped he would be arrested, Pugliese directed his musicians to continue playing it in a loop. The dancers complied by dancing the longest *La cumparsita* ever, until the police finally gave up and left. As Pugliese ended his epic version, his audience cheered for him.[71]

Tango artists faced even more challenges in the next decade, especially after a 1943 military *coup d'état* led to the 1946–1955 presidency of Juan Perón. In this era of the "New Argentina," his right-wing military government espoused Catholicism, nationalism, and championed the laboring classes idolizing his wife Eva ("Evita"), who had grown up in poverty herself. Under Perón, *tango* became an Argentinean symbol of national pride – but not before undergoing censorship. In an attempt to make Argentine Spanish less "vulgar," Italian-inflected *lunfardo* was banned. Racy *tango* lyrics were sanitized to reflect Catholic morals and no longer portrayed *milongueras* as betrayers or prostitutes, thanks to the maternal Evita, who advocated for the rights of women and the disenfranchised. Instead, the earlier nostalgic theme of the loving, self-sacrificing mother returned.[72] During the Perón era, people danced in large masses to big bands playing *tango* tunes with minimal, innocuous lyrics.

After Perón was ousted by a *coup* in 1955, Argentinians experienced more decades of political strife and censorship. Yet some artists managed to keep *tango* moving forward, such as composer and musician Ástor Piazzolla (1921–1992), an acclaimed bandeneónist who played in several famous orchestras. Influenced by jazz and avant-garde music, he founded *Quinteto Nuevo Tango* in 1960. Piazzolla influenced countless musicians, as well as dancers. He collaborated with female lyricist Eladia Blázquez on many compositions and toured with the famous *tango* duo, Juan Carlos Copes and María Nieves. Piazzolla and his family had recently moved to Italy when a military *coup d'état* occurred in Argentina in 1976. By avoiding the censorship that ensued in Argentina during the next decade, Piazzolla was free to pursue his highly adventurous, experimental work that would have been repressed in Argentina during the era of *La Guerra Sucia* – the Dirty War.

The Dirty War: *La Guerra Sucia* (1976–1983)

From 1976 until 1983, Argentinians were oppressed by a brutal dictatorship whose ideology included state-sponsored terrorism, censorship, and the torture

Think about:
Can a form that has been "sanitized" by a political regime ever retain or regain its original characteristic flavor?

Figure 8.15
Junior Cevila and Mariana Parma perform in *Tango Noir*.
Image: Jack Vartoogian, Front Row Photos.

or murder of alleged subversives. During this time, over thirty thousand citizens – clergy, artists, scholars, students, or dissidents – mysteriously disappeared, and they became known as *los desaparecidos*. Political statements or critical artistic expressions were censored by the military, and an edict was passed against public gatherings, which affected dancing *tango* in *milonga* social clubs. *Tango* had been a target of censorship even before the days of the Perón government, and political pressure on *tangueros* surely did not dissipate in the next few generations. Interviews by cultural anthropologist Arlene Davila of older *tango* dancers present after Perón's fall in 1955 included unpleasant memories of being questioned and harassed by police on their way home from *milongas*.[73] Scholar Ana Cara, who did fieldwork in Argentina during the "Dirty War," observed that the reluctance to engage in *milongas* was due to fear, and finding *tango* lessons or dancing publicly in Buenos Aires was difficult.[74] Instead, people watched staged *tango* performances and listened to *tango* music, although many lyrics had been censored. In the wake of the Falklands War in 1983, the military regime folded and was replaced by a democratic government. Cara asserts that after this transition, because traditional *milonga* gatherings allowed Argentines to congregate, dialogue openly, and express themselves freely, that *tango* fostered political and social healing.[75] In Argentina, a "*tango* renaissance" developed slowly, while abroad – stoked by the emergence of a show that became a worldwide hit, *Tango Argentino* – it erupted.

Produced by Claudio Segovia and Hector Orizzoli, *Tango Argentino* made its debut in Paris in 1983 and toured internationally for over a decade throughout Europe, Japan, and the United States. Its *tangueros*, who came from all walks of life and were all shapes and sizes, included couples such as Nieves and Copes, and Milena Plebs and Miguel Angel Zotto. After their success in *Tango Argentino*, Plebs and Zotto created *Tango X 2* in 1988, which further contributed to *tango*'s revival. In 1992, *Tango Argentino* was performed in Argentina for the first time and reignited the interest of *tango* in its place of origin. The *tango* dance resurfaced with an unexpected force, especially in the resurgence of *milongas*. Ironically, this was yet another case of *tango* leaving Argentina, and coming back triumphantly.

Tango dance

In Argentina, Uruguay, and beyond, there are innumerable ways to dance *tango*, but one universal rule is that it is most important to develop mutual communication with one's partner – but without words or visual signals. Cara identifies the difference between "export *tango*" and "home *tango*": flashy export *tango* is devised for tourism and touring, while the more understated version is practiced devotedly in *milongas* by Argentinians (and adept foreigners).[76] In the *milongas*, as the music starts, *tangueros* often pause in their embrace and sense each other before they begin to dance. *Tango* is completely improvised – steps can be put in any order and be big or small. Playing with rhythm and phrasing is part of the enjoyment, such as when a couple takes a momentary pause during their counterclockwise journey. Although a leader guides the follower in what is called *la marca*, the latter has equal power. As the leader uses body pressure to indicate a move, the follower has to be skilled enough to interpret their intent and has the power to slow down, speed up, or embellish the steps with fancy footwork. When a couple dances in a locked embrace with their upper halves pressed together, the leader may be marching counterclockwise as the other executes fast footwork and *quebradas* (hip twists), or *ochos* – pivots in a figure-eight pattern. Although their lower bodies may be dancing different steps, the follower has equal power, and, as Cara points out, there is a reciprocity that is reflected in the old adage, "it takes two to tango."[77]

Despite the scintillating spectacle of stage *tango* (which contains flashy moves that are actually not allowed in *milongas*), intimate, fleeting moments do occur. In a *lustrada*, a shoe is polished on the back of the opposite calf, or, more seductively, a

Figure 8.16 (p. 249)
Argentinian *tango* dancers Gachi Fernandez and Sergio Cortazzo perform in *Tango X 2*.
Image: Jack Vartoogian, Front Row Photos.

foot can be slowly dragged up a leg in a *humero*. In a *sentada*, one partner bends low while the other momentarily perches on their thigh. Eroticism is further conveyed when one executes *a gancho*, a hook of a leg around a partner's leg, or waist. In a *calesita*, one balances on a leg while the other bends and presses against the partner's side and is promenaded around on the ball of the foot. The final two notes of a *tango* – the *chan-chan* – is a Ki-Kongo term translating as "step it down."[78] The dancers will end with the *chan-chan* in a *corte* (cut) – a statuesque pose that embodies *tango*'s glamour, passion, and soulful elegance.

Current trends

Tango, now a globalized form, thrives in communities in Japan, France, the United States, Finland, and beyond – a subject beyond the scope of this chapter. In Argentina today, many *tangueros* who perform at *milongas* also make a living as teachers or as stage performers. People dance at *milongas* for their own pleasure, but the reality that one will be watched, and judged, is real. Anthropologist Marta Savigliano, an Argentinian herself, observes that *tango* is an addiction of the passionate in Buenos Aires and that the rules of the *milonga* scene are ruthless. At all costs, one has to have mastered the dance to participate. She writes:

> In the milonga everything means something else, and everybody pretends to be someone else . . . Every new arrival is observed, carefully pondered, discretely discussed, casually engaged in conversation when necessary, and eventually, trotted around the dance floor. Every look, exchange, and invitation to dance (whether given or received) is a test.[79]

Gaining proficiency to dance weekly at a *milonga* is the aim of many, and students will dance in group *practicás* or take *tango* lessons. Although there are tea time *milongas*, in general, people arrive around midnight and stay until dawn to dance *La cumparsita*, customarily the last *tango* of the night. In a testament to their passion, some *tangueros* attend *milongas* at least twice weekly.

Buenos Aires *milongas* range from sophisticated to family oriented. *Milonga Paracultural* at Salon Canning is popular with all ages, while *La Viruta* and *El Yeite* are the hippest, loudest, and latest spots, as is *Practica X*, where *nuevo tango* is performed. The Sunderland Club in the *barrio* of *Villa Urquiza* is attended by generations of families. Beginners can take lessons at *Le Catedral del Tango* and then stay on after the band arrives. Queer *tango* is very popular – at *La Marshall* gay couples dance openly and women enjoy leading, breaking traditional barriers. Other queer Buenos Aires artists include Walter Perez, who, along with his partner, Leonardo Sardella, established their company, *Malevaje Tango*, in NYC in 2011. Sid Grant and Claudio Marcello Vidal – who dances in five-inch heels – are another duo.

Outside of the *milongas*, *tango* tourism is an enormous boon to the Argentine economy. *Piazzolla Tango* offers elegant, revue-like *tango* performances, as does *La Esquina*, a dinner theater in historic Abasto, where Gardel grew up. On a more national level, Gardel's birthday, December 11, is *Día Nacional del Tango*, and is celebrated with dancing and music, while the *Gran Milonga Nacional*, also held in December, is a massive outdoor *tango* festival. Buenos Aires is a beacon for international competitions: *El Campeonato Metropolitano de Tango*, a tournament sponsored by the city of Buenos Aires, occurs annually, and every August, the *Tango* World Championships are held. In whatever capacity – as a romantic offering for tourists, as a passionate pursuit for beginners, or as a way of life for longtime *tangueros* – *tango*, just like Carlos Gardel, is a ubiquitous presence in Río de la Plata culture.

Discussion questions: *tango*

1 Like *flamenco* – also originally a diverse cultural expression of those low down on the social scale – *tango* has an equally complex and multiethnic history. What happens to a dance form when it leaves its place of origin and is appropriated by another group?

2 Identify the effects politics had on *tango* in the twentieth century, and discuss why and how *tango's* resiliency has prevailed.
3 What happens to the concept of "authenticity" when a dance form becomes globalized?

Notes

1 Welch, James, and Paul Stekler. *Killing Custer: The Battle of the Little Bighorn and the Fate of the Plains Indians,* 45–46.
2 Mooney, James. *The Ghost Dance Religion and the Sioux Outbreak of 1890*, 69–70.
3 Welch and Stekler, 77.
4 Hillstrom, Kevin, and Laurie Collier Hillstrom. *American Indian Removal and the Trail to Wounded Knee*, 55.
5 Ibid., 55.
6 Mooney, 2; Hillstrom, 63.
7 Mooney, 92.
8 Ibid., 35.
9 Ibid., 30.
10 Ibid., 179–180.
11 Brown, Dee. *Bury My Heart at Wounded Knee*, 409.
12 Ibid., 411–412.
13 Frazier, Ian. *On the Rez*, 59–60.
14 Kehoe, Alice B. *The Ghost Dance*, 23.
15 Mooney, 139–140.
16 Brown, 418.
17 Mooney, 34.
18 Ibid., 131–132.
19 Frazier, 120.
20 Crow Dog, Mary, and Richard Erdoes. *Lakota Woman*, 65.
21 Ibid., 42–43.
22 Warrior, Robert Allen, and Paul Chaat Smith. *Like a Hurricane: The Indian Movement from Alcatraz to Wounded Knee,* 230.
23 Crow Dog and Erdoes, 142.
24 Frazier, 17.
25 Welch, James, and Paul Stekler. *Killing Custer: The Battle of the Little Bighorn and the Fate of the Plains Indians*, 51–52.
26 Michel, Claudine. "Vodou in Haiti: Way of Life and Mode of Survival," 34.
27 Zinn, Howard. *A People's History of the United States: 1492–Present*, 5.
28 Ibid., 5.
29 Desmangles, Leslie D. "African Interpretation of the Christian Cross in Vodou," 41.
30 Daniel, Yvonne. *Dancing Wisdom*, 69.
31 Brown, Karen McCarthy. "Afro-Caribbean Spirituality: A Haitian Case Study," 2.
32 Desmangles, 41.
33 Michel, Claudine, 30.
34 Brown, Karen McCarthy, 8–9.
35 Danicat, Edwidge. "A Year and a Day," 1.
36 Brown, Karen McCarthy, 12.
37 Dunham, Katherine. *An Island Possessed*, 91.
38 Brown, Karen McCarthy, 11–12; 14.
39 Dunham, 106.
40 Brown, Karen McCarthy, 11.
41 Desmangles, 46.
42 Daniel, 7–8.
43 Brown, Karen McCarthy, 13.
44 Daniel, 70.
45 Daniel, Yvonne. "The Potency of Dance: A Haitian Examination," 69.
46 Michel, Claudine. "Vodou in Haiti: Way of Life and Mode of Survival," 33.
47 Dunham, 135.
48 Beenish, n/a.

49 www.ayikodans.com/index.php/about-us
50 Brown, Karen McCarthy. "Afro-Caribbean Spirituality: A Haitian Case Study,"
   13–14.
51 Savigliano, Marta E. *Tango and the Political Economy of Passion*, 45.
52 Collier, Simon. "The Tango Is Born: 1880s–1920s," 20–21.
53 Savigliano, Marta E. *Tango and the Political Economy of Passion*, 47.
54 Thompson, Robert Farris. *Tango: The Art History of Love*, 61–62.
55 Ibid., 66–67.
56 Thompson, Robert Farris. *Tango: The Art History of Love*, 138–139.
57 Ibid., 121.
58 Ibid., 151.
59 Thompson, 276.
60 Castro, Donald. *The Argentine Tango as Social History (1880–1955)*, 91.
61 Ibid., 157.
62 Collier, 45; Savigliano, 50.
63 Collier, 51.
64 Ibid., 57.
65 Cooper, Artemis. "Tangomania in Europe and North America: 1913–1914, 67.
66 Ibid., 72.
67 Savigliano, 119.
68 Castro, 177.
69 Ibid., 250.
70 Azzi, María Susana. "The Golden Age and After: 1920s–1990s," 140–141.
71 Paz, Alberto. https://elfirulete.wordpress.com/1999/07/25/
   when-the-tango-was-in-jail/
72 Castro, 230.
73 Davila, Arlene. *Culture Works: Space, Value, and Mobility Across the Neoliberal
   Americas*, 139.
74 Cara, Ana C. "Entangled Tangos: Passionate Displays, Intimate Dialogues," 444.
75 Ibid., 459.
76 Cara, 430.
77 Cara, 453.
78 Ibid., 127
79 Savigliano, Marta E. "From Wallflowers to Femmes Fatales: Tango and the
   Performance of Passionate Femininity," 105.

Bibliography

Visual sources

YouTube

"Aaron Huey: America's Native Prisoners of War," YouTube video, TED TALK, 15:59,
   posted November 10, 2010, www.youtube.com/watch?v=8tEuaj4h8dw
"American Indian Movement," YouTube video, 6:24, posted by "kweetsadee,"
   July 24, 2014, www.youtube.com/watch?v=BlKc19OUR54
"Juan Carlos Copes und Maria Nieves," YouTube video, 2:33, posted by "Tango Ffm,"
   April 14, 2016, www.youtube.com/watch?v=2BBp0hqEXfE
"Meet the Vodou Priestess Summoning Healing Spirits in Post-Earthquake Haiti,"
   YouTube video, 14:39, posted by "VICE," May 6, 2016, www.youtube.com/
   watch?v=QPuAJzB425I
"Mingo and Esther Pugliese Dance to Osvaldo Pugliese," YouTube video,
   4:17, posted by "tanguero2/4," February 26, 2008, www.youtube.com/
   watch?v=VoXe4bmeUEI
"Tango X 2 – Miguel Angel Zotto 'Su Historia' – bailan Romina Levin Leandro Oliva,"
   YouTube posting, 2:38, posted by "lavana6 Video Tango," November 1, 2014,
   www.youtube.com/watch?v=vSJEK_BzddM

Written sources

Azzi, María Susana. "The Golden Age and After: 1920s-1990s." In *Tango: The Golden
   Age*, edited by Simon Collier, 114–156. New York: Thames and Hudson Ltd., 1995.

Bellegarde-Smith, Patrick. "Resisting Freedom: Cultural Factors in Democracy – the Case for Haiti." In *Vodou in Haitian Life and Culture: Invisible Powers*, edited by Claudine Michel and Patrick Bellegarde-Smith, 101–116. New York: Palgrave Macmillan, 2006.

Beenish, Ahmet. "Why Vodou and Lesbians Get Along." *Ozy, The Daily Dose*, November 15, 2016, www.ozy.com/rising-stars/why-vodou-and-lesbians-get-along/72362.

Brown, Dee. *Bury My Heart at Wounded Knee*. New York: Holt, Rinehart and Winston, Inc., 1970.

Brown, Karen McCarthy. "Afro-Caribbean Spirituality: A Haitian Case Study." In *Vodou in Haitian Life and Culture: Invisible Powers*, edited by Claudine Michel and Patrick Bellegarde-Smith, 1–26. New York: Palgrave Macmillan, 2006.

Cara, Ana C. "Entangled Tangos: Passionate Displays, Intimate Dialogues." *The Journal of American Folklore*, Vol. 122, No. 486 (Fall, 2009), *Latin American Dance in Transnational Contexts*, 438–465. Published by University of Illinois Press. Stable URL: www.jstor.or/stable/40390081.

Castro, Donald. *The Argentine Tango as Social History (1880–1955)*. Lewiston, NY: The Edwin Mellen Press, 1991.

Collier, Simon. "The Tango is Born: 1880s-1920s." In *Tango: The Golden Age*, edited by Simon Collier, 18–55. New York: Thames and Hudson Ltd., 1995.

Cooper, Artemis. "Tangomania in Europe and North America: 1913–1914." *In Tango: The Golden Age*, edited by Simon Collier, 66–100. New York: Thames and Hudson Ltd., 1995.

Cosentino, Donald J. "It's All for You, Sen Jak!" In *Vodou in Haitian Life and Culture: Invisible Powers*, edited by Claudine Michel and Patrick Bellegarde-Smith, 199–216. New York: Palgrave Macmillan, 2006.

Crow Dog, Mary, and Richard Erdoes. *Lakota Woman*. New York: Grove Press, 1990.

Danicat, Edwidge. "A Year and a Day." *The New Yorker*, January 17, 2011. www.newyorker.com/magazine/2011/01/17/a-year-and-a-day.

Daniel, Yvonne. *Dancing Wisdom*. Chicago: University of Chicago Press, 2005.

Daniel, Yvonne. "The Potency of Dance: A Haitian Examination." *The Black Scholar*, Vol. 11, No. 8, *Black Anthropology*, Part 2 (November/December 1980): 61–73. Published by: Taylor & Francis, Ltd. Accessed November 25, 2016, 16:52 UTC. Stable URL: www.jstor.org/stable/41068017.

Davila, Arlene. *Culture Works: Space, Value, and Mobility Across the Neoliberal Americas*. New York: New York University Press, 2012.

Deloria, Vine, Jr. *Custer Died for Your Sins: An Indian Manifesto*. New York: The Macmillan Company, 1969.

Desmangles, Leslie D. "African Interpretation of the Christian Cross in Vodou." In *Vodou in Haitian Life and Culture: Invisible Powers*, edited by Claudine Michel and Patrick Bellegarde-Smith, 39–50. New York: Palgrave Macmillan, 2006.

Dunham, Katherine. *An Island Possessed*. Chicago: University of Chicago Press, 1969.

Frazier, Ian. *On the Rez*. New York: Picador; Farrar, Straus, and Giroux, 2000.

Griner, Alison. "A Leap of Faith." *Aljazeera Magazine*, July 25, 2015. www.aljazeera.com/indepth/features/2015/07/magazine-haiti-dancer-leap-faith-150712094316787.html.

Hardy, Kevin. "Near Standing Rock, Pipeline Protest Meets a Spiritual Movement." *Des Moines Register*, October 16, 2016, 6:51 a.m. www.desmoinesregister.com/story/news/2016/10/08/near-standing-rock-dakota-access-pipeline-protest-meets-spiritual-movement/91567854/.

Hillstrom, Kevin, and Laurie Collier Hillstrom. *American Indian Removal and the Trail to Wounded Knee*. Detroit: Omnigraphics, Inc., 2010.

Kehoe, Alice B. *The Ghost Dance*. (Case Studies in Cultural Anthropology). Orlando, FL: Holt, Rinehart and Winston, Inc. 1989.

Martin, Richard. "The Lasting Tango." In *Tango: The Golden Age*, edited by Simon Collier, 157–170. New York: Thames and Hudson Ltd., 1995.

McAlister, Elizabeth. *From Slave Revolt to a Blood Pact with Satan: The Evangelical Rewriting of Haitian History*. Middletown, CT: Wesleyan University, Studies in Religious History, 2012. https://works.bepress.com/elizabeth_mcalister/37/.

Michel, Claudine. "Vodou in Haiti: Way of Life and Mode of Survival." In *Vodou in Haitian Life and Culture: Invisible Powers*, edited by Claudine Michel and Patrick Bellegarde-Smith, 27–36. New York: Palgrave Macmillan, 2006.

Mooney, James. *The Ghost Dance Religion and the Sioux Outbreak of 1890.* Chicago: The University of Chicago Press, 1965. Originally published as Part Two of the Fourteenth Annual Report of the Bureau of Ethnology to the Secretary of the Smithsonian Institution, 1892–93.

Paz, Alberto. "When the Tango Was in Jail." *El Firulete*, Copyright 1999–2011, Planet Tango. Accessed December 26, 2016. https://elfirulete.wordpress.com/1999/07/25/when-the-tango-was-in-jail/.

Savigliano, Marta E. "From Wallflowers to Femmes Fatales: Tango and the Performance of Passionate Femininity." In *The Passion of Music and Dance: Body, Gender, and Sexuality*, edited by William Washabaugh, 103-114 Oxford and New York: Berg, Imprint of Oxford International Publishers Ltd., 1998.

Savigliano, Marta E. *Tango and the Political Economy of Passion.* Boulder, CO: Westview Press, 1995.

Smith, Paul Chaat. *Everything You Know About Indians Is Wrong.* Minneapolis: University of Minnesota Press, 2009.

Taylor, Julie. *Paper Tangos.* Durham and London: Duke University Press, 1998.

Thompson, Robert Farris. *Tango: The Art History of Love.* New York: Pantheon Books, 2005.

Warrior, Robert Allen, and Paul Chaat Smith. *Like a Hurricane: the Indian Movement from Alcatraz to Wounded Knee.* New York: The New Press, 1996.

Welch, James, and Paul Stekler. *Killing Custer: The Battle of the Little Bighorn and the Fate of the Plains Indians.* New York: Penguin Books, 1994.

Zinn, Howard. *A People's History of the United States: 1492–Present.* New York: HarperCollins Publishers, 2001.

Glossary

'Ailolo: a sacrificial pig feast, which occurs after a *'ūniki* graduation ceremony and marks the official entrance of *haumana* into the guild of *hula* performers.

'Ayāna: a woman possessed by *zār* spirits, who seeks the help of a *shaykha*.

Adavu: basic dance step patterns in *bharatanatyam*.

Agem: an asymmetrical posture and the fundamental stance of Balinese dance.

Aharya abhinaya: decorative aspects such as costumes, jewelry, and make-up in classical Indian dance.

Ahchi dede: the chief of the *tekke* kitchen, who guided dervish initiates through a multitude of daily chores during their retreat.

Akua: the major gods of the Hawaiian pantheon in its polytheistic religion.

Ali'i: the noble class in old Hawaiian society.

Alta: a red dye that accentuates a classical Indian dancer's palms, fingertips, and feet.

American Indian Movement: an Indian activist organization, founded in Minneapolis in 1968, that staged radical militant occupations of Alcatraz prison, Wounded Knee, Mount Rushmore, Plymouth Rock, and the Bureau of Indian Affairs in Washington.

Andalusia: a province in southern Spain and the birthplace of *flamenco*.

Anga suddha: translates as "clean body line." A *bharatanatyam* dancer uses precision in extending the limbs of the body, beating the feet on the ground in time with the music, and articulating *mudras* between the rhythms, text, and song.

Angarakha: a long-sleeved, wide dress, cinched at the waist, worn in the Muslim style of *kathak* costuming.

Angika abhinaya: concerns the movements of the whole body in classical Indian dance.

Angkor Wat: a colossal Hindu temple, dedicated to the Hindu god Vishnu. It is decorated with many carvings of *apsara* dancers.

Angsel: sudden bursts of movement that highlight the percussive accelerations of the Balinese *gamelan*.

Aotearoa: translating as "Land of the Long White Cloud," the home of Māori people was called "New Zealand" by European explorers.

Apsaras: celestial dancing nymphs in Hindu mythology. The royal Cambodian *lakhon lueng* dancers were considered to be living symbols of the divine *apsara* dancers.

Ara orun: translating as "beings from beyond," a Yoruba term for ancestors.

Aragoto: introduced by Ichikawa Danjuro I in militaristic Edo, this bombastic, "rough style" featured *kabuki* actors wearing exaggerated make-up who performed warrior stories filled with bravado fighting.

Araimandi: a half-seated *bharatanatyam* position, in which the feet are turned out with the heels touching, and a diamond shape is created in the legs as the knees bend out to the side.

Arangetram: a solo dance performed by a *devadasi* at the conclusion of her training.

Asson: a rattle used by Haitian *manbo* or *houngan* priests to summon *lwa* spirits.

Atua: gods and goddesses in the Māori polytheistic religion.

Auto-da-fé (act of faith): a method of torture implemented during *La Reconquista* in Spain, which people were burned at the stake.

Awa: the male masking society, whose members organize and perform in the Dogon *dama*.

Awiran: shimmering cloth panels worn by a *baris* dancer, silk-screened with gold and edged with a colorful pom-pom fringe.

Bailaoras: female *flamenco* dancers.

Bailaores: male *flamenco* dancers.

Bali-balihan: secular Balinese ceremonies held in the outer courtyard of a temple the *pura*.

Ban zhu: the master of a *jingju* troupe, who acted as director, playwright, composer, and teacher of apprentices.

Bapang: a decorative bib-like "armor" covering the chest, shoulders, and upper back of a *baris* dancer.

Baris: a Balinese ceremonial male dance in which the performers become symbolic bodyguards for the gods. Baris translates as "line," while *baris gede*, a group dance for men, means "great line."

Barrios: urban neighborhoods.

Bata de cola: a torso-hugging *flamenco* dress with a wide skirt that extends into a long, ruffled train.

Bebali: semi-sacred Balinese dances, performed in the second courtyard of a temple.

Bedhas: articulate movements of the head, neck, and eyes in *bharatanatyam*.

Bedhaya: a Javanese court dance traditionally performed by nine highly trained women, which pays tribute to the glory of the ruler and exemplifies the serene self-containment of the Javanese way of life.

Bharata Natyasastra: a dramaturgical text written by the Indian sage Bharata in the second century.

Bharatanatyam: theater or dancing to the principals of Bharata, found in the *Bharata Natyasastra*. This term replaced *sadir* of the *devadasis* in the 1930s.

Bhava: the *rasa*, or communication of emotion in a skilled classical Indian dancer will create *bhava*, or mood, in an audience.

Bindi: an auspicious red dot placed on the forehead, traditionally worn by an indian bride.

Black-beard *tati*: hunters and dwellers of the forest, as well as schemers, who have dark faces and wear a white *chutti* flower on their nose *in kathakali*.

Bols: abstract vocal syllables, such as *ta thei thei tat-ta thei thei an Indian tai*, recited by the dancer to a *tala* cycle before beginning a *kathak* solo.

Bukkaeri: translating as "sudden change," a *kabuki* actor's onstage costuming alteration demonstrates a lead character's emotional or physical change. For instance, a man may be instantly transformed into a spider by three *koken*.

Buong Suong Tevoda: a ceremony to bring rainfall, performed as an offering in the Cambodian court or the temple during times of drought.

Buta: malevolent Balinese demons that bring evil and misfortune.

Butai: made of Japanese cypress, a *noh* stage has a peaked roof supported by four corner pillars and references the architecture of a Shinto shrine.

Butoh: a subversive dance genre that arose in Japan in the chaotic wake of World War II in reaction to the war's atrocities and the Westernization of its culture.

Cafés cantantes: intimate venues for watching *flamenco* that emerged in the mid-nineteenth century, which led to the commercialization of the form.

Cajón: a wooden box played by a *flamenco* musician that is struck while sitting upon it.

Cak: a Balinese male chorus, who energetically chant the monosyllable "cak" (pronounced "chak") repeatedly in interlocking rhythms once the *sanghyang* enter the trance state of *kerawuhan*. This chorus was also incorporated into the *kecak*, which emerged as tourist entertainment in the 1930s.

Cakkyars: Brahmin actors famous for their *abhinaya* acting and dancing in spiritual Sanskrit dramas in Hindu temples of Kerala.

Calonarang: a ritualistic Balinese dance drama that serves to drive away negative powers in a community. The main protagonists are Rangda, a witch who represents destruction, and the Barong Ket, a lion-like creature who keeps demonic forces in check.

Candombe: a polyrhythmic African Kongo dance that became the foundation for the *milonga*, a predecessor of *tango*.

Cante jondo (deep song): a *flamenco* singing style, often described as raspy sung by a cantaor/a

Canyengue: a dance from Kongo culture that influenced *tango*, in which one bends low, with the knees pressed together.

Carmen Amaya (1913–1963): a female *Gitano flamenco* artist and international star, who shattered norms by dressing in a tight matador's *traje corto* suit and performing the fierce, lightning-speed *zapateado* reserved for the male dancer.

Carnatic music: a small Indian orchestra including a singer, drums, flute, violin, and a drone, conducted by a *nattuvanar*.

Chakkars: fast spins in *kathak*, possibly derived from the dance of Turkish Sufi dervishes.

Chan-chan: during these final two notes of a *tango*, a couple ends with a statuesque pose that embodies *tango*'s glamour, passion, and soulful elegance.

Chauri: a long braid attachment that extends down to the waist, typically worn by Indian brides.

Chille: a sequestered retreat for a dervish initiate, lasting for 1,001 days.

Chille tennuresi: a long black gown worn throughout the 1,001 days of a dervish initiate's education.

Choli: a tight bodice with short sleeves worn in the Hindu style of *kathak* costuming.

Chou: a clown in Chinese *jingju*, who serves as a humorous foil to a leading character, and can be of any social rank, age, or gender.

Chutti: a beard, or knobs for the nose or forehead, crafted from thick white paper and affixed with rice paste, which give the *kathakali* actor a superhuman appearance.

Chutti pattam: jewelry covering the middle part of the hair and framing the forehead of a *bharatanatyam* dancer.

Chwal (horse): at Hatian Vodou rituals, a pleased *lwa* might descend into a devotee, who in a state of deep possession trance becomes a *chwal* that is "ridden" by the *lwa* and used as a medium to communicate with the community.

Clandestinos: high-class bordellos in *Porteño* neighborhoods in Buenos Aires.

Compadritos: poor Argentine slum-dwellers who adapted the dress of *gauchos*, but were underworld thieves, brothel owners, and pimps.

Compás: rhythmic patterns in *flamenco* that predominantly fall into two categories: *grande* (big, heavy) such as *siguiriya* and *soleá*, and *chico* (light), such as *alegrías*, *tangos*, and *bulerías*.

Conventillos: squalid slum tenements for immigrants in southern Buenos Aires.

Crazy Horse (1842–1877): an Oglala Sioux and celebrated warrior, who, like Sitting Bull, refused to be relocated to a reservation and fought in the Battle of the Little Bighorn. He died from a bayonet wound in an Army prison.

Daaq: a percussive rhythm or beat, which is a catalyst for summoning *zār* spirits. Drawn by their respective *daaq*, the *zār* spirits descend into the bodies of an *'ayāna* and her *shaykha* during a *zār*.

Dama: a collective funeral ceremony held approximately every twelve years for Hogons or important elders. In these rituals, the descendants honor the departed through masked dances that shepherd the souls of the deceased to the spirit world, where they will then attain the rank of ancestor.

Dan: female character roles in Chinese *jingju*, which include *quigyi*, a virtuous woman of high status; *huadan*, a flirtatious female; *lao dan*, an elderly lady; and *wu dan*, an acrobatic female warrior.

Darwish (sill of the door): a Persian word, written in Arabic and Turkish as *dervish*, that metaphorically depicts one who seeks the door of enlightenment.

Dasiattam: dance of *devadasis*.

De cintura para abajo (from the waist down): refers to the dancing and the sound of *zapeteado* footwork in the male *flamenco* style.

De cintura para arriba (from the waist up): concerns female *baile*, in which the majority of the *flamenco* movements are with the torso and arms.

Dede: the title given to an initiate after the successful completion of dervish training.

Dege: wooden statuaries of Dogon ancestors, housed in the altar of the *ginnu*.

Dengaku: rooted in Shinto fertility rites, this folk entertainment was a musical offering to the gods from rice farmers wanting to insure a good harvest, and influenced the development of *noh*.

Devadasi: translating literally as "female devotees of god," they performed ritual duties in temples and danced in royal courts in South India from the sixteenth to the early twentieth century.

Dhoti: a single cloth, wrapped around the legs and pleated at the waist, worn by men in *kathak*.

Dodot: a floor-length skirt of batik cloth with a long train in the front, which drifts backward in between the ankles of a *bedhaya* dancer as she moves.

"Down to the Countryside" movement: a policy during the Cultural Revolution that exiled members of privileged families to the country to work and be "re-educated" by peasants and farmers.

Duende: translating as "goblin-like spirit," this term embraces the charisma and fiery passion that remarkable *flamenco* performers possess.

Dupatta: a scarf worn over the shoulder and across the torso by a female *kathak* dancer.

Egungun: Yoruba ancestral spirits who can be invoked to help the living by giving advice, granting blessings, or punishing wrongdoers for being ritually honored on earth.

Egungun maskers: Yoruba believe that ancestor spirits physically manifest themselves by descending into the bodies of *Egungun* maskers – members of a male society who demonstrate the power of ancestors to their descendants through dance in festivals throughout Nigeria and Benin.

El baile: dance, which in *flamenco* reflects the percussive footwork of Indian dance and the serpentine arms seen in that of the Middle East.

El cante: *flamenco* song, which is infused with the rhythms and vocalizations of Arab and Jewish music, sung by a *cantaor/a*.

El toque: *flamenco* guitar playing, played by a *tocaor/a*.

Elewe: *Egungun* masks of the Igbomina Yoruba, which represent an ancestral lineage of chiefs.

Émna: the various masks used in the *dama* funeral ceremony, which are carved from sacred wood by blacksmiths. When the performers are costumed and masked, they are also called *èmna*.

Escuela bolera: the classic school of Spanish dance, which evolved in the eighteenth century and synthesized French ballet with popular folk dances such as *fandangos*, *malagueñas*, and *boleras*.

Escuela Sevillana: the Seville School of classical *flamenco*, developed by Pastora Imperio and Matilde Coral.

Farah ma'a al-asyād ("wedding with the masters"): in this private, initial *zār*, the *'ayāna* enters a union of sorts with her possessing *zār* spirit(s), known as *asyād* masters.

Farruca: a predominately male *flamenco* dance, in which rapid-fire *zapateado* footwork is performed while keeping the body relatively still.

Federico García Lorca (1898–1936): an Andalusian poet, playwright, avant-garde theater director, and a great supporter of *flamenco puro*. Lorca was executed in 1936 by a firing squad in the first month of the Spanish Civil War, due to his leftist politics and homosexuality.

Flamenco: a form of music and dance originating in the Spanish province of Andalusia, whose varied roots tap into the music, song, and dance of Arabs, Jews, Africans, and North Indian Gypsies.

Flamenco puro (pure): the *Gitano* style of dancing and singing before its commercialization.

Fort Laramie Treaty of 1868: the terms of this treaty established the Great Sioux Reservation. Although the sixty-million-acre tract was designated for their absolute and undisturbed use and occupation, the agreement craftily brought the Lakota Sioux under governmental control, and has been violated numerous times.

Gat bhaav: short narrative pieces in which a *kathak* dancer pantomimes mythological episodes, performed to songs without words.

Gauchos: immigrants who worked as rural cowboys on the Argentine *pampas*, or plains.

Gede Iwa: these Haitian Vodou spirits represent the realm between life and death, and their color is black. They include tricksters such as Papa Gede, spirit of death and sexuality, and Baron Samedi, guardian of cemeteries.

Geerewol: a dance in a Wodaabe Geerewol Festival in which the most confident and beautiful men compete and are judged by three unmarried women, who pick three winners, or "bulls."

Geirahan: a Balinese hand gesture in which the palms flex and face down so that the fingers arch upward, trembling and fluttering.

Gelungan: a triangular headpiece, that can feature two "horns" of frangipani blossoms or be adorned by hundreds of mother-of-pearl shell fragments; worn in a *baris* dance and by *legong* dancers.

General George Custer (1839–1876): a US Army commander who led an expedition into the Black Hills in 1874, where gold was discovered. He and his Seventh Calvary were later killed in the Battle of the Little Bighorn by the victorious Sioux, who were defending their land.

Genzai (realistic) noh: involves a living protagonist, who suffers tremendously from the loss of a spouse or a child.

Gharanas: stylistic schools of *kathak*. The three existing today are the Jaipur, Benares, and Lucknow *gharanas*.

Ghazals: ancient odes to both love and the bittersweet pain of separation.

Ghunghru: ankle bells in *kathak*.

Ginnu: a Dogon family compound.

Gisalo: an all-night *sing-sing* between two Bosavi-Kaluli clans involving singing, dancing, and cathartic inducement of deep grief and violent pathos in Papua New Guinea.

Gitanos: Rajasthan people who migrated to Spain in the fifteenth century.

Gitanos: a distortion of the word *Egiptanos* (Egyptians) which came to represent the

Golpe: a striking step against the floor in *flamenco*.

Guru-shishya: a reverent one-on-one teacher-student tutorship in India.

Gur-wando: masks of bush spirits used in eastern Mossi funerals that represent a family of a father, mother, and child. The *yali* mask is worn by a small boy, while the *wan-zega* representing the father, and the *wan-sablaga*, the mother, are worn by men.

Gwo bonanj (big guardian angel): a soul-like presence in a Haitian Vodouisant, which must depart from the body before a *lwa* takes possession. The absence of the *gwo bonanj* explains the loss of cognizance and the lack of recall in the devotee.

Gyaku-yunyu: the concept of "to go out and come back." An artist or company is unlikely to be recognized in Japan until they get an international stamp of approval.

Habanera: an Afro-Cuban form, brought from Havana in 1850 to Buenos Aires, which influenced nineteenth-century music and dance such as jazz and inspired the beat of the *milonga* and the *tango*.

Hadra: a weekly public *zār* in Egypt.

Haitian Vodou: an Afro-Caribbean faith having antecedents in the ancient West African religions of Vodun and Yoruba, which aims to heal individuals and maintain the well-being of a community. A spiritual pantheon exists with a Supreme Being at the top, while the numerous deities below are all manifestations of and conduits to this androgynous presence.

Haka ngārahu: a means of inspection by Māori elders and experienced warriors who judged if the participants were emotionally and physically ready for fighting.

Haka ngeri: a Māori dance to rouse a group to achieve its aims, such as in sports.

Haka peruperu: a Māori war dance preceding a battle. Fierce facial expressions and the waving of weapons warned their opponents of their fate and invoked Tuumatauenga, the god of war.

Haka poi: a gentler dance performed by Māori women who twirl *poi*, a string with a ball on the end.

Haka taparahi: a ceremonial Māori dance to express joy or contemporary grievances.

Hanamichi: translating as "flower walk," this ramp for entrances and exits in *kabuki* extends from the back of the theater to the stage through the audience. Three-tenths of the way along the ramp is the *shichi-san*, a trap door that allows for characters to mysteriously emerge.

Haole: the Hawaiian term for whites of European descent.

Hashigakari: a passageway that connects the *noh* stage and the dressing room, and is a symbolic bridge spanning the realm of spirits (backstage) to this world (the stage).

Haumana: *hula* students. Originally, *haumana* would live within the confines of the *hālau* under the strict guidance of their *kumu hula*.

Hayashi: *noh* music, made up of a small ensemble of drums and flute. The *jiutai* chorus is made up of six to ten men who intone *utai*, vocal music.

Hirqa: a long black overcoat with wide sleeves worn by dervishes in the *sema*, which represents the grave, or death itself.

Hogon: elder spiritual leaders in Dogon communities, who preside over all agricultural and religious services.

Hokotai: the basic *butoh* walk in which the knees bend, the torso drops down, and the body seems to float lightly as the feet slide lightly along the floor.

Hong: a Māori exchange, in which two people shake hands, and touch their noses and foreheads together, mingling their breath in a show of unity.

Hounfort: a Haitian Vodou temple.

Houngan: a Haitian Vodou priest.

Hounsi: a Haitian Vodun initiate, who must master the phenomenon of possession trance to become skillful in controlling the arrivals and departures of *lwa* spirits.

Huabu opera: this form, which influenced *jingju*, is based on historical folktales and popular with the working class.

Hula: a Hawaiian dance that evolved from a sacred form of worship known as *ha'a*, practiced at outdoor temples called *heiau* under the auspices of a *kahuna* (priest).

Hula 'auana: translating as "drifting dance," this secular genre of *hula* dance, with its Western-influenced songs and instruments, developed in the early 1900s and catered to tourists.

Hula 'ōlapa: translating as "agile," a *haumana* earns this title after completing their *'ūniki* graduation.

Hula hālau: a consecrated *hula* training ground run by a master teacher called a *kumu hula*.

Hula ho'opa'a: translating as steadfast, this titled is given to *hula* students who have earned a higher degree of training, who may become assistants to the *kumu hula*, and perform *mele* chants and play instruments.

Hula kahiko: translating as "ancient dance," this sacred form pre-dates European contact and is accompanied by *mele* chants and indigenous Hawaiian instruments.

Hula ku'i: translating as "to join old and new," this term refers to the revived *hula* of Kalākaua's court, which emerged through experimental innovations and new influences in music.

Iwi: Māori clans.

Jeroan: the innermost courtyard of a Balinese temple.

Jiang Qing (1914–1995): Mao's fourth wife, also known as "Madame Mao," was a member of the "Gang of Four" that presided over the Cultural Revolution.

Jing: a painted face type in *jingju*, whose bombastic nature is manifested in the outlandish patterns of his painted face. Always male, loud, and rough, they can represent characters such as judges, landowners, outlaws, or supernatural beings.

Jingju: also known as Peking or Beijing opera, *jingju* is a highly stylized genre of popular entertainment that emerged in mid-nineteenth-century China during the Qing Dynasty.

Jinn: less powerful **zār** spirits, yet annoying and malevolent.

Jo-ha-kyu: a crucial aesthetic *noh* concept. *Jo* means beginning; *ha* means breaking; and *kyu*, rapid, or urgent. The contained energy within this introduction, development, and conclusion governs the movements, gestures, and sections of *noh* plays.

Juehuo: conventional *jingju* acting "tricks" that include fan manipulation and artful pantomime.

Ka mate: a popular Māori *haka* song by Te Rauparaha, a chief of the Ngāti Toa *iwi* (clan), telling the tale of fleeing from another clan. Its lyrics include *Ka mate! Ka mate!* (I die! I die!) and *Ka ora! Ka ora!* (I live! I live!).

Kabuki buyo: classical *kabuki* dance, which evolved from three styles: *mai, odori,* and *furi. Mai* derived from the slow glides of *noh,* while rhythmic, airborne *odori* originated from folk dances. In the pantomimic form of *furi,* a dancer uses a fan to represent elements such as a falling leaf, a sake cup, or a letter.

Kabuki plots: most of its 350 plays – some adapted from *noh* – include *sewamono* (domestic dramas) or *jidaimono* (historical plays), both drawn from real-life situations.

Kain: a long piece of gold batik silk fabric that winds tightly around a *legong's* body.

Kaja and *kelod* axis: the Balinese use sacred Mount Gunung Agung to orient themselves. **Kaja** translates as "toward the mountain" and is a sacred, positive direction, while *kelod,* meaning "toward the ocean," is a dangerous and negative trajectory since demons inhabit the sea.

Kake-goe: deep, resonant, and meaningless syllables that are made by drummers, who use them as signposts in leading the rhythm in *noh hayashi* music.

Kalaripayattu: a South Indian martial art dating back to the thirteenth century, practiced by the *Nayar* warrior caste.

Kami-mono (noh god play): involves a deity who descends to bestow blessings on mortals.

Kan'ami Kiyotsuga (1333–1384) and Zeami Motokiyo (1363–1443): a father and son who were crucial in the development of *noh,* and wrote many of its plays.

Kanaga èmna: a *dama* mask with a headpiece of a vertical piece of wood, crossed horizontally by an upper and lower blade that symbolically connects the spiritual world above with the physical world below.

Kanzo: Haitian Vodou *hounsi* initiates undergo a trial in which they are exposed to heat, which "cooks" them, strengthening them and rendering them impervious to harm.

Kapa: a material for traditional *hula* costuming, made from pounded mulberry bark, decorated, and fashioned into wrap-around skirts called *pa'u.*

Kapa haka: "*kapa*" translates as "to stand in row or rank," while *haka* means dance and the song that accompanies it. Many Māori *haka* are grouped under this term and can welcome guests, belittle an enemy before a battle, address concerns, or be performed ritually at Māori tribal gatherings or at funerals.

Kapu: strict rules of the *hula* **hālau** kept by *haumana-hula* students.

Karanga: a towering vertical plank mask worn by male dancers in northern Mossi funeral ceremonies.

Kari types: black-faced witches who wear fangs, high headpieces, and fake breasts in *kathakali.*

Kata: codified patterns of movement and dance in *kabuki, noh,* and Japanese martial arts.

Kathak: a North Indian dance form, which synthesized into lavish court entertainment from Rajasthan, Persia, and Turkey. Some historians posit that *flamenco's* origins are rooted in *kathak.*

Kathaks: male storytellers who enacted Hindu devotional tales at North Indian royal courts.

Kattai kuchi: a rectangular piece of wood, beaten with a stick by a *nattuvanar* to control a dancer's rhythm in classical Indian dance.

Katti (knife) type: in *kathakali*, a green-faced *pacca* type; however, the red lines thrusting up from his nose onto his forehead indicate his flawed nature, as do two *chutti* knobs that sit awkwardly on his forehead and nose.

Kazuo Ohno (1906–2010): a Japanese dancer considered to be a co-founder of *butoh* with Hijikata, who helped direct Ohno's choreographic visions, such as *Admiring La Argentina* (1977). This *tour de force* solo catapulted Ohno into international stardom, and he enjoyed a long career as a dancer and teacher.

Kazura-mono (noh woman play): a lovelorn female is wronged or abandoned by her lover.

Keli: drums, gongs, and cymbals draw the audience at sunset to a *kathakali* performance.

Kerala Kalamandalam: an academy founded by Vallathol Narayana Menon in 1930 that offers institutional training in *kathakali* and *kuttiyattam*.

Kerawuhan: an altered somatic state in Balinese rituals, which translates as "to be entered."

Keris: a large Balinese dagger.

Khmer Rouge: led by Pol Pot, this communist group ruled Cambodia from 1975–1979. Millions of Cambodians were victims of genocide during this era, during which religion, education, and commerce were banned.

Kidung: sacred Javanese poems.

King Kalākaua: known as the "Merrie Monarch," during his reign from 1874 to 1891 Kalākaua reinstituted the *ali'i* court custom of maintaining resident *hula* performers and fostered the resurgence of indigenous practices to strengthen Hawaiian cultural identity.

Kiri-mono (noh demon play): in this last, faster-paced play of a *noh* cycle, evil beings preside, or sometimes magical animals.

Kiritam: a tiered tower headpiece backed by a large circular disk painted in a mix of gold, green, and red, and adorned with small mirrors that sparkle, worn by *pacca* and red-bearded *tati* in *kathakali*.

Koken: as in *noh*, *koken* are onstage attendants to the *shite*, or lead actor, who handle any properties, changes costume accessories, and prompts actors forgetting any lines, all while maintaining an "invisible" presence. He is a *noh* master, who can take over a role if necessary.

Koobgal: an arranged Wodaabe marriage, brokered between cousins (*waldeebe*) of the same lineage.

Kouche: a stage in Haitian Vodou initiation in which *hounsi* initiates are blindfolded, led through an unsettling, spiraling dance, and then taken to a room where they lie down like infants for several days.

Kraton: royal Javanese palaces; the two largest are in Yogyakarta and Surakarta.

Kris dancers: devotees of the Barong in the *calonarang* dance drama, who often fall into trance during the dramatic battle against Rangda, and turn their daggers (*krisses)* against themselves.

Kuahu: an altar in the *hula hālau*.

Kumadori: the make-up of *aragoto kabuki* characters, featuring thick lines of red, black, brown, or blue, painted in patterns that appear as blood vessels, distended due to violent or victorious feelings.

Kunqu opera: a highly sophisticated literary entertainment for aristocrats that originated in the fourteenth century and contributed to *jingju's* evolution.

Kupe'e: Hawaiian wristlets and anklets of whale teeth, bone, or shells.

Kurta: a long shirt extending to the knees worn in *kathak*.

Kuttiyattam: a theatrical form that preceded *kathakali* and was supported by royal patronage.

Kyogen: translating as "mad words," a *kyogen* is a short comic interlude, interspersed twice in the traditional cycle of five *noh* plays, that has antecedents in the humorous form of *sarugaku*.

La Reconquista: a crusade launched by Ferdinand and Isabella in the fifteenth century in an attempt to unify Spain by establishing Catholicism throughout the Iberian Peninsula.

Laka: goddess of the *hula*, to whom *hula* students (*haumana*) pray for protection.

Lakhon lueng: the sacred female palace dancers of the king, who performed dances as offerings to ancestral spirits, asking for rainfall to bring fertility to the land, and to the Khmer (Cambodian) people.

Lakota Sioux: also known as the Teton Sioux, this enormous band comprises seven sub-tribes, including the Hunkpapa, Oglala, and Minniconjou.

Lasya: a feminine dancing style in classical Indian dance that is gentle, sensual, and sometimes erotic.

Lave tet (head washing): a spiritual cleansing in which a Haitian Vodou initiate's *mèt tet*, or master of the head, is determined.

Lebe èmna: a towering plank mask decorated with geometrical patterns representing Lebe, the Dogon snake god.

Legong: a Balinese court dance inspired by the movements of the *sanghyang dedari*, traditionally performed by pre-pubescent girls, who are also called *legong*. Unlike *sanghyang*, *legong* are highly trained and, while performing, they neither speak nor enter into trance.

Lehenga: a long, full skirt, worn on top of *chudidaar* (pants) in *kathak*.

Lei: garlands of vines or leaves worn on the head, shoulders, anklets, and wrists by *hula* dancers.

Leyaks: harmful witches who convene in Balinese graveyards and appear in the guise of animals.

Liangxiang: an entrance by a *jingju* actor, in which one strides through the curtain, walks along a curved path, stops at center stage, and strikes a pose before announcing their character.

Lunfardo: a working-class dialect of Italian and Spanish that developed in the *conventillos* of Buenos Aires.

Lwa: a deity in the Haitian Vodou pantheon. Followers seek help from the appropriate *lwa*, who acts as an intermediary between the Supreme Being and humans.

Ma: translating as "the space between," this experiential concept awakens self-reflexive moments in *butoh* performers and their audiences.

Mai: the low and grounded dance of *noh*. A *jo-no-mai* is a quiet, graceful dance for a female character, while tormented warriors and madwomen dance an agitated *kakeri*.

Maile: a type of greenery that represents the spiritual power of gods and demi-gods, used for decorating *hula* altars and in costuming.

Makahiki: a religious festival dedicated to Lono, Hawaiian god of fertility.

Malo: a Hawaiian loincloth worn by men.

Mana: a spiritual life force, or power, extending from the gods to a king in both Māori and Hawaiian culture.

Manbo: a Haitian Vodou priestess.

Mandi: a full-seated posture in *bharatanatyam* in which the dancer sinks down low and perches on the balls of the feet.

Manifest destiny: a nineteenth-century US doctrine that justified the expansion of white settlement westward, and influenced the government to decide that Native Americans should be contained on Indian Territory.

Mao Zedong (1893–1976): a communist revolutionary who became the autocratic ruler of the People's Republic of China in 1949. "Chairman Mao" was the author of the *Little Red Book*, which all Chinese were required to carry and recite from daily.

Māoritanga: the ideals of Māori culture.

Marae: a sacred meeting area, which includes the *wharenui*, a community meetinghouse. Ceremonial Māori gatherings and games occurred in this communal place.

Marcaje: silent marking steps in *flamenco* that emphasize a dancer's musicality.

Meh fīls: intimate performances of poetry, music, and *kathak* dance in the music rooms of nobility.

Mele: chanted poetry that is a repository for Hawaiian mythology and history, and often accompanies *hula*.

Mele hoʻoipoipo: Hawaiian chants about people, places, or historical events.

Mele inoa: translating as "name chants," these sacred compositions celebrate Hawaiian genealogical history of gods and chiefs, and their lyrics are not open to interpretation or change.

Melismas: an athletic *flamenco* vocal technique in which one syllable is catapulted into a range of notes by a *cantaor/a*.

Mèt tet **(master of the head):** the protective deity of a Haitian Vodou devotee.

Mevlana Jalalu'ddin Rumi (1207–1273): a Sufi poet, teacher, and the inspiration behind the organization of the Mevlevi order of dervishes, which espouses a doctrine advocating tolerance, positive reasoning, charity, and awareness through love.

Mevlevi dervishes: members of a Sufi Islamic order founded in the thirteenth century in Konya, Turkey, whose followers seek divine truth and knowledge through their union with God.

Mewinten: a Balinese cleansing ritual that entails a special diet, abstention from sexual activity, and avoidance of corpses for at least twenty-four hours before performing a *calonarang*.

Milonga: a quintessential dance of the working class, which blended *gaucho* folk traditions, *candombe* movements, *habanera* rhythms, and the *abrazo* (embrace) of European ball dances It is also the term for Argentine social clubs where *tango* is danced.

Milonguitas: female *tango* dancers.

Minukku: female *kathakali* characters and Brahmin priests, whose golden facial make-up indicates their gentle nature.

Monoguri-mono (noh madness play): the protagonist, often a woman, is driven to a deranged state by extreme duress or jealousy.

Mudras: codified hand gestures in classical Indian dance that communicate words, feelings, or concepts in conjunction with the lyrics of a song. These are sometimes called *hastas*.

Mugen (fantasy) noh: in these plots, a sleeping *waki* sees the ghost in a dream.

Muti: a conical *kathakali* headpiece decorated with vibrating silver spangles, worn by Rama and Krishna.

Nacionalflamenquismo: during Franco's regime in the 1950s, *flamenco* was forged into a propaganda tool that became a joyous symbol of Spanish national identity that displayed no trace of its *Gitano* origins.

Naga: a huge sea serpent, which legendarily spawned thousands of *apsaras*. Its serpentine nature is reflected in Cambodian dance patterns.

Nakomsé: translating as "people of power," this is the ruling class of political chiefs in Mossi society.

Nasyons: the "families" of Haitian Vodou deities, with the Rada, Gede, and Petro being the most prominent.

Nattuvanar: a male *guru* (teacher) who served as choreographer, rehearsal director, and orchestra leader for Indian dance and music.

Nautch: a distortion of the Sanskrit word *nāch* (dance), and a derogatory term used by the British for Indian street dancers, associated with prostitution.

Navarasas: the nine expressions of emotion shown, through facial expression and body language in classical Indian dance, are love, laughter, sorrow, anger, heroism, fear, wonder, disgust, and serenity.

Nayika: A heroine, portrayed by a *bharatanatyam* dancer, who might express love or dismay at having to wait for a lover.

Nelik: an intense, wide-eyed stare of a Balinese dancer expressing anger or fear.

Ngelayak: translating as "tree laden with blossoms swaying in the wind," entranced *sanghyang* sway from side to side or arch dangerously backward as they are carried on men's shoulders throughout a Balinese village.

Nian: an actor's recitation in *jingju*, which imparts the narrative.

Nityasumangali: the eternally auspicious status of a *devadasi* "married" to a deity, who was exempt from widowhood due to his immortality.

Noh kata: highly stylized actions, such as scooping water, pouring sake, thrusting a sword, reading a book, or writing are executed with a fan. Abstract *kata* are included in dancing, and include zigzag traveling patterns and stamping.

Noh theater: a highly refined aristocratic entertainment that emerged in fourteenth-century Japan. Its moralistic plays served as exclusive entertainment for the *Shogun* and the elite *samurai* class.

Nritta: non-narrative interludes in which a classical Indian dancer dancer does precise, rhythmic footwork in time to the music, and executes ornamental arm and hand gestures that have no specific meaning.

Nritta drishti: translating as "dance of the eyes," *kathakali* students perform these eye exercises daily.

Nyama: a Dogon term for the soul, or life force that is released at the moment of death, and must be contained so that no harm comes to the living.

Nyonyosé: Mossi farmers who perform the spiritual masking traditions used in initiations and funeral rites.

Odalan: Balinese temple celebrations.

Okina: a sacred invocation that opens a typical *noh* play cycle, in which the descent of a god is celebrated by a *kamigaku* (divine dance), and then is royally sent off with a lively dance called a *sanbaso*.

Omote: *noh* theater masks, with which an actor magically conveys a variety of expressions by merely changing the angle of the gaze.

Onnagata: a *kabuki* convention in which highly trained male actors specialize in female roles, offering a hyper-real version of a woman in looks, gesture, voice, and movement.

Ópera flamenco: a theatrical and narrative form accompanied by a large orchestra that became popular in the 1920s.

Orisa: a deity in the spiritual West African Yoruba pantheon.

Ozu tonnolo: in Dogon philosophy, the dualistic concept represented by decorative zigzag or serpentine motifs on religious altars, carvings, and in choreography.

Pa: ancient, fortified Māori hilltop settlements.

Pacca type: a heroic *satvik*, or virtuous character in *kathakali*, identified by a green face, white *chutti* beard, a red bow-shaped mouth, and a mark of Vishnu painted in the middle of a yellow patch on his forehead.

Padams: a dialogue or soliloquy in first-person narration that accompanies *bharatanatyam* dance passages.

Paha Sapa (the Black Hills): located in the US state of South Dakota, this epicenter of the Lakota spiritual world was illegally appropriated by the United States government in 1876.

Pākehā: The Māori term for whites of European descent.

Palmas: hand clapping in *flamenco*.

Palos: various *flamenco* styles, classified by *compás*, or rhythmic patterns.

Pedjalan: the crouching, stylized walk of a *baris* dancer.

Pendopo: the dance hall of a Javanese *kraton*.

Petro lwa: these Haitian Vodou spirits signify the evolution of African-based religions due to New World influences and are associated with the color red. Petro spirits are more violent, such as Ogou, the *lwa* of iron and thunder.

Pihuang (orchestra): the music of *jingju*, which is divided into two categories: *wen chang* and *wu chang*. *Wen chang* music supports the emotion behind the melodic singing, while *wu chang* accompanies acting, recitation, dancing, fighting, and scene changes.

Pitos: finger snapping in *flamenco*.

Porteños: the educated elite of Buenos Aires.

Poteau mitan: a tall pole in the middle of the *péristyle*, an outdoor courtyard in the *hounfort* (temple), from which the *lwa* emerge during Haitian Vodou ceremonies.

Pottukkattutal: a symbolic "marriage" ceremony uniting a *devadasi* to a deity, in which a red thread, or *pottu*, is tied around her neck.

Pōwhiri: the Māori welcoming ceremony, in which the host party, known as the *tengata whenua* (people of the land), meets their *manuhiri* (guests).

Pratima: wooden doll-like effigies. Hindu-Balinese believe that when the gods descend during an *Odalan* temple festival, they enter these effigies and are guarded by *Baris* dancers.

Puja: a *bharatanatyam* dancer's salutation to Mother Earth before and after dancing.

Pukana: the rolling of the eyes in *kapa haka*.

Pukari: the wide-eyed staring in *kapa haka*.

Pura: Balinese temples. These have three courtyards in which three different categories of dance are performed.

Puranas: Hindu scriptures and mythological tales from the *Mahabharata*, the *Ramayana*, and other epic poems.

Purapattu: a *kathakali* duet danced by a *pacca* hero and his companion behind a half-lowered *therissila* (curtain).

Quebradas: twists of the hips in *tango*.

Queen Ka'ahumanu: the powerful wife of Kamehameha I, who converted to Christianity in 1823 and then banned *hula* dancing.

Rada lwa: these benevolent old-world spirits of Haitian Vodou are rooted in Africa, and associated with the color white. Damballah, the venerated snake *lwa*, presides over this cult along with his wife, Aida Wedo, Erzili Freda, the spirit of love, and motherhood, and Legba, the *lwa* of the crossroads.

Ragit tika-tika: a pattern in which the nine *bedhaya* dancers line up in three rows of three, reflecting the auspicious nature of that number in Hindu culture and the sacred trinity of Shiva, Vishnu, and Brahma.

Rasa: translates as emotion, or taste. A classical Indian dancer's innermost feelings in storytelling are portrayed through *rasa*.

Reamker: a Cambodian dance drama based on the *Ramayana*, an ancient Hindu text.

Red-beard *tati*: an evil *kathakali* character, with a red face, black eyes and lips, an oversized *chutti* moustache, and *chutti* balls on his face.

Red Guards: A mass of Chinese students, recruited by Mao, who engaged in the violent persecution of millions and the destruction of ancient artifacts during the Cultural Revolution.

Redoble: rapid stamping in *flamenco*.

Robam boran: the classical royal dance of Cambodia, and one of the oldest court traditions in Southeast Asia.

Roppo: translating as "six directions," a *kabuki* actor will make a spectacular entrance or exit that reveals the inner landscape of their character.

Ruume: in this first dance of a Wodaabe *Geerewol* Festival, men gather in a large circle to dance and chant about love, the beauty of women, and their own masculine charms.

Sadir: the solo form of *dasiattam*, danced by *devadasis*.

Sakoku: a period of Japanese isolation that began in 1635 when the *Shogun Iemitsu* expelled all missionaries and most foreigners by sealing off Japan's borders until 1853, when the US Navy's Commander Matthew Perry forced them to open.

Salangai: *bharatanatyam* ankle bells, stitched onto padded leather in rows.

Samapadam: a *bharatanatyam* standing position in which parallel feet and legs touch.

Sampeah: a respectful gesture to the forehead in Cambodian dance, in which the palms meet and the fingers arch to create a V shape.

Sampur: a scarf tied around the waist that falls to the floor and is flicked to accentuate movement in Javanese dance.

Samurai: a society of Japanese warriors during the *Shogun* era who lived by *bushido* – a strict moral code upholding attributes of obedience, frugality, loyalty, honor, and Buddhism.

Sanghyang: ancient Balinese dances involving ritual possession by spirits or celestial deities for the purpose of exorcising illness.

Sanghyang dedari: meaning "honored goddess nymphs," these Balinese pre-pubescent girls become possessed by divinities, who give advice on how to heal the community.

Sanskrit: an ancient Indo-Aryan language, in which many Hindu scriptures, poems, and mythological stories were written.

Sarugaku: *noh* derived from this acrobatic entertainment from China, which grew into a form of humorous mime at shrines or temples to expel evil spirits and bring good fortune.

Sastras: Hindu scriptures.

Sati: the Hindu practice of a widow being burnt alive on her husband's funeral pyre.

Satimbe èmna: a *dama* mask honoring women. Its wooden superstructure is a seated naked woman with jutting breasts, whose bent elbows are held tightly to her ribcage.

Satvika abhinaya: the representation of the psychic condition of a character through facial and bodily expression in classical Indian dance.

Seb-i Arus: translating as "wedding night," or "night of unity with God," Mevlevi disciples celebrate this December anniversary of Rumi's death.

Seiza: a formal kneeling pose, which *kabuki* artists must master for as long as an hour.

Selams: the four periods of dancing and music in the *sema* known as *selams*, or "salutations."

Seledet: rapid eye movements of Balinese dance that dart up and down, or right to left, in time to music.

Sema: a whirling dance performed by Mevlevi dervishes that induces a state of religious ecstasy in a follower.

Semadhi: the Javanese form of the Sanskrit word *samadhi*, through which intense religious focus leads to a mystical union with the divine.

Semahane: a circular dance hall in the dervish *tekke*.

Semazen: a "whirler," or performer in the *sema* dance.

Semazenbashi: a dervish dance master.

Sembah: a Hindu salutation of prayer, in which the palms are brought together and held in front of one's face.

Seppuku: ritual suicide, which a *samurai* would commit facing dishonor or failure by slicing his own abdomen with a sword, thereby freeing his spirit.

Shaykha: a female spiritual medium presiding over *zār* ceremonies who brokers an agreement with the spirits troubling an afflicted woman.

Sheikh: the spiritual leader of the dervish *tekke*.

Sheng: male character roles in *jingju*, which includes *lao sheng*, a middle-aged to elderly man; *wu sheng*, a warrior; and *xiao sheng*, a young, handsome man.

Shite: a *noh* protagonist, or lead actor (pronounced *shee-tay*).

Shogun: translating as "great general," these Japanese military rulers presided over lords and *samurai* warriors, and frequently were more powerful than the emperor.

Shozoku: the colorful silk robes of *noh* theater, referencing the dress of fourteenth-century nobility.

Shura-mono (noh warrior play): a fallen hero's story.

Sigi so: a secret language used to address and give praise to the *èmna* during a *dama* ceremony.

Sikke: a tall, cylindrical dervish hat, made of camel's hair, which represents the tombstone.

Sing-sings: ceremonies of singing and dancing by indigenous peoples in Papua New Guinea, such as the Bosavi-Kaluli.

Sitting Bull (1831–1890): a Hunkpapa Sioux holy man who refused to live on the reservation and fought against Custer in the Battle of the Little Bighorn. A longtime leader in the Indian resistance to the ruinous policies of the US government, he was killed in 1890 by Indian police who came to arrest him during the Ghost Dance movement.

Slokas: narrative sections of songs or Sanskrit verses that describe situations or surroundings.

Sob: a mussel shell rattle attached to a long string, which a *gisalo* dancer strikes against the floor as he bounces slowly in place, with knees bent and torso tilted forward.

Sollukattus: syllables, such as "*dhit-dhit-teis, dhit-dhit-teis*," recited by a *nattuvanar* and paired by a *bharatanatyam* dancer's footwork.

Spanish Civil War (1936–1939): a vicious conflict between the leftist Republican and the right-wing Nationalist Falange Party, which mirrored the Fascist regimes in Germany and Italy. Generalissimo Francisco Franco's Nationalist army was the victor, and he reigned as dictator until his death in 1975.

Sringara: the expression of love in song, danced out by a *devadasi* in the solo form of *sadir*.

Sun Dance: an annual religious Lakota rite that US authorities perceived as barbaric and consequently banned in 1883.

Suri-ashi: the gliding gait of *noh* is executed while in the stance of *kamae* in which the torso is tilted forward, the knees slightly bent, and center of gravity is low.

Swaraj: the Indian movement for independence from Britain; the literal translation is "self-rule."

Tabi: thick white Japanese socks, split in between the first and second toe.

Tablaos flamencos: intimate urban nightclubs geared for tourists that became popular in the 1950s and 1960s.

Tachimawari: the term for *kabuki* stage acrobatics and combat, based on martial arts from the days when *samurai* were always poised for battle.

Taksu: a charismatic performance quality that every Balinese dancer aspires to gain.

Talas: rhythmic metric cycles in *kathak*, played by the drums that can transition between three speeds, or *layas*.

Tandava: an energetic, masculine dancing style, legendarily danced by Shiva in his manifestation as Nataraja, Lord of the Dance.

Tango-canción: an era in the 1920s and 1930s in which *tango* lyricists were largely men, the narratives were sung from a male point of view and revealed confessions, insecurities over women, or their dependence on a forgiving mother figure.

Taonga: a Māori cultural treasure.

Tapu: Māori spiritual restrictions and imposed rules that must be followed, or the wrath of the gods could be invoked.

Tari kraton: the respective lineages and distinctive court dances of each Javanese palace. These are considered to be *pusaka* – sacred and treasured royal heirlooms.

Tati: a characterization of three *kathakali* bearded types: red, white, and black.

Tatsumi Hijikata *(1928–1986)*: a Japanese choreographer and dancer who made highly provocative works that were seen by many as shocking and sexually perverse. He called his dance *ankoku butoh*, or "dance of darkness."

Tawaifs: highly literate, female Muslim court performers who sang and danced, and were often courtesans of nobility.

Te Reo Māori: the Māori language, which was officially recognized by the government in 1988.

Tekke: a spiritual dervish lodge and conservatory for philosophical teachings and training master performers of Turkish music and *sema*.

Tengabisi: translating as "people of the earth," they are a Mossi working class of blacksmiths, weavers, and merchants.

Tennure: a long white dervish robe, symbolic of the funeral shroud of the ego.

Teppu: masked *kathakali* animal characters such as lions or birds.

The Cultural Revolution: a radical movement (1966–1976) that enforced Mao Zedong's Communist ideology by purging China of any capitalist or bourgeois elements. Millions of scholars, artists, landowners, and religious figures were persecuted or killed, and innumerable historical artifacts and temples were destroyed.

The Dirty War, or *La Guerra Sucia* (1976–1983): a period in which Argentinians were oppressed by a brutal dictatorship during which over thirty thousand citizens mysteriously disappeared.

The Edo, or Tokugawa, era (1603–1863): in a shift of power, the Tokugawa *Shogun* moved from Kyoto to Edo (today's Tokyo).

The Ghost Dance: a religious movement founded in 1888 by Wovoka, whose followers believed that by dancing this circular dance, their ancestors and the buffalo would return, and white people would be obliterated. This movement ended when hundreds of Sioux were brutally massacred at Wounded Knee by the US government in 1890.

The Muromachi era (1336–1573): the period when the *Shogun* of the Ashikaga family ruled from Kyoto.

The Wodaabe: known as "people of the taboos," these nomadic shepherds travel with their families and cattle throughout the Sahel steppe in southern Niger.

Therissila: a portable rectangle silk curtain, hand held by two men, and used in various ways in *kathakali*.

Theyyam: ritual folk dance honoring Hindu deities, by performers wearing enormous headpieces, voluminous costuming, and painted orange faces.

Thumri: poetic songs ranging from the sacred to the sexual, interpreted by a *tawaif* through *abhinaya* gestures in *kathak*.

Tingetange èmna: a *dama* mask representing water birds that is worn by dancers who perform on tall stilts.

Tira-nokku: standing on a stool, a *kathakali* actor will grip the top of the *therissila* and ominously lower it to give the audience a glimpse of his character.

Todayam: a preliminary *kathakali* devotional dance, done by student dancers obscured by the *therissila*.

Toya mili: a Javanese technique translating as "flowing water" in which dancers move their necks and heads in a floating serpentine fashion.

Treaty of Waitangi: In 1840, when Māori chiefs and the British signed this treaty, the Māori unwittingly ceded their governance in exchange for the possession of their lands, forests, and fisheries, much of which was gradually taken away from them.

Tsure: traveling companions to the *waki* or *shite* in *noh*.

Tuol Sleng: Pol Pot's secret prison, also known as "S-21," where millions of Cambodians were tortured before being executed in the Khmer Rouge Killing Fields.

'Ūniki: a graduation ceremony from the *hula hālau*.

Utplavanas: dynamic vertical jumps with bent legs in *kathak*.

Utu: the Māori concept of compensation, or balance, which requires reciprocating friendly gestures as well as seeking compensation for offensive acts.

Vachika abhinaya: verbal expressions of syllables, poetry, or song in classical Indian dance.

Vèvè: designs that represent each Haitian Vodou *lwa*, made by a *houngan* who passes a thin stream of cornmeal, coffee, or flour through his fingers onto the dirt to attract the spirits.

Ville-aux-Camps: a mythical place in Haiti below the sea where the *lwa* (deities) reside.

Vodouisants: Haitian Vodou adepts, or followers.

Vodun: a deity in the spiritual Haitian Vodun pantheon.

Vueltas de tacón: turns on the heel in *flamenco*.

Wagoto: this realistic, "soft style" *kabuki* genre, popular in refined Kyoto, whose gentle, meek hero was desired by the most popular courtesans in the pleasure quarter, was created by Chikamatsu Monzaemon (1653–1724).

Waiata: traditional songs that pass down Māori ancestral knowledge and history, and are used at funerals, to welcome guests, as lullabies, or to reflect social or political concerns.

Wajd: a blissful, mystical state, in which a dervish sees God in everything.

Wakashu kabuki: translating as "young men's *kabuki*," young boys replaced women in roles.

Waki: a secondary *noh* actor, who always enters first, and serves as a foil to the *shite*. The *waki* appears as an unmasked mortal and never plays a female.

Wali: sacred Balinese dances, performed in the most inner temple courtyard, closest to Mount Agung.

Walu èmna: a *dama* mask representing the antelope, a beloved animal in Dogon culture.

Wasichu: this Lakota term defining non-indigenous people has taken on a pejorative connotation: "those who take the best meat."

Whatero: the protrusion of the tongue in the *kapa haka*. Since this is symbolic of the phallus, it is the domain of men only.

White-beard tati: the beloved and beneficent monkey general Hanuman of the *Ramayana*, wearing *chutti* side-burns, is an example of this *kathakali* type.

Wi aledo: a Bosavi-Kaluli term for those who have shared meat – an important social obligation and a fundamental way of showing friendship and affection.

Wikasa wakan: sacred Lakota medicine men.

Wiri: the distinctive, quivering movements of a *haka* performer's hands.

Wovoka (1856–1932): a Paiute Indian mystic who in 1888 prophesied the annihilation of the white race not through fighting, but by dancing the devotional dance he had envisioned. This became a religion for many, including the Lakota Sioux, who called it *wana'ghi wa'chipi*—the Ghost Dance.

Yaaba sooré: a sacred ancestral Mossi pathway between earth and the afterworld. After a person dies, spiritually charged masks, dancing, and drumming at funerals are essential in pointing the soul of the deceased toward this route.

Yaake: a dance contest in a Wodaabe *Geerewol* Festival in which three women judge the men's charm and personality.

Yangbanxi: eight state-sponsored or "model works" that promoted Mao's ideology and were the only condoned entertainment during the decade-long Cultural

Revolution in China. These included two dance dramas, *The Red Detachment of Women* and *The White-Haired Girl*.

Yanvalou: translating as "I beg of you," this dance attracts Legba, who allows the Haitian *lwa* to enter the *péristyle* through the charged *poteau mitan*. Damballah and Aida Wedo also are attracted by the undulating *yanvalou*.

Yaro kabuki: translating as "men's *kabuki*," the *Shogun* decreed in 1652 that only mature males could be *kabuki* players, which has continued to this day.

Yugen: another aesthetic *noh* concept, translating as "invisible beauty," that is a quality enhanced by an actor's experience and age.

Yu-jo kabuki: translating as "pleasure women's *kabuki*," Okuni's presentations brought many to the "pleasure quarter," a designated area where actors and prostitutes plied their trade. To rein in *samurai* mixing with this lowest class of society, the *Shogunate* banned all female performers in 1629.

Zapeteado: percussive *flamenco* footwork, usually done with heeled shoes studded with nails to enhance the sound.

Zār: a healing rite, predominantly practiced by women in North Africa, in which maladies caused by possession of "*zār*" spirits are cured through music, dancing, and sacrificial feasts.

Zār spirits: known as *asyād* in Egypt and as *zayran* in Sudan, these spirits are generally considered to be benevolent, but might inflict sickness in the person they possess when their demands are not met.

Zikr: the dervish practice of honoring God through frequent repetition of phrases, such *la'illaha il'Allahu* – "there is only God."

Index

Italic page references indicate boxed text. **Boldface** references indicate photographs and illustrations.